B. Baker
work 291-3338
x1631

THE PRISON COMMUNITY

THE PRISON COMMUNITY

by

Donald Clemmer

DIRECTOR, DEPARTMENT OF CORRECTIONS,
DISTRICT OF COLUMBIA GOVERNMENT

With a Foreword by
DONALD R. CRESSEY

HOLT, RINEHART AND WINSTON
NEW YORK • CHICAGO • SAN FRANCISCO
TORONTO • LONDON

June, 1966
21474-0118

Printed in the United States of America
Library of Congress Catalog Card Number: 58-11040

CONTENTS

FOREWORD BY DONALD R. CRESSEY

The Prison Community fits into three intersecting research contexts. First, it is a sociological study. Although the character of American sociology has changed since the early 1930's, when Clemmer's research was conducted, most of the basic or "core" concepts and principles of sociology have remained unchanged. Among other things, there has been a decided shift toward use of sophisticated statistical techniques for testing precise hypotheses and toward emphasis on research dealing with social structure rather than with social processes or with norms and values (culture). But principles regarding the relationship of the individual to the group, the development of personality, the adjustment to conflicting roles and cultures, and integration of groups and society have remained fairly constant. It is with these basic sociological principles that *The Prison Community* deals. Although the premise is unstated, the book deals with the prison as a social microcosm in which the conditions and processes in the broader society are observable. Consequently, it is an effective "casebook" for sociologists and sociology students.

Second, the volume is a report on a study of social organization. Sociologists have examined the effectiveness and efficiency of different kinds of organization in a wide variety of settings, ranging from broad administrative systems to specific factories, military hierarchies, and mental hospitals. Also, the conditions under which various types of organization arise, persist, and change have been studied. *The Prison Community* was one of the first organizational studies of this kind, and its author pioneered in developing the concepts "informal" and "formal" organization (pp. 143, 294). Similarly, the study is among the first to stress the notion that the events occurring in a factory, hospital, prison, or other organization occur because there is an organizational "place" for them to occur.

Third, *The Prison Community* is a study of a prison. As such, it contributes to criminological and penological knowledge. Although in America such knowledge is primarily sociological — because most researchers in criminology and penology are sociologists — there is a demand for it by persons who are not necessarily sociologists. Among these are legislators, wardens, prison workers of various kinds, and informed citizens. While some prison conditions have changed in the past twenty-five years, the fundamental aspects of prison life described by Clemmer have continued. Sentences are shorter, food and sanitary conditions are better, emphasis has been placed on "rehabilitation" or "treatment" of inmates, amenities of various kinds — such as radios and canteen privileges — have been introduced, and restrictive legislation has curtailed the amount and kind of work inmates can do. But any current observer of prisons certainly will see that the basic processes and conditions observed in the institution which was Clemmer's subject of study are still in operation. In fact, many of the more recent prison studies were inspired or, at least, highly influenced by this volume. Yet no subsequently published study has this book's scope and detail; after the almost twenty years since it was originally published, *The Prison Community* remains as the best and most comprehensive published study of a prison.

We cannot expect *The Prison Community* to use the language of contemporary social science or, for that matter, to make certain kinds of observations. It is a study of what Erving Goffman in a recent essay appearing in the Proceedings of a Walter Reed Army Institute of Research symposium on psychiatry calls "total institutions." In these institutions, such as mental hospitals, prisons, and monasteries, men live together twenty-four hours a day, with the result that the organization directly meets all of the personal needs which are going to be met at all. Accordingly, social relationships take on a peculiar form, and the relationships in one type of total institution resemble the social relationships in other total institutions. But Clemmer could not make a comparison of his prison and, say, mental hospitals for the simple reason that the idea of comparing them was not part of the sociological culture of the 1930's.

A similar omission which is a consequence of the perspective of the times is failure to *account for* the conditions which were observed. Perhaps the kind of administrative organization devised to attain the goals our society has set for prisons has inadvertently produced the kinds of relationships which develop among prisoners. Clemmer hints at this in numerous places (e.g., pp. 143, 177, 193, 294-298), but the notion was not studied as an explicit hypothesis. More specifically, it is a logical hypothesis that phenomena such as inmate stratification (p. 107), the proportion of inmates in groups (pp. 115-120), the answers to questions about fellow inmates (p. 123), and evidence of both loyalty (pp. 118, 154-155) and disloyalty (pp. 108, 157, 297-298) to inmates are products of official and unofficial administrative policies.

Both a prison's objectives and its means for achieving them are determined by authority outside the institution. As prisons have grown in size and as society's concept of their function has changed, new services and roles have been added without special regard for those already existing.

For example, prisons have always been expected to keep inmates quietly and securely confined, and to a large degree a prison's success is measured by absence of "trouble" in the form of escapes, riots, or violence. During a short period in the early history of prisons few organizational problems arose in connection with meeting this objective. Society expected prisons to do very little except confine inmates, and during this period administrators were permitted to use effective means for achieving this end — all prisoners were to be placed either in solitary confinement or in institutions such as the Walnut Street Jail where only peripheral control was emphasized. But we soon came to expect that prisons would *also* have rehabilitation programs and would maintain themselves at least cost to the state. Prisons are now expected to engage inmates in production, housekeeping, maintenance, educational, and treatment activities while, at the same time, efficiently repressing them. This expectation effectively limits the means available to prison administrators for keeping inmates quietly confined, yet these officials continue to be held responsible for the prisoners' orderly confinement.

Prison administrators have worked out two principal kinds of solutions to this problem, and both are apparent in the findings of *The Prison Community*. One is to keep inmate society as unorganized as possible, to prevent individuals from joining forces. To this end, psychological solitary confinement is substituted, to the fullest extent possible, for physical isolation. This permits inmates to work and to participate in prescribed activities, but it minimizes the danger of violence, revolt, or riot. To facilitate the state of unorganization or anomie, administrators always admonish inmates to "do your own time," and, consistently, officially distribute rewards such as parole and good-time allowances to inmates who remain isolated from other prisoners. The high percentage of "ungrouped" inmates which Clemmer found (pp. 119-123, 295) seems attributable to this official system for maintaining control.

A second kind of solution to the problem is to enlist, unofficially, the aid of inmates themselves. When inmates far outnumber staff members it is extraordinarily difficult, if not impossible, to keep each of them psychologically isolated by official techniques alone. But control is facilitated if inmate elites propagate and enforce norms and values which promote psychological isolation among the other inmates. The inmate culture, then, performs useful administrative functions. For example, the inmate "code" contains admonitions which are the exact counterparts of the officials' admonitions. These include directives to be rational, to not bring "heat" by antagonizing employees, to not cause trouble by stealing from fellow inmates, and, generally, to "do your own time." Of course, the code is frequently violated — in enforcing it, the inmate elites necessarily violate it.

Although even most inmates perceive the inmate culture as "anti-administration" in emphasis, the leaders who arise to carry and enforce it (pp. 107, 141-147) help the administrators maintain general control over prisoners.

It would be expected, then, that power of various kinds would unofficially be *assigned* to inmate elites, rather than seized by them. This seems to be the case. Inmate leaders appear to be men who, like the administrators, have a vested interest in maintaining the *status quo*. They seem to be men who have unofficially and perhaps even unintentionally been permitted to violate minor prison rules and to avoid some of the hardships of prison life in return for their cooperation with employees. Such "corruption of authority," as Gresham Sykes called it in an article appearing in the March, 1956, issue of *Social Forces*, is characteristic of prisons. The inmate rules for behavior of prisoners, in turn, protect the elites' privileged positions and operate in such a way that they help keep the bulk of the inmates in a condition of anomie and, thus, under control. To take an oversimplified example, an inmate might be allowed by a guard to steal a little coffee from the kitchen in return for working hard and, generally, for not causing trouble. This man is then likely to take a dim view of other inmates who would steal coffee in such a manner and measure that the guard and his superiors would put all coffee under strict control. Moreover, other inmates are prohibited from making inroads on his coffee-stealing privileges by a culture which emphasizes the importance of doing one's own time, not bringing heat, and not "ratting." The prison's coffee supply is thus protected by an inmate elite that steals from it while enforcing a code which, in these circumstances, prohibits others from doing the same.

There are other kinds of evidence of alliances between a prison's administrative organization and its inmate organization, but they cannot be discussed here. *The Prison Community* has most effectively shown some of the consequences to inmate relationships of such alliances, but it leaves to future researchers the twin tasks of documenting the nature of the alliances and of specifying in detail the processes by which they produce the observed effects.

D.R.C.

Los Angeles
April, 1958

PREFACE TO THE 1958 REISSUE

As this volume is reissued, it is well to emphasize its original purposes. It was intended as a compendium to cover the formal and informal organization of a conventional prison. It did not seek to test particular hypotheses. It is descriptive and analytical. It is objective but lacks full scientific precision. It implies cause and effect but does not always prove it. It was written for contemporary students and has also a historical context in that it can serve as a case study of a prison of the 1930's for students a century ahead. Its shortcomings are noted in the text and in the methodological note. It locates the areas for additional research. Further comment is unnecessary, for the volume must speak for itself.

It would be interesting to know whether or not the structure and functions of the prisons of the late 1950's are the same or similar to those which are described in this study of a conventional penitentiary for adult felons of the 1930's. It would appear that conclusions would be difficult to ascertain. The data for *The Prison Community* were collected in the Depression Years of the 1930's, and throughout the book there are references to the fact that the culture of the prison reflected the American culture, for the prison was a culture within the larger one. Since then, to employ just a few word symbols, we have seen World War II, urbanization, television, Korea, a peacetime draft, rocketry, cold war, automation, Sputnik, inflation — and so on. It's a different world. The prison of today operates in this changed social world, and it is guided by legislators and administrators, operated by employees, and peopled by inmates who have, in varying degrees, been a part of this dynamic environment. But, wait — has the prison really changed very much in these twenty years? Has all this impact of the world around it affected the community of the prison in noticeable ways? Are the concepts in this now old book still applicable? Has there been a ponderousness in American penology that lags behind all technological advances and behind almost all social changes in this dynamic society?

These and related questions cannot be answered with any precision. Answers with some merit might be obtained after months of research if the methods and perspective which were applied in *The Prison Community* could be applied to a similar type of prison today. Such a comparative study has not been made and probably never will be, for, like everything else, research techniques in sociology and its related sciences have also been dynamic. Comparison must be made by broad evaluation, and it remains therefore to apply the best judgment possible from general observation to determine in what ways the prisons of the late 1950's compare with the one described twenty years ago.

This writer has been active in prison work for almost thirty years. He is currently responsible for four institutions holding some 4,800 inmates, and he inspects one or more of them six days a week. He has also visited dozens of American prisons and worked and studied with other prison officials. Out of this experience and with the concepts of *The Prison Community* in mind, he may be qualified to guess.

Some 40 per cent of American prisons appear little different today in basic organization, institutional program, or the subtle aspects of the unseen environment of the prisoners' world than they were twenty years ago. This is believed to be so because, in part, they are being operated in the same old plants and under a routine and a regime little different from those found in the old bastille institutions. The criminality of the inmates of the current time, as judged by technique and type of crime, is only slightly more sophisticated than it was in the 1930's; in other words, the basic component of prisons — the human element — is fundamentally the same. Also, these prisons are administered in large part by politically appointed officials and operated under a patronage system. In view of these several basic factors it follows that, by and large, the picturization in this book still applies, and a good guess is that it applies in four out of every ten institutions.

It is believed that some 60 per cent of the penal institutions across the country differ in varying degrees in their formal and informal organization and operations from the one this volume describes. The differences vary from slight to marked, with the greatest differences found either in prison camps or in the newly built institutions for 500 men, providing private living quarters, featuring a versatile work and training program, and operated by trained, career-type personnel. The architecture of such plants and the various programs for the inmates and the quiet influence of good leaders combine to thwart the harmful aspects of the informal group interaction among inmates, as noted in *The Prison Community*.

Among this 60 per cent or so of American prisons which have changed or improved in the last two decades, it could be demonstrated that certain complex influences have been brought to bear upon them. The doctrine of humanitarianism in its slow and jagged climb has touched the minds of policy makers in legislative halls and administrative offices, for example. Also, there have come to the prison services men of goodwill with appropriate training who have been able to work in career status under protection of increasingly competent employee merit systems. The academic disciplines which deal with human nature have added some new techniques and concepts over the decades. The improvement in American prisons, in short, stems from increasing humanitarianism, good people, and scientific advances. There have been other influences, but these three seem basic.

While these three forces account for much of the improvement evident in the majority of adult prisons over the last twenty years, they have not been of sufficient intensity to bring about organic changes in the system. In spite of the many ingenious programs to bring about modification of attitudes or reform, the unseen environment in the prisoner's world, with few exceptions, continues to be charged with ideational content inimical to reform. Except in a few bright new institutions, prisoners today tend to affiliate in informal group life much as they did twenty years ago. The prison world is drab and graceless in spite of the television sets and flowers on the campus. There is monotony and even stupor, in spite of group counseling and psychotherapy. Homosexuality is about as prevalent now as of old, in spite of classes in sex education and liberalized visiting. By and large there is disinterest in work, in spite of vocational training and occupational aptitude tests. And so on. The improvements suggested among 60 per cent of prisons are real but have been only in degree, for the old patterns continue.

If this evaluation may appear pessimistic, let it be recalled that there have been 105 riots or serious disturbances in American prisons since 1950. These riots have occurred in institutions with progressive programs as well as in some of the 40 per cent which are regarded as unimproved in the last two decades. The resistance to therapies, and the elements for riot as well, evolve from the subculture, so to speak, in the prison community. What remains to combat in most modern prisons is the unseen environment, which is a stronger force for evil than the programs are for good.

As humanitarianism increases, as more good men enter prison work, as the much needed institutions for smaller populations are constructed, and as the sciences which deal with the nature of human nature invent improved tools for treatment, the criminality of some offenders, which is now increased by the existing prison culture, may well be decreased in that brave new world somewhere ahead.

D.C.

Washington, D.C.
April, 1958

PREFACE TO THE 1940 EDITION

The purpose of this book is to present to the reader an accurate representation of an American penitentiary. A typical prison, strictly speaking, does not exist but the institution here studied has many features common to all American penitentiaries. It is typical as to size, varying only 200 in population from the average of fifty-one major correctional institutions. It is not atypical as Sing Sing or Joliet would be, prisons whose populations are made up almost exclusively of men committed from the metropolitan areas they border. Our prison is fairly typical in respect to discipline, labor, and the various practices found in most other adult correctional institutions. It has been described by a distinguished penologist who has inspected every American penitentiary as, "just another place where men do time."

The approach used differs from the more common one in which a survey is made of prison administration, discipline, industry, labor, sanitation, and the like, for it aims at a description of the *culture* of the prison. Thus, since the interest of the book centers on the structure and social relationships in the prison community, it is more concerned with social processes than with incidents. Attention is focused on such phenomena as class stratification, informal group life, leadership, folkways, and various other social controls. The writer hopes that he has been able to make clear the pattern of prison life woven of those salient social forces which influence and prescribe the attitudes and behavior of prisoners, or, in other words, that he has been able to make understandable the extent and degree to which the culture of the penitentiary determines the philosophy of its inhabitants.

While the reader of this book is dealing with the social aspects of one contemporary prison as a concrete entity, he should keep in mind the social philosophy which has initiated and sponsored the prison movement. The history of penology from the Middle Ages to the present time, the various public opinions concerning crime, and especially the social, political and economic organizations in this more recent society have pertinent relationships with the social life of a prison. Today's penitentiary is not a closed culture. Society has fostered prisons for some of its members, and these members have brought into prison the *ways* of society. These ways are controlled, however, and the prisoner community, in a conflict between control and tradition, fuses into a unique societal combination.

The point of view of this study may be said to be a sociological one, since its chief concern has been the making of an analysis of social patterns as the determinants of behavior. As a community the prison is a social phenomenon and for that reason an attempt has been made to emphasize the social processes in operation. Processes become evident, however, in events or series of events which occur in time, and these studies cover the period 1931-34. Much of the literature dealing with prisons is in the nature of emotional muckraking, or is so specific in its emphasis that the reader loses the sense of the whole. It would therefore seem worth while from an historical standpoint to have a report on a fairly typical American prison in the present decade, for a few years hence, as social inventions are adopted, our penal institutions may not have the heterogeneous characteristics so common now.

In no sense is this study an attack on prisons, the people in them, or the ones who manage them. The prison world is interpreted as a natural outgrowth of social trends, and pains have been taken that these interpretations shall be objective and dispassionate. No effort has been made to prove or disprove any particular doctrine. In a way the study is a compendium, for it attempts to cover the most important aspects of an American prison in the nineteen thirties, and perhaps we may think of the institution described here as the "Middletown" of American prisons.

This book was made possible through the writer's work in the prison as sociologist of the Mental Health staff, a professional staff consisting of a psychiatrist, a psychologist, a physician and a sociologist, and which later became known as the Classification Board. While the materials which compose the book were gathered for the most part by the writer independently of his routine staff duties, data collected by the members of the Classification Board in the day-by-day discharge of their work have formed valuable additions. The regular duties of the writer consisted largely of interviewing inmates. In these examinations social histories were collected and inmate personalities were evaluated with respect to criminality. Information thus obtained was combined with the findings of the psychiatrist, psychologist, and physician, and was available to the Parole Board, the wardens, and the superintendent of prisons.

I am indebted to a number of persons for help in the preparation of this volume. I am particularly grateful to Dr. Paul L. Schroeder, my chief of staff, who made possible the assembling of the materials for these studies. To Mrs. Lilian Davis who read and edited the manuscript I express my sincere thanks. Invaluable counsel and aid of other kinds has been received from Albert C. Welge, sociologist, Dr. Luton Ackerson, psychologist, Dr. R. G. Barrick, psychiatrist, Richard C. Garrison and Clifford C. Shaw, sociologists, my parents, Dr. and Mrs. Franklin B. Clemmer, and my wife, Rose Emelia Clemmer. Acknowledgement is made to Professor Donald R. Taft for his helpfulness during my eight years of penal work. To my Warden, respects are paid for his early progressiveness and permission to conduct some of the studies here reported which were made after he took office. But chiefly my deepest and most heartfelt gratitude goes to the countless inmates who knowingly or unknowingly contributed to the making of this book. A few of them I can now mention by the names I have always called them: To Pug, Will, Jim, Paul, Pat, Sparky, Fitz, Jim R., Slinky, Harry, Joe, Danny, Shorty, Irish, Marvin, Glenn, Swede, to my football teams and to the memory of Bill, I am greatly indebted and I thank them all.

D.C.

1940

THE PRISON COMMUNITY

The Prison Community

CHAPTER I

Culture Antecedents of the Prisoners

Our 2,300 inmates live in a walled-in area of thirteen acres. Their isolation is more geographic than social. Though living in an unnatural environment, unnatural because of limited choice, they perform a good many of the customary acts of life. In living together they have relationships with one another, and the character, type, and degree of these social relationships depend on a wide variety of conditions. An important determinant of relationships in prison is the type of experiences a man has had with other persons before he came to prison. In a sense, the very fact of penitentiary residence is symptomatic of disturbed social relations in the free community.

Man is a political animal. What he is as an adult is largely the result of what he has learned through infancy, boyhood, and youth. His personality is only partly determined by heredity and biologic factors. His personality is predominantly the expression of his association with other people. The man is what he has learned to be. We are to be concerned in this first chapter with some of the things which our inmates have learned before commitment. Such knowledge provides a basis for understanding the relations within prison and offers a foundation for appraising the effect of penitentiary culture on inmate personalities. To understand the causation of crime is not our central purpose. Rather, we wish to know the wishes, ambitions, drives, habits and attitudes of our men because it is these forces which bring to the prison community some of the factors which make it unique and determine its culture.

Attitudes, ambitions, and wishes are the resultants of association; they are group bred. Not only do the intimate or close associations make the personality, but the bombardment of ideas from impersonal sources shape man's ideations. Every social experience is important. Every item in the national life, in the schools and churches, in government and in industry, contains conditioning influences which affect human beings. Our inmates, no less than others, are the product of human interaction. We wish to see what the culture of the free community has done to them, and we desire to know the phases or items of culture which they carry into prison. We shall attempt to do this by scanning three sources of phenomena. First, we shall briefly look for the major characteristics and the broad social trends in American life which are likely to influence indirectly the attitudinal structure of the person who comes to prison. Secondly, by delimiting our search, we can seek for more direct influences in the regions or areas whence our inmates have come. Thirdly, we can inspect even more closely the intimate contacts and social relationships which the persons have had before incarceration.

Some Broad Social Trends

Few persons will deny that in the American scene there is a melting of morals, an uncertainty in creeds, and an indecision in defining situations. In every institution, the family and home, the church and school, in business, industry, and in government there are bewildering social problems. One need only read *Recent Social Trends* [1] to perceive the utter complexity of social phenomena. The social problems, these authors say, are products of changes in all phases of life, material and social, but most particularly in social organizations and social habits. The changes are interrelated and one change affects another, but effects are often delayed and maladjustment results. We cannot say, of course, that the social changes wholly account for crime, or prisons, but we must concede that the social changes affect the social institutions and influence people. Those social trends which are most prominent in modifying the personalities of men who become inmates will be briefly reviewed here. We cannot ignore the broad factors even though the observable connectives may seem to be slight. The broad social trends influence the minute social relationships. Perspective is everything.

The distribution of a population in any nation is a determinant of the social processes in the culture. The most significant movements of peoples in recent decades relate to their concentration in cities. The question is arising as to whether the cities are becoming too crowded for comfort, economy,[2] and honest relationships. City life has a fast tempo. Values fluctuate in importance, yet for every value a myriad of attitudes exist. There are thousands of contacts among the inhabitants of a city, and impersonal relationships abound. Because of the anonymity of urban life the conduct of a city's people is less subject to stringent social controls than for-

---

[1] Report of the President's Committee on Social Trends. *Recent Social Trends in the United States,* McGraw-Hill Book Co., Inc., New York, 1933

[2] *Ibid.,* p. lvii.

merly. Individualism flourishes. Cities and metropolitan areas are productive of maladjusted personalities, some of whom we call criminals, and the urban centers are much more productive than are the rural areas.[3] Cities develop neighborhoods where crime is a common way of life. To a large extent[4] men commit crimes because of social conditions and the social conditions of cities are conducive to many forms of crime.

The distribution of the population is probably not as important as, though related to, the rapid changes in the material culture. The differences between the personality of the ten-year-old child today and a child of similar age in 1900 are not a matter of heredity. Scientific inventions have literally changed the way of life. "More and more inventions are made every year, and there is no reason to think that technological events will ever stop."[5] It takes about thirty years for inventions to be adopted,[6] and while they make for comfort they also aid in making life more complex, and more confused. One need but listen to the radio a few hours to be presented with an array of bewildering and contradictory attitudes. Driving a car in Sunday traffic brings thousands of perceptions concerning one's fellow-man and the devices and means he uses to obtain what have come to be optimal conditions. The more variable and complex the culture, the more variable and unpredictable is the behavior of persons within it. The matter of making a living is no longer simple. Machines have taken the work of many hands. "In 1870 77 per cent of the gainfully occupied persons in the United States were engaged in transforming the resources of nature into objects of usable form through manufacturing, mining, agriculture; in 1930, only 52 per cent."[7] Inventions cause the gravest problems in unemployment, in leisure time practices, in morals, in education and law. The speed of material and mechanical inventions has far outstripped the advancements of social inventions and maladjustment has resulted.

In a natural economy which flourishes in one year and flounders in another, can be found the reciprocal causes for much of the social instability. The halcyon days of 1925–29 can be matched only by a great depression in contributing to social problems. "The income of a whole population (in depression) falls by 10 or 20 per cent; in extreme depressions by a substantially greater figure. And these average losses are accompanied by appalling individual tragedies in millions of cases scattered through all classes of society, but

[3] E. H. Sutherland, ***Principles of Criminology,*** J. B. Lippincott Co., Chicago, 1934, p. 122.

[4] ***Recent Social Trends, op. cit.,*** p. xxiii.

[5] ***Ibid.,*** p. xxv.

[6] ***Ibid.,*** p. xxv.

[7] ***Ibid.,*** p. xxvii.

commonest among those who have few resources."[8] Great wealth and luxuries for the few, a comfortable living for the many, but poverty for about one-third of the people, are facts well known and well understood in their significance to the social order. There are differences in the distribution of wealth and privilege. Our customary emphasis upon private initiative, self-help, rugged individualism, and the holding of private property have brought material advantages and comforts of a high order to a large number of people but have left an even larger number deprived of what has come to be considered, the essentials. Poverty and dependency go hand in hand with an economic system such as ours. Death rates are considerably higher in the low income group. "Until a point is reached where the present death rate does not vary according to income, it seems paradoxical to claim that wage earners are receiving a living wage."[9] Labor organizations have arisen in protest to domination by capital as expressed in low wages, long hours, unsafe working conditions. Since the World War of 1914–18, some adjustments have been made and labor conditions, while still in a sorry plight, are said to have improved.[10] "From the beginning of the century until the depression beginning in 1929, labor's standard of life has been raised about 25 per cent, as measured by the purchasing power of wages, although this increase prevailed through only a few of the thirty years. In the two years following 1929, the aggregate money earnings paid to American employees fell about 35 per cent while the cost of living declined 15 per cent."[11] Can we say that our national wanderings in economics are not intimately related to crime, to prisoners, to the penal environment?

The economic structure in our national culture affects many institutions and none more important than the family. The family has, to a large extent, been displaced as an occupational institution and as an educating and recreation center, and to a lesser degree, as a major social organization. The family is exceedingly important as "the cradle of personality." It meets the need for affection.[12] It changes the biologic organism of the infant into a human being, but there is evidence to show that many functions of the family have been lost and not completely replaced, and that the former sturdiness of the family has waned. "Divorces have increased to such an extent that, if present trends continue, one of every five or six bridal couples of the present year will ultimately have their marriage broken in the divorce court."[13] Women and housewives have become

---

[8] *Ibid.*, p. xxxl.
[9] *Ibid.*, p. xxxv.
[10] *Ibid.*, p. xlii.
[11] *Ibid.*, p. xlii.
[12] *Ibid.*, p. xlii.
[13] *Ibid.*, p. xlii.

emancipated and are finding their places in occupations outside of the home. Families are slightly smaller than thirty and ten years ago, especially in cities.[14] The changing conditions of modern life make the rearing of children more difficult, even though greater stress is being given the subject. There is a widening of the gap between parents and children, brought about by the differences in education and by social changes.[15] "Such differences joined with the growing individualization of the members of the family, and the complexity of the new urban environment, reduce the conscious control of the parents over the children." [16]

The government of a nation, state, and city affects every personality included in its scope. The growing complexity of government, the inertia of the people, the tendency toward the decay of democracy, and the self-interest of many persons active in government agencies, form patterns which influence every relationship. Our legislatures as bodies do not hold the general respect of the people.[17] Corruption and graft in the government of cities is almost the expected thing. The services rendered by political bosses are frequently personal and temporary and too seldom are a public benefaction.

The police are frequently regarded as corrupt, brutal, and inefficient.[18] State's attorneys are known to indulge in graft. The judiciary is ridiculed frequently for inefficiency and outright dishonesty. In practically every form of government, there is, at times, evidence to indicate marked inefficiency, dishonesty, or both. Thus, many governmental agencies and functions are held in disrespect. "Aside from the fear of punishment one would generally prefer to be caught breaking almost any of the laws (except those relating to the most serious felonies) rather than to eat peas with his knife, and in certain groups even the felonies are less serious than breaches of etiquette." [19] Competition, conflict, and self-interest abound, not only individually but among groups. People who are otherwise honest feel it legitimate to dodge some form of taxes. Laws which do not have the support of public opinion are considered as something to ignore or evade, and even when there is a cohesive public opinion, minority groups and individuals, in self-interest, justify their evasions by pointing to what others have done. All of these factors and many more have resulted in the

[14] William F. Ogburn and Clark Tibbets, *The Family and Its Functions,* pp. 683–685.
[15] *Ibid.,* p. 699.
[16] *Ibid.,* p. 699.
[17] E. H. Sutherland, *op. cit.,* p. 164.
[18] *Ibid.,* p. 164.
[19] *Ibid.,* p. 165.

construction of a great amount of legislation which frequently is held in disrespect.[20]

The broad social conditions and trends which we have briefly mentioned here cast influences on all men and operate with other factors to determine their lives. The criminal often does not see the beauty of American life, the slow, but inevitable progress of our nation and the ideals of kindness, service, and honesty which are common in many persons. He does not understand or consider social trends. He does not compare the standard of life, nation with nation. He does not objectify the perceptions he receives. Seldom does a prisoner speak a good word for government in the abstract. The criminal is, by and large, the sheer individualist. He is not the worst of the individualists and he is less canny than most. He is a residue of our individualistic society; he is left after the more clever, more lucky, more socially literate persons are sifted out.

The man presently "destined" for prison arises in the morning to a life in which the newspapers scream of crime, and make dramatic news of a robbery. He walks to work through streets of poverty, filth, and destitution on the one hand, and of luxuries, comforts, and riches on the other. He reads as he walks and notes that a former government official was found guilty of embezzling a hundred thousand dollars and was granted probation. He works in his shop long hours for small pay, doing the same job over and over. He comes home at night past gambling establishments and prostitution in full flourish. He sees a former friend who had less schooling than he and who has never worked, sleek, well groomed, driving an expensive car in the company of smart, beautifully gowned women. He eats a tasteless supper in a cheap, crowded, and noisy restaurant. No one talks to him. He does not ponder either the state of the nation or international affairs. But things do not seem fair to him. He never gets any breaks, he says. There is the friend with the expensive car who tells him, "Only saps work." He knows that the precinct committeeman gets a cut from the hand-book. He knows that the mayor of the city is only in his office an hour a day. He thinks his employer will lay him off because orders are not good. He joined the union, but there are grafters in that, too. In short, it is only the social conditions that touch this man directly, which influence him. He does not perceive the broader aspects out of which his immediate environment has been made, but the student of human nature cannot ignore the social trends if a true perspective is to result.

---

[20] *Ibid.*, p. 163.

Regions and Areas Which Produce Our Inmates

The penitentiary in which this study was made serves an area in one state of 34,000 square miles. This state is a diversified territory. Included in it is a portion of a large metropolitan district. There are two cities which approach 100,000 in population, and several cities varying between 25,000 and 60,000 inhabitants. There is also an extensive agricultural area in which corn, the grains, and fruit, especially apples are raised. It is further diversified by having an extensive coal mining area. In a small portion of the territory is an oil field. This diversification of economic activities in the territory which it serves gives to our prison much of the character, we believe, which makes it fairly representative of all American prisons. The variety of regions from which our population comes not only makes it fairly typical of all American prisons, but gives rise to interesting social relationships in the prison by men conditioned in different geographical and economic situations.

Too much stress should not be given to the characteristics of the particular state, however, because men who come to prison are a nomadic lot. Slightly over half of our inmates are native to the state in which the prison is located, and a large proportion are native to three bordering states, but a number have been highly mobile. In seeking to determine the regions which have had the greatest influence on the inmates' lives, case histories have been studied. Thus, the region or area in which a man has lived longest, and which seems to have had the greatest influence on his life, has been designated as the predominant conditioning region. In Table I the findings are presented for a random sample of 800 cases. The coal mine areas are, of course, the towns and small cities near the mines where the central occupational pursuit is mining. The open-country item refers to the completely rural situation and the tabulation includes men who have lived predominantly in farming situations near an agrarian village. In the town-and-village category we have included those inmates whose lives have been spent largely in communities up to 15,000 population. The Bureau of the Census designates that towns of 2,500 population or over should be classed as cities, but many communities of less than 15,000 do not contain the social characteristics of cities. In the table the item "cities" refers to all urban areas with a population over 15,000, excepting metropolitan districts. Metropolitan areas are, of course, cities and their satellites such as New York, Chicago, St. Louis, Los Angeles. While only one metropolitan area is included in the territory which our prison serves, many of our inmates have lived in such districts in other states. In the mixed category we have recorded those cases in which no one area can be singled out as being predominant, or where our data are inconclusive.

TABLE I

The Predominant Localities Wherein 800 *Inmates Have Been Culturally Conditioned*

	White		Negro		Total	
	Number	Per cent	Number	Per cent	Number	Per cent
Coal Mine	56	8	5	4	61	8
Open Country	95	14	5	4	100	13
Town and Village	190	28	23	20	213	27
City	160	23	37	33	197	25
Metropolitan Area	121	18	33	29	154	20
Mixed or Uncertain	64	9	11	10	75	9
Total	686	100	114	100	800	100

The significance in presenting this information rests in the fact that personalities are what they are, in large part, because of the cultural forces that have played upon them. Personal behavior and social organizations are correlatives [21] although individual differences in personalities and other factors as well need to be understood. Professor Hiller states, "It is now clear that certain uniform ways of behavior which characterize a group depend less upon unique capacities than upon culturally induced attitudes." [22] As indicated in the foregoing section, the men who become inmates, as well as most other people, feel the influence of the social forces expressed in culture patterns directly, only if their individual lives are touched. Without referring to individual persons we will attempt to characterize what seems to be a representative sample of each of the five natural areas shown in Table I. If we have understanding and know the meaning of the broad culture in which the prisoners have lived, we have a part of the foundation necessary to appreciate the personal relationships which develop in the penitentiary.

Let us first take the coal-mining community. "Coalville" is a town of 7,000 people located in the heart of the coal country. It is the county seat. There are four other large towns in adjacent counties which are also coal centers. It has hot summers and reasonably mild winters. It has a concentrated business district which centers around the streets which border the county court house. One large and gaudy movie house, six pool rooms, about fourteen saloons or taverns (since repeal), five churches, two labor union halls, various lodge rooms, a golf course, and the school houses,

[21] E. T. Hiller, *Principles of Sociology,* Harper and Brothers, New York, 1933, p. 499.
[22] *Ibid.,* p. 499.

take care of its extra-family life. Also, due to excellent state roads, there is much travel to the larger towns nearby. The major occupational activity is mining. The mines are located a few miles from the town, and are owned by a corporation with headquarters several hundred miles away. The mines are worked seasonally, but, until the depression of 1929, were active about ten months a year except during occasional strikes. Strikes have been frequent, due, the union members say, to low wages and unsafe working conditions. The miners are paid the union scale, however, and work the prescribed number of hours. The mine owners have added much new machinery to the mines, thus creating a situation in which the labor supply is greater than the need. With the coming of the depression coal mining became sporadic, and a still larger volume of relief funds was necessary than already existed due to the technological unemployment. Next to mining, farming is the most important occupational activity and Coalville is a small agricultural center. Two railroads offer transportation in addition to the trucking on state roads. There are the usual number of merchants in a town of 7,000 and the chain stores thrive although the policies of their corporations have been anti-labor.

About 12 per cent of the total population are foreign born.[23] The male–female distribution and the distribution of children are typical of small American cities. Of the 564 families on relief in 1932, 265 were miners; 148 were ex-miners who even in normal times had no work due largely to technological unemployment; 76 were common laborers; and 78 were other types of workers. About 25 per cent of the relief clients were outright or partial owners of their own homes. Over three-quarters of such clients had lived in the town for more than five years. The median size of families was 4.8 members per unit. Though some old-world traits continue, customs in family life are Americanized. The homes provide a shelter and a center of affection, but most other functions, including recreation, except for the very young, are found outside the home.

The great effort in Coalville is making a living. The miner, the striker, the two competitive unions, and relief, both private and public, are major topics in the folk talk. Politics and political affiliation are largely a matter of issues, and not men, as they so frequently are, and the main issue deals with which party can do the most for a man or his union.

An important extra-familial activity among both the older and the younger men is drinking. Before repeal they drank in speakeasies, now, in saloons. They are hard workers and hard drinkers who, in

---

[23] United States Department of Commerce, Bureau of the Census, Fifteenth Census of the United States, Population, vol. III, Part I, Reports by States, United States Government Printing Office, Washington, D. C., 1930, p. 599.

drink, are argumentative and assaultive and fights are frequent. Gambling is widespread throughout the community. It occurs less frequently in homes than in the back of saloons or at private meetings. Much of the wagering is professionally operated by "housemen"; dishonesty is common. There is not much providence in the community. The men who work hard for their money spend it freely, often for immediate pleasures. Gambling, drinking, automobiles, union dues, and commercial recreation such as movies, pool, and carnivals, take the greater part of the wages which are not spent for the essential living requirements. During the depression the failure of the three banks added to the financial distress of an improvident community.

Coalville is not vicious. It is not ridden by especially corrupt public officials. In the past it has been a hard-working, free-spending, social organization where prestige results, in the main, from the possession of typical American luxuries and personable masculinity. The hard worker, the union man, the fighter, the drinker, the family-man who treats his family well but who is not opposed to occasional promiscuity—such are the men held in esteem in Coalville. The town is something like a frontier; it is for hardy people. Except for the professional group there are almost no persons with higher education. There is a tradition of a type of courage among the townfolk. "We've been fighting these mine owners so long that we are used to fighting. . . . We have as much right to live as anyone else. . . . Why should people in ———— get more relief than we do? Why shouldn't we have cars and radios and decent homes and good times just like they (the owners) do? We do the work and they sit in their offices and tell us what to do and how to live." While a solidarity based on the mutual low economic status exists, there is also considerable disassociation. Jealousies over possessions and authority are common. Occasional dishonesty in the unions and considerable dishonesty in personal relations is common. A good proportion of relief clients lie, as they hoard supplies. Business men cut prices. In spite of superficial civilities and some community loyalty, there is a dog-eat-dog philosophy among the sample of the population studied.[24]

Crime in Coalville includes all types of offenses, but murder and manslaughter are more common than in most communities. Most of the offenses in the past twenty years have not been of a professionalized type, with the exception of those committed by a mob

[24] The material presented here on this and other communities has been compiled from census data, chamber of commerce leaflets, findings of relief organizations, and, more important, from the writer's six months of activities in administering relief in twenty-two counties. Also, the homes and neighborhoods of some inmates have been investigated by the community-approach method.

which flourished during prohibition in bootlegging activities. What Capone was to Chicago, two brothers were to the coal counties. They manufactured whiskey; they delivered it throughout the coal areas and to the largest cities within two hundred miles; they shot down their would-be competitors in true gangland fashion; they fought among themselves; they controlled some public officials and double-crossed others; they lent terror and drama to the jazz age in the coal country. Though one of the leaders was hanged and another killed, their exploits are still much talked of. The activities of the gang set a pattern; it brought gangsterism to the coal towns. Ten years later we notice the influence of this gang on our twenty-year-old youths who are coming to prison now. The gang functioned outside the law, but not outside public opinion, for prohibition was never popular in the coal-mine towns.

So in Coalville and the mining centers which are like it, we find a population whose bread winners are idle a good share of the time due to depression, strikes, technological unemployment, and weather. We have a community in which higher education is relatively unknown. There is solidarity in the community which unites the members when in conflict with a dominant financial group, but we find petty dishonesty, jealousies, and corrupt practices in the ordinary life. Drinking is traditional and tolerated. The aggressive, personable male is prized. Most desired are luxuries for comfort and aggrandizement, yet money and wealth are not easily acquired, and in some six hundred families extreme poverty is avoided by a pittance of relief. Many are becoming pauperized; space for gardens stands empty. There is much talk, many meetings, a humming social life, and many accusations on all sides, but things do not change much. About 8 per cent of our inmates have been conditioned in such a regional culture.

As fairly representative of one type of open-country region in which 13 per cent of our prisoners were predominantly conditioned, we will take Farm County. This county has an area of 733 square miles. The population in 1930 was 19,130, of which 19,050 persons were native born.[25] There were two Negroes. There were 3,100 farms totaling 375,000 acres. In 1930 the farms were valued at more than twelve million dollars, and in 1935, at about eight million dollars. The major occupation is farming except in the county seat, with a population of 3,500, wherein two manufacturing concerns have a total weekly payroll of five thousand dollars. There are also four small towns in the county ranging between 150 and 300 in population.

Corn and the grains are raised, as well as fruit on the southern

[25] United States Department of Commerce, Bureau of the Census, op. cit., p. 601.

border. The barns and farms seem well cared for, but the houses were the tenants live are shabby, for the most part, except those on a few estates. We have no reliable data as to ownership, but it is estimated that two-thirds of the 3,100 farms are operated by tenants or share-croppers.

It is the custom of the farmers to work long hours during eight months of the year. Hard work, neat fences, shiny machinery, tall corn, large yields per acre, thrift, several children, fat hogs, an automobile, and membership in the county farm organization, are held in esteem. Recreation for the farm people consists of the weekly trip to town for shopping and a band concert, attendance at fairs, picnics, the movies, and political meetings. Interests are narrow and local, except in regard to agriculture, and in that the national scene is watched. For the younger folk of the farm families the dances at the county seat, movies, girl-courting, and motoring are the prevalent recreations. Drinking by young folks is largely secretive and occasional, and is not condoned. The existence of paved roads, refreshment stands on the borders of town and nearby cities, make for considerable mobility in seeking recreation. Also, those who wish to indulge in more exaggerated recreational forms leave the county, as gossip travels fast, and is a means of control. There seems to be a breakdown in social distance between the rural and urban peoples, evidenced in the personal relations between farm boys and the girls who work in the factory at the county seat. These girls are paid about eight dollars a week. Money contributed to the support of the home, and for clothes in the Ginger Rogers style, consume their incomes, so their recreational expenses are cared for by the young men, many of them from the surrounding country.

Government is honest in Farm County. Graft is almost unknown. There is close relationship between each township supervisor and his constituents. People are interested in politics for self-interest, but also as entertainment and pastime. In 1932 the county voted 5 to 4 Democratic, but previously had been predominantly Republican.

The occasional crime that occurs in this county, and in others like it, follows no set pattern. A hired man on a farm may steal twenty dollars from his employer. A share-cropper may steal three head of sheep from a farm ten miles away. A farm boy may steal a car for a joyride, and an intellectually dull farm hand may rape a fourteen-year-old girl. An occasional murder may result from marital infidelity. Most of the crimes are of a personal-social nature. The petty, predatory crimes, if they happened in a city, would never call for penitentiary placement, but the state's attorneys, for a number of reasons, including their desire to be "convicting prosecutors," send men to prison in whom criminality is no more advanced than in the average "sharp" business man, if as much so.

Farm County is different, however, from another type of rural region, of which "River County" is fairly typical. It is not necessary here to give any but the barest details. River County, as its name implies, is bordered on one side by a large river. It is a hilly and wild country. Farm land is hard to till except for the "bottoms" along the river. The operators of the farms are largely tenants, and their farming skill is limited. Hunting, trapping, fishing, bootlegging, square dances, and picnics are the pleasurable activities. Men marry young girls. There is a flavor of "Tobacco Road" in River County. Esteemed traits among the men are physical prowess, hunting and fishing skill, the ability to hold liquor, the domination of women, the provision of a decent living and personableness. The general culture might be designated as "hillbilly." Portions of River County are a frontier in a more real sense than Coalville is. For the state as a whole the percentage of illiteracy is 11.5 in the rural districts, but for River County it is slightly higher.[26] In the country areas the boy who has finished the eighth grade at twenty years has done "right well."

The crime, as might be suspected, is largely theft with assault, in which drinking is frequently a contributing factor. The men who come to prison from River County and the regions which are like it, are somewhat naive and quaint in the penal population. They are frequently stupid and gullible but for sheer physical courage and uncontrollable temper they "out-tough" the city's gangsters. One section of this region is described by the state's attorney as follows:

> I am in receipt of yours of June 1st in which you refer to the young men set to prison from and about ———.
>
> This is strictly a farming and bootlegging neighborhood. A great deal of rich farming land lying in the river bottoms and overflowing each year is cultivated by tenant farmers and they devote the time not used in the cultivation of these lands to moonshining. Perhaps ninety per cent of the land has been owned in the past by a half dozen landlords who were not too strict in the morals and standing of their tenants, with the result that there has a psychology developed in this community that the usual status of living is on the border line of the criminal law.
>
> The cultural standards are very low; in fact, very few of the older inhabitants can read or write, and many of the younger generation are similarly handicapped.
>
> There is no great prevalence of feeble-minded in this community, but there is a feeling for one to be really an accepted member of the social structure there he must watch and despise "the law" and must not snitch.

[26] *Ibid.*, p. 610.

It was in this vicinity that Federal prohibition agents were fired upon two years ago and one of them severely wounded.

The lads that have been sent are typical products of the *toughs* of this community.

The 13 per cent of our inmates who have been predominantly conditioned in regions such as River and Farm counties, as we shall see, contribute to the heterogeneity of the prison population and affect the relationships in strange ways.

To represent the city in which twenty-five per cent of the penal population have lived for the longest period of their lives, we will take a community of 57,000 people and call it "Leeds." The population is about equally distributed between male and female, and also has a typical distribution in age groups. Three per cent are Negroes and 4 per cent are foreign born.[27] Leeds appears to be a fairly typical, small American city. It has the customary business district with "small" skyscrapers. A section of the city is composed of excellent, well-cared-for residences and pretentious apartment buildings; another section has smaller, but neat and tidy homes; a third section has somewhat tumble-down houses with children's toys strewn about; and yet another area is slum like, with old, two-story flats and weather-beaten frame houses. Around one edge of the city is an industrial district dominated by a massive plant where several thousand persons work. Three railroads and several bus lines connect it with two large metropolitan centers less than two hundred miles away. The city has 700 acres of parks and an artificial lake constructed many years ago at a cost of two million dollars. The school system is modern and probably progressive. A college of 500 students towards the south end of the city seems to play only a slightly greater part in Leeds, than did the college in Middletown.[28] There is the customary, humming social life with women's organizations, Rotary, Kiwanis, the Country Club, drama clubs, American Legion, and so forth. There are movies and taxies, hotels and restaurants, dance halls and saloons, lodges and libraries, handbooks and prostitutes, and all the other institutions that go to make up an American city. Anonymity of a sort exists, but chiefly between classes. Most of the hoodlums know each other in the same way that most of the elite do. And the politicians know every one for different reasons.

In one respect Leeds is not typical in its agencies for dealing with delinquency, for it is reported to have an advanced and socialized probation department, but in spite of this there are many repre-

---

[27] *Ibid.*, p. 610.

[28] Robert and Helen Lynd, ***Middletown***, Harcourt, Brace and Co., New York, 1929, *passim*.

sentatives of Leeds in our prison. The police seem little different than the police of other cities. They go about their duties in the regular way, extending privilege where it counts. The honky-tonk provides most of the arrests, a great share of the arrested being itinerants or drunks. Gambling flourishes in a semi-open manner. There is no isolated red light district, but any cab driver will tell the inquirer where to go.

The crimes which occur in Leeds and other cities like it are predominantly offenses against property. Burglaries, theft of cars, armed robberies of stores, shops, gas stations, and theatres, are common. The offenders, in the main, want the luxuries and pleasures that they cannot, or will not, get otherwise. The thief in Leeds is generally not envious of those who work for their luxuries; he has no hatred of class, but he simply wants things for himself. He wants the superluxuries, if he has any to start with, and if not, like the Negro, he wants food for his stomach and bright ties for his neck. However, many of the offenders from Leeds have been stealing for a long time. They seem to have learned to steal first little things, for fun, then bigger things, and many of them started in their home neighborhood. In fact, there is some dishonesty in practically all of Leeds' neighborhoods. People do not always pay their bills. Gossip is often untruthful. Business men may lunch together in the finest fellowship on Tuesday noon and plot to ruin each other on Wednesday morning. But there is civic spirit in Leeds, and the citizenry coöperate in most matters and are, by and large, essentially decent. Some phases of life would seem to be artificial and make-believe, but there is nothing artificial in the way they handle the law violators, or a part of them, as our prisoners can well attest.

Leeds is a prototype of "Metro." To represent the one metropolitan district within the territory served by our prison, and metropolitan areas in other states, we will briefly picture Metro in which some 20 per cent of our inmates have been predominantly acculturized. After all, we need take little space to describe Metro, as its features are already well known. To say that Metro is corrupt in government from the mayor's office to the living-room of the least-important precinct committeeman, is a commonplace. There is always the exception, and even the corrupt in municipal government perform some services. The student of social phenomena takes the long view, and when he knows that the police of Metro cuff the hands of suspected offenders (who, in the eyes of the law are still innocent until proven guilty) and beat them without mercy, and, in the next hour receive a "cut" of the "sucker's" money from a gambling establishment, he ponders the facts and wonders why social progress remains so retarded. Yet, only a short time ago, historically speaking, men were put to death by torture for a great number of offenses against the law. All policemen are not beaters, and all aldermen are not dishonest, but in the past and the present among Metro's officialdom dishonesty has cut a wide swath. The Metro which concerns us most is probably not typical of metropolitan American. It is worse. Corruption in relief, and dishonesty and graft in the department of juvenile probation, may be taken as indicators that the municipal system is alive with chisellers. The story of graft is an old story but it is important to us because the awareness of it on the part of men who come to prison plays a part in the relations they have among each other.

Metro has the usual districts, business and industrial, the main stem, the white way, the honky-tonk, and various assortments of residential neighborhoods. The ways of life are essentially the same as those of Leeds though the tempo may be faster. There are also greater economic extremes, dire poverty and vast wealth. The most debased area of Metro has prostitution, gambling, disease, "dope," poverty, and filth, but it is small and its habitues are relatively few. The great majority of Metro's population are decent, law-abiding, family-loving, sympathetic, generous, and aim to be honest. They build and maintain progressive schools, libraries, playgrounds, but they are apathetic towards government, and those best qualified to take part in it avoid it.

Metro's crime includes the entire array of unlawful acts. Not all the worst criminals come to prison. The bandits and the burglars, the car thieves, the murderers, and the rapists are the ones sent to the penitentiary. The grafters, the stock swindlers, the bank embezzlers, the dishonest advertisers, the gamblers, and the stone-hearted landlords, though their behavior may cause far greater social distress, are seldom convicted. Motivation for crime, as in Leeds, includes desire for comforts, luxuries, needs, pleasures, thrills, hate, revenge, and sex satisfaction.

For the village and town wherein 20 per cent of our men have been primarily conditioned, "Cardo," a community of 8,500 inhabitants, seems fairly representative. Cardo has only 2 per cent of foreign-born and a Negro population of 3 per cent. Cardo is in an agricultural area, but also has a railroad shop employing, in good times, 400 men. There is a small flour mill which works about 100 men in three shifts, and a small clothing factory employing 350 persons, most of whom are girls on small wages. There is a catsup factory which provides seasonal work, and the town includes the customary merchants and business men. The schools are modern, and the small library up-to-date. The Red Cross, the American Legion, the Business Men's Association, the various women's clubs, and so on, provide the interest-group activities. Cardo is a small

Middletown, and the functions noted by the Lynds are also observable here. Radio, hard roads, metropolitan newspapers, and other factors of communication, have broken down the isolation and entity that formerly was the small town. Yet there is a strict class differentiation between the people who live on one side of the railroad tracks and those who live on the other. The demarcation is largely economic, for Cardo has the typical American democracy, and snobbery in the European sense, is rare.

Cardo's youth are "wilder" than their brothers and sisters in Leeds, though exaggerated commercial recreation takes place away from the home town. The adult recreation is largely centered in the homes or in interest groups.

The criminals produced in Cardo have usually lived on the "wrong" side of the tracks. They have spent their lives in unpretentious surroundings, but have been impressed at every hand by the importance of money and wealth. Only a few of their crimes are committed in their home town. They go to the cities, where additional social influences are added to an already-formed predisposition towards crime. They steal for luxuries or needs and when they are caught they can't explain how they ever became "that way." The crime in Cardo itself is usually petty and trivial, except for an occasional murder resulting from a love triangle, or drunkenness, or insanity. As in the open country areas the thieves who commit their offenses in Cardo would seldom come to the prison if they had committed the same offense in a city where work-houses, jails, and probation are more commonly used. But the people and officials of the small town are in horror of the type of conduct which is stipulated as crime by the law. That, in the ordinary day-by-day goings-and-comings of Cardo's citizenry, many acts more unsocial than the offenses of criminals occur, there is not the slightest doubt.

These thumb-nail sketches of regions deal with much that is obvious. We have presented them here for the purpose of perspective and to further integrated thinking. The balance of the book will be given over to the more or less direct association of the inmates and the remaining portion of this first chapter will serve to illustrate the types of relationships which existed prior to segregation.

Direct Social Influences Preceding Imprisonment

We cannot hope, in one chapter or even in many volumes, to present a complete picture of the antecedents of prisoners. We can only point to some of the more frequent conditions and trust that by illustrating some of them the unmentioned factors will, as a result, come into the general understanding of the reader. A logical manner in which to approach the investigation of prisoner antecedents would be to divide arbitrarily, and then to measure and compare, the institutions or levels of activity in which the men have performed. Thus, the family, school, neighborhood, work life, and so on, might be investigated. This has been done, and is presented in the next chapter. We wish now, however, to think of the inmate's background in the free community as an entity of interrelated patterns. This is attempted by a presentation of portions of case studies, autobiographical statements by inmates themselves, and by the letters to inmates and officials, from mothers, sweethearts, wives, and children. While the letters are addressed to the men as inmates or to officials, they reflect the total pattern relationships that existed before incarceration. We wish also to present briefly an independent study which reveals intimate and direct social relationships before commitment.

In 1923 the Federal Bureau of the Census conducted a statistical study of 19,080 men who had been committed to prisons or reformatories during the first six months of that year. Some of the findings may prove helpful in furnishing background information. The Bureau of the Census found that 61.9 per cent of offenders were living with relatives at the time of the crime which caused their imprisonment, and 38.1 per cent were living alone or with non-relatives.[29] Over 69 per cent of the men were employed at the time of the crime.[30] The income of the sample showed that 53 per cent were receiving between ten and nineteen dollars a week, 30.5 per cent between twenty and twenty-nine dollars, and 3.4 per cent over seventy-five dollars a week.[31] It was also found that the divorced population furnished a disproportionate number of prisoners.[32] We cannot provide data for our prisoners for comparison with these for the findings of the Bureau are sixteen years old.

In the home life of our men will be found both love and care, indifference and brutality. In this first chapter we are emphasizing the culture antecedents of our inmates as entities of interrelated patterns, rather than as selected particular culture traits. Thus, letters by the relatives of inmates reveal a totality of the culture in which the inmate formerly moved. The thoughts conveyed, the use of words, and the feeling tones expressed in the letters of mothers, wives, and children, shed light on the nature of the social relationships and the culture in which they were fashioned.

---

[29] United States Department of Commerce, Bureau of the Census, Prisoners' Antecedents, United States Government Printing Office, Washington, D. C., 1929, p. 25, Table XV.

[30] *Ibid.*, p. 35, Table XXIII.

[31] *Ibid.*, p. 32, Table XX.

[32] *Ibid.*, p. 23.

Darling Son:

Sunday before Christmas and how I would love to be with you. You never told me about any change in your work. I hate to think of you doing that kind of work but the fresh air will do you good. I am sending you $2.00 and tomorrow will start on your Christmas box. It makes me happy to be able to send you one. I bought you a nice Christmas cake, too. It will be about like your Thanksgiving one. Can I send you fruit for New Year?

I sent my usual wreath to my father's grave yesterday and I am buying small gifts for the babies. That's all this Christmas. There is a nice radio here just now; it is playing "Memories." I am glad I have sweet ones of my children. Well, dear, there is so little news when I don't go any place, so will close with all my love.

Mother.

Dear Son:

It's been a long time since I last heard from you, and I have been worried. I sent you the underwear, I also sent the Thanksgiving food, but you didn't answer, how come you don't answer, have you been sick, you know how a mother feels, I am always worrying, although worrying don't do much good, you know, your Aunt L—— and I have been having bad dreams about you, so that is what kept us worrying all the more. Son, please write a letter to me if you can, let me hear something about you, your sisters, cousins, Aunt L—— send Love and kisses,

Your loving mother.

Illustrative of the relation between children and their fathers, are the following letters:

Dear Daddy:

I am sure you mean good if you got out. I have written to Mr. J——— to see if there is no way out for you. And besides you know you are guilty. If you will faithfully promise never more to do that again I will see what I can do. Because I don't want you to suffer. You may think I have a hard heart, but I have not. I have been feeling pretty good lately with the exception of a little cold. I wrote to A——— the other day but he hasn't answered yet. I have learned a lot of things here and I mean to make use of them later on. I am just beginning to learn how to crochet. Is Mom taking care of our things? And may I send for my Mother's crocheting things? I am sorry for N———. Say, did you know Uncle E——— was married again? I got a letter from Aunt T——— the same day I got yours, and I bet you can't guess who I got a letter from the other day. They said to tell you Hello.

As it is nearing Easter and we are having Holy Week I think I will give you a little prayer to say for your Holy Week's penance. "Oh, dear God, how I have grieved Thee by my wicked almost unforgivable sins. I pray you to forgive me and may I live a Holy life ever after." Please say this little prayer for me, will you, daddy? I think I will send you an Easter card if I can get one. My penance for Holy Week is to keep from getting angry at what some of the girls say. We had somewhat like the backend of a cyclone the other day some say it hit D———, others say it came from O———. It snowed but has all gone now. Well I will close now and pray I may yet get you out. Now that is no sign you are not guilty because if you do say you're not, you'll have to answer for it at the judgment seat of God, and so God bless you and N———.

Your loving daughter.

P. S. Be sure and say that little prayer and do some more penance for Holy Week.

The sixteen-year-old daughter quoted above was the co-party of her father's crime in incest. Her attitudes, interests, and use of words reveal something of the social relationships in which our inmate spent his earlier years.

The following portion of a letter from an eighteen-year-old son to his predatory father reflects the character of the relationships this inmate had with his family in their city home.

. . . . I guess the University of Southern California didn't take Notre Dame into camp. Was I glad? Anna how! Esther B——— used to go with some sap from there and I didn't like him. He was a great, big husky guy so I didn't tell him so. He went with her after I quit her and when I tried to step back in she wanted him to share half her time, so I just stepped back out again. Wasn't that the proper thing to do? If I stayed in I probably would have got my eyes blacked. I like these one man women like Mom, don't you? Mom never will love anybody but you, do you know that? Funny, ain't it? I always thought Mom had good taste, but since I have grown older I find she lacks both good judgment and good taste. Right? You're a liar, it ain't right! You're the one without the judgment. You know I have got into fights and almost into them, lots of time, over you. People always want to keep a man down when they get him there, don't they? And when they do that in front of me I try to lift you up and them too. I lift them up, though, by socking them under the chin.

Some letters addressed to the Mental Health Office and answers to questionnaires are revealing.

Dear Sir:

You have given me the privilege of telling you in
regard to my sons case.
This seems but a dream to me
It sure was a terrible shock
When the news came to me. My
Son never had an enemy as ever I new of.

He was well loved and Respected By all and made friends
wherever he went
I honestly believe he was influenced by leaders into
this crime. For he had no cause for doing it.
If you can help him in any way I sure would appreciate
it. For I have been a heart broken mother since this
happened for I need his support and care.

Yours very truly
Mrs. G——— B———.

Dear Sir: Just a fue lines on this side in Regard to Bill. he had an Invleid Father and I had to Work so hard being away from home nearly all the time to make a living and I Broke myself down and I had to keep Bill out of school to help me then his Father died in 1926 and he worked at C———'s on a farm. Then he worked at the Furniture Factory at F———, and worked 1 year and he another boy were scuffling and got layed off he done good work. he gave me from 10 to 15 per week and was good to me.
In regard to School We mooved to B——— on Georgy Ridge Mountains and they had school 2 months a year and that was July and August and the school was 5 miles away and my Children wasen't able to stand the walk he lost 4 years off scholin the Children made fun off him because he was so back in his studies and I diden't have money to get him clothes Fit to wear to school. When Bill Was a baby he had Indegeston and likes to off died Would die away and I would rub him to bring him back to life had to Dr. him so nearly a year but he is Very nervous yet will get up in his sleep and walk around. The man he stayed With last winter is dead he died 2 months ago. I think I have told you as clear as I can how my Son had to do.

thanking you I remain,
Mrs. H——— B———
a Broken hearted Mother.

Dear Drs.

I am writing something which I have never told anyone.

Not long after conception M———'s father did something which made me very angry. I worried and worried—tried to sell a small farm I had to get money to leave on. I have always thought that the reason G——— is like he is. Then too, a tree fell on him when he was 3 or 4 years of age. I have four other children, not any of them like him. He was good to get up mornings and help me in the kitchen. Also was neat about his clothes. No matter how late at night when he came in they were always in place. If you could help him, God alone knows how it would help me.

His mother
Mrs. L. M. S———.

The two preceding letters reveal conditions of poverty and underprivilege in a small town, and the following portions of letters reflect the same conditions in a city's slums. Poverty is a powerful determinant of the character of social relations.

Dear Dr.

My son W——— was a social & good boy easy to get along with & had no what you would call Bad unruly ways when under my control. But after going away from home to work he finally got in Bad Company. & W——— D——— is the Man Put him where he is today. & I sure Feel sad to know what Bad Bad Co. lead him astray. G——— & I have attend Good Serves Sunday School & all good places for Mother's to have their Children go, as to keep them in good Co. & help Keep up their Repetation. I all Ways have Been a good Christian Mother & I exs. to Die a Praying for My Son in hopes that he can soon be a free Man as he sure was a noble and true Boy and Child for me.his sad Broken-Hearted

Mother.

. . . His father died when N. was 5 year old. He never was very strong. But being a poor widow with two smaller children I could not give them all the care and nourishment they needed.

So please do what you can for my son, and give him a chance. Of course I want him to do what is right and be honest. And that is what I have taught him, but why he has done this I can not understand. May I ask you to let me hear from you again sometime in regard to my sons case.

Yours truly,

Mrs. A——— B———.

Other relationships in the homes, schools, neighborhoods and workshops of our men become clear in the following portions of case studies.

Home Conditions and Relationships: The home relationships were dominated by the alcoholic behavior of the father. The informant (mother of the inmate) remarks that the father was, "bad . . . and chased the children." Before any of inmate's siblings married there was considerable overcrowding in the home, as the houses where subject had lived seldom had more than four or five small rooms. Only one of the six residences in which inmate spent the first twenty years of his life had any plumbing, and judging from the present abode, the housewifery was careless.

The first few years of the parents married life were apparently harmonious. But with the husbands turn to heavy drinking and with increasing poverty, marital conflict became more pronounced, and finally ended in a separation when inmate was eleven years old. Prior to the separation, the children were constant witnesses to the quarrels of the parents, and W———, the oldest child, killed himself at the age of 19 due to the unhappiness brought about by the father's conduct, the Informant reports. . . . Indicative of the family disintegration are the following: 1.) the children and mother would eat alone; the oldest daughter would then serve the father, who always ate alone; 2.) When the father was intoxicated he would pick up the furniture and throw it at the children; 3.) The mother and children frequently told neighbors of the father's conduct and the neighbors reported the conditions to the police. Officers would arrest the father, keep him in jail until he became sober and turn him loose. . . .

Such were the conditions in the home of one of our men during the first eleven years of his life. In a portion of another case study we find pertinent references to the type of neighborhood in which an inmate was reared.

Neighborhood: This man was born and reared in Y———. This is a community which has had a high rate of delinquency for three decades. It is a neighborhood in which Italians have replaced Poles, and Poles replaced Slovanians. Recently, some Negroes have been settling on the borders of the community. In spite of the changes of nationality composition, the delinquent patterns which have existed for so many years have continued. The neighborhood is a semi-business district through which a street car line passes. The street on which our inmates lives is one block removed from the car line, and the buildings there are all frame and of ramshackle appearance. The streets are dirty and littered with refuse. There is no grass on the parkways or in the yards. Casual glances into the buildings indicate that filth and uncleanliness prevails. Rents are low in the area and vary between eight and twenty dollars a month. For the most part the property is managed by agents for landlords who live in far better sections of the city. The families living here usually have large numbers of children. The youth of the community gather on street corners and in alleys. Boys' gangs roam over the area and, even before the members of the gangs are 10 and 12 years of age, they engage in petty preditory activity. The gangs of the younger boys are sometimes loosely affiliated with gangs of older boys who are bolder in their activities and more mobile. It is in such a community that inmate X——— has been reared.

From another study we will extract one short paragraph dealing with the interests and recreational activities of one of our men during his boyhood years.

Interest and Recreation: As a boy, offender wished to be a barber like his father before him. He had heard his mother speak of how nice the family had lived before his father's death. . . . When he became a little older, about 12, his interests were primarily in things mechanical. It seems to have been something of a fad in the various neighborhoods for the boys to make push-wagons and roller-skate cars. Informant accounts for this interest by stating that the boy is a "natural-born mechanic." His step-father did some carpenter work and L——— frequently borrowed his tools and made various wagons, carts, and little houses. . . . He was never a good mixer and preferred to play with his brothers and sisters rather than with the neighborhood children although he never shunned or stayed away from them when his siblings were playing with them. Street baseball, infrequent swimming trips, camping excursions, and grade school basketball made up his play program. . . .

A brief comment included in the case history of another inmate refers to a change in attitude during the inmate's youth following his mother's remarriage.

Control and Supervision: Before the death of offender's father, the mother states that L——— was always a kindly, obedient and quiet boy. His father never whipped him for slight misdemeanors but simply talked to him about it. When he was a little boy, informant states, she used to spank him, "just easy," whenever he ran away from home. . . . When the mother married B———, however, punishment for L——— increased and his attitude toward it changed. Whereas L——— took punishment gracefully from his parents, when the step-father whipped him for "teasing the dog" or "talking back," L——— would laugh at him which only made the step-parent more angry and he would whip the boy harder. On a few occasions, informant states, B——— became so rough that the mother stepped in and made him stop. This caused marital conflict with an attendant disposition on the part of the boy to run to his mother whenever the step-father became cross with him. Discipline by the mother was infrequent and probably lenient. "He was my first child and I never felt he needed much spanking. . . ."

In the material collected concerning the life adjustment of one of the inmates we have the following notation concerning his school life. In such instances as this portion of the case portrays, we find the customary paucity of educational opportunity in an impoverished rural area.

School: Offender attended the rural public school at X——— intermittently until he was twelve years old. He completed the third grade. . . . His school attendance was irregular and he wasn't "specially smart with books." The schools in this county were opened in late July and were closed before Christmas. This odd school period was necessitated by the conditions of the roads. There were no hard roads and the spring rains made walking to and from school an impossibility. Concerning his schooling the offender remarks, "My father made me work on the farm in the summers and in the mines during the winter." . . . On the Stanford-Binet examination this man was found to have a mental age of eleven years and six months, which indicates borderline intellectual capacity.

Indicative of the occupational adjustment of some prisoners is the following excerpt from their work record.

Work Record: John was first employed by the American Brass Foundry located at ———. He started working there on July 1st but was laid off on August 3rd. His duties consisted of polishing small brass parts which were passed along on a movable belt. He was paid $11.00 a week and worked nine hours a day. After leaving the American Brass Company, John was unemployed until November when he received a job as a truck driver's helper for the Smith Department Store. He worked steadily during the last two weeks of November and all of December, but was laid off on December 30th. For assisting the truck driver in the delivery of Christmas packages he was paid $15.00 a week and worked on an average of twelve hours a day. John's next job came in April, after he had been out of work almost three months. During the three months of idleness he made applications for employment at seven different concerns. Finally, through the influence of an older friend, he was employed by the Georgeville Steel & Iron Company. This is a concern that during normal times gives work to several hundred men. . . . John was classified as a laborer and for eight hours a day he used a shovel and a wheelbarrow in the transferring of sand from one location in the plant to another. His salary was $22.00 a week. This job lasted only to the end of July, a total of three months. Our inmate was out of work until November when he finally procured another job of a seasonal nature which lasted for only two months. . . .

From another case record we learn that the occupational adaptation of the inmate was directly related to his crime.

Work Record: Wilson had been working for the F. D. L. Company for nine years. He was considered, according to the letter from the concern, as a steady, reliable, and capable employee. With the coming of the economic ebb our inmate, along with two hundred other employees, was laid off. Wilson attempted to procure other jobs but was unable to do so. He applied for relief and the case-workers greeted him with respect, but because the machinery of relief distribution was slow in organizing, our inmate, his wife and three children were actually facing starvation. Reliable informants tell us that before Wilson broke into the grocery store, he had sought the aid of relatives, of friends, and of the local politician—all to no avail. Friends and relatives were as impoverished as he and the local politician had no funds available. It was from facing this crisis that Wilson committed the burglary which brought him to us. . . .

While the brief references given here reflect genuine desire for work and occupational adequacy on the part of our men, a number of the prisoners have been, ostensibly, unwilling or incapable of holding jobs even after having received several new opportunities from their employers. Such a case is that of inmate Brown.

Brown's longest job was for the Akin Packing Company, a large concern which employs several hundred men. He worked for the Akin concern for seven months during which time he was absent on eleven occasions and tardy for work fifteen times. It was suspected by the employers that

Brown's occupational irregularities were due to drinking and a member of their personnel department verified this. He was dismissed from the Akin concern, but upon his persistent pleas, he was re-employed after some three weeks of idleness. He worked steadily for another two months, but once again started being irregular in attendance and after an additional sixty days, during which time he was absent from work on seven occasions, he was again discharged. Two years later this man was employed again by the same firm and after some three months of fairly steady employment he again became irregular in attendance and was finally released.

While the social relationships set forth in the foregoing comments have more or less omitted the love theme, there is no reason to believe that there is less intensity in the sex and love life of prisoners than in that of men of any other class. As we shall later see, promiscuity may be somewhat more prevalent, and, in some cases the love emotion may be more superficial, yet in others the love development has the same aspects as among non-criminals. The following letters are revealing of these relationships. The first comes from a young wife to her young husband, destined for a long imprisonment.

Darling Sweetheart:

Just a few lines to let you know I am almost heart-broken. I was just talking to R——— and he said there is no hopes whatever of ever doing anything. He asked me if I wouldn't get a divorce, as I could come to see you just the same, but it would be better for both of us that way, he said. I've been bawling all morning. Divorce is such an ugly word. Oh, honey, it would be a horrible thing to do. I told him I don't think I could do it. He told me to talk it over with you and see what you thought of it. He said I'd be sacrificing my life in vain as there doesn't seem to be any hope. It's awful but there must be a way, it can't be as bad as all that. Just because they have millions of dollars they can't wreck people's lives like that. He said they have a trust fund up to see that both you and B——— stay there. Honey, what good does it do them to be so mean? They can't be happy knowing they are keeping an innocent man in jail for a crime he never committed. I don't know what to do. I just keep thinking over and over that there must be some mistake. It can't be that bad. There must be a way. Oh, why are they all so afraid of those mean old ———? They all promise until they hear about the "X" then it's like someone who has leprosy. They all stare and say they are sorry but can't try it. It seems that even the Lord is afraid of the "X." It's just like bucking a brick wall the same thing from every one. "Sorry, but it's too tough." Well, I don't know what to do or say. I hated to tell you, but R——— says it's best that you know as it won't seem so hard as living in hope and always expecting something to turn up. Well, who could ever stop hoping? Daddy darling, don't worry about it. It won't help matters any. We've just got to make up our minds that that is the way our life was meant to be. The pages are written up there before we are born and no matter how we try, nothing can change it. Fate has cut it out that way. There is no dodging it. It's bad no matter what we do, but that's life, a bed of thorns for some and all roses for those who don't appreciate it. If I didn't have the baby I'd go to the end of the world, away from everything that has brought this on, away from eyes that try to show pity when it is really mockery. I could kill everyone who says, "I'm sorry," cause they aren't, they are happy about it. Hypocrites, all of them.

Life, life, hell for some, oh, I could just strangle some people. They cheat on every thing that they get in contact with yet they reap the harvest of life. Those who plod along trying to be right get the raw end of the deal.

I'll square this if it's the last thing I ever do. I swore that someone would pay and they will. Just wait and see. I'm so sick of trying to be good and getting hell and raw deals. It seems that the rottener a person is the better life treats you. I'm going to be as rotten as I've been good; maybe I'll get a good deal for a change. The only good deal I ever got was that God blessed me with an angel for a father. Without him life would have been a worse hell than it is. That's all I have to be thankful for so far, and my baby. A few months of heaven with *you,* the rest all hell from the day I was born. The few months we lived together were the happiest I ever had in my life. I thought my troubles were over then. I thought life was just beginning and it ended before I had a good taste of it. I guess that little bit of happiness was given to me just to bring more torture in the years to come. When I look back on those day I could give my life for just a few more days of that kind of happiness. That was heaven. This is hell. How easy it is to say, "Forget." I wonder if they could forget as easy as they ask others to do it? I wonder if those happy days wouldn't haunt them as they haunt me night and day? I wonder if those to blame aren't haunted by the wrecks they made of two lives. I hope they are. I hope they never find peace.

Love and Kisses,

Your own—.

After five years of apparent loyalty, evidenced by letters and visits, this girl, resident of a large city, obtained a divorce and has since remarried. Her husband has continued in prison for ten long years.

Indicative of relations in a rural situation between an essentially non-criminalistic young man and his sweetheart, is the following letter.

Sunday Noon

I LOVE YOU DEAR: B———, M———,
Nov. —, 193—.

Mr. W——— R. P———.

My dear lover. Will drop you A few Lines as my thoughts are of you. I truly hope and trust you are O. K. As for myself. Just fine and still

Trusting in Christ Jesus. i would Love to see you today. Say dear, I can see your loving Picture, When I can't see you. Oh, dear boy. you were so dear to me when we were together, only it were a sad ending. Mabe someday it will be a Happy Meeting. Wan't it dear? Don't worry about your troubles you used to have, because I don't Hold that against you—or nothing else for only i do love you and will always. A——— and B——— C——— and D——— and C———'s sis was over Thur eve. of course B——— were telling me of the Wedding Wed. Did i Tease her. D——— said she wrote you a Letter and sen't in care of your mother. Don't guess you got it yet. Say, dear, this is a blue Sunday, so rainy looking. M——— were over yesterday she sure is funny. Ha Ha i Guess We will go to Church tonight. It seems so lonesome without Martin and his wife. Altho we have some good times in the lord, before The lord can work i really wan't To do what is right, for the lord has done so much for me i can never turn away from him. The reason i never did wan't to go to the Park is i Wen't this summer and i got to goin with unsaved company and there was so much Temptations was leading me back in sin, only the lord knowed and he brought me back and never let me go back in sin and now am i glad? That is one reason i don't wan't to go any where only to Church for the devil trys me every way he can, only im going thru with Jesus, for hes our only friend. You pray a lot dear. The lord will save you, someday if you will only look To him. He will save you. The promise is for us. You read a lot and pray. Also, and i will always continue Praying for you. You know, dear, i will always love you. i sure did hate To hurt you over that verse, only dear, I believe dear you will forgive me wont you dear. Write and tell me in the next Letter. I sure did Worry about it. i love you always, and i do pray dear, that when we meet again we will never be parted and unhappy again. Im going read all your letters in a few moments from now. I wish you could be with us Today—fer its so lonesome & sad. Oh, dear boy. You are my dreams. You can Guess how i feel today sad, lonesome, and worried, and will be that way until i see you again. Oh dear i love you and can't help it. The lord only was my —— (picture of a heart) i have just got to close this letter until noon. Love is something that works on your heart. By-by.

Many of our prisoners marry when young and drift away from their even younger wives. Such a wife writes the sociologist:

Dear Sir:

I will try and answer a few of your questions as near as I know how. W——— was not a mean sort of a man. But he was not raised right. His father died when he was Just 9 years Old and his mother never Staid at home before his Father died and after he died. She took them to her brothers to Live and as Soon as they got big enough to work they had to make their own way. There was 3 boys in the Family. W——— was the Oldest. They never did have it very easy In their lives. W——— was 18 when I married him and I was 15 and we have 2 girls and one Boy.

He acted like he thought enough of me when he was with me But he would leave me and stay a week or 2 then he would come back and maybe he would stay with me a year or too before he would leave again. I would ask him why he left me and he never could seem to answer it. And I don't know why he left for he never would stay away very long. Well If I Could talk to you I Could tell you a lot more but I can not write It So I will Close.

Yours truly

Mrs. W——— Y———.

Some prisoners' relationships with their wives have been lacking in sympathy, as shown in the following letter:

Do you remember when you were out on Bonds all the abuse you gave me just because I put a little dent in your fender? Do you remember telling me you would have been better off without me? That if the Court freed you, you were going to get a divorce? When I reminded you of all I've done for you you said I had only done what a tramp you could pick up would do. How many women would have done what I have for you? How many would take the abuse I took and still go for you like I did? Do you remember the awful names you used to call me and the mean treatment you gave me when I was sick in bed? Do you remember how you'd lock me alone in the house when I was sick in bed and I've had to wait till my mother could get there at night to cook me some things? Do you remember how I cried and begged you to stay with me one night when I felt pretty sick and you laughed at me and told me you had a date with a girl and couldn't be bothered with me, I was only your wife and you said you didn't get a kick out of taking me out or spending any time with me. Do you remember when I was lying sick in the hospital and you came to tell me you had been out with another woman all night? I'm not rubbing it in, I'm just trying to make you realize all I took from you and still went for you when you needed me and how I lied to my Dad and always told him you were good to me. Think back, do you think you will do it again. I'm just refreshing your memory a little because if things go right you may be home again and I'm hoping you won't do those things over again. I'm hoping and praying that this thing has changed you and I'm hoping we can forget the past and start all over again. I hope our future together will be happier than our past has been. Of course there were a few happy moments in the past, but so few that they are hard to remember. Misery was so great and the unhappiness so much that the happiness is lost in it. Well, I'll let you know how our angle progresses.

An intelligent ex-wife tells pointedly of some of the social situations in the life of her husband, and the relationships, direct and indirect, positive and negative, that existed for thirty-five years.

Thank you so much for your letter. It was most kind of you to want to comfort one whom you do not at all know, and blessedly kind to be willing to help a fellow-man unable to do much for himself. I apologize for the delay in replying, due partly to the lack of a free hour and partly to a hope for another letter from X———, with, perhaps, some further information or instructions. His writing privileges are limited to twice a month and it may have been necessary to use that privilege otherwise. It is quite right that you should know the facts, and such as I have I will try to make clear. To do so, I must go back a long way.

He and I were married June —, 189—, I sixteen, he about twenty. I was attending a business college where his father was director. Neither of us had good sense but we were madly in love and eloped to W———. His father was a man of remarkable intellect, an interesting, lovable individual. We were in G——— for a while; later C——— went to L——— where his brother and family lived, and after a few months I joined him there. In 189—, our daughter was born.

Life there was primitive; we were seventy-five miles from a town, our nearest neighbor ten miles distant, the stage bringing mail twice a week. It was dull and it was difficult to be, in a way, dependent, though we both contributed much in the way of service. We secured work at the ———, some thirty miles from his brother's place. An opportunity to teach school in N——— was promised him if he passed the preliminary examination, which I am sure he could have done easily. The excitement of civilization proved too much for him; pending the examination he drank, gambled, forged three checks and vanished. I managed to get to L———, secured work in an office and eventually persuaded the saloon keeper to give me the checks, so there was no record against him. I was to have gone to B——— as clerk in the legislature, but illness of my small daughter prevented. Instead, I went to the home of his mother.

His father and mother had been separated for many years; both fine, intelligent people but with radically different outlooks on life. He was the youngest of three children and I am inclined to believe their differences may have contributed much to his restlessness of spirit and general instability. Among his forbears are many splendid folk, some distinguished for solid achievements. The brother was on the place I mentioned, later was in T———, and has since passed away. The sister was then in B———, a very fine woman, indeed, but with a somewhat narrow outlook. . . . In fact, my daughter and I constitute their principal contact with the outside world, the husband being an invalid. (This explanation is made now, merely to indicate that there are no immediate relatives who may be relied upon for understanding or help.)

To resume: It was essential that I earn money: Y——— afforded few opportunities so I secured work in a law firm in N———, B———, leaving my daughter with her father's mother, paying as much as I could for her care. Infrequent letters came from him, always with the request that we join him, to which I replied that I would when he could show some qualities to be depended upon—that I did not mind for myself, but that I could not subject a small child to uncertainties. He insisted he had as much right to the child as I and would so demonstrate. I was frightened—did not know then that it was said merely as pressure—took the only course open—divorce, which gave me custody of my daughter.

Previous to our marriage there had been some difficulty with rich relatives, ending in a term in some prison in L———. I am not sure, but I think he was pardoned. I knew nothing of this until long after, so it had no bearing on the divorce.

From S——— I came on here; later his mother joined me and for a time we lived in O———. Once I heard from him there, with request for permission to write to his daughter. I answered saying she was unsettled and emotional and feared it would make for further difficulties. He interpreted that to mean "fear of contamination" and again vanished into oblivion. That must have been about 19— and from that time until last April there had been no word from or about him. Indeed, it was supposed that he could not be living. And of all that might have happened in that period of some thirty years I know very little.

I do not believe he is in any real sense a criminal. I blame myself for not having been wiser in those early days. I believe, with Keyserling, that marriage is not so much for happiness as for growth; that the "field of tension" created thereby constitutes unparalled opportunities for soul expansion. There is no music—no depth of tone—from loosely anchored strings. If I could have talked with him, even once, I could have helped him understand many things. My daughter wrote to him and had many letters from him—writing seemed to serve as a release. . . .

A number of our men have had contacts with religious persons.

Dearest Bro. in Christ Jesus.

I will write you a few lines this morn. as Sis is writing. How are you? Well and still happy in Jesus, I Pray. This leaves us all well and happy.

A——— fell and hurt his Breast one day Out in the feild Husking corn he was kicking down the corn in his wagon as he drove across the end & fell across the Bump Board he said it knocked the Breath Out of him for a while its Still Pretty sore he has over a week husking yet. I'm glad you are still trusting in Jesus Don't ever think of turning Back for theres nothing to go back to. Pray for us and for the Church. Some Of the Saints have gone Back in sin & are working against the Elder. Its the last days now for we can see the Bible being full filled. It says in the last days there will be a falling away of the Saints. We know only a few will enter in at the gate—I want to be ready to meet Jesus for he will come in such an hour as we think not.

I wish you could be here to go to Church. The time will soon pass. We will all Pray for you that god will keep you. I believe you when you say you want to be saved. The Word say if we hunger & Thirst after righteousness we shall be filled Matt 22:13 read. Just hold to god's unchanging hand. M——— said she dreamed last night Something said to her she was called to Preach, said she could see a light & was following it said she sure felt happy. Dont worry about sis for the lord is keeping her for you. I know she Will be true. Pray for all of us & we will always remember you in prayer.

Maybe some of us can come and see you next summer if you are still there. How far is it from here. I must close. I remain as ever your sister in Christ.

B———.

From autobiographical and self-evaluating statements of prisoners, valuable insight may be gained concerning their pre-penal relationships. The statement which follows shows the extent of contacts and hints at the incalcuable experiences in one life. It is not atypical, but rather fairly representative of any number of autobiographies which might be presented. The major facts in this report have been verified.

I was born on a farm about 8 miles north of P———, M———, on April —, 189—, of quite poor but respectable parents. My father was born in I——— of Irish and English descendants, and my mother was born at N———, I———, her people being Pennsylvania Dutch. Her name was H——— T———. About the first thing that I remember is my first pair of boy's clothes, that is, shirt and pants; the wife of an elder cousin of mine made them and dressed me up in them on May 30, after I was 3 years old in April. I remember the fight I had that night when we started to church for the Decoration Day services, a fight which I won and I wore the pants. I started to school at 5 years of age. I always got along well at school as far as getting my lessons was concerned, but was often lined up for other things I did, maybe no more than any other live boy would do under the same conditions, but I will own up to having been a pretty bad boy. I guess the rest of my boyhood days were like other farm boys of that time, school, home work, and play. I have always liked to work, the only thing that seemed to interfere with working was that I like to do things that required me to think my way through. I have always enjoyed studying and while my school days were cut short at the age of 16 years, I have put in lots of time with books, understand pretty well all mechanical and electrical work as well as the building trades, and am greatly interested in live-stock and farming. I like to hunt and fish, and have done lots of both in the northern states, especially in Wisconsin and Minnesota. I like to read as long as the book is founded on facts, but have never been able to become interested in fiction.

From my boyhood days on the farm until I entered the Army in 1917 I spent the time at shop work, working as a machinist and die maker. I have always made good money but never saved much, not that I just fooled it away, but spent quite freely for books, clothes, and just seeing places and things, and while I have always been more or less of a drinking man, I don't think I ever was what one would call a drunkard, and I can pass up drinks without exerting my will power. In 19—, I bought a race car and spent two seasons on the dirt tracks, this is where I used my first dope. At one of the races I had my right foot injured and just couldn't keep the pressure on the gas, so took a shot and won the race. I used it after that before each race, and it will put an extra 20 miles per in a car, as well as add to the driver's nerve. At this time and until 1923 I never used it otherwise and never had the drug habit.

I met my wife in 19—, a nice girl not taken to flirtation, etc., and a girl with an honest and decent purpose in life. I enjoyed her company and we were often together at shows, parties, etc., but at the same time I was keeping company with another girl in a town 45 miles from my home, a different type of girl, a stepper. I led a kind of double life with these two girls, nice boy at home, but a big time sport with my other girl. I always had a job, car, and money, so could get by at the game pretty easy. Now this fast girl, L——— we call her, I really loved, but she was not a girl one would trust so far, while my girl at home, M———, who later became my wife I really never cared much for, only she was nice and respectable to be with and she trusted me in every way.

I was trying to talk her out of a kiss one evening when she asked me something like this, "Fritz, will you always be good to me?" I answered "Of course I will." I got the kiss and she took it for a proposal of marriage and started right in getting ready to become a bride. I never just had the heart to try to tell her that I didn't want to marry her, but thought well, I will think myself out of the mess some way. I never did, tho, and we were married, something that I didn't want to do, but she was and is a nice girl, honest, straight, and smart, and we should never have had trouble, only I just never wanted to, or tried to have the home for her that I should, I always thought I was nuts for getting married and while it was never my desire to mistreat or be ill-mannered with my wife this relation between us caused me to seek other company at times, which, of course, causes some bad feeling at home. My wife has no passion and wanted no children, but being neutral on the question myself, we never had any trouble over that.

In 19— I tried to put over a radio manufacturing company in C———, together with A——— B———, inventor of a set we were to build. We organized a stock company with $200,000 capital and started, but we failed to get by with the set because of patent failures, and separation of stations with the set. During the long hours' work trying to build up this business, I got back on the drugs again, but had no trouble stopping the use of them in 19—, at which time I went to northern W——— and spent two years just hunting and fishing and taking life as easy as one in moderate circumstances could.

My mother died in 1928, so arrangements were made for my wife and myself to return to O———, to be with my sister who is a very successful business woman, and has accumulated quite a lot of property, part of it at this time being 80 acres of land 8 miles west of S——— in need of lots of improvement to put it in first class shape. When we returned to S——— I went to work die making, while my wife worked at the University for the first year. I then went out to this farm and started building fences, gates, new buildings, etc., fixing it up for the time we were to have a home out there and just take it easy, and in 1930 I bought equipment and was farming the place myself. For the first year my wife and sister lived in town and I stayed on the farm.

At this time I had quite a lot of trouble with my teeth and in order to get sleep I drank quite a lot and the next year the wife and sister moved out, and of course started kicking every time the odor of booze was noticed, so I cut out the drinking and went back on the drug again. I guess I let my nerves get bad on me this time, for I got till I couldn't carry on, and just had to quit the farm, and when I got in this trouble I was just running around doing nothing. I was not in need of money, and never thought of committing a crime to get money but at times I have been a little loose with the check-book, but used my own name only. I have no ill feeling toward anyone, but I did during the past few months while I was in jail tell a few people that I was getting a raw deal, and expected to get even some day. I have no such notion at the present time, though, and feel that it is only right that I pay for anything I may have done.

As a general thing my nerves are very good. I can go down in a mine shaft, or up in an airplane without any reaction as far as fear is concerned. I have spent time in large cities, also been in the woods and mountains alone and feel at home and at ease either place. If there is anything I am afraid of in particular I don't know what it is. I don't like to see anything suffer, especially animals, but don't seem to pay much attention to suffering myself and have been able to always adapt myself to my surroundings, at present while I of course feel sorry for my wife and sister, I don't for myself, and have always had the complex that I could take it, and make the best of it.

In drinking I have never been a steady drinker, if I get a little too much I can't bear the thoughts of it for a few days. The first few drinks I take seem to loosen up my tongue, and I talk maybe too much, when I get too many my eyes seem to glare up and take on a wild look, but I don't get drunk in the feet, that is, I don't fall around but can walk straight regardless, in fact, I will always get sick and have to stop drinking before I will stagger. Other habits such as tobacco, etc., I have always used moderately if at all, and was never bothered with boyhood or sexual vices and habits.

I don't remember ever getting real angry when I was sober, but could always laugh off my troubles and be a good loser if I had to lose, but at the same time I will play hard to win. I have always been active and don't tire easy, and most things I enjoy doing I do well, such as baseball, golf, bowling, and such out-door sports, and like to do such problems as cross-word puzzles, jig-saw puzzles, etc. I play cards well, but at times when I am behind will be a little reckless in bidding and betting.

I have no trouble at all in following orders and rules, and it does not in any way work a hardship on me to follow the rules of this institution, at the same time I have spent a great part of my life giving orders rather than taking them. I like boxing and am fair with the gloves, but never had but one grudge fight, and lost that one, this party and I are good friends now.

I have full confidence in myself and am sure that I will be able to do my time here and go out a better man than when I came in, and just fall back in line with the world, without asking favors of anyone in particular.

I have one sister and one brother living, and two sisters dead. All my people are good, honest, common folks, or I guess just the average people on sees doing well and enjoying life. I know of no one of them that was ever in serious trouble outside of my brother who did a year on probation years ago, I think for some kind of larceny charge though I may be wrong about that.

I guess this is all that I can think of, but will be glad to answer any other questions that you care to ask me.

While I will admit that I am a good liar, I have, to the best of my knowledge, told the truth here.

And so we see that when the offender comes to prison there is much behind him. Every relation in life has gone into the making of his personality, and every personality is a product of experiences in social groups even though, as our documents tend to show, the man who becomes an inmate seems not, as a rule, to have been closely affiliated with integrated social groups. As we proceed we will determine the significance of this observation.

As a last effort to illustrate the pre-penal relations of inmates, we believe it may prove helpful to summarize a study dealing with the boyhood ambitions of prisoners. Ambition is a complex thing and reflects not only native and inherent traits, but social situations as well. To know a person's ambition is a short-cut to understanding the totality of that person. "If I know the goal of a person, I know in a general way what will happen. . . . If I am acquainted only with . . . the reaction-times, the ability to repeat, and such facts, I am aware of nothing that actually takes place in the soul of a man." [33] A person's goal reflects the values of the social organization in which he lives; the goal is determined by social relationships.

Boyhood Ambition [34]

Ambition is a term seldom encountered in scientific literature, yet the understanding of a person's goal in life will reveal fundamental information about him and the associations which he has had. Ambition is related to the tissue conditions of the body which give rise to stimulations such as hunger and the sex urge which excite the organism to activity. As such it is a problem of native, or original human nature. While the tissues of the body are the sources of energy which activate the human organism, the social situation in which it moves is the orienting force which formulates the pattern of life. Inasmuch as the social milieu is the patterning agent of an individual's goal, and inasmuch as there may be changes

[33] Alfred Adler, *The Theory and Practice of Individual Psychology,* Cosmopolitan Book Corporation, New York, 1929, p. 3.

[34] Unpublished study of the *Boyhood Ambitions of Two Hundred Prisoners* by the writer, summarized and reported to his Director, 1933.

in the milieu, it follows that ambitions may change. To the Adlerian school of psychology we are indebted for emphasis of the principle that the unit-organism, man, is a dynamic whole moving through a life pattern towards a definite goal. That goal is the maintenance of life. The desire to maintain optimal conditions for oneself is practically universal. But to have an ambition is not universal, even though the potentials of it are rooted in every individual. Ambition is something that is acquired through social interaction. To some degree it corresponds to a "wish," and in other respects to an "attitude." It is not our purpose here to present a theoretical discussion, and it will be sufficient to set forth what is meant by "ambition." We say that ambition is a desire, an eager desire to achieve a certain rank in society. The desire (wish, drive, attitude) will seek expression on an occupational and "social" level. Ambition is a pointing towards a goal. It is a variable state of an individual and is not homogeneous among mankind. It is basically produced through the organic conditions of the body, but is patterned and moulded in a social milieu. . . .

Two hundred prisoners were systematically interviewed in regard to their ambitions as boys,[35] and an effort was made to classify the reported ambition, and then to locate relationships between types of ambitions and other factors. Strictly speaking, we have not studied ambitions but responses to inquiries concerning ambition. Ambitions could probably be studied only at the time of their inception and formulation by observing the behavior they set in action, yet a retrospective-introspective method offers at least a partial understanding. We have found that the ambition of men who later became prisoners developed between the twelfth and twentieth year. Frequently more than one ambition existed, but we have selected the one for tabulation which seemed to be the most real one and consistent with the total personality and social situation in which the inmate functioned. We have reason to believe that most of the responses were truthful and genuine.

The replies elicited from the two hundred men cover a great variety of occupations and social roles. The most logical grouping has indicated that the ambitions fall into four general categories. In the first category have been placed those whose ambitions exceeded their father's occupational and social placement and led them toward the professions. Physicians, lawyers, school teachers, musicians, actors, mechanical engineers, and other occupations constituted some of the boyhood ambitions of this group. Not only was it their ambition to be professional persons on a work level, but also on a "social" level. The authenticity of this boyhood wish

[35] The method of study is detailed in Appendix A.

was demonstrated by most of the men who could talk intelligently about their chosen field. In this group were found thirty-one, or 15 per cent, of the two hundred men. Two of them realized their boyhood ambition, and seven of them had occupational roles similar to those they had desired. In addition to this number eleven more made active efforts to obtain their goal, while the life record of eleven shows no indication of effort to approach the situations toward which their boyhood ambition had pointed them. Many of their statements indicated that as boys they had had a service ideal; they desired through their work to be of some assistance to society. How "real" such an attitude was is a question. Their desire for service was probably prompted by a more basic desire that they should receive recognition. Among this group were two men of borderline intelligence whose so-called ambitions were more probably wishful thinking and resulted from the frequent thwartings of everyday life, so that they set for themselves an ambition which was compensatory for their frustrations in daily interaction. The following case summary gives some indication of the life experiences of one member of this group.

This is a 26-year-old man who as a boy had ambition to become an architect. S——— was the fourth of seven children born to a poor family in a city of a million people. His father was the foreman of a bridge gang on a railroad. The home was located in a low-rent area adjacent to the industrial section of the city. The mother was a kindly person without much education but with a dominant desire that her children be successful. At great sacrifice all the children were sent to school. S——— had an aptitude for drawing that was first noticed when he was in the sixth grade. At about the same time he was allowed to accompany his father on working expeditions. He first learned of trestles, stresses, and elevations from the railroad engineer who directed his father's work gang. S——— finished the eighth grade at fourteen. After one semester in high school his father died and the family moved to a city of 20,000 inhabitants where the older boys worked. S——— had to quit school and found work in a garage. His associations there were deleterious. His working companions drank, gambled, and pursued unsavory feminine companionship. "Hot cars" were handled at the garage and while S——— was instructed to work on them he had nothing to do with the illicit dealing. Two years after the father's death the mother married a member of the Salvation Army and at about this time S———'s adjustment at home began to grow less satisfactory. In the interim he had purchased drafting tools and had done some studying on his own initiative. One winter he attended night school with his ambitions still set on architecture. Until he was nineteen years old his recreational life had been passive. Through his work associates he met a girl four years older than he with whom he fell in love. She was worldly and attractive. She encouraged the ambition and vigor of this immature, aggressive boy. They were married when S——— was twenty and shortly thereafter S——— enrolled in a correspondence course in mechanical drafting. After a year of married life, S——— lost his job and for several months was unable to find work. The young couple had to live with the groom's parents which caused the first marital disharmony. S———, through an old friend of his father's, finally found a job on a railroad section. The young wife, not having a home of her own, spent her leisure time with former girl friends. She eventually became promiscuous and was discovered by her husband. He blamed himself for not being a good provider and in an effort to furnish the clothes and trinkets his wife desired, sought the companionship of his old associates at the garage. He met another woman who promised to adjust the broken situation between him and his wife. She told him of a hardware store where he could steal guns, with no chance of being caught. After some planning he entered the store and stole 42 revolvers of various kinds. His woman associate showed him where to hide them. They were to be sold later but when negotiations had been completed for their disposal the woman doublecrossed him and he was eventually caught. It was his first offense. He still wants to be an architect. His wife is now divorced from him.

This man is of superior intelligence and without marked physical pathology. Since his twelfth year his ambition has played an active part in his life except during his first year of marriage. Even with the stigma of prison upon him he has a strong drive to succeed in his chosen field, get a job as a draftsman, own a home, and "live like a man should." He not only desires to put his talent to work but he yearns for the status that such work could give him so that he can "show them."

In the second category of ambitions are 90, or 45 per cent of the offenders. This group is made up of those men whose boyhood ambition was to exceed only their father's occupational role. These offenders were not interested in a higher "social" position from the angle of status in a group, except in so far as such status would yield them more economic security. There seems to be no yearning to leave the primary group relationships of their boyhood and seek a higher strata of society. This category includes miners' sons who wanted to be boss-mechanics; laborers' sons who wanted to be miners; boys from the homes of tenant farmers who wanted to be stock farmers or have land of their own; sons of small merchants had ambitions to become wholesale grocery salesmen or chain-store managers; several from poor homes had ambitions toward becoming air pilots or airplane mechanics. None in this group expressed a service ideal. Ambitions for them were concerned generally with the increase of income in order that life might give more pleasure. About half of these men achieved their boyhood ambitions for short periods. Exact data in regard to this observation cannot be obtained.

Falling into the third category are those men whose only predominate boyhood ambition was to occupy the same occupational and social notch as their fathers or breadwinners had. If their fathers were tenant farmers or miners, they, too, sought such rôles. On the other hand, they evidenced that anything of a lower rôle would not suffice. To this extent they have ambition. While there is an awareness of class distinction there seemed to be no marked dissatisfaction with their social position. "My father was a poor man —he done all he could for me—I wish I could have been as well sot as he is." In this group are 26, or 13 per cent. All but four of the families from which these men came were of the laboring class. As boys and young men the 26 offenders had as a goal the same work as that of their family head or at least some work on the same level. There was no drive for a more prominent "social" recognition except in the case of a few miners who were ambitious to become leaders in their local labor organizations, but as leaders they hoped to improve the situations of their own group. Nineteen of these 26 "achieved" their boyhood ambitions for a short period before becoming involved in crime.

In the fourth class are 53, or 26 per cent, of the 200 offenders. This category we have called the "ambitionless." At no time during their youth was there any well-defined ambition. Their thoughts of the future were confined to what means was to be employed in order that the necessities of life might be procured. This type of offender is characterized by a trait of haphazardness and a lack of appreciation of the difficulties likely to be encountered during life. The philosophy of many is to take life as they find it and meet the situations as they arise. They have no drive towards securing recognition by persons other than their primary group associates, and many are largely indifferent about this. Whereas these men had no ambition during youth, as the term has been defined, yet they have exhibited a homogeneous motivation towards maintaining optimal conditions. Where there is no goal of any sort, distracting stimuli are more likely to swerve a personality than in those instances where a pathway is outlined. The men in this group are more like one another in all respects than are the members of the other groups as classified. The story of T——— is a fairly typical one.

T——— is now 28 years old. He came to prison this time for armed robbery. He is of low average intelligence and there is no marked physical pathology. His mother had been a prostitute. The early home life was in continuous turmoil. His father drank heavily but had a reputation for being a hard worker in the small southern city where the family lived. There were three other children in the family, two older than T———.

As a boy he advanced to the sixth grade in school. He then quit, not because of incapacity, but because there was no incentive. Both parents thought schooling was silly, "cause he had to make his living with his back, anyhow." T——— got a job working in a factory for a few dollars a week. At no time in his life, he states, did he have any desire to do any particular kind of a job. "I just wanted to work so that I could have spending money." He had seven short-time jobs, all menial, between his twelfth and sixteenth years. He had never read a book. He knew no one who had. All he desired as a boy was pocket money for cigarettes and candies. His associates were few, although T——— is a friendly person now. One time, when out of work, he and another boy broke through the skylight of a pawnshop and stole two suitcases full of jewelry. He was caught in two days and spent two years in prison. Upon release, still without a life plan, he went on a bumming tour of the country and worked at 11 different kinds of labor during 14 months. He was arrested again on a robbery charge and spent three more years in a prison. When released he jumped his parole and got a job as a bus boy in a hospital in a large city. He became acquainted with a waitress and soon married her. A baby was born in seven months. For being negligent at work he was discharged from the hospital. He could find no work in the city. His brother came up from the South and brought two revolvers. In one night the two brothers boldly "stuck up" two drug stores and two restaurants in a large city and obtained about $700. T——— was caught later the same night and is now in prison.

The contributing factors in this man's offense are many, but three things stand out prominently. First, his home and neighborhood were very unwholesome. Second, there was a paucity of beneficial associates during adolescence. Third, and as a result of the first two factors, the boy never had a life plan or ambition. . . .

Thus, among the 200 cases analyzed, 31, or 15.5 per cent, were ambitious to have a professional occupation and social status, thus improving their condition over that of their parents. While but two of them achieved their goal, 18 others made efforts and prepared a pathway toward their goal. In the second group were 90, or 45 per cent, whose boyhood ambitions did not exceed the level of their father's social status but who were desirous of a higher occupational placement. In the third group were 26 or 13 per cent whose ambitions did not rise above either the social or economic level of their primary group. In the fourth group were 53 men or 26 per cent whom we have characterized as ambitionless. Obviously none of the two hundred men had ambitions to become prisoners, and during their formative years, none of them had ambitions to become criminals. Relationships have been sought between the four categories and numerous other factors, which it is not necessary to report here. Regardless of the complex webb of causes for the various attitudes dealing with ambitions, it is sufficient to know that the large majority of men who come to the penitentiary have not been favored with that set of situations out of which ambitions of service, efficiency and ideals result.

* * *

The interrelation of factors producing or failing to produce ambitions, the direct relationships of home, school, occupation and neighborhoods, some culture traits of the regions producing our men, and some broad social trends in America, have been briefly set forth in this opening chapter. The presentation has been descriptive and generalized and should aid the reader in understanding the complexities of the prison community. Let us now turn to more specific information about the men themselves.

CHAPTER II

The Composition of the Population

The composition of the population is usually viewed from such standpoints as births and deaths, race and nationality factors, occupational, age, and sex distributions. To know the composition of a population is to know, in short, certain fundamental facts about the people who comprise it. The facts gain full meaning only, however, when they are interpreted in terms of the total culture. We wish here to discuss our penal population in terms of certain specific culture traits, personal capacities, and achievements. The preceding chapter presented various facts concerning the cultural antecedents of the men. These facts, when considered together with the data relating to the composition of the population which are presented in this present chapter, suggest certain general conclusions. The obvious, but most important item, that the prison is an all-male population, indicates to the careful student that behavior patterns similar to a frontier society may develop, and similarly, some activities found in a sexually mixed population will not exist except in a modified form. The fact that a population is all masculine, however, indicates what the situation will be only within broad limits. To gain a fuller knowledge, other facts are needed, facts pertaining both to the material and social aspects of culture, as well as additional facts about the population make-up. Introductory to an understanding of the penal culture is this chapter which examines the population in search of fundamental information.

Age, Race, and Nationality

On a specified day during the period of study the average age of the 2,347 prisoners in residence was 34 years and 8 months. Thirteen hundred were under 33 years of age, and 1,047 were over 33 years of age. The youngest inmate was 17, and the oldest was 90. This relatively high average age is related to the condition that the state has an institution for younger offenders. The few instances in which youths have been sent to, or kept in, the prison have been at the discretion of the trial judge or the Classification Board. The ages of greatest incidence on the specified day were between 25 and 31, but the age groups from 35 to 50 are well populated. Differing with the age of the prisoners on a selected day is the average age at time of commitment, which has been found to be 30 years, 2 months. The extremes of commitment age were 15 and 87. The modal age was 23, and the ages of greatest incidence were between 21 and 23. The great scatter of ages, as we shall see, constitutes an important fact in the social life of the prison.

The population varies from day to day for distributions such as age and race, although the changes are slight and do not destroy the trends. On a specified day when exact data were tabulated, 409 Negroes composed 22 per cent of the total population of 2,304. At other times the Negro population has risen to 28 per cent. No Orientals were in residence. Among the Negroes were some who are part Indian, but the number is negligible.

Only 103 of the inmates, or a trifle less than 5 per cent, are of foreign birth. They represent 25 nations, the greatest number being of Italian, German, Austrian, and Canadian nationality. All but nine of the forty-eight American states have native sons in our prison. About 52 per cent were born in the state in which our prison is situated, and another 17 per cent are native to three bordering states. The place of birth has no especial significance unless such facts are considered together with predominant residence.

Intellectual Capacity

The relationship between crime in general and mental deficiency, which has been studied and restudied during the last three decades, is now generally agreed to be slight.[1] We shall therefore not be unduly concerned with this topic, and pause only to show that the inmates of our prison are essentially of the same intellectual capacity as the general population. Because there is controversy as to whether or not the testing devices actually measure native intellectual capacity, the term "intelligence" as here used refers to whatever mental attribute the tests measure. Year after year the results of the tests are nearly the same, and in spite of occasional perplexing evidence that at different times the same inmate will obtain somewhat different scores, the persistently similar results for annual samples of around 500 cases would seem to indicate that the method is generally reliable and that the capacity measured is, by and large, an entity. For our subjects the Army Alpha test was used, and those who for any reason failed because of physical defect or illiteracy

[1] E. H. Sutherland, *op. cit.*, p. 96.

were individually tested by the Stanford-Binet examination or by performance tests.

By transposing Army Alpha scores into mental age (M.A.) it has been possible to find the median for the total population. For 1,901 white men the median M. A. was 13 years and 7 months. For 403 Negroes, no distinction being made between those from the North and those from the South, the median M. A. was 11 years and 5 months. These results are in essential agreement with, or slightly higher than, the draft army of 1917.[2]

It has been agreed by psychologists that persons whose M. A. was below 11 years and 2 months, or below an I. Q. of 70, were mentally defective. In our prison 21.2 per cent were found to be in that category.[3] In the selected sample of the draft army, 23.9 per cent were so classified. For another group of 93,955 white men in the draft army the percentage of mental defectives was 17.6,[4] and for 18,891 Negroes who were drafted, the percentage having an I. Q. below 70 was 64.[5] Thus, our penal population differs only slightly in the proportion of mental defectives, no matter what criteria are used. If the all white draft army is used as a basis of comparison, our population shows a slightly higher percentage of mental defectives; if the selected representative sample is used, which is generally assumed to be typical of the national population, our percentage is slightly lower. The proportion of men in the other categories, the borderline, the average, and the superior groups, agrees essentially with the findings of the draft army. For example, 4.6 per cent of the selected draft group were found to have superior or very superior intelligence, and 5.6 per cent of our prison population are in that classification.[6]

It will be noticed in Table II that the Negroes score considerably lower, which is not inconsistent with previous findings. The category in the Table which bears the item "Borderline," includes a portion of men in the higher limits who, when clinically diagnosed, are called "Dull Normal" rather than "Borderline."

---

[2] Memoirs of the National Academy of Science, Vol. XV, *Psychological Testing in the United States Army,* Robert M. Yerkes, Editor, Government Printing Office, Washington, D. C., 1921, p. 790.

[3] This percentage has been computed from individual tests scoring an I. Q. below 70, and these individual tests were given to all men who failed to score above C 30 on the Army Alpha. In arriving at the I. Q. the age of 16 was used as representing mental maturity, and as the divisor of the total months scored correct on the individual tests. Since this study here reported was made the psychologists assigned to our staff have designated that 15 should be used as representing mental maturity. Had the divisor 15 been used in the tests appraised here, the percentage of mental defectives in the prison community would have been approximately 17, rather than 21.2 as shown.

[4] *Ibid.,* p. 790, Table 333.

[5] *Ibid.,* p. 790, Table 333.

[6] *Ibid.,* p. 790, Table 333.

TABLE II[7]

Number and Percentage Distributions of 2,295 Prisoners According to Intellectual Capacity, in Four Major Categories

	White		Negro		Total	
	Number	Per cent	Number	Per cent	Number	Per cent
Superior and Very Superior	124	6.7	3	.8	127	5.6
High Average, Average and Low Average	970	51.8	84	19.9	1,054	45.9
Borderline (or Dull Normal)	475	25.2	151	35.8	626	27.3
Mental Defectives	304	16.3	184	43.5	488	21.2
Total	1,875	100.0	422	100.0	2,295	100.0

The central thesis of this book does not demand exactitude and preciseness in reference to intelligence. For our purposes it is sufficient to know that between 17 and 20 per cent of our men are inferior in "brain power," and that fact should be kept in mind as we observe and evaluate their individual and collective behavior. Reference will be made from time to time to the intelligence factor as it seems to affect sociological phenomena. One other general point should be made. There is considerable difference in intelligence among the various crime groups. For example, 16.9 per cent of men committed for frauds rate as superior as opposed to 4 per cent of sex offenders, and 5 per cent of the murder group. The robbers appear to be "smarter" than other thieves, and the crime group most typical of the entire prison population are the larcenists.[8]

Body Build and Health

While authorities are somewhat uncertain as to the importance of health and anthro-biological factors in the causation of crime,[9] there is no reason to believe that health is not a most important factor in the evaluation of a community. A healthy population,

[7] These data were collected in two batches. The conventional class intervals were used in one, that is, I. Q. from 60–69, 70–79, etc. The class intervals used in the second batch, consisting of slightly over half the total number, were I. Q. 61 through 70, 71 through 80, etc. This was purposeful and administrative in order to give aid to a parole board. It is believed that this slight inconsistency does not destroy the reliability of the four general categories. For the most recent appraisal of the intellectual capacity of prisoners see, Andrew W. Brown and A. A. Hartman, *A Survey of the Intelligence of Illinois Prisoners,* Journal of Criminal Law and Criminology, Vol. XXVIII, No. 5, January–February, 1938, pp. 707–719.

[8] For a discussion of intellectual capacity among police officers see Fred E. Haynes, *Criminology.* McGraw-Hill Book Co., New York, 1930, p. 91.

[9] John Lewis Gillin, *Criminology and Penology.* The Century Co., New York, 1926, p. 103. See also, Ernest Hooton, *Crime and the Man,* Harvard University Press, 1939.

other things being equal, will mould a different culture than an unhealthy one. We cannot attempt to give a complete appraisal of our inmates in this regard, except to point out certain general conditions affecting personalities, which, in turn affect the culture.

The median weight of the prisoners is 150.7 pounds, and the median height is 67.71 inches. The range in weight extended from 105 to 280 pounds. In height the range extended from 4 feet, 10 inches, to 6 feet, 4 inches. The medians were computed from the entire population.

The venereal infections are not uncommon among our prisoners. In a population of 2,330, 47 per cent, or 1,119, admit to a history of gonorrhea. Of these, 49, or 4.2 per cent also had the complication of bubos. There are usually 15 to 20 men being treated for active or chronic gonorrhea at one time. Syphilis infected 247 of the 2,330, or 10.6 per cent, as measured by the Kahn or Wassermann blood tests. Of the 1,119 men who gave a history of gonorrhea, 39, or 3.7 per cent, also had syphilis.

No dependable figures are available as to the number of visual or auditory defects. Two of the prison physicians tentatively stated that the inmate populaton probably have about the same proportion of these deficiencies as would be found in a non-criminal population of the same age span and economic condition. Only a few inmates are blind, and less than a dozen are deaf enough to demand especial administrative attention. The dentist believed that the teeth of inmates are generally in somewhat poorer condition than are the teeth of a comparable sample of non-prisoners.

A division of inmates known as the "crank gang" is made up of between fifty and sixty men who, because of various disabilities and infirmities, are unable to perform the regular duties. In this group are the crippled and deformed, the blind, the rheumatic, a few diabetics, and sometimes, psychopathic personalities, as well as men who are not actually psychopathic, but who are not suited to work with other men.

Seldom are there more than twenty men in the hospital at one time. The tubercular ward has between ten and fifteen patients regularly, though many persons with tubercular lesions are assigned to regular duties.

The number of deaths a year varies between nine and twenty, and for four years averaged about one a month.

The greatest number of complaints by the resident population concern abdominal distress, headaches, and colds.

Home Structure and Ordinal Position

In the opening chapter we descriptively portrayed the interrelationships between the organization of family life and community pattern. It remains here to supply additional facts which tend to support the implied evaluation that the culture of home and community in which our inmates have lived is disorganized, inconsistent, and sometimes conducive to lawlessness.

Explanations of the causation of crime run in fads. At one time it was thought that broken homes were a major cause of crime. More recently, however, various studies have indicated that when controls are set up for age and neighborhood composition, the factor of a broken home is relatively unimportant in producing delinquency among juveniles.[10] In dealing with adult prisoners it is even more difficult to determine whether or not a broken home has significance in terms of crime. The average age of commitment is 30 years, and slightly over half of the men who come to the prison have never been incarcerated before. At least for this portion, one wonders whether or not a broken home during youth would have much relationship with a crime committed, on the average, ten or more years after most young men become independent. Of course many factors are operating and knowledge, except in extensively studied individual cases, is lacking as to the intimate relationships in the homes.

Whether the problem is important or not, a sample of 800 unselected cases has been studied, and "broken home" has been defined in this somewhat unorthodox way. First, if our records revealed that either parent was missing from the home during the major portion of the inmate's boyhood from the ages, roughly, of 5 to 18, the home has been considered broken, and, secondly, homes have been tabulated as "broken" if the relationships between the family members were persistently so affectionless as to provoke serious conflicts, since such homes are broken in harmony. A home, for example, in which the father died during our inmate's youth has not been considered as broken if the mother's second marriage provided a reasonably cohesive social situation. However, a home where one parent was absent during the entire youth of our inmate has been tabulated as broken, even though the relationships among the remaining members of the family were harmonious. Conversely, homes in which hate, distrust, abusiveness, lack of loyalty, and extreme pathology of any form existed, have been tallied as broken, even though the family was intact. Table III shows the distribution by race.

---

[10] Clifford R. Shaw and Henry D. McKay, *Report on Social Factors in Juvenile Delinquency,* National Commission on Law Observance and Enforcement, Government Printing Office, Washington, D. C., No. 13, Vol. 11, pp. 261–284.

TABLE III

Broken Homes, as Defined, According to Race, shown in Numbers and Percentages

	White		Negro		Total	
	Number	Per cent	Number	Per cent	Number	Per cent
Organized	385	56	33	29	418	52
Broken	216	31	64	56	280	35
Unknown or Uncertain	85	13	17	15	102	13
Total	686	100	114	100	800	100

Judging from the fact that we have placed 13 per cent of the cases in the "Unknown or Uucertain" category, it is clear that decisions have been hard to make, and that all of our records are not adequate in this regard. Deducting the 102 cases which have not been included, we find that 40 per cent of our population had broken homes, as defined. As to whether or not this is a causative factor in crime, no opinion is ventured. It is definitely asserted, however, that this fact affects the prison culture. About one-third of our prisoners have almost no visits and receive almost no mail. This condition makes for the most lonely and deadening of existences. Men who are isolated from the normal community even as to visits and letters come largely from broken homes.

In the search for the "causes" of crime, investigators have sought an answer, or partial answer, in the order of birth. Many studies seem to indicate that ordinal position is related in some degree to delinquency, while others fail to show a relationship. Professor Sutherland concludes that it is now very doubtful if ordinal position has any association with personality and behavior.[11] Case studies of some of our prisoners would seem to indicate that certain correlations exist between crime and personality and those factors of personality which result primarily from being, for example, an only child, or an eldest child.

In order to test the hypothesis, and also to further our knowledge of the penal population, a sample of 975 unselected cases was inspected.[12] From this we procured data on the average size of family among our inmates, which was 4.1 members per unit. In this we did not distinguish between half or step-siblings. This finding is higher than any found by Ogburn who studied a much larger block of census data in 9 types of cities.[13] When he had

[11] E. H. Sutherland, *op. cit.*, p. 150.

[12] An unpublished manuscript by the writer with the assistance of Frank Hart, entitled, *Family Placement of Prisoners and Types of Offense.* Submitted as a report to the writer's Director, 1934.

[13] William F. Ogburn, *Social Characteristics of Cities*, The International City Managers Association, Chicago, 1937, p. 13.

eliminated one member families he found the largest median family unit to have 3.45 members in cities of between six hundred thousand and a million, one to three hundred thousand, and fifty to one hundred thousand. The larger median of our prisoner's families is probably associated with the large proportion reared in villages or open country.

In search of significance of ordinal position, we found that 6.2 per cent of our sample were only children, that 19.1 were eldest children, and that 15.5 per cent were youngest children. The 575 other cases comprising 59.2 per cent of the sample were "in between" siblings. The absence of control data prohibits conjectures. To the 40 per cent of only, youngest, and eldest children, we ascribed the name of "distinctive" family placement, but were unable to find any outstanding relationship even with type of crime. This little study adds nothing to criminological knowledge, although the item of "distinctive" placement may be a point of departure for more intensive investigation. The student should keep in mind, however, that in a two-child family, both children have "distinctive" placement. While statistically there is no support for the contention that a relationship exists between ordinal position and crime, the hypothesis is held that in the penitentiary the large proportion of inmates who had distinctive family placement is associated with certain grouping tendencies which will be discussed in Chapter V.

School Achievement and Religion

The procuring of reliable information from inmates as to school attainment presents difficulties not encountered in gathering data, such as type of occupation, place of birth, and the like. The inmates who declare they have advanced farther in school than they actually have, do so partly to save face and partly in the hope that they may obtain a better work placement in prison. Inmates are queried about their school record by both the prison authorities and the Mental Health staff. The figures presented here were gathered by the latter group and have proven more reliable. The reliability is greater because the sociologist and the psychiatrist question each inmate carefully, and have, in more than 1,000 cases, directed questionnaire letters to parents. Table IV is considered fairly accurate because of the care with which the data were procured and the essential consistency with intellectual capacity and home conditioning. Many deductions might be attempted as to the relationship between education and crime. We are not interested here primarily in causation, however, and must interpret these data in terms of the formal educational knowledge which inmates bring to the prison environment.

TABLE IV

Educational Attainment of 2,348 Prisoners as Shown in the Mental Health Office Records

	Number	Per cent
Attended Common School	1,818	77.4
Attended High School	306	12.9
Attended College	37	1.6
No Schooling but Literate	36	1.2
Illiterate	143	6.5
Unascertained	8	.4
Total	2,348	100.0

Common School

Grade Completed	Number
1	18
2	90
3	155
4	238
5	189
6	226
7	256
8	646
Total	1,818

High School

Year Completed	Number
First	102
Second	105
Third	33
Fourth, or more	66
Total	306

Higher Education — College

Year Completed	Number
First	9
Second	16
Third	6
Fourth, or more	6
Total	37

Per cent who have completed eighth grade	29.4
Per cent who have completed high school	3.0
Per cent who have completed college	0.2

Among 60,250 native-born whites who were drafted for military service in 1917–18, the percentage of those who had completed eighth grade was computed at 25.4; those who finished high school comprised 4.1 per cent, and those who had four years of college, comprised 1.1 per cent of the native, white draft.[14] When it is

[14] Memoirs of the National Academy of Sciences, *op. cit.*, p. 758.

considered that even twenty years ago the native white draft army had more formal education than our prisoners, we are warranted in stating that the prisoners, as a group, are considerably below the average in formal education.

Upon entrance to the prison each man is queried as to his religious preferences. Except in a negligible number of cases no verification of the statement is obtained. The Mental Health Office has found that ministers and priests who are named by inmates among eight other types of potential informants are the least responsive. Only 12 per cent of the letters are answered while the responses of employers and parents is 63 and 82 per cent respectively. When an inmate cites a certain denominational preference he does not necessarily imply that he is affiliated, but rather that he has either attended certain church functions occasionally, or has other reasons for his choice. Community studies reveal in general that our inmates have had little or no part in the activities of church life with the exception of the Roman Catholics, who usually observe the minimal duties, and also of certain sex offenders whose religious zeal often carries over into their life in prison. On a selected day 51 per cent or 1,191 of the 2,343 prisoners had declared that they had no religious preference. Among the balance the largest group was of the Catholic faith: 308 men, or 13 per cent. The remaining 844, excepting 3 members of the Jewish faith, gave Protestant affiliations to twenty-two denominations. Of these, the largest number were Baptists, comprising 294, and Methodists with 258 adherents: 12 and 11 per cent respectively. Negroes cite affiliation with these two denominations in large proportions.

Occupational Status

Information as to the work life of the prisoners has resulted from careful interview by the sociologist, and questionnaire replies from employers and parents. It has often been stated that information from prisoners about their work life is unreliable.[15] We found in our studies that the statement which the men give as to the type of work they have done is in essential agreement with the replies from employers and parents. It is not the type of work or the place of employment about which the men are occasionally untruthful so much as it is the regularity of their work. An inmate will frequently report that he worked three years steadily for a certain employer, while investigation will often reveal that he had worked as reported over a span of three years, but that he was employed on the average of only two days a week, or five months a year. A small percentage, usually the more or less professional offenders, lie outright, or give

[15] E. H. Sutherland, *op. cit.*, p. 160.

fictitious establishments which they claim are no longer in business. It is not difficult to gauge the work record of men who have been previously incarcerated as the length of their servitude in other institutions is at hand. So, while no great exactness is claimed for the data presented here, the general indications shown would seem to represent the factual situation. Only 800 cases have been inspected for work record. Had a larger sample been taken, scrutiny for reliability would, of necessity, have been less thorough.

The categories in Table V are self evident except for the "Semi-Skilled" group into which have been placed those engaged in such trades as barbering, truck driving, some of the less skilled carpenters, bakers, restaurant cooks, and automobile mechanics. The table does not propose to show regularity of employment, but only the type of work done.

As can be seen from the table only 11 per cent of the men had no type of employment and never had worked. Unemployment in American was at its worst when most of the men here considered entered the penitentiary. Actually, a sizable portion of those included in the "common-labor" and "semi-skilled" categories had not worked regularly for some time, but by their previous occupa-

TABLE V

Occupational Status of 800 Prisoners Who Entered the Penitentiary During 1931–1934

	White		Negro		Total	
	Number	Per cent	Number	Per cent	Number	Per cent
Common Labor	162	24	74	66	236	30
Miner	41	6	4	4	45	6
Farm Labor	98	14	8	7	106	13
Skilled	38	5	0	0	39	5
Semi-Skilled	189	28	16	14	205	25
Own Business	19	3	1	0	20	2
Own Farm	14	2	0	0	14	2
Clerk, Salesmen	48	7	1	0	49	6
Unemployed	76	11	10	9	86	11
Total	685	100	114	100	800	100

tions qualified to be tabulated in one of these two designations. Of the fourteen men who have been categorized as working on their own farm, twelve were tenants. The nineteen men cited as owning their own business include proprietors of small garages, restaurants, confectionery stores, saloons, and taxi companies. In the "clerk-salesman" category of forty-nine men are sixteen bank employees who were convicted following the bank failures of 1931–32. In the New York Prison in 1920 it was found by the State Prison Commission that 80 per cent of the prisoners had mastered no trade.[16] The data here offered are in close agreement if we consider our category of "semi-skilled" workers as not having mastered a trade. Even evaluating this category as possessing a trade, we still find 49 per cent of our sample as having engaged only in the most menial of work. Our data are conclusive enough to warrant the evaluation that the inmates as a group have been placed in the lower occupational brackets. This well-known fact has significance in the study of causation, but it is more important to us now as we appraise the prison culture. It is important because a heavy majority of our inmates bring into the prison environment the inefficient work habits, the unskilled techniques, and the apathy and indifference to failure on the occupation level.

Marital Status

In this section we may confine our interest to a statistical consideration of prisoners who are married, widowed, divorced, separated, or single. In Chapter I an effort was made to depict some of the psycho-social aspects which our inmates have had in their marital experience or in the pursuit of feminine companionship, and it here remains to show the marital status and related factors.

Two studies conducted independently, and with somewhat different data,[17] reveal similar findings which lend reliability to the conclusions. Dr. Martin found 39.8 per cent of the inmates were single, 40.0 per cent were married, 5.2 per cent were separated, 8.2 per cent were divorced, and 6.7 per cent were widowed. The writer's study showed, for the same categories, the percentages to be: 37.7, 38.6, 10.7, 8.4, and 4.4. These figures have been computed from the statements of inmates shortly after admission, and are subject to the criticisms of such methods. I believe, however, the proportions are logical and the data are reasonably accurate. The tabulations of both Martin and the writer show that about 60 per cent of our prisoners have been married. In the general population in America in 1930, 60.5 per cent of all persons 15 years of age and over were married.[18] While we cannot compare this figure with the data we have secured about prisoners because of age and sex differences, yet we can see a general indication that prisoners, at least, are not greatly different from the general population in the matter of marriage. Many other comparisons leading to more refined conclusions might be drawn, but they would add little to the central thesis of this book.

---

[16] *Report of the Prison Survey Committee,* State of New York, Adolph Lewishen, Chairman, J. B. Lyons and Co., New York, 1920, p. 31.

[17] The writer inspected 1,239 cases selected at random in 1933, and Dr. Walter Martin appraised 2,125 cases in 1930 to determine the marital status of the inmates.

[18] William F. Ogburn and Clark Tibbets, *op. cit.,* p. 680.

In the writer's study the relationship between marital status and intelligence test scores were computed and no significant relationships were found. For example, 10 per cent of the single men are feeble-minded and 20 per cent are high average or superior in intelligence (a score above 105 on the Army Alpha). Of the married men, 8 per cent are mentally defective and 14 per cent are high average or superior. These findings were computed from 387 single men and 411 married men. Among the inmates who are separated from their wives or divorced, 19 per cent are feeble-minded and 26 per cent are high average or superior. The slight tendencies for the single men to be somewhat more intelligent, and for the separated and divorced persons to share the extremes of the intellectual scale, need further investigation before conclusions are warranted.

In using another random sampling of 400 cases, we found the same proportion of single men, but in this instance tabulated all the men who had married (neglecting divorce, separation and widowhood) and counted them as married. This system was devised in order to calculate age only, as it was believed that the two major samples, referred to above, sufficiently indicated the proportion of broken marriages. In this particular sample we found that 37 per cent of the men were single, and that 64 per cent had been married. The median age of the men who had been married was 34 years. In the age span of 18 to 29, 45 per cent of our inmates had been married; in the span of 29 to 35, 82 per cent; and 85 per cent in the span of 35 to 82. Facts such as these may be of aid to the reader in later chapters as he makes his own interpretations of certain practices in the prison community.

The Crimes

Each man who enters the penitentiary has been sentenced for a specific crime or crimes, and is therefore tabulated as a murderer, rapist, robber, and so on. While there is some value in such a tabulation the students of criminology should keep in mind that at one time of life a sex offender may have been a burglar, or that a man tabulated as a murderer may actually have been a robber who shot during a hold-up. Likewise, a so-called rapist might not even be in prison if his willing "victim" had been a few months older. Or, again, a man indicted for murder may be convicted for manslaughter. However, the classification of offenses reveals in broad terms something of the criminality of the population and will be presented here for that purpose.

TABLE VI

Offenses of 2,353 Prisoners
Classified According to Type of Crime

	Number	*Per cent*
Burglary-larceny Group	819	34.70
Robbery Group	608	25.64
Murder Group	543	23.08
Fraud Group	151	6.75
Sex Group	150	6.41
Destruction of Property Group	28	1.13
Miscellaneous Group	54	2.29
Total	2,353	100.00

The 819 men sentenced for various property offenses comprise the largest group and include 282 cases of various types of larceny, including automobile stealing, 70 for plain burglary, 420 for burglary and larceny (a single crime), 29 for receiving and concealing stolen property, and for attempting burglary and (or) larceny, 18. This group totals 34.7 per cent of the total population.

In the robbery group are 457 men convicted for robbery while armed, 119 for plain robbery which usually consists of a strong-arm offense, and 32 for assault or attempt to rob, the entire group totalling 25.6 per cent of the population.

In the third largest group are 283 sentenced for murder, 93 for manslaughter, 66 for assault to murder, and 1 for mayhem, all of which comprise 23 per cent of the prisoners.

In the fraud group are 99 forgers, 25 confidence game offenders, 18 embezzlers, 4 sentenced for issuing fictitious checks, 2 for withholding public funds, 2 for accepting deposits illegally, and 2 for attempt to commit confidence game. The fraud group included 6.7 per cent of the resident population.

Among the sex offenders are 74 sentenced for rape, 19 for assault to rape, 26 for indecent liberties, 17 for incest (with daughters, except in 2 instances), and 14 for crime vs. nature. The sex offenders total 6.4 per cent of the prisoners.

Among the 28 men whom we have included in the destruction-of-property group, are 26 sentenced for arson or attempted arson, 1 for possessing explosives, and 1 for injury by dynamite. The group totals 1.1 per cent.

In the miscellaneous group have been placed 3 sentenced for kidnapping, 3 for abduction, 2 for extortion, 6 for perjury, 4 for bigamy, 18 for escaping from the state penal farm and 3 for attempted escape, 1 for liberating prisoners, 2 for malicious mischief, 3 for violation of the prohibition act, and 6 under the habitual criminal act. These 54 classed under miscellaneous crimes comprise 2.2 per cent of the men in prison.

It is not the purpose of this volume to deal sensationally with the crimes the men have committed, but the reader should become well aware that the great bulk of the penal population is comprised of awkward, amateurish and occasional offenders. Most typical of burglars are those who break into a house or store and carry away loot or money seldom exceeding eighty dollars—not those who tunnel under a street and steal sixty thousand dollars worth of gems from a jewelry store. Most typical of robbers are men who hold up a gas station or a pedestrian and obtain ten to fifty dollars—not those who sweep down on a bank with a high-powered car, armed with tear gas and sawed-off shot guns and swag eighty thousand dollars in three minutes. Most typical of forgers are men who write ten or so twenty-dollar checks which they cash at stores or with acquaintances—not those who forge wills and concoct schemes yielding fabulous thousands. Most typical of murderers are men who anger easily and impulsively assault their victim with gun or knife—not those who carefully plan the crime of the century and cautiously rip the nails from their victim's toes before they encase him in concrete and drop him in the lake. Most typical of sex offenders are men with poor inhibitions who press their sex attentions too strenuously on sometimes none too unwilling victims—not those who snatch the little child and carry it off to a life of sadism in the mountain cabin. There is no such thing as the typical prisoner, but if the reader thinks that the prison is populated with the type of men whose cases get into the newspaper, let the impression be corrected.

No one knows what proportion of prisoners are actually professional criminals but this writer estimates that less than 20 per cent should be so classified. Another 5 to 10 per cent are psychopathic or sociopathic and the heavy majority are awkward, occasional or accidental offenders little different from the non-penal population except for an "unfortunate" attitudinal structure which happens to be functioning and guiding behavior in a particular concrete situation.

Recidivism

Even in the better textbooks on criminology there is no exact definition of recidivism. The dictionary defines the word as a tendency to relapse into crime. While the term is used somewhat differently by various investigators, it is generally agreed that a recidivist is a prisoner who has previously been in correctional custody. The problem at once arises whether or not men who have been on probation should, when committed to prison, be termed recidivists since, technically, they are in correctional custody and have broken a law. Similarly, should an inmate who has been previously in a boy's school for petty stealing be considered a recidivist? Again, should a prisoner whose only previous record consists of a 30-day jail sentence for drunkenness be considered a recidivist? In the prison system with which this study deals, the professional staff diagnoses recidivism, not according to previous record alone, but largely on the basis of personality make-up. Thus, a "two-time loser" may not be designated a recidivist, and, conversely, a man who has never been arrested before may be diagnosed as a recidivist. This individualized understanding of each case by the professional staff is not shared by the practical prison officials who generally take the position that every man who has served time before is a recidivist. For practical purposes the data offered here on recidivism will take the conventional form.

On a selected day when the population figure was 2,355, there happened to be exactly 1,000 men whose records showed that they had been previously incarcerated in other prisons, reformatories, workhouses, penal farms, jails, chain-gangs, or boys' correctional schools. Thus the raw recidivism rate was 42 per cent on the selected day. Sutherland, in his *Principles of Criminology,* reports that in 1933, 48 per cent of all offenders who were committed to such institutions and reformatories had been previously committed to such institutions, and that in Massachusetts penal and reformatory institutions in 1927, 59.8 per cent of the offenders were recidivists.[19] Our prison with 42 per cent has a slightly lower proportion of persons who have been previously institutionalized. In Table VII may be seen the type of custody which our so-called one thousand recidivists have had.

TABLE VII

Number and Percentage Distribution of 1,000 Inmates Who Are Officially Designated as Recidivists, Classified According to Type of Previous Incarcerations

	White		*Negro*		*Total*	
	Number	*Per cent*	*Number*	*Per cent*	*Number*	*Per cent*
Prison or Prisons	349	49.4	108	62.4	457	45.7
Reformatory or Reformatories	180	25.5	36	20.8	216	21.6
Correctional School or Schools	52	7.4	7	4.1	59	5.9
Prisons and Reformatories	65	9.2	18	10.4	83	8.3
Prisons and Schools	21	3.0	3	1.7	24	2.4
Reformatories and Schools	28	3.9	1	.6	29	2.9
Prisons, Reformatories and Schools	11	1.6			11	1.6
Farms, Jails, Workhouses and Chain Gangs, Only[20]					121	12.1
Total	706	100.0	173	100.0	1,000	100.0

[19] E. H. Sutherland, *op. cit.,* p. 546.

[20] In tabulating the number of men who had served at penal farms, work houses, jails, and chain gangs, the race distribution was neglected and, as shown in the table,

Of the 457 men who were previously in other prisons, 300 have been in one other, 114 have been in two, 27 have been in three, and 16 have been in four or more. Including their present incarceration the average is 2.7 commitments for each of these 457 inmates. Similarly, the average of the 216 men who were previously in reformatories is 2.1 commitments per man. Excluding 121 men who have been in jails or workhouses, penal farms, or chain gangs only, 879 of the recidivists have served an aggregate of 1,407 correctional terms. This is an average of a little over one and one-half terms (1.6) per recidivist. Because the workhouse (misdemeanor) group has not been included, and because our records may not be complete, the figure cited is probably too low. Differing slightly with the expected condition, our data show that Negroes are no more recidivistic than are whites. Excluding the 121 misdemeanants, there were 174 Negroes and 705 white recidivists in a total population of 2,355 on the selected day. In the total population there were 466 Negroes and 1,889 whites, and the percentage of recidivists was 37.32 for each race. Another study reveals that recidivists are slightly more intelligent than non-recidivists.[21]

Pointing, as we are, to an understanding of the total culture of the prison, these facts concerning recidivism are of considerable importance since, when men have had residence in other prisons they bring with them the attitudes and customs they have assimilated there and disseminate them in the culture of our prison. The major crime problem is essentially the recidivist problem. Professor Sutherland says that recidivists ". . . provide more than their fair share of the failures on probation and parole and more than their share of disciplinary problems in penal institutions. Massive walls and other devices are needed principally for recidivists." [22]

---

has been included only in the "Total column" as 121. In addition to the 121 who have been charted as penal farm, workhouse, jail, and chain gang incarcerants, there are 103 others who also had a major institutionalization and they have been properly included in other portions of the table. The error is considered too inconsequential to demand a laborious retabulation insofar as the important trends are shown. It is the writer's opinion that if the records were absolutely accurate the recidivism rate would be higher. This applies to workhouses, jails, penal farms, chain gangs, and correctional schools especially. Many investigators do not consider that residence in a boys' correctional school only, is sufficient to designate a rating of recidivism. The reader may make corrections for the item of correctional school only, if he sees fit.

[21] An unpublished study by the writer, entitled, "Some Observations on the Relationship of Recidivism and Intelligence at the ——— Prison." Submitted to his Director, 1934.

[22] E. H. Sutherland, *op. cit.*, p. 546.

CHAPTER III

Organization of the Penitentiary

The first chapter of this book attempted to summarize the culture conditioning of our inmates. The second chapter continued this theme and set forth in broad terms the personality equipment of the men in prison. In this chapter we wish to observe the formal organization of the community in which the personalities thus conditioned, live. It is a perspective and a bird's eye view of the total situation which is now in order so that the subsequent chapters may be interpreted in relation to the total situation. We are for the moment interested in such facts as the survey type of study reveals.

While our major concern is with the "unseen environment," there is need of understanding the community set-up in which the "unseen environment" exists. In evaluating the penal community it is necessary, for example, to know that the prisoners are allowed to attend a ball game on Saturday afternoon under the scrutiny of eight guard towers, though it is more important to know why the inmate spectators habitually cheer for the outside, visiting team. Similarly, we must give attention to the fact that the average ration is 2,675 calories per day for each inmate, yet we have more concern, from our frame of reference, in understanding why, for example, gravy served for five consecutive breakfasts, creates, collectively, a configuration of attitudes which, if ignited by leadership, might precipitate a riot.

The survey type of study will tell us that the prison walls are thirty feet high, but it will not usually reveal that when an inmate sees and learns about a certain wall, attitudes inimical to reformation develop.

For the moment we will leave the more abstruse sociological problems in favor of a quick survey of the prison as an administrative unit.

The Plant and Its Equipment

Our 2,300 prisoners live in and with property valued at nearly two and one-half million dollars. The land is valued at $84,554, the buildings at $1,755,060.33, and personal property at

$660,317.82. The prison proper is surrounded by thirty feet walls, or cellhouses which serve as walls, and occupies about thirteen acres. The farm unit operates 1,650 acres owned by the state, and leases about 100 acres from private owners.

All three cellhouses are of the block type. The two oldest, as well as the walls which surround the prison grounds are built of sandstone, and the newest is made of concrete and cement blocks. Cellhouse *A* was built in 1878, *B,* in 1888, and *C* was completed in 1932. A two-story brick building serves as a dormitory. Though old and penologically obsolete, cellhouses *A* and *B* are in good repair. The administration building was constructed about the time the cellhouses were, and in architecture and arrangement of quarters, is typical of American architecture in 1890. The buildings which house the various industries are old but fairly adequate in heat, light, and ventilation. Industrially speaking, the pride of the prison is the knit shop whose new machinery, installed in 1933, is modern in every respect, and valued at $57,000. The two quarries, one inside the walls and one outside, but nearby, are expansive and about sixty feet deep and have the machinery adequate for quarrying and preparing crushed limestone.

The headquarters of the prison farm are located about three miles from the prison proper. A dormitory of recent construction houses about 120 prisoners. The farm uses 500 of its 1,650 acres for corn. Cantaloupe, potatoes, broom-corn, and many vegetables are raised. Part of the farm work also consists in caring for some 120 cows, 2,000 hogs, and a few thousand chickens.

Security equipment, in addition to walls and iron bars, includes the locking devices and firearms. All windows facing the outside have iron bars three-fourths of an inch thick which are inspected daily. Several of the buildings within the walls also have barred windows. In the two oldest cellhouses each cell may be individually locked, and in addition has a long rod running the length of the gallery, which is operated by hand, and which may prevent any or all doors (which swing outward) from opening. In the newest cellhouse, *C,* there is a modern pneumatic system for locking and unlocking cell doors collectively. An armory strategically placed in the administration building, has telephone connections with the sixteen guard towers and all other likely trouble-spots in the prison. For use in preventing escapes or quieting riots are some 185 articles including guns, sub-machine guns, revolvers, tear and gas grenades, and the like.

Administration and Personnel

In the state in which our prison is located the legislature makes a biennial appropriation of between five and seven million dollars, depending upon building needs, for all correctional institutions, including schools for minors, and male and female adults, a total of eight institutions. Our prison's portion of this amount is around one million dollars for the two years. The annual per capita cost for the years with which study deals has been:

1931	$278.45
1932	227.45
1933	190.43
1934	156.55

The money is appropriated by the legislature from the general revenue fund and is assigned from a budget to the Department of Public Welfare. Included in this major department, administered by the Director, is the Division of Prisons, headed by the Superintendent of Prisons who has charge of five institutions for adult offenders. While the warden of each prison is appointed by the governor, administratively, he is responsible to the superintendent of prisons, who, in turn, is responsible to the director of the public welfare department, who is responsible to the governor.

Appointments to the wardenship are made almost completely on a political basis. The only experience of a criminological nature which most wardens have had consists of a term or two as deputy or county sheriff. During the period of this study there have been two wardens, one succeeding the other in the Democratic victory of 1932. The first, a Republican, had been warden for eight years. He had been, prior to his appointment as warden, a postmaster in a small city, and a deputy United States marshal. His social vision was limited to the narrow boundaries of the state over which he was political boss. He was known as a strong party man and had many affiliations. He was kind to his friends, and severe with his enemies. His guidance of the penal colony was uneventful; he fostered no reforms and allowed his lower officers practically to manage the prison. He had no particular penological policies other than to keep the prison clean, prevent riots and escapes, and use his position for the strengthening of old or the making of new political ties. His administration was so poor that he was unaware that his subordinate officers practiced brutal disciplinary methods. He was either held in contempt or vigorously hated by all but a few inmates who served as his flunkies.

The second warden, a younger man, was 39 years of age when appointed early in 1933. He had attended high school and was in the Navy during the World War. Prior to assuming the wardenship he had served as a deputy sheriff for four years, as a sheriff for four years, and had been a county treasurer for about three years before his appointment. While his appointment was essentially political, the governor considered him to be suitable material to administer the lives of 2,300 inmates and 230 employees living and working in an institution valued at two and a half million dollars. Soon after taking office the warden gave evidence of possessing a humanitarian point of view. He allowed inmates who were assigned to indoor shops to have the freedom of the athletic field for an hour each noon. While he insisted on strict discipline, he demanded that brutal punishment be stopped, and in one case discharged a senior officer, who belonged to the same political party as he, for kicking an inmate. He stopped much needless waste and reduced operating costs. He initiated football and boxing. He coöperated with all employees, and for the first time gave some prestige to the Mental Health Staff. The new warden was a marked improvement over his predecessor and when one considers the confusing complexities of penal administration one can but wonder that prison officials operating in a society such as ours handle the situation as well as they do.

The assistant and second assistant wardens, as well as eight or ten captains, are the contact men in the operation of the penitentiary. The assistant warden and the second assistant have about the same background as does their warden, but their political prestige is usually less. In dealing with inmates the second assistant warden is the key man, as he has direct charge of work assignment and discipline. Of the two who held the position, the first was lazy, dull, and inefficient, and the second has proved ineffective and opposed to change. Neither has had a broad social perspective. The eight or nine captains are in direct charge of the guards and spend their time going from gang (work unit) to gang, and are on hand for special assignments or in case of trouble.

Practically all of the 160 guards and keepers reach their positions, as do their superiors, through political channels. Their duties vary from spending twelve long hours alone in an isolated wall tower, to unlocking and locking a steel-barred gate one thousand times a day. The guards are the wheel-horses of the prison. They get the inmates up in the morning, march them to breakfast, dinner, and supper, observe their work during the day, put them to bed at night, and watch over them while they sleep. The duties are many and varied. While the actual physical work of the keepers is small, the constant surveillance and caution they must exercise is nerve racking and tiring. As a group the guards have had little education and do not come from the "higher walks of life."

In addition to the personnel briefly mentioned, there are numerous special employees. The following tabulation will show the approximate number of employees in the various work categories and the salaries they received in 1936:

Number of Employees	*Position*	*Salary per Month*
1	Warden	$358.33
1	Assistant Warden	235.00
1	2nd Assistant Warden	150.00
170	Guards	112.50
32	Guards	103.50
8	Deputy Wardens	135.00
4	Industrial Superintendents	135.00 (average)
4	Clerks	134.00 (average)
3	Teachers	118.00 (average)
1	Dentist	157.50
2	Chaplains	125.00
1	Storekeeper	150.00
1	Steward	125.00
1	Steward	115.00
1	Fingerprint Expert	150.00
1	Chief Clerk	200.00
1	Master Mechanic	225.00
1	Mason	125.00
1	Gardener	125.00
1	Censor of Mails	125.00

It will be observed that the salaries are small, although practically every position carries full or partial maintenance. The guards, who comprise the majority of the workers, may eat three meals a day at the prison, and may get their laundry, pressing, and barbering practically free. Most of the single men are provided sleeping quarters. Such advantages, however, do not balance the low salaries and the twelve-hour day.[1] The twelve-hour day is not demanded of clerks, chaplains, the physician, and a few other of the specialized employees.

Since 1905 civil service has been on the statute books of the state wherein our prison is located. Around 1911 it flourished in theory and practice. In 1917 interest waned, and certain legislation took the teeth out of the previous laws so that a virtual spoils system has been practiced in most departments since. While a Civil Service Commission has existed for many years, it has been virtually powerless to enforce a proper or complete civil service. This is so partly because an administrative officer may remove an employee for any number of reasons, and the employee has no recourse unless he can prove his discharge is the direct result of political, religious, or race prejudice—a very difficult thing to do. Most guards discharged on such grounds accept their fate and take no retaliatory steps because they realize that through precisely similar methods a vacancy

[1] Since this study was completed three shifts of eight working hours have replaced the two twelve-hour shifts.

was created for them when they procured their position. When the warden discharges a man he has the power to appoint an officer and may fill the position temporarily, and renew such an appointment. Eventually, a temporary employee may take a civil service examination, which is relatively simple, and become a certified employee. In practice, this procedure is an unbridled spoils system and is not peculiar to this state alone, but is part and parcel of government practices in most states.

Paradoxically enough, in 1932 and 1933 this procedure did much to improve the staff of our prison. Those were the years when national unemployment was at its worst and many able men were without work. The change in political administration, coming as it did at this time, replaced many of the older, poorly trained, poorly disciplined, and lazy job-holders with younger, more interested, and efficient men. However, changes in personnel were not made so fast that the safety of the institution was impaired, but within a year all save a handful of the employees of the previous administration had been replaced. Taking into consideration the rapid turnover caused by the spoils system, and the fact that guards have almost no chance for advancement and so leave the service whenever a better job is offered, it is not surprising that the average tenure of a guard is about four years and that the better men leave and the less capable remain as long as they can.

Admission and Release Procedures

New men are brought to the prison in custody of the sheriff in the county where they were convicted. The sheriff has in his possession a mittimus which is the official instrument which places the responsibility for the offender's custody and safe-keeping in the hands of the warden. As the sheriff delivers the mittimus to the record clerk, an assistant clerk asks the new prisoner a few questions such as his home address, age, religion, and so forth. The new inmate is then ushered to the rear gate which enters into the prison yard. In the custody of a guard now, he is first searched, and then escorted across the prison yard to the Identification Office. Here the new man is finger-printed and photographed. A record is made of tattoo marks, scars, color of eyes and hair, and height and weight. The next procedure is in the clothing room where he is dispossessed of his civilian clothes, except for the shoes which he may retain if they pass the clothing-room guard's inspection. The fact that some newly admitted men have had steel files secreted in the leather layers of their shoes demands that the inspection be more than cursory. The new inmate is allowed to retain his summer underwear if he wishes, as none is provided by the prison. His new clothes, consisting of two pairs of denim trousers, two hickory shirts, one pair of hose, one pair of shoes, a cap, one handkerchief, and a face towel are given him. While the neophyte is under the shower in a room next door, an assistant stamps all of his new clothing with his prison number. The bath is taken in the general shower room which incidentally has capacity for eighty-four men at one time. Following the bath the new inmate is given antiseptics as a safeguard against the spread of vermin. He then dresses in his prison clothing, leaving in the clothing room one outfit into which he may change a week or more later. The man is then taken to the barber's chair where he is shaved and his hair is entirely clipped off. The admission process thus far may have been for one or several new men. The next step, however, is an individual interview in the office of the second assistant warden. An inmate stenographer procures certain identifying data. Age, schooling, marital status, nationality, previous record, and similar information is obtained. The neophyte is also allowed to tell briefly his version of his crime. A trip to the hospital is next in order. There a medical history is taken by an inmate hospital worker and under the direction of a physician each new prisoner is innoculated for smallpox and typhoid fever. A specimen of his blood is also obtained for the Wassermann test for syphilis. The prison physician then examines the man and records his findings. Next he is again interviewed by the second assistant warden who briefly explains the rules and gives the inmate a rule book and a copy of the Progressive Merit System regulations. At this time the new prisoner is also assigned to a work division or "gang," as it is commonly called. If the series of events making up the admission procedure takes more than one day, which is usually the case, the new incarcerant is assigned to a special gallery in *A* cellhouse known as the "fish gallery."

The sentences of men admitted to our prison are both determinate and indeterminate. The criminal code of the state provides indeterminate sentences for sixty-eight different crimes varying, for example, from "Possession of Burglar Tools," which carries a sentence of one to two years, to "Robbery, Armed," which sentence is one year to life. (See Chapter II for distribution of type of offenses.) The crimes of murder, rape, habitual criminal, and kidnapping carry "flat" or determinate sentences, such as ten years, sixty years, or whatever the trial judge chooses to fix. Some offenders are unfortunate enough to have received both an indeterminate and a determinate sentence such as forty-five years for murder and one year to life for armed robbery. Somewhat similarly, a prisoner may have been sentenced on three charges of larceny (a one to ten-year sentence) and each sentence to "run consecutively," which means that the minimum term of one year on each of the three sentences must be served before the man is eligible for parole.

Release from the institution depends upon the type of sentence imposed. Men with indeterminate sentences are released when the parole board says they should be, and within the limits of their sentence. Men with determinate sentences are released when their time is served. However, both types of sentences are subject to certain time allowances which will be discussed later. There are many details, both statuatory and pertaining to parole board regulations, which guide the release of prisoners, and which it is not necessary to take up here. It is sufficient to know that slightly over seventy per cent of the inmates must follow parole requirements upon release from prison.

The inmate with an indeterminate sentence sees a committee made up of two members of the parole board after he has served about eleven months, if he has a minimum sentence of one year, which all but six of the sixty-eight such sentences provide. This interview with the parole board committee is a crucial event in the prisoner's life as four weeks later a letter is sent him either declaring that he will be immediately paroled, or giving him a "set," that is, stipulating a certain future date when parole will become effective. The Parole Board has seven members, one of whom is the chairman. Two of these members comprise a committee and visit the prison for three to five days, beginning on the first Monday of each month, excluding July and August. For several hours the first day the committee listens to the pleas of the friends, relatives, or victims of prisoners. They then interview each man individually allowing anywhere between five minutes to an hour for the "hearing." For study, and to assist in evaluating each man's case, the parole committee has at their disposal the following data: (1) statement of trial judge and state's attorney regarding the crime; (2) work and conduct record in prison; (3) medical report; (4) mental health and classification reports; (5) criminal record; and (6) a statistical prognostication by the acturial-sociologist. They usually have favorable letters from relatives and friends urging release, and proffering a job and sponsorship, or they may have letters or petitions from the victims and other persons who do not wish to see an inmate paroled.

When the inmate is called to the office for an interview, the members of the committee already know something about him. Questions and answers are recorded in shorthand, and a rather complete summary is subsequently dictated by the committee. Questions deal with the crime, the likelihood of its being repeated, the kind of work the prisoner would do if paroled and other such inquiries. When the parole committee have finished their work at the prison they return to the state capital where the entire board of seven members meets and determines what action shall be taken. The inmate is informed of their decision within four weeks.

The amount of data on each man and the apparent separate consideration given each person would suggest that the treatment of each case is individualized. It seems, however, that with some exceptions all robbers get about the same "sets," and that in each specific crime group each offender fares about the same. The parole board has the most difficult job in a penal system: prediction of human behavior. The members of the board are political appointees, and while they are intelligent men, but few of them have been trained for their difficult task. They are subject to pressure on all sides: from the press, the government, political and financial groups, and friends and enemies of inmates. Most men in prison hate and distrust the board. Those who get quick paroles may be more kindly disposed, but their pro-feeling does not affect the prison culture because they are not of it.

When the time comes for the prisoner's release the local parole officer informs him of the rules he must obey on parole and gives him a number of blank reports. He is to send one of these in each month after it has been signed by both his sponsor and employer. He is then barbered, given a fairly presentable suit of clothes and other furnishings, ten dollars in cash, and a railroad ticket to his home, unless it is out of the state, in which case he is given carfare to the boundary of the state. A few friendly words from the warden, and he is gone.

Classification

Legislation was passed in the summer of 1933 which set into operation a classification and segregation system. The laws stipulate that each of the four prisons in the state are to be used for a particular type of prisoner, and, in addition, one new institution is to provide a residence for the insane criminals who heretofore were segregated in a special hospital which was not under the jurisdiction of the prison authorities. The laws and regulations provide that one institution be set aside for recidivists who are without gross mental pathology, another for young "normal" first offenders, another for more mature "normal" first offenders, and a fourth for mental defectives. An advisory commission made up of prominent psychiatrists in the state was appointed by the governor to assist in the formulation of various policies concerning state wards. This commission provided a more feasible system of classification of prisoners based on the concept of "improvability." Thus, inmates are not diagnosed as first offenders or recidivists, but rather as "improvable," "questionably improvable," or "unimprovable." Before such a diagnosis can be reached, the Classification Board weighs factors of age, intelligence, mental condition, criminality, and so on. This system of classification with its sub-classifications is a complicated one, the details of which are not pertinent to our present discussion. It is sufficient for us to know that the institution with which we are concerned was originally designated as the residence for those prisoners who were mentally defective. It should be stated here that during the time of the investigation presented in this book there were no transfers of mental defectives to our prison in sufficient numbers to disturb the *status quo,* as the laws provided that the classification program should be put into operation only as fast as administrative facilities could be arranged. Even though the innovation of classification effects only the last year of the three years covered by this book, and has not materially changed the composition of the population, a brief description of the procedure followed will indicate the manner in which the classification program was initiated.

Provided by the legislation is a stipulation that the examination of prisoners to determine their place of residence should be carried on by members of the mental health staff whose major duties before had consisted of examining all inmates who were to be considered for parole, and of caring for those men who developed psychoses. Under the direction of the state criminologist the same staff, composed of a psychiatrist, a sociologist, and a psychologist, undertook the classification of prisoners by much the same professional methods as were used in examining men for parole. The approach to this work, known as the multiple approach to the study of personality was, and continues to be, four-fold, as in addition to the three specialists mentioned, the prison physician also contributes by giving an evaluation of the health and physical factors. Thus, each new man who enters the prison is studied from these four points of view and a classification report is prepared which recommends the institution to which he should be sent, the type of work he should do, any special education he may need, and medical treatment if such is necessary. The sociological study consists of the gathering of a social history of the inmate by personal interview and by check-up correspondence with relatives, employers, social agencies, friends, and on occasion, ministers and physicians. The sociologist weighs the social factors in an effort to understand and integrate the broad cultural influences which have been instrumental in developing the particular attitudes which have led to the offense. The sociologist's special contribution has been in the diagnosis of criminality. The psychologist administers intelligence tests and determines the mental age of the inmate. The psychiatrist integrates the findings of sociologist, psychologist, and physician, in addition to lending his own psychiatric appraisal of the personality. The Mental Health Staff became known as the Classification Board with the psychiatrist as chairman. The reports of this board and the recommendations they include, the law provides, should be advisory only. The final institutional allocation of prisoners is the function of the superintendent of prisons. Only rarely has the superintendent failed to follow the suggestions of the professional staff.

Punishment and Rewards

The punishment for infraction of prison rules consists of solitary confinement, loss of privileges, and, in some cases, loss of "good time." Considered as rewards are the weekly letter, a small portion of tobacco each seven days, and the opportunity to decrease the length of servitude by good conduct. The essential principle in these topics of punishment and reward is the "Progressive Merit System" which became effective in 1920.

The Progressive Merit System provides that inmates who maintain excellent conduct shall have the length of their stay in prison reduced. Five grades of conduct-status are used, known as *A, B, C, D,* and *E., A* indicating the best conduct-status and *E* the poorest. When a new man enters prison he is placed in *C* grade, which carries no good time allowance. After three months, if he maintains good conduct, he is promoted to grade *B*. For every month he serves in grade *B,* he earns five days of "good time." After another three months of good conduct he will be placed in grade *A,* and he will earn ten days of good time each month that he remains in that grade. Thus, in the first year of incarceration the inmate will earn two and one-half months of good time. When the inmate sees the parole board after his first eleven months, the "set" which they give him will be materially reduced if he stays in *A* grade. For example, a man who enters the prison on January 1, 1935, on an indeterminate sentence of one to twenty years, will see the parole board early in December of the same year. If they give him a "set" of ten years, that is January of 1945, he will be eligible for release in six years and three months providing he remains in *A* grade, and would then be paroled in October of 1941. This date is arrived at by subtracting four months from each year of the "set" except for the first year, when only two and one-half months are deducted.

Almost all of the infractions of rules are punished in other ways than by reduction in conduct-grade. However, when an inmate persistently breaks the rules, or when his infraction is serious, he may be reduced in grade from *A,* for example, to *D,* or *E.* Such demotions affect the length of his servitude, as for every month he spends in grade *D,* he loses five days, and if in grade *E,* he loses ten days good time. Furthermore, the inmate will lose all the good time previously earned in grades *A* and *B* if he is demoted, and, in addition, must remain in *D* or *E* grade for one year, that is, three months each for grades *A, B, C,* and *D.* After a demoted inmate has been shifted to *C* grade, he must remain there for as many days as he held *E* grade status before he can be advanced to *B,* and again earn good time. A man who is not in *A* grade is deprived of seeing the parole board until he attains that status.

With some exceptions the whole system of punishments and rewards is tied up with the Progressive Merit System. For example, inmates in *D* and *E* can write letters but once a month, whereas men in the other grades may write once each week. Men in the higher three grades may have a visitor every two weeks, but men in the two lower grades are permitted visitors but once in six months. Men who are not in *A* grade are not eligible for Honor Farm placement, trustieship, or parole.

The Progressive Merit System is not a law but merely a regulation in the Division of Prisons. There is a law, however, known as the Statutory Good Time law which provides certain reductions from the sentence imposed unless an inmate participates in the most rebellious type of conduct, such as assaulting an officer, or fomenting a riot. It is not necessary for our purposes to give a detailed account of this legislation, except to say that it operates in much the same way as the Progressive Merit System. It permits men who are committed on flat sentences to serve half the time which the sentence states, plus fifteen months. Thus a twenty-year flat sentence means the inmate will serve eleven years and three months before discharge, providing his conduct is not seriously rebellious. This figure is reached by deducting so much time for the first year and increasing the amount of time deducted with each year until five years have been served, when six months is deducted for that year and each succeeding year of the sentence imposed. The Statutory Good Time law also operates in indeterminate sentences and allows the inmate to reduce the amount of time he will serve even though the parole board have given him the maximum setting. In essence, both Progressive Merit System and the Statutory Good Time law are measures instituted to maintain the peace of the prison and give an incentive for good conduct. They serve the double purpose of rewarding the inmate and protecting the prison.

Other punishment methods which may or may not affect the merit standing of an inmate include solitary confinement for any period between one and twenty-one days, and loss of certain privileges such as attending the weekly movie or a ball game. A man who attempts an escape will usually be demoted to *E* grade and given twenty-one days in solitary confinement as well. For talking in the dining room an inmate may simply be cautioned, or deprived of a movie, or forced to serve four days on bread and water in a solitary cell, the length of time depending on his previous conduct and the circumstances. The conduct infractions most frequently followed by solitary confinement include: talking in line or dining room, insolence, refusing to work, loafing at work, fighting, cooking food in the cell, carrying food from the dining room, and less frequently, escape, or attempting to escape, homosexual activities, or assaulting an officer.

The twenty-four solitary cells are in a small building known as the yard office, which also contains the Identification Bureau and the office of the second assistant warden. "Solitary" is set off by itself and is heavily barred and isolated. The cells themselves contain no furniture. The one window is small, and the iron bars of the door have another wooden door which keeps the light from entering. The cells are cold in winter and hot in summer. The inmate is given one blanket and must sleep on a wooden slab raised about two inches from the cement flooring. One piece of bread and a necessary amount of water is allowed each day.

The greatest reward which an inmate can earn is his Progressive Merit time. However, the warden may recommend additional good time for efficiency at work, or for other reasons, up to ninety days. Such a recommendation is considered by the parole board and only occasionally refused. Most of the "industrial good time" grants are for thirty or sixty days.

The Daily Routine

The daily routine varies somewhat with the season of the year. Generally, the men are aroused earlier in summer than in winter. The daily schedule also varies with conditions such as an occasional fog in the morning, which delays the breakfast hour until the density of the fog has cleared enough so that there will be no danger of an escape. Other situations such as a primary or general election will change the daily routine because a large proportion of the employees return to their home communities to assist in electioneering. When an escape does occur, and if the warden believes there is a chance of capturing the escapers he will order that all work cease and that the men be locked up in order that a large number of guards may engage in the man-hunt. Once, a few notorious prisoners made their escape and the warden received word that they were hiding in the surrounding territory. He kept the majority of the prison population locked up for two days, and sent their warders to search. Food was served in the cellhouses, and the various gangs were given exercise by marching. In spite of some changes in the daily procedure, however, each day is enough like another to become deadeningly monotonous, as we shall later see. A typical summer schedule is as follows:

Arising Bell and Count	5:30 A. M.
Guard Change	6:00 A. M.
Breakfast (long line)	6:30 A. M.
Breakfast (short line)	7:15 A. M.
March to Work (long line)	7:15 A. M.
Sick Call	7:30 A. M.
March to Work (short line)	7:45 A. M.
Dinner (short line)	10:45 A. M.
Dinner (long line)	11:30 A. M.
Return to Work	1:00 P. M.
Supper (short line)	3:30 P. M.
Supper (long line)	4:30 P. M.
Evening Count and Whistle	between 5:00 and 5:30 P. M.
Guard Change	6:00 P. M.
Warning Bell	8:45 P. M.
Lights Out	9:00 P. M.

In this schedule the designation of "long line" and "short line" refers to two assortments of work gangs, which, for purposes of eating, are lined up together, each "line" eating at slightly different times. The dining room will hold but 1,200 men. The "long line" fills it, and the "short line" occupies about two-thirds of its capacity.

In the morning between the arising bell and breakfast, the men must dress, wash, make their beds, and clean their cells. A glance at the schedule would seem to indicate that about thirty minutes are allowed for each meal. Careful timing for one complete week, however, showed that the actual time elapsing in the dining room for eating purposes averaged thirteen minutes. With one exception noted later, the hour between twelve and one at noon is spent in the cell. Washing before breakfast is done in the cell, but washing before the other two meals must be done in the shops or from barrels of water in the quarry.

The item on the schedule noted as "count" refers to a most important daily activity. At a day's end, officials never breathe easily until they know that all inmates are present. The counting process takes place at least twice a day in the cellhouses. Two guards of each work unit must count the men assigned to them and report their findings to a captain. Other such reports are made, the process taking about ten minutes. When it is learned that all men are present, a whistle, known as the "O. K. whistle" blows. The inmates, except the trusties and special detail men, are all locked in their cells during the counting process, and must stand facing the front with their hands on the bars.

The rules, all of which are given in Chapter VIII, govern the daily routine. Like all regulations they prescribe what may and what may not be done, and their central theme is the maintenance of order and the setting of a standard for conduct of the prisoners and for the cleanliness of the institution.

System of Housing and Sleeping

The prisoners reside in cellhouses *A* and *C* except for 125 men who live in the farm dormitory or annexes, and 372 who reside in the dormitory inside the walls. (During the first year in which data for this study were collected, cellhouse *B* was also used, but during the balance of the time it was undergoing reconstruction.)

A house has 400 cells. This building is of the block type in which the block containing the 400 cells stands in the center of a long, rectangular building. There are four galleries, one of which is on the ground floor, and the others directly above. In *A* house the cells are 7 feet long, 6½ feet high, and 4 feet and 8 inches wide. Between each cell is a solid stone and cement partition of 8½ inches. The back and sides of the cell are of solid concrete, painted gray. The steel-barred gate constitutes the front part of the cell. Each cell is equipped with a double deck, gas-pipe-frame bed which is moveable. The mattresses for the beds are of cheap construction and filled with excelsior. Two blankets, a pillow and slip, and one sheet are provided. The cells also contain two stools, a wash basin, a can of water, and a covered bucket used for toilet purposes. In each cell is one 25-watt light. In this oldest building ventilation is provided by blower fans which are not very effective. The narrow windows are also opened on occasions. The heating system operates effectively except for the cells on the ground floor and the "monkey-cages." The cells are scrubbed once each week, and the mattresses are aired and sunned about once in six days. By use of an insecticide and by blow torches, an effort is made to keep the cells free from cockroaches and bed bugs. The so-called "monkey-cages" are steel-barred, moveable cells which are placed on the ground floor and used because of over-crowding. They contain the same equipment as the cells of the regular block, but are even smaller and more reminiscent of early penology at its worst than is the cell block proper. In general, *A* house is a miserable domicile. The toilet buckets, in spite of daily care and disinfecting, lend a putrid odor. The small windows and the antiquated ventilating system do little to cleanse the atmosphere from 420 toilet cans and 850 male bodies which are not too frequently bathed. In summer the walls collect moisture. On cold winter nights the air is warm and stuffy, as the few guards on duty object to opening the windows completely as the cold air would make them uncomfortable. The mattresses are generally lumpy. The 25-watt bulbs are so weak that a yellowish gloom pervades the cellhouse and reading is difficult. More than any other place in the prison, one gets here the impression of caged animals in cramped quarters.

Cellhouse *C*, completed in 1932, is a less unhappy place for the 1,000 men who occupy its 500 cells It is also of the cellblock construction, being 5 galleries high. The cells here are 7½ feet high, 10 feet, 3 inches long, and 6 feet, 5 inches wide. The cells are of solid concrete construction except for the "front door" which consists of strong steel bars. The partitions between cells are 9 inches thick. Ventilation in this newer building is modern and the large glass windows admit light and air. The cell equipment consists of a modern toilet with running water and a small wash stand. The two beds in each cell are attached to the wall with iron chains and may be swung upright and parallel with the wall to provide more room. The bed equipment is otherwise the same as in *A* house. Two stools and a shelf for storing necessary articles are also included. In general, the living conditions of *B* house are hygienic.

The inside dormitory, a building formerly used as a shop, has two stories and holds 180 men on the first floor and 190 on the second. There are no cells here, although the windows and doors are barred. The beds are double-decked cots which are placed in long rows. Each inmate has a locker which is stored under the bed. Every man is also provided with a stool. At one end of each floor an open space is left for recreational purposes. A wash room contains toilets, showers, and wash stands of modern type but insufficient in number to care properly for the number of men who must use the facilities at one time. The inmates who live here have no special privileges other than the fact that they are not confined to cells. In general, the dormitory is clean, hygienic, and furnishes a fairly decent physical environment. The 120 men who live and work on the Honor Farm are provided with good living conditions in a new dormitory.

The System of Food Provision and Eating

The general mess hall (colloquially called the "con dining room") seats 1,200 men. There are four sections of tables, each of which provides for 300 men. Everyone faces the front of the building and occupies an individual seat. The table tops are of oak and are cleaned after each meal. The kitchen from which the food is served is adjacent to the dining-hall and contains one 150-gallon coffee urn, one 100-gallon coffee urn, one electric potato peeler, one electric meat and vegetable cutter, a coffee grinder, a bread slicer, four ranges, nine 80-gallon cooking pots, four vegetable boilers, an electric silver and glass washer, a large refrigerator, and a cold storage room. The bakery has an electric dough mixer and an oven which has capacity for 400 loaves of bread. The prison cannery, which prepares the summer's produce for winter use, has eleven vegetable steamers and other comparable equipment.

The inmates enter the dining room in double-breast formation and march to their seats. They immediately sit down and the men who enter first are served as the balance file to their seats. One guard accompanies each work group and several captains are in attendance. Seated high above the population in a barred perch, is another officer who has gas and firearms in the event of a riot. The inmates are not allowed to talk as they eat, and the sight of 1,200 men stoically eating in silence is gruesome. The inmate waiters pass among the tables with huge pans which they hold by means of leather straps around their necks. They ladle out the more liquid foods and hand the bread to each inmate with their hands. Everything is placed on one metal plate which often makes an unpalatable appearing mess. Coffee or tea is poured into the tin cups which the men bring with them. Second helpings may usually be had, although a rule exists that the plates must be cleaned. In quantity the food is adequate, although the monotony of the diet and the unappetizing preparation and serving are the cause of much complaint.

The food served to the inmate population in the summer of 1936, was said to average 2,675 calories per capita per day. Meat is usually served at six of the seven noonday dinners, four of the five suppers, and three to four of the seven breakfasts per week. In the summer, fresh vegetables and some fruits are provided. In the winter, cabbage, turnips, carrots, parsnips, and sweet potatoes are served three or four times a week. Gravy is often served. The cost of meals per capita in 1934 was about 11 cents a day as compared with 23 cents a day for the officers' mess. This cost is based on current market prices because the farm, which operates as an industry, sells its produce according to prevailing prices.

On Sunday there is no evening meal but at the noon dinner each man is given a sandwich which he may take to his cell for supper. The inmate store, or commissary, also supplies food for those prisoners who are able to buy it, and often such supplies are used for the Sunday evening meal.

The officers' dining-room serves substantial food for the guards and other lesser officials, and is open practically all hours of the day, as the guards have to take turns eating. In connection with the officers' dining-room is another small eating quarters for some twenty to thirty inmates who have semi-trustie status, such as office workers. These men eat the same food as the officers and are often envied and disliked by the population who call them "politicians." The dining-room at the Honor Farm serves meals somewhat better than those which are given to the general population. The smaller number to feed and the handiness of fresh supplies account for the more appetising meals. The daily per capita cost for this unit is around twenty cents.

Industries, Maintenance, and Labor

The prison's labor and industrial activities operate under a state-use system of production and distribution. In its earliest days a modified indenture system was used in which the inmates were "rented" outside the walls to manufacturers. Somewhat later, a contract-system was used. By this method the prison itself was turned into an industry. A civilian contractor would furnish machinery, raw materials, and technical supervision. He would pay the state about 50 cents a day for each inmate's labor and sell his prison-made goods on the open market. About 1905, legislation was passed which abolished the contract system and established a system of production for the prisons of the state, the guiding principles of which, as stated in the law, were to train inmates in industry and to provide useful products for the state and its political subdivisions. Through the years there has been other legislation, amendments, and administrative orders which have set up industries to produce materials suitable for use by other public institutions. The most recent legislation was passed in 1931 and provides a number of stipulations which emphasize the continuance and broadening of the state-use system. Adoption of the state-use system in our state, as well as in others, is, of course, the result of pressure by manufacturers' associations and organized labor. Such organizations have objected strenuously to prison industry and fostered legislation, both state and Federal, opposing the marketing of prison-made goods. Some manufacturers have even objected to the sale of any prison produce to other state-controlled institutions. The recently enacted laws, however, make it mandatory that the state and its subdivisions purchase supplies from the various tax-maintained institutions if the material they need is manufactured or produced. This law has not been vigorously enforced. The state has not had enough money in its revolving fund to set up many new industries during the depression, and as a result unemployment and idleness, like that in all other American prisons, has prevailed in the three major units of our state. In the prison which we are studying, unemployment has been a less severe problem than in most, although, while every inmate has been assigned to a job, there is still much idleness and too many hands for the work to be done.

It is impossible to cover adequately the labor and industrial situation as the topic itself is worthy of a book. In order, however, that the reader may have a general idea of the occupational aspects, we will outline the work program and describe in brief fashion one or two of the most prominent industries, and then give passing attention to the maintenance workers.

The work activities which are designated as industries are:

Knitting Mill—Hosiery	Farm and Garden
Knitting Mill—Underwear	Dairy Production
Clothing—Woolens	Hog Raising
Brick and Post Shop	Poultry Raising
Stone Quarry	Bakery

Manning these production units are about 1,200 men. More men are assigned to the industries when the orders for finished products are large. Quarrying uses the largest number of men, about 650. The knitting mills give employment to 130 men, and 120 find work on the farms. The men are permitted to talk as they work. They receive no wages, and are treated no differently than are the men who do the maintenance work.

The 650 prisoners who work in the quarry are divided into six groups or "gangs" each having about 100 men. These work units are known by number as "4-gang," or "5-gang." They are watched over by two or three guards in addition to those on the walls. After breakfast each morning they are marched to the quarry in the back part of the yard, where they get their tools from sheds down in the 60 feet deep hole. The quarry process includes the removal of surface soil by hand shovels, dynamiting (done at noon when the men are at dinner), "making little ones out of big ones," that is, breaking the dynamited rock with 30-pound sledge-hammers and chisels, wheelbarrowing, loading the broken rock into the small, cast-iron cars which are on a track, pushing the cars to the stone-crusher where it is ground or pulverized according to what is needed. The inmates have various jobs. Some are "shovelmen," some are "hammermen," and some are "pushers." The work is heavy, hard, and dirty. There is some idleness, however, in waiting for the cars to go and come from the crusher with their load. The guards preserve order and give general instructions as to the work which they, in turn, have received from the superintendent of the quarry industry. From one-quarter to one-third of the six different quarry gangs are made up of Negroes. Usually the most dangerous and unruly men are assigned to this type of work. The finished product is used for state or country roads, except for a small portion of limestone dust which is sold to local farmers for fertilizer at sixty cents a ton. This one exception to the state-use act is provided for by law. The yearly output of the quarry gangs is around 70,000 tons.

The knitting mill occupies both stories of an old, but well-cared for, building wherein work the 130 men who furnish the labor. In addition to two guards, the mill is presided over by a superintendent who is in general charge. In 1933 modern machinery was installed to manufacture a large number of garments. The raw product used is cotton yarn. From it is knit hose for men, women, and children as well as eleven various types of men's underwear and at least fourteen various styles of women's underclothing. The garments are of light and winter weight. About 120 dozen pairs of hose are knit each day, and twenty-five dozen suits of underwear. These garments are manufactured only when ordered by other state prisons, correctional schools, mental hospitals, and the like. The inmates' work consists largely of loading and attending the machines, sorting, stocking, and preparing the goods for shipment. The men assigned here are usually the younger, white prisoners, except for a few Negro porters and manual laborers.

The stone quarry and knit shop are examples of industries which retail most of their product to other state institutions. From an accounting and administrative angle, certain of the other work units in the prison would not technically be called an industry, but they are operated in much the same way. The bake-shop, for example, "sells" all its produce to the prison in which it operates. The 146,000 loaves of white bread baked during the fiscal year of 1932, for example, were sold to the prison for $5,790. The tin shop, the broom shop, the farms, and other units sell most of their goods to their own prison.

The prison is kept clean, in good repair, heated and operated under the administration of officials, by the balance of the inmates who are not assigned to the industries. The exceptions to this are a "crank gang" (the aged, the blind, and crippled) composed of about 75 men, and about 100 other inmates who attend school a half day. Among the maintenance group are 50 clerks. One hundred men keep the two cellhouses and dormitory clean by scrubbing, airing the mattresses, and by disinfecting; one hundred and eighty men prepare and serve the meals; thirty-five are barbers, forty-eight attend to the heating; twenty-five help the physician and dentist in the hospital; and many other groups clean the walks and streets, take care of the outside lawn, flunky for the officers, teach in the school, and maintain the farming equipment. The largest extraindustrial group, excepting those preparing the food, is known as the master mechanic's gang. There is one civilian plumber, one machinist, one electrician, one mason, and one carpenter. These qualified workers are assisted by 105 inmates, many of whom have had experience in the trade to which they are assigned. Because the plant is old, repairs are constantly being needed, and no maintenance group is considered so important as the unit headed by the master mechanic.

There is no formal vocational training. However, men may learn the barbering trade and receive a certificate after a prescribed amount of training. While there is no formal instruction, the inmates assigned to the hospital are in a position to acquire knowledge of nursing. Persons with an aptitude for music will find experience and encouragement in the band. Some knowledge of tailoring and knitting by machinery can be acquired. The men in the quarry develop strong backs.

Education, Religion, and Recreation

The prison school occupies the second floor of a shop building. The eight grades of the common school curriculum are offered under the direction of a civilian superintendent of education, who supervises the inmate teachers. The superintendent reached his position through political channels. He had been graduated from high school, and had had one year of normal college training, and one year of teaching experience prior to his appointment. His salary is $125 a month with partial maintenance. The inmate teachers are placed in the school by the second assistant warden, who usually selects the teachers without consulting the superintendent, or learning from the mental health office whether or not an inmate is intellectually capable of teaching. Thus the inmate teaching staff has been made up of persons who profess more than average education, according to prison standards, and whose glibness has impressed the deputy warden. A few of the teachers appointed by him have been intellectually inferior, but he has insisted upon retaining them as teachers in spite of their unsuitability. The eight classes are all held in one large room. The students sit around long tables with an inmate teacher at the head of each table and a blackboard on the wall behind him. The books and supplies are furnished by the state. The texts used are the same as those commonly found in public grade schools, and are not suitable for adults.[2] The inmates who attend school do so on a half-day schedule, dividing

[2] Educational methods have improved somewhat since 1936.

the day usually between schooling and quarry work. The assigning officer, the second assistant warden, places in the "school gang" practically all inmates who admit to illiteracy. Almost all such persons are illiterate because of various degrees of mental deficiency, so the educating of them is a most difficult process. In general, school attendance is not obligatory and an illiterate person who is strongly opposed to attending school is not compelled to do so.

For men who desire high school or other semi-advanced education, a correspondence system has been arranged. These so-called "cell courses" provide mimeographed text matter, some books and instructions for study. The students are assigned to regular work during the day and may study at night. They prepare their lessons and hand in their written answers to lessons as rapidly or slowly as it pleases them. Some 200 men at a time study the following subjects: English composition, American history, orthography, geography, algebra, Spanish, French, elementary book-keeping, and so on.

The prison library, under the supervision of the Protestant chaplain, has a catalog of about 6,000 books, most of which are light fiction. There is a monthly circulation of 12,000 books, indicating roughly that each book is assigned at least twice a month.

Recreational activities provided by the administration include weekly ball games with outside teams during the summer, a weekly movie during inclement and winter weather, boxing matches, radio programs, intramural softball for the shop-workers each noon during the summer, and occasional other events on holidays. A commissary provides tobacco, candies, cookies, and cake, some canned goods, and fruits for those inmates who have money in the commissary fund. About $2,500 is received each month from relatives and friends of inmates. No inmate is allowed to spend more than $3.00 a week for commissary luxuries. The profits of the commissary department, averaging between four and five hundred dollars a month, are used to support the recreational program.

Religious services are held in the chapel on the third floor of the administration building. Each Sunday morning the Protestant and Catholic chaplains conduct services for all inmates who wish to attend. Both meetings are quite typical of church procedure in the normal community. The chaplains are assigned to full-time duty, receive $125 a month with partial maintenance, and spend about six hours a day in the prison. In addition to their church duties they hold interviews with inmates and assist in the holiday activities. The Protestant chaplain receives his position by political appointment.

Physical and Mental Health

During the tenure of this study a new hospital was completed. It is a modern, three-story building with a capacity for housing thirty-three patients comfortably, or forty-three in the event of an epidemic. There are no private rooms. The wards contain between four and seven beds, except for the tubercular ward on the third floor which has a capacity of ten beds. A modern operating room and X-ray machine make for good surgical work even though the surgical instruments are old. The hospital also contains the dental department, a laboratory for urine analysis, and, during the greater period of this study, the mental health office.

In charge of the hospital is the prison physician, who was graduated from a Class A medical school and who is assisted in the medical work by a staff of twenty-four inmates who keep records, do the nursing, assist with first-aid and surgery, and keep the place clean. One guard is assigned to this unit who assumes charge when the physician is not present. During various periods covered by this study a junior physician was also on duty. When an inmate is not feeling well he is allowed to join the sick-line which forms every morning after breakfast at the hospital door. This line, of about ninety men, marches into the hospital where an inmate clerk locates the medical record which is handed to the physician who queries each man as to his complaints.

Many men on the sick line are quickly disposed of by prescribing laxatives or pills for colds. When an inmate gives evidence of critical illness the doctor examines him more carefully after the sick-line is finished. He may prescribe hospitalization, surgery, X-ray, a milk diet, or a change of work. Seldom are there more than twenty patients in the hospital at one time. Treatment for syphilis with injections or mercury rubs, occurs Thursday mornings routinely, and treatment for active gonorrhea is given Thursday afternoons. First-aid is given whenever an injury occurs. Operations are usually performed on a set day unless there is an emergency. While the physicians make an effort at maintaining their professional point of view, the fact that malingering is common among prisoners tends to make them severe in their dealings with men. Much of the inadequate medical care results from lack of drugs and equipment, a condition related to the insufficient budget. The full-time dentist is confronted with the same problem of inadequacy of supplies. Plates, and some dentures, cannot be provided unless the inmate has the money to pay for the materials, although actual suffering is not allowed.

A psychiatrist has been in attendance at this institution on the average of only two days a month, except for a period of a year and nine months when the same doctor was both psychiatrist and head physician. The duties of the part-time psychiatrist were for the most part occupied in a brief examination of inmates who were eligible to be seen by the parole board. In his hurried examinations of some 80 men in two days he would often spot incipient mental disease and would make this fact known to the warden and to the physician. If, during the absence of the psychiatrist an inmate exhibited insanity, the officials and physician would provide safe keeping and refer the patient to the psychiatrist when he next called. In general, the work of the psychiatrist has been almost entirely diagnostic with little time for therapy. The most pronounced mental cases are transferred to an institution for insane criminals, but in the population are many psychopaths and pre-psychotics.

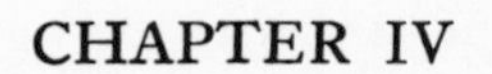

CHAPTER IV

Social Relations in the Prison Community

In a general way the preceding chapters have described the types of persons who compose the population of the prison, and have presented something of the conditioning which has made them what they are. We have also inspected the material situation in which the inmates live, as well as certain aspects of the organization which guides their lives. The following chapters will be given over to the study of the social relations of the inmates, for we have yet to learn of the more fundamental and subtle processes which exist in the environment of the penitentiary. The present chapter is devoted to some initial phases of social relations.

The emphasis in this book is pragmatic. We are not to be unduly concerned with theory, unless theory can serve as a helpful tool in the explanation of phenomena which otherwise might be lost in a myriad of bewildering and confusing facts. Some sociological theories will prove to be helpful. Sociology is essentially, and in its simplest terms, the study of the relations between individuals. It is a study of their conduct toward, and with reference to, one another and the standards by which they are regulated.[1] The title of this chapter is, of course, too broad, as the subsequent chapters will also deal with social relations. Yet it seems wise to begin thinking in terms of social relations in a broad sense, and to reserve for later chapters some of the more specific delineations of relationships.

Reference has been made to the prison as a community. To be sure, it is a unique community since it is held together by walls and guns, laws and rules, yet in it, regardless of the reasons for its existence, there are social relations, communication which makes the relations possible, and other social processes. Not only are there relations between persons in prison, but the individuals within the prison communicate and have relations with persons beyond the walls. So this chapter sets forth, in a preliminary way, the techniques of communication which lead to, and at the same time are, the social relationships between prisoners themselves, between prisoners and officials, and between prisoners and persons without the walls. While tracing these means of communication we shall

[1] E. T. Hiller, *op. cit.*, p. 3.

become aware of various attitudes and opinions which the prisoners hold, and though supplementary to the main purpose now, the knowledge of attitudes and opinions will aid our understanding of the prisoner.

Fundamental Principles

The prison, like other societies, is dynamic. The population is in constant flux. About 600 new men enter the community each year, and a smaller number leave. There are also changes in the official personnel. Indeed, within one period of fifteen months, some 200 officers were replaced. The persons coming into the community have a wide scatter of ages. Between a fifty-year-old man and a twenty-year-old boy there is a wide variation in habits and perspective. Men also vary according to the regions in which they have lived, and the experiences which they have had. These conditions give the prison environment a changing or dynamic character. In spite of these dynamic characteristics, however, the controls which guide the conduct of the prisoners, and the behavior of the officials has changed little from year to year. Forty years ago the flippant or irascible prisoner was punished by solitary confinement and sometimes beaten just as he is now, and forty years ago the prisoners held physical courage, gambling skill, or clever thieving techniques in high esteem as they do now, yet forty years ago it was a considerably different prison population in terms of personality make-up which arose in the morning, formed the bucket brigade, went to breakfast and to work. There are variations, but the patterns are essentially the same. This tendency toward the establishment of controls and values which continue year after year in spite of great social change is in the nature of a paradox. It is of sociological importance that the same paradox exists in the free community, though in prison the condition is more pronounced. In normal communities the continuance of old controls and old values may be attributed to what might be called institutional vigor. For example, we know that the institutions of marriage and the church have changed to some degree, but they persist tenaciously and vigorously, and are still institutions. So in prison the system [2] of living, the system of working, the system of disciplining, have persisted tenaciously, in spite of the dynamic characteristics of life and the dynamics of the peoples who are in them and compose them. Our first basic principle, then, is that the behavior of those who

[2] For the prison community the word "system" is used to designate the manner in which things are done. The "system" of living, of work, of education, is prescribed and permanent. We use this term rather than the more specific sociological term "institution." An institution in a free society is "the approved or even the prescribed and relatively permanent usages governing an activity." Thus, "system" and institution are similar, though not precisely the same phenomenon.

compose the prison community, both officers and inmates, falls into channels which are established and have a history, and notwithstanding the fact that the peoples whose behavior is canalized, are a social dynamic.

Like the similarity between a free and a prison community in regard to the vigor of established systems, is another condition which applies equally to both communities. We here refer to one variety of social relations known as impersonalization. In the non-penal world the relations among the great majority of peoples are touch-and-go. Impersonal social relations have arisen in society as the result of a number of factors. Urbanization and the character of city life, with its high mobility and constantly changing population, have developed it. The tendency towards, or the partial breakdown of, primary group bonds has fostered it. Specialization in industry and other occupations has made it unnecessary for people to deal personally with each other. Our inmates have been conditioned to this general type of relationship before they come to prison, and the organization of the penitentiary facilitates the continuance of such rôles. This does not mean that in many instances cohesiveness is foreign to prisoner relationships. In the normal community, as we know, strong affiliations remain. Villages and towns, rural areas and some portions of cities, have a relatively high degree of personal, sympathetic relationships among the peoples. Even an aggregation of people who are contacting each other impersonally will, in the event of a disaster, change to an association of like-minded, sympathetic persons who deal personally with each other. Though less pronounced, and with some variations, the same phenomenon will occur in prison. Yet, in cities as in prisons, impersonalization is the general rule, and this is our second basic principle.

The third and a more obvious principle is that the prison, like other social groups, has a culture. "Culture may be defined as those artificial objects, institutions, modes of life or thought which are not peculiarly individual, but which characterize a group and have both spacial and temporal contiguity; or, in the oft quoted words of Tylor, as 'that complex whole which includes knowledge, belief, art, morals, law, custom, and any other capabilities and habits acquired by man as a member of society.' Culture, therefore, is supra-individual. The individual is a carrier and transmitter of it and he may modify it; but no individual creates more than an infinitesimal portion of the culture he acquires through membership in a group." [3] Thus, those thoughts and behavior sequences which

---

[3] Wilson D. Wallis, *The Analysis of Culture,* Publication of the American Sociological Association, 1927, vol. 21, pp. 158–60, as indicated in Kimball Young, *op. cit.,* page 15.

are highly characteristic of our inmates are part of the prison culture. The high stone walls and the strong iron gates are sometimes considered not a part of the culture, but simply an occasion for it.[4] The feelings of men toward or against such material things are, however, a definite phase of the culture. It is of course evident that the prison culture is not distinct, or even greatly different from the culture in a free society. The difference may be no greater quantitatively than that between Arizona, on the one hand, and Vermont, on the other, or, more precisely, between the gold coast and the slum. It is to point out these differences and to show to some extent how the culture molds the prisoners that we proceed.

To understand the culture of the prison, knowledge of certain fundamental processes of human interaction is necessary. To the sociologist culture is societal structure, and the social processes are functions. Except abstractly, it is difficult to think of these two aspects separately, as structure and function are so intimately related. On this point Kimball Young says, "When we analyze the social processes we are concerned with the social functions, the interactional patterns of individuals and groups. When we analyze the social organization and culture, we are dealing more especially with the framework or structure of society. Truly structure and function go hand in hand, and it is useless to try and treat one and not the other."[5] In our study of the prison we shall not overtly attempt to show theoretical distinctions, but to delineate the behavior of the men as it operates by and in the culture. Not all of the recognized social processes are applicable to the prison, or at least to our data, so we shall pause here only to mention briefly the processes which most often appear.

Conflict sometimes arises when a person or a group with one set of values and attitudes comes in contact with a person or a group of a different set. When a clash occurs, it is conflict if it is personal and conscious.[6] There are, of course, all degrees of conflict. Rivalry and competition do not classify as conflict, though competition is a separate process by itself. Conflict is purposeful, and though it may long endure, eventually ends. In the prison two men may fight, or the members of a work unit may strike. The behavior of flying fists in the first instance, and the idle workers in the second, are illustrations of conflict. When adjustments occur between the parties of the conflict, an *accommodation* may be said to have taken place. Accommodation is that process which ends conflict by mutual agreement or by superior power and skill. In our analogies when

[4] E. T. Hiller, *op. cit.*, p. 3.
[5] Kimball Young, *op. cit.*, p. 347.
[6] Robert E. Park and Ernest W. Burgess, *Introduction to the Science of Sociology.* The University of Chicago Press, Chicago, 1921, p. 347.

one prisoner overcomes the other so that he can fight no more, accommodation has occurred, and when the strikers resume work after official coercion, the adaptive behavior is accommodation. However, the beaten prisoner may plan for a month to harm his foe, and the strikers may never stop work again. Thus accommodation may lead to further conflict, or to a stable adjustment. *Assimilation* is a more or less unconscious process during which a person, or group of persons, learns enough of the culture of a social unit in which he is placed to make him characteristic of that unit. Sometimes, of course, the persons or group of ingress will also influence the social unit into which they move, thus creating a fusion of cultures. Assimilation and the cultural fusion which may take place are gradual processes. Conflict and accommodation are usually abrupt. Fundamental to these processes which have been mentioned and to others as well is *communication*. Communication is the method by which ideas are exchanged through language (speech and writing), and by other complimentary sensory experiences. It is by communication that processes operate and the operation of the processes contributes to the culture.

It is our fourth general principle that in the social world of the prison the processes above described will be found. Other supplementary processes are also at work in the penal environment, but it is unnecessary to mention them apart from the material which will illustrate them.

We have been assuming rather confidently that the prison is a community. The term *community* has had a number of definitions which are reviewed by McClenahan. After a concise summary of the various definitions, she concluded, ". . . that communities may be defined as areas of common life, with indefinite boundaries, or with boundaries more or less arbitrarily fixed from two points of reference: communities may be areas of service from the standpoint of institutions or organizations such as stores, banks, parks, playgrounds, churches, improvement associations; or they may be areas of participation, from the standpoint of persons living in the locality and sharing the activities."[7] There is no arguing the point that the prison has fixed territorial boundaries that are definitely established! In a sense, the prison is both an area of service and an area of participation. The differences between the prison and the normal community in the quoted definition are self evident. Other definitions give greater stress to the thought that a community has consensus. To explain the differences between the locality where 2,300 men live behind walls and the more conventional community,

[7] Bessie Everne McClenahan, *The Changing Urban Neighborhood,* Univ. of Southern California Studies: Social Science Series, No. 1, 1929, pp. 104–107, as included in Kimball Young, *op. cit.,* p. 9.

we may simply precede the word "community" with the word "prison," and think of it as a somewhat different type of aggregation. It is methodologically helpful to think of the penitentiary as a prison community.

The Techniques of Communication

It is communication by which consensus and positive relations are developed, just as it is by communication, in part, that opposition and negative relations are established. It is by language, of course, that people are able to share one another's ideas. "Language is the carrier of a vast amount of what we call culture." [8] Language is probably also the most important medium by which a culture is expressed, therefore it is necessary for us to understand those aspects of language which are characteristic of our prisoners since by its use various contacts and relations develop and the culture is reflected.

The type of communication which is most important as implied in the foregoing paragraph, is language as used in speech and writing. Communication results from sensory experience and while we must not ignore the composite sensory stimuli of gesturing it is considerably less important. Communication may be thought of as being direct, that is, face to face, or indirect, that is, remote.[9] Direct communication, for example, is the conversation between prison partners. Indirect communication exists through letters between an inmate and his mother. This distinction between direct and indirect communication does not involve positive or negative relations because the inmate who corresponds with his mother may have a much closer sympathetic bond, a positive type of relation, with her than he has with his cellmate. It is frequently true that some prisoners respond with positive relations to direct communication as they would not otherwise do were it not for the peculiar environment of the prison. Radio and reading matter are indirect communication which we will discuss in a later chapter. We wish now to turn our attention to prison argot, and also to observe the indirect communication which exists with our men and outsiders.

From several hundred autobiographies or writings on particular topics by prisoners as well as through conversations, the writer has formed a "dictionary" of 1,063 slang words and terms.[10] Such collections are not rare and it is doubtful if the one at our disposal is unique in any particular way. Its collection was incidental to other investigations. No great effort has been made to determine the etiology of the words, and it is doubtful if many of them had

---

[8] Kimball Young, *Social Psychology,* F. S. Crafts and Co., New York, 1936, p. 203.
[9] E. T. Hiller, *op. cit.,* p. 130.
[10] See Appendix B.

their beginnings in the prison which we are studying. Argot, such as exists in a prison will usually be found in other all-male groups, as among hoboes and in armies. Only five per cent of our words, however, have a flavor or vagabondage, while sixty per cent refer to crime and prisons. The words have been classified as shown in Table VIII, and it is interesting to note that of the 116 words which have a sex reference, over half have a homosexual significance. A portion of the "dictionary" is included in Appendix B, and in comparing the words with the figures in Table VIII, the reader can observe the topics of emphasis.

TABLE VIII

Classification According to Reference of 1,063 Words and Terms in Fairly Common Usage in Prison

	Category	*Words*	*Total Number*	*Per cent*	*Total Per cent*
A.	*Sex*		116		10.90
	a. Homosexual	64		6.02	
	b. Heterosexual	52		4.88	
B.	*Crime*		320		30.08
	a. Technique	137		12.87	
	b. Police, etc.	79		7.43	
	c. Loot, etc.	31		2.91	
	d. Escape, etc.	30		2.82	
	e. Guns, etc.	43		4.05	
C.	*Body Parts*		59		5.54
D.	*Description of Individuals*		83		7.80
	a. Race, etc.	20		1.89	
	b. Associates	63		5.91	
E.	*Alcohol*		34		3.19
F.	*Gambling*		13		1.22
G.	*Drugs and Narcotics*		37		3.48
H.	*Prison*		345		32.44
	a. Equipment	12		1.13	
	b. Authorities	20		1.88	
	c. Articles of Daily Commerce				
	1. Money	31		2.91	
	2. Clothing	9		.84	
	3. Food	22		2.07	
	4. Miscellaneous	186		17.48	
	d. Mental Status	16		1.54	
	e. Punishment	11		1.06	
	f. Sentence, etc.	38		3.53	
I.	Vagabondage		57		5.35
	Total		1,063		100.00

It is difficult to say definitely why a particularistic vocabulary develops in a prison, jail, or other male group. It is probably a combination of factors, among which the following are important.

First, of course, the use of the vocabulary results from a learning process. Our prisoners use these words because former prisoners used them, and thus the language is handed down. Second, the regular vocabulary of many inmates is limited, and profanity and slang are substitutes. Third, there are elements of humor in some of the words. Fourth, an in-group of sympathetic affiliates makes use of uncommon language to exclude others from participating with them. Fifth, many men in prison realize the inferiority of their social position and a particular jargon is used as a device to impress listeners and bolster their status. Sixth, possibly the development and practice of a particularistic vocabulary may be a collective, unconscious device to keep a unity, although other evidence to be offered later would contradict such a supposition.

The basic interest here in vocabulary is due to the manner in which it affects the growth of relations either positively or negatively, and this is best explained by point four of the preceding paragraph. Not all men in prison make use of the terms mentioned, but practically all, excluding the lowest of the feeble-minded and the most provincial, know the meaning of them. It is even probable that some mental defectives know as much of the prison jargon as they know of common language.

At least one term deserves special mention for, so far as can be learned, it is native to the prison. Every inmate knows its meaning and a great portion of them use the word. The term which seems unique in the prison is the word "hoosier." A "hoosier" seems to be any person, inmate, or otherwise, who is objectionable. More specifically, it is used for stool pigeons, stupid persons, and officials. It seems to have no reference to Indiana and its etiology could not be learned.

Two inmates were asked to give their opinions regarding prison language. The first is a fairly typical prisoner and the other is more criminalistic and highly intelligent.

Profanity and Slang

> Profanity in prison is the most vulgar ever to fall on my ear. Men who never swear in a free world go forth from prison one of the worst to be found.
>
> Monotony of prison life, poor food, poor government of prisoners, ill treatment, favoritism of the politicians and the Negro, all help to dishearten the faint-hearted convict. Miscarriage of justice in the courts and case handling by the parole board, all bring about the vilest profanity.
>
> I have heard guards go to extremes in criticising convicts and curse them most vehemently, but this is rarely done.
>
> "Playing the Dozens" is the most common way a convict has of using profanity. The term used really means anything of the vilest and worst

that can be said about anyone's people. Instead of cursing one direct, they talk about the mother, sister, wife, or sweetheart of the other. This one thing alone, has caused more fights among prisoners than any other cause during my five-year term and observation. Slang is easily adapted to prison life. By reading the papers and magazine articles, and also by visits, one learns the new slang of the streets. Of course there are many, many underworld slang phrases heard in prison which are not familiar to the social life.

Following are a few words heard among the prisoners which are names of something: Bum Rap, Stool Pigeon, Rat, Fink, kite, stiff, rocks, shive, pill, hoosier, gunsel, Screw, Fish, Bull, snitch, Punk, yegg, Buddy, Bo, Bug, Fixer, J. P., Pimp, jolt, Stretch, Sky Pilot, Bug Doctor, Far.

Slang

Slang, apart from the prison vernacular, is much the same among prisoners as it is among the corresponding class of free men. By corresponding class, I mean the lower strata of society, though prisoners, of course, are drawn from all strata. Slang reaches a prison quickly by means of new prisoners or visitors, and it is speedily adopted. It spreads rapidly and the speed with which it spreads seems to be determined by its pungency or humor. I know of no slang phrase which originated in prison unless some of the vernacular phrases which are sometimes pungent and apt are to be classed as slang. The vernacular is always the same—a guard is a "screw" and so is the key with which he locks or unlocks the doors. The prison physician is always the "croaker," and the solitary is always the "hole." (The term "screw" may come from the twisting motion used in locking or unlocking a door, and it may be applied to the guard because he is the one who unlocks, or unscrews, the doors.) Calling the prison physician a "croaker"—which means one who croaks, or kills another person or a patient—is a more or less satirical commentary on the political appointees who fill such a post. The practice of calling the solitary the "hole" probably originated when the solitaries were dungeons, or were actually below ground level. "Rap" may mean the charge for which a prisoner is committed, or a protest against his release, or a report for violation of the rules, and its application is obvious. None of this vernacular shows much originality.

Nicknames are more clever, occasionally, though most of them are stereotyped. Blackie is common, for a dark-skinned or black-haired prisoner. Shorty is even more common, and Slim and Skinny are made to fit nearly anyone above the average height who lacks fat. The name "Timber Leg" for a peg-legged prisoner or guard, is slightly more humorous and original than the usual term "Peg," and "Step-and-a-half" describes the gait of a cripple in apt terms. "Meat head" is a fair description of a prisoner with a large head and fat face, and "Fish mouth" leaves nothing to be desired for a man with a large mouth if one thinks of a cat fish instead of a small-mouth bass. "Big town" is applied to men who continually speak contemptuously of small towns, and "Pork chops" is the nickname of a thick-lipped Negro. The list could go on indefinitely. Some of the more derisive names are applied to the officials or guards, such as "Eagle eye" to a watchful and alert Deputy, "Red muzzle" to another red-faced deputy, "Butter-and-Eggs" to a prosperous looking and fleshy officer, "Nocky," "Chisel Chin," and "Bad eye," to others.

Profanity is so very common that it has lost its strength and it is my theory that it is used because of a limited vocabulary and to take the place of adjectives. When a strong term is necessary the much-used terms which are considered as very strong by free men are too mild, and some of the most frightful and disgusting phrases are freely used.

Other officials have been known as follows: "White Hope," so-called because of his having killed a Negro who ran amuck; "Gander Neck," a term of derision based upon a long, thin, neck and a penchant for making trouble; "The Goat," which animal the inmates claim, the officer resembles when chewing tobacco; "Weenie Jim," "Pimp Head," and others. Possibly the most interesting name was given to a guard who came from a rural district. His real name is forgotten by the men, but his legend remains. He was called "The Bee Hunter." He wore glasses with very thick lenses and continually peered through them as if he were seeking something afar off.

An inmate who has been incarcerated for many years and who, by personality type is classified as a decided extravert, was asked to write out the nicknames of all the prisoners or members of the underworld with whom he was acquainted or knew about. Within an hour and a half, he had compiled a list of 192 nicknames. Some of them are:

Akron Jimmy
Army
Baby Face
Bad Eye
Belly Robber
Big Duke
Big Six
Black Jack
Blondie
Blue Steel
Bubble Jaw
Bugs
Bullets
Buzzy
Carnation Jimmy
Chinatown
Dago
Deacon
Dead Eye
Diamond Tooth
Dog Face
Dressed-up-Johnny
Eddie-the-Immune
Farmer
Friggie
Germany
Gimp
Goldie
Hammer
Hard Rock
Hot Sam
Hunkie Bill
Iron Jaw
Jew Boy
King
Koonzie
Leftie Louie
Legs
Little Bit
Maggots
Meadows
Measley
Meathead
Mike-the-Pike
Muckle
Nick-the-Greek
Nig
Pappy
Peanuts
Pin Head
Pinkie
Polock Joe
Pooch
Poogie
Pretty Boy
Prince Arty
Puddles
Roundy
Scoop
Single Shot
Slick
Smiley
Snakie
Snookie
Sparky
Step
Stormy
Stuffy
Tar Baby
Toledo
Tubby
Umbrella Mike
Whiskey Pete
White Alley
Wild Bill
Yellow

The more common names as "Red," "Slim," "Mike," have been omitted. It is evident from this list that the nicknames are significant of: (1) locality, (2) nationality, (3) physiognomy and stature, (4) criminal technique, and (5) some outstanding personality trait. Nicknames are less used in direct face-to-face relationships than they are for reference. It is seldom that Christian names are used except between two men. In a larger group the men address each other by last names, nicknames, or not at all, but begin a conversation with "Hey, you." Nicknames add color to the conversation and are also a means for classifying persons.

Communication exists in the prison not only by speech, but also by written language. The latter is much rarer, but "kites" (written messages) are common enough to warrant mention. "Kites" are usually exchanged between men who work in different gangs, and who are thus unable to see each other. They are usually used for matters of some importance to the men. They may deal with escape plans, food, prison discipline, or they may be employed in love affairs and sex pursuits. "Kites" are carried by "runners" (errand boys) or by other men who have the freedom of the yard. They are, of course, contrary to prison rules, and anyone apprehended with one is severely punished. There is probably more communication by "kites" than the officials know. While the writer's position was not a disciplinary one, nevertheless he was under obligation to inform officials if he had knowledge of "kites" which in any way threatened the administration. The two or three which came into his possession did so long after they were written.

The first "kite" presented here is a request for money from a supposedly wealthy inmate. The sender was a man who was serving a life sentence for murder. He had first been sentenced to death, but that sentence was commuted to a life sentence:

> D———,
>
> You perhaps know that I have a petition going around trying to get together enough money to appeal to supreme court again. My trial lawyer is getting together the procedures of the last trial and just as soon as I have ample money for filing fees he will file these papers in supreme court and as soon as this is filed I will be given release from here pending a hearing from the supreme court. It is certain that the case will be reversed and I am more than certain that it shall be cleared up in another trial. But so far I have gotten only $10 of the required $100 and I have only 35 days to get together the other $90. I have a few friends here who would donate the entire amount, but at the present time they are not in position to do so. But I know that your circumstances will allow you to do otherwise, D———, that is why I am putting this before you. I am not asking you to donate me the money. But merely asking a loan of you for whatever you can spare, that is, any amount up to the required

$100, and you need not worry about it being repayed, because it will be within 4 months time. You perhaps know S——— L——— of H———. He has two places at H——— that I have mentioned. But at present time the income of these places is tied up or being used for the purpose of clearing up a minor charge against L——— that is now pending in supreme court, and I can expect very little help there until the charge against him is cleared up. You understand that the money I have mentioned will be needed within the next 35 days because I was given only 60 days to complete the appeal. I would not ask you for this, D———, if I was not sure the affair will be cleared up. After then I shall be able to return any amount you let me have. I hope, D———, that you will consider this thoroughly as you know the nature of the case against me, also the circumstances that I am facing, and that you will help me to at least a good portion of this required amount, because I hardly think that the full $100 can be made up among the fellows and friends that I have here. M——— and I were over to see you this morning, but you were busy with your work and we did not want to disturb you. I would like to discuss this with you in person, but as that does not seem logical so as I probably won't have a chance to see you in person I am sending this and a petition which I hope you will pass around. I will be gratified for any amount that they can give and I hope you will not fail in considering what I have asked of you. If you care to do what I have requested naturally the collection will be stopped and any further steps in this matter will be discussed solely between you and myself. Please give me your opinion outright on this as soon as possible. I am

Yours in hopes,
K——— E———.

E———,

I am very sorry that I do not seem to be able to interest anyone up here in your collection, and am unable to do anything for you myself. When you were under sentence of death everyone had a lot of sympathy for you, but you must remember that all of us are serving time, and there is very little sympathy for a common ailment. My own opinion is that it will be a very hard matter for you to get any sum which would approach a hundred dollars from the prisoners, considering the hard times inside and outside.

As far as the possibility of getting any such sum from me is concerned, that is entirely out of the question. I have had to spend a great deal of money on my own case, though I have served a very long time, and times are hard for me as for anyone else. I feel sorry for you, but that's how things stand.

Sincerely,

Letters between inmates are "kites" but letters illegally sent by an inmate to an outsider are called "underground kites." The word "underground," refers to an illicit communication which is smuggled out of the prison, theoretically under the walls, but actually in the pocket of a visitor, officer, or trustie. A bearer of "underground" mail, if an employee, is subject to dismissal and possible indictment, depending on the nature of the message. In spite of the severity of punishment and the matter of betraying trust, a few guards and visitors have been prevailed upon to carry out "underground kites." When an inmate has some civilian who frequently carries out mail, such a channel of communication is called a "route." Such letters deal with matters which ordinarily will not pass the prison censors, such as escape, criticism of officials and the parole board, attempts to raise money, or communication with persons in the underworld who are well known. Sometimes the letters contain nothing of any antisocial significance, but the men who send them find the one weekly letter permitted them insufficient.

The inmates may legitimately correspond with relatives. They may also write to the warden or any other official on printed request sheets. Examples: I respectfully request (printed) "an interview personally and privately in regard to a change of work and some matters I think you should know." Another, ". . . . to speak to you the way these guards are doing me it semse (seems) like they are hard losers." A third, ". . . . to see you at once for an advice concerning some property of a missen aunti of mine, and I am sure you will interview me at once."

In Chapter I there were presented types of correspondence which relatives and friends send to the men. There are offered here copies of a few letters which were sent through the prison censor. In reading them one should bear in mind that censoring always prohibits free expression. The first letter was written by a heart-sick, non-delinquent boy who lies to his mother bravely:

Dear Mother:

Again the time comes when I am allowed to write to those I love, and knowing that you are always interested in how I am getting along will say that everything is just going fine with me. I like my work, like the food, in fact, if it were not for few liberties which we are denied and that are obtainable outside, I would say that altogether its not any worse than being in the Army. Of course, we are kept away from our loved ones, but that is the price that must be paid for wrongdoing. The future looks bright to me and I hope that it will not be too long before I will be with you again.

An old, defeated man writes to his daughter:

Dear G:

Well, Honey, the cruel war is over. I have met my friends, the enemy, and they took me like Grant took Richmond. Our plans, our hopeful dreams, our everything now lies a sordid mess—a fit item of the general depression. Our particular portion of the Brain Trust has said its say and, being omnipotent, the Old Man is fated to be but a social liability from here on out.

It seems a shame, in a way. Had we been given a Chinaman's chance at this time, then society, too, would have had an equal chance. But, as it looks at present, I am to be held for years as a dead load upon the social body and then released either as a physical and mental wreck, or such a hopeless loser that I can play the game out in but one way.

At the tail end of the Board meeting I was called in and treated to a twenty-second interview. Mr. X——— merely remarked, "We are going to recommend that you be given a sentence." It would seem that the 14 years with which I am already burdened are not sufficient. Being something of a literary gent, Mr. X——— has evidently decided that a simple sentence is inadequate in my case—I am to be given a complex affair, perhaps a compound sentence, maybe a whole paragraph.

When the slip comes from the Board it will probably indicate 8 years and 3 months as the proper amount of punishment for such a terrible menace as I. That is but a lesser matter even two years would serve the purpose as well. They might as well give me the chair, for evidently they intend that my days shall be ended in prison, to the end that life and property shall be made safe.

Money is important to prisoners in order that they may purchase tobacco and a few sweets. Here is a boy thanking his mother for money:

I got your letter with the three dollars enclosed and it sure came in handy. I was beginning to think that I was never going to hear from you and was beginning to worry. Everything is alright now and I forget my worries. . . . I realize that things outside are tough and I appreciate those few dollars, mother. . . . I feel pretty good for the time I have put in, but will feel a whole lot better when I am out. . . . Will close with love. . . . Give my regards to step family.

An inmate tells a new-found friend of his sentence.

In one of your letters you asked how much time I was doing, and when I would get out. Well, I'll answer those two questions with figures of speech. . . .

Winter is already here, you might say. When spring rolls around I'll have six years in. Mine is a ten-to-life sentence. Four more to go after spring. . . . When I first entered prison, a mountain of time—ten years—stood before me. Before me stood the immovable mountain of TIME. For five years—stumbling, bruised, filled with heartaches and longings, I plodded up one side of the mountain of time. Six months ago I pulled myself up to the top of the hill—the halfway mark—five long years filled with hopes and despairs and longing that beset the heart of every imprisoned human. But—the top has been reached. I am now descending the other side. Behind me on the other side are heartaches and agonies that

> may stay with me long after I am released. But I try not to think of them as I descend. My thoughts are on what lies way down below me on the downward climb. Far down below lies a valley. It is the valley of Freedom. . . . If I do not falter somewhere along that downward descent, if I can suppress the impatience with which every human being is seized when within a sight of his ambition, or goal, the beautiful, panoramic views of the valley, coming nearer and nearer with each step, will be a pleasure instead of a hardship. Yet, on that downward climb one tormenting doubt creeps into my mind, and it is this:
>
> On the day that I set foot on the fringe of that valley of freedom, will my journey's end meet with disillusion? Will the valley evanesce into one of those mirages? Or will a human Fate see to it that the valley turns not into a mirage, but remains as I view it, allowing me, after a journey of ten years, to enter it? I only hope . . .

Letters frequently deal with arrangements for parole, or other aspects of the inmate's "case." Here are a few sentences which an inmate addresses to his attorney:

> I want to ask you something. If the Parole Board turns me over to the U. S. government, is it possible for me to be called back before Judge ——— and get a bench parole or suspended sentence on the grounds of slight evidence in the case, or upon the fact that I have served 10 solid years here, or upon the state of my health? . . . I don't know how the Parole Board came to call me at the February meeting, ahead of time, but even though I had not a thing in my behalf, the Parole Board appeared favorable. But a fellow can't depend on anything that appears—they often appear favorable and do the opposite, or nothing at all.

Many of the letters are less intelligently constructed than these presented here. Perhaps most typical in language and form is the one in which the inmate thanks his mother for the gift of money.

A type of direct communication which in the past has sometimes been considered mysterious, especially by the pulp magazines, and occasionally by newspapers, is the "grapevine." This term has been used to describe the rapidity with which a bit of information circulates. It is, of course direct communication by word of mouth, from man-to-man. In our prison a bit of information may originate with a clerk. He tells a Runner, who, in the ordinary discharge of his duties, walks around the yard. The Runner will tell other men, and soon most of the population has the knowledge. Important and exciting things are communicated more quickly than is other news. Error and inaccuracy are frequent. An "oldtimer" comments on the "grapevine" thus:

The Comic Strip of Penology

Any reference to the "grapevine telegraph," or so-called underground communication within prison walls, is good for a laugh from any oldtimer who knows his stuff.

Just when this bunk originated I know not, being entirely too young to have done a jolt in the first of all prisons, but I can tell you *why* and *how* it started. All set, let's go.

Convicts are the most consistent gossips on earth. Almost any group of "numbered men" can, and do, make an old ladies' sewing circle seem as serene as a silent prayer in the Little Brown Church in the vale. In addition to this, no matter how busy you keep them during the day, or how much reading matter may be in the cells of an evening, their minds are sure to ramble all over in search of recreation.

Among the first prisoners there was undoubtedly some crafty wise-guy who sensed that outsiders considered lockups as very mysterious places. Fair enough! Why not kid the folks along? 'Twould be good sport! So the game started.

Before long it was discovered that even the keepers fell for it. Eventually, the cons themselves (some of them) implicitly believed that messages floated straight through stone walls. People have said to me, "But, I got this straight. That information was broadcast among the prisoners even before the officials knew of it. It seems supernatural."

Yes, I have heard those stories, too—in fact, have started many of them, and can assure you that sensible investigation and a proper analysis of the tale will show a solution something like this in the test tube:

Fertile imagination	98%
Coincidence	1% plus
Clever connivance	A trace

Here is some "case stuff," a typical incident:

During two years of my sojourn as a guest of the state of X———, I acted as night cook in the con's kitchen. Among other duties I was expected to prepare the midnight meal for the power house bunch. Two of the firemen would come to the kitchen at that hour and carry the food to the engine room. One night a stoker named "Whitey" asked me if I had any cash; not an unusual question ordinarily, but a bit queer in this case because he and I had never been intimate. Incidentally, there was something like ten thousand dollars in real money floating around the prison. But I had a hunch that something was coming off. Sure enough, about 2:00 A. M., as I stood in the kitchen door looking past the front gate, toward the powerhouse, here came Mr. W——— sauntering casually along toward the entrance carrying a heavy mason's hoe over his shoulder. There was little necessity for haste. Though two screws "infested" the prison yard all night, they were superannuated old birds who should have been sleeping in some Old Folks' Home.

Whitey walked boldly up to the wooden stockade built around the gate, climbed the palings, hooked the blade of his hoe over the coping on the wall, and over he went. The night captain happened to be making his outside rounds and spied the disappearing get-away. Each shot from his pistol scored a clean miss, but the racket sure started something. Wall guards began to walk thier posts in a military manner; electric searchlights flashed brightly from corner to corner; the aroused deputy warden ran to the cellhouse for sheets from the escapee's bed, so that the bloodhounds might get the scent—all was excitement.

I heard the hounds bay as they caught the trail, run barking in a bloodcurdling way about one hundred yards, then go into a huddle and loudly tell their troubles to the moon.

I was relieved by the day crew at 4:30 A. M., at which time I would go to the cellhouse and to my "room." On this particular morn I sauntered slowly along the range and detailed the incident of the night to several of my friends who were awake. They, in turn, told the day-time range men, who were unlocked a half hour earlier than the "main-line." These messengers further spread the news. When the day screws came to unlock they found that the convicts, just getting out of bed with their eyes full of sleep, knew more of the details of the escape than did the officers who had been on duty at the time.

This thing is still given as convincing proof of the mystery of the underground telegraph. It is to laugh!

The "grapevine," the language, the "kites," and letters give us some insight into the means of communication, and reveal some of the subtle aspects in the prison world. When inmates, as well as other persons, address each other, the speech is directed to themselves as well as to the listeners. Thus speech is both stimulus and response. One becomes especially aware of this duality in speaking with prisoners.

Inmates seem more distractible than are other types of persons. A fifteen-minute conversation may involve a number of different topics which are only slightly related. Many of the men enliven their discussions with anecdotes which have very little reference to the original topic. Anecdotes are preceded by such introductory phrases as, "Now in my case . . ." or, "Look what happened to me . . ." or, "When I was in a spot like that I said to so-and-so . . ." or, "I don't know what you did, but I know what I would have done . . ." or, "Listen to this . . ." or, "I know that answer. Listen . . ." And the irrelevant stories continue with, as a rule, considerable self-reference.

Many of the inmates' anecdotes are intended to show that: (1) they are smarter than one would think; (2) though they may be in prison they have love and charity in their hearts; (3) that they are even more criminalistic than one would think; (4) that they have known many fine and important people; (5) that their status before incarceration was high. To be sure, the principle of self-reference in conversation is not characteristic of prisoners alone, nor do all prisoners evidence it to the same degree. It is rare, however, that one finds much objective, impersonal talk among prisoners even though the central idea of the topics under discussion would seem to be impersonal.

Relationships: New Prisoners and Cell Mates

The initial contacts which the men make when they enter the prison seem to be important to them. One cannot become well acquainted with a prisoner without learning sooner or later something of his first impression of the penitentiary and the men in it. The inmate seems to rely greatly on his first impressions of people, and though he will modify his behavior if he finds he was wrong, he will yet insist he was correct in his first decision, and will say, "The guy's changed." Even though a man may have served for six or seven years, he still remembers his first contacts. "The first guy I seen in this stir was Ratty. The sheriff marched me up past the front door, and he really had me tied. You'd think I was a mobster or something—all the crap he had on me. He had that Oregon Boot on my leg, and cuffs besides. When he brought me in, there was Ratty. Of course I didn't know his name then, but was he impressed! He looks at me with real respect. He sort of smiled, and I smiled at him, and as I was waiting at the gate, he says to me, under his breath, 'Too bad, kid. Watch the gray-haired guy!' He meant J——— (a deputy warden). You know, I've liked Ratty ever since. I didn't get to know him well until he got busted and put in the quarry."

Another inmate tells of his first contacts with officials and inmates:

> Although I didn't like those deputy sheriffs that brought me here, they treated me pretty good on the way down, and after the questioning by that clerk they turned around and shook hands with me and wished me luck, and though I hated both of them, when they left I felt like I had lost my best friend. There were some other "fish" there, and a couple of them were laughing at me. Just then the receiving officer came up and asked us some more questions. He asked me what my "rap" was, and when I told him he said, "You'll do plenty of time." Isn't that a hell of a way to start a man off in prison? As we were going across the street (in the prison yard) one of the guys that laughed at me said, "I know that old son-of-a-bitch. I been here before, and that guy is poison. Watch your step with 'em." I thanked him for that tip, and he sure was right. I haven't talked to that lug since, but I'll never forget his tip.

The contacts which the men have as they first enter prison are fleeting. Not until they are assigned to a cell in the evening of the day of their arrival, is there much chance for talk. Sometimes the new incarcerant will spend the first few days and nights in a cell alone, but most frequently two "fish" are placed together. Sufficient knowledge is not at hand to describe the relationship which develops by simulating their conversation. From talking with hundreds of them, however, the general topics discussed include: (1) comments about the prison officials; (2) comments about other contacts which they had as they were hurried through the busy day; (3) comments concerning other aspects of the present, or of the immediate future, such as the type of work they will do in prison; (4) comments about their crime, trial, and the journey with county officials to the prison. With older men who have never before been in trouble, conversation is usually held to the minimum. If two new inmates who have not been accustomed to custodial treatment are celled together the first night, and if they are relatively non-criminalistic, there will be vows and pledges as to the lawfulness of their future conduct. They will make plans concerning their good behavior while in prison. A mutual sympathy will develop, and probably never would they be better risks for parole than after the first night in prison and before the penal culture has had a chance to engulf them.

When parole violators return to the same prison which they have left a few months or years before, they find the resuming of contacts painful. Regardless of the stories they may have ready to account for their return to prison, the irrefutable fact that they are there, signifies their failure. They may have failed in their illegal enterprises, or they may have failed to adjust in a non-criminal life because of inability to live and work in one place, inability to convince police of their lawful pursuits. Conversations between a returned parolee and inmates he knew before release follow much the same pattern: "How come, Johnny, what are you back for?" "Not a thing. I was on the 'legit' but Snooks planted some hot silver in my room and the law came and found it. They held me on ten thousand bail and I couldn't have raised a hundred. I couldn't snitch on Snooks, but I told the copper it wasn't mine and that I could account for every minute of my time. They didn't indict me, but I gotta see the Board, and you know what they will do." "Well, what did you let Snooks use your room for?" "He . . . you know how it is." And Johnny knows that he used poor judgment; he knows that he failed and his ego is deflated. An inmate will say to a parole violator whom he knew prior to his parole, "I guess you like it here, you come back so often. I wish they would give me a chance. I'd never come back"; or, "You must be a sap. What's a matter with you?" Or, "I see you're slippin'—you can't even steal good anymore"; or, "You guys that go out and come back make it harder for us that ain't gone out yet. You're really makin' us serve more time." The redevelopment of relations between a parole violator and his former acquaintances is frequently accompanied by an increase in social distance. Among some of the more advanced criminals relations may be re-established with considerable sympathy, but this is not the general rule.

Many of the new men feel "swallowed up" when they first come to the prison. The "swallowing up" process is transitory and differs from assimilation as will be pointed out later. The feeling of loss of identity is especially pronounced among persons who are not markedly criminalistic, and who have been residents of smaller communities where anonymity does not exist. Such a man will feel "swallowed up" whether or not the relations he develops the first few days are positive or negative. The response is to the total situation and is not the result of contacts with any particular men or groups of men. The new man is intensely aware of his number which is stenciled on every garment he wears. He is never referred to by name. He is one of a thousand men who silently file out of the cellhouse twice daily. He is one of a hundred workers in a gang. He is one of the 1,200 who eat in the dining room. The height and thickness of the walls, the mass of the buildings, the impersonal contacts with officials and inmates, all contribute to this feeling of being "swallowed up." His family and friends are far away. The routine of prison life for the first few weeks absorbs him. A few men never recover from the effects of the "swallowing-up" process, and seem to lose a sense of their own individuality. The greater number of them do, however, recover, as other relationships, either positive or negative, develop.

As a result of contacts between cell mates, types of relationships develop which are interesting to observe. Including the nine hours supposedly given over to sleep, cell mates spend between eleven and fifteen hours a day in each other's presence. The time in the cell is spent in reading, card playing, idleness, studying, listening to the radio, or in other similar activities. So far as we have been able to learn, there is not much talk between men who have been in the same cell for sometime. After a few months they have told each other as much of their life histories as they wish to, and, except for occasional anecdotes, confine their conversation to current events in prison or outside, to plans, and yearnings. It is not infrequent that cell mates thoroughly dislike each other. Even when an adjustment is ostensibly good, it is frequently found that neither respects the other. Attitudes toward cell mates were brought out by the answers the men gave to the questions, "Do you like your cell mate? Why, or why not?" Some answers follow: "He is a nice, quiet fellow." "Joe is a little 'punchy' from serving so long, but he keeps his half of the cell clean, and don't bother me much." "He is always dopey and won't never talk. I can hardly stand being with a man for hour after hour who just sits there and never says a word." "Dan is alright, but he is always reading his Bible and quoting things to me." "I never liked him from the first day. He told me some of the worst lies I ever heard. He must think I'm dumb to believe all the stuff he puts out about his rich relatives. If they're so rich, why don't they get him out of here?" "My cell mate is dirty; he doesn't keep himself clean and he snores at night, and he has bowel trouble, and our cell is a mess." "It doesn't make any difference to me who I cell with. I'm doing my own time, and all 'cons' are alike anyway."

A number of men were asked to write descriptions of their cell life. The excerpts presented here are fairly typical and reveal, in addition to the relationships between the cell mates, something of the personality of the writers:

> I had my first look at the man whose cell I was sharing. I don't know why I do, but I invariably always analyze a man upon first meeting him, and instantly like, or dislike him. In the case of Bunch, although I had no reason, I had talked to no one about him, and had never seen or heard of him before, I disliked him.
>
> He was a nice-looking, big, athletic fellow with blond hair and blue eyes, and an intelligent-looking face. As we sat down on our stools he started questioning me as to how much time I had, where I came from, and if I ever did time before. After answering him, he told me that he had "life" for killing the jailer in an attempted jail delivery, which I afterward found out to be all lies. He was, in reality, here for stealing clothes out of a country store.
>
> When he finished telling me how tough he was, he asked me if could play cards. "Yes," I answered. "Can you play coon-can?" he eagerly asked. "I can play," I answered, "but I'm afraid not good enough to compete with a good coon-can player." Without bragging I wish to state that at that time and now, I found very few men that could defeat me playing coon-can.
>
> Bunch got his cards off the shelf and we started playing on the bed. He explained before the first game was over that it was customary to play for packing the toilet can. At that time it was necessary for one or the other of the occupants of each cell to dump the toilet can. It was about a good city block from the cellhouse to the sewer where the toilet cans were dumped. Each man would dump his toilet can and then hang it on a rack with the cell numbers on it and march on into the dining room. Each coon-can game was to represent one trip with the toilet can, etc.

Report 2

> I am writing this from my own cell life. Everyone has a different cell life in some respects. I put in the most of my time in the cell studying, reading, or writing.

On the walls in our cell we have sixty pictures taken from magazines, most of them movie stars, also ten or fifteen of our people. They are in frames made by my cell partner. They are hung in such a way as to form a border around the cell, with others scattered here and there. Above this writing shelf we have a piece of cloth about two feet by three, with pockets sewed on it. In this we keep pencils and any small thing. We also have a small one above the wash bowl for our combs, tooth brushes, and tooth paste. We have cord tied along the wall for our towels to hang on. I have the upper bunk, as I like to lay on it to read. The light is better there. We get clean sheets and pillow cases every Thursday. We have two blankets.

A convict's day starts when the lights come on at about five-thirty. I always sleep a little later. Sometimes hardly have time to wash before going out. If it is a bad day we come in at noon. I always get my lessons then, or, if we got out on the ball diamond, I get my lessons the first thing when I come in at night. We are counted as soon as we come in at night and must stand up to the bars. By that time it is almost five o'clock. I usually spend from five till six on arithmetic or orthography, then we have another count. Soon after the six o'clock count the Guard passes out the mail. That is one of my happiest cell moments. Library books are left in cell bars two days a week. I always read my book through the same night I get it. We also get several daily papers from fellows around us. Things like this I am writing now I write just in my spare moments. I always read a little of the Bible every night. Sometimes I get the blues and just want to sit and think, or daydream. The radio starts again at seven and continues until about eight forty-five. At nine the lights go out.

The conversation which takes place within the cell is usually moderately quiet except for occasional oaths during argument. However, there is frequently talk between cells. Because the men in one cell cannot see the men in any other cell, when they wish to converse it is necessary for them to raise their voices. Much of the talk from cell to cell is coarse, vulgar banter. Some nights the cellhouse is a babble of voices, loud enough to drown out the radio. An inmate gives the account, reproduced here, of the conversation between men in different, but adjacent, cells.

In the cellhouse when work gangs consist of a mixture of white and colored men, the Negroes are gathered into a group and cell at one end of the gallery. That condition exists in the gang to which I am assigned, and I happen to cell in No. 39, alone. The next cell to me, No. 40, is occupied by another white man who has no cell partner. No. 41 is occupied by two Negroes.

A few mornings ago I was smoking the last cigarette before breakfast and waiting for the doors to be opened. The nigger in cell No. 41 called over to the lone white man in cell No. 40 and asked, "Hey, 40, have you got any paper?" "What kind of paper?" asked the Caucasion intellectual.

"Any kind of paper," said Sip, who is commonly called "Mississippi" after his native state. "No! I ain't got any," stated the inhabitant of 40—a typical farmer. I had been idly listening to the conversation, and when it reached this point I began tittering. The colored brother in 41 was annoyed, it seemed, and he growled, "Well, if you ain't got any paper why in hell did you ask me what kind I wanted?" "Oh," explained the member of the supreme race, "I thought you might want white paper." "I does want white paper," stated the Afro-Mississippian. "Send some over." "Didn't you hear me?" asked the farmer, "I told you I ain't got any paper at all!"

I could still hear the nigger talking—evidently to himself—and I thought I had better butt in for a moment. I called over to the white man and asked, "Say, 40, is Gracie Allen your sister?" The question seemed to confuse him; possibly because I had never before shown any interest in him or in his relatives. He denied any relationship or acquaintance with the lady I had mentioned. "Who is she?" he asked. Before I could answer, the nigger in 41 blurted, "You does too know her, and you *is* some relation to her. She's that damned fool woman who talks just like you, over the radio."

When cell mates adjust to each other poorly, one or both of them will seek out an official and ask for a change of cell partners. The officials are often reluctant to make changes because the men cell on the gallery according to the work unit in which they are employed, and a change in cell mates uusally means that one of the men must be assigned to a different gang. Some officials are unaware, or ignore the fact that to keep together for thirteen hours a day two men who hate each other is hazardous to any chance of reformation. Considerable subterfuge and conniving is used to effect changes in cell partners. The cellhouse clerk (an inmate) will accept a bribe on occasion if he believes that officers will not become aware that a change has been made. An inmate who wishes to be rid of his cell partner may treat him so badly that the partner will beg officials for a change. One man may "frame" another, and have him sent to solitary confinement, thus gaining a few days' respite. Any number of motives may prompt desire for a new cell mate. A prisoner may wish to live with someone from his own town. He may wish to share a cell with a man in order to learn a new technique of crime, or in order to replace a noisy cell mate with a quiet one. He may desire a certain cell mate for sex purposes. While two men occasionally may share the same cell for years, the average length of time that a cell is shared by the same two men is eleven months and it is not uncommon for an inmate to have four different cell mates a year. It is an occasion of some importance when a new cell partner is acquired. The following dialogue, though not typical, describes a celebration tendered a new cell partner (N. C. P.) who is a waiter in the officers' dining-room:

Dialogue

(An old friend gets a new job and moves into my cell.)

We go in at 8:45 and are razzed all along the line. When the night guard unlocks the cell we enter and the following conversation takes place:

N. C. P. What the hell is that on the floor? Which is your bunk?
Me: I don't know. The hoosier (galley boy) usually keeps this joint pretty clean. Your bunk's the top one, but if your mattress is better than mine, we'll sleep there.
N. C. P.: Some one's been eating peanuts and dropped 'em on the floor. I have to get up at 5:00 o'clock don't I? Will he remember to call me? (The night guard.)
I: You have to go out at 5:00 o'clock and he wakes you up at 4:00 so you can get dressed. If he don't call you, the screws won't get any breakfast.
N. C. P.: That hoosier better not bother me at 4:00 o'clock. What the hell do I care whether they get any breakfast or not! Oh, the dirty bastard!
Me: What's the matter?
N. C. P.: Look at the rice—all over the bed!
Both of Us: Oh, the dirty bastard!
N. C. P.: That's what was on the floor. Oh, Johnny, Oh, Johnny. Oh, you dirty bastard.
Johnny (trying to sound innocent and injured): What's the idea?
N. C. P.: You know what's the idea, you dirty bastard. Why in hell didn't you cook it and put sugar and cream on it?
Johnny: You two bastards have been framing this for a long time. I'd like to watch you tonight.
N. C. P.: Anyone could watch if I had you over here, baby. Hey, look what that bastard did to my bed; put the sheets on top and the blanket underneath.
Moi: That's all right for one night. Sleep on top of 'em and fix 'em tomorrow. (Zero weather.)
N. C. P.: Hey, will that hoosier call me?
I: Yeah, at 4:00 o'clock. You're a politician now!
Me (at 4:00 A. M.): Cut out that goddam noise.
N. C. P.: Jesus Christ! That bunk is high! I like to broke my goddam feet when I hit the floor.
Me: Get a stepladder, or cut some holes in the end wall and climb down. You could hold to the shelf.
N. C. P.: Yeah, or I could get a pole and slide down it like a goddam fireman, and tie my clothes to the bottom of it so I could slide into them. When will he open the door?
Me: In about twenty minutes.
N. C. P.: Why, the son-of-a-bitch, waking me up like this. I'm going back to bed.

The door opens and he goes out.

Me: Hey, wait! Send me in a cup of jamoke.
N. C. P.: Yeah, I'll send it in by Brown. Come in when you get up!
Me: You're a politician now. See you way late.
N. C. P. (going down the gallery): To hell with a politician!

Some Broader Aspects of Relationships

Another factor affecting the relations among prisoners is the apparent existence of social classes. In an artificial and highly controlled group of 2,300 men, class distinctions cannot be clear cut, but the attitudes of certain types who are more or less alike in orientation toward other types of men, give indication that some stratification exists. From our study we feel warranted in designating three general categories: the élite class, the middle class, and the "hoosier" class.

The three classes are not definitely demarcated. The criteria used in the formulation of three classes refer to the attitudes the men hold regarding who is the equal of whom. These attitudes towards others are built upon not only individual complex psycho-social items, but also on the reputation men have before they come to prison, their behavior while in prison, especially in reference to officials, and certain other personality traits. In the class which we have termed the "élite," are the more intelligent, urbanized, sophisticated offenders who, for the most part, do not toady to officials, and who set themselves apart, and have their relations chiefly with each other. Criminal experience and anti-administration attitudes will generally be found among them, although there are some who are not basically criminalistic and who behave neutrally toward officials. Intelligent, quiet, and dignified prisoners as well as those with money, who are otherwise not too objectionable, may be included. The élite are aloof from the "hoosiers" but not from the middle class. They have no particular or strong loyalty to each other as members of a class, nor are all of them aware of a class distinction in the population. They may sometimes rub shoulders with the "hoosiers" at work, but they maintain a social distance. The social distance is maintained, not as a specific awareness of their belonging to a class, but more as a consciousness of whom they feel, as isolated individuals, are their social equals.

The middle class is composed of the great mass of the men who are generally not outstanding as criminals or as "characters." They are scarcely aware that some prisoners feel, and occasionally act, superior to them. They are not aware that they constitute a class except that they dislike the "hoosiers" and do not voluntarily associate with them. In the great middle class are persons qualified for inclusion in the élite group but the circumstances of work assignment or individual wishes to have none but necessary contacts with any prisoner, prohibits mixing. The "hoosiers" are designated as such by the other two classes. They are unaware that they compose a class and there is no proletarianism among them. When they are subjected to snobbery by the élite, they refer to the élite as "big-shot hoosiers." This third, or lowest class, includes practically all the abnormal sex offenders, the dull, backward, and provincial persons, the lower range of the feeble-minded, some of the known stool pigeons, the persons who show a marked lack of physical courage, the confirmed "suckers," the extremely pious, the habitual braggarts, and some sexual perverts.

Marked inconsistencies in the assignment of certain men to their class become apparent in such instances as the following: A man accepted as a member of the élite class may be continually acting as a stool pigeon, but in so clever a way as to avoid detection; a man may be designated as a "hoosier" because of a rural background, little knowledge of crime, gullibility, or for other reasons, while in the basic character values which are held in esteem by the prisoners he should classify as a member of the élite; the élite may include as a social equal a person with considerable money, who, otherwise, would be termed a "hoosier." It is quite possible for a man in the middle group to rise to the upper group through behavior which bears the stamp of the prisoners' approval, such as assaulting an officer or refusing to give information to authorities, even though punished. Similarly, a member of the élite class may lose caste and no longer be treated as a social equal by his former companions through behavior which is contrary to the class code. Likewise, a person once classed as a "hoosier" does not always remain one. A twenty-two-year-old feeble-minded boy was released after serving a three-year sentence. While in prison he had been used for sex purposes and had been a stool pigeon. Immediately upon his release he was committed to a feeble-minded colony. While there he piled a number of mattresses together and set fire to them. Considerable damage was done by the fire and newspaper publicity followed with the result that he was returned to prison for *Malicious Mischief*. Upon his return he was at first accepted as a social equal by some of the élite and middle-class men because of his belligerant rebelliousness, but as months passed he gravitated again to the lowest class.

As has already been stated, the prison community should not be thought of as having a strict social stratification since the classes are not sufficiently clear cut. While there is some assumption of superiority by the élite it is not shared by all, and though a few in the "hoosier" class are aware of their rank, most are not. In a community where free choice of work, residence, and associates does not operate as in an unrestricted community, some of the customary processes do not occur. This lack of freedom prohibits the formation of distinct social classes but even in a loosely stratified society, relationships are influenced thereby.

The relations among the prisoners are further influenced by certain responses of personalities to the culture. The behavior of individuals in any society is determined not only by personal-social relationships which are non-standardized and non-conventional, but also by the conventionalized, group-accepted forms of conduct commonly called "cultural patterns." [11] To these two types of influences operative among prisoners may be added a third, the "prison culture." The so-called "prison culture" is too complex and too little understood to admit of analysis here. However, it is important to show how these three determinants affect the behavior of men in prison. For example: Prisoners *A* and *B* had an argument as to whose duty it was to clean the cell, and a fight ensued. *A* whipped *B* and, as a result, *B* nursed a grudge. So far the behavior was determined by personal-social determinants. For revenge, *B* mutilated *A*'s Bible and while *A* knew that *B* had done it, and hated him for it, yet he did not inform the officials. In not giving information against *B, A* was responding to an item of the prison culture, an item which prescribes that one inmate shall not inform officials about another. In possessing a Bible (which few prisoners do), *A* was responding to an item of the general culture, i.e., the institution of religion. Inmates who learned of the affair began to admire *A* whom they had considered, up to this time, merely a religious fanatic. Thus, through conforming to the code of prisoners he lessened the social distance between himself and certain other prisoners, and contributed to the development of positive relations. Another man is in the habit of leaving a group immediately when vulgar or indecent jokes are being told. This behavior is partly a personal-social response, and partly a response to the general culture of the inmate's background. It is, however, a response which develops negative relations with the group of inmate story tellers. In general, the responses which are in harmony with the prison culture develop positive relations with the majority of inmates, and responses to the general culture develop negative relationships on those levels (usually the mores) where the two cultures clash. The personal-social contacts may stimulate either positive or negative relations, depending on circumstances.

Some men become integrated into the prison culture and some do not. In either case, such men have no particular conflicts. However, a portion of the men become only partially assimilated and may be said to be on the border, or in the shadows of, two cultures,

[11] **E. T. Hiller, *op. cit.*, p. 142.**

and not acculturized to either. These men may reject some standards or items of the penal culture and adopt others, but they will not reject all the items of the general culture, nor accept all the items of the prison culture. They are thus in the shadows of both cultures, and their behavior seems confused and illogical to those other inmates who have become assimilated and cling tenaciously to the precepts of one culture or the other. The conflicts and difficulties arise, of course, on the level of the mores, customs of conduct, and matters of right and wrong, and do not refer to habits of sleeping, eating, or dressing, for example, which are essentially the same for both the penal and the non-penal cultures. For example, a man on the border of the two cultures may approve of some crimes against property and not of others; in one circumstance he will condone cheating at gambling and not at another; in one instance he would not divulge and peddle information to officials, and in another instance he would. Behavior of this sort is incomprehensible to men who are completely in and of one culture or the other. "You can't be both ways," the inmates say over and over again, and this attitude stressing conformity is an important force in the development of positive or negative relationships.

CHAPTER V

Social Groups in the Prison Community

In the foregoing pages the word "group" has been used to designate a collectivity, or simply a number of persons. The men in the penitentiary may be thought of as a prison group. Similarly, the one hundred inmates who work in the knit shop are a shop group, and, again, the six hundred men who reside in A-Cellhouse may be called the A-House group. We also have used the word "group" in referring to murderers, mental defectives, and so on. "Group" in this sense is a numerical aggregation of persons who classify as being similar in some way. It is a convenient way of categorizing people.

In this present chapter we intend to use the word "group" in a different way, and as a concept. Preliminary to applying the concept to the penal population, a few words as to the meaning of the concept and some of the ramifications involved may prove helpful. When a baby is born he comes into the world as an individual, as a biologic organism. As he is reared by his parents and other persons who surround him he acquires "human" qualities and comes to have status. Status is position in society.[1] He first has status in his family and, later, with other groups in his immediate environment. As a child acquires status he becomes a person; a person is an individual with status. "The individual inevitably has some status in every social group of which he is a member. In a given group the status of every member is determined by his relation to every other member of the group." [2] Not only does the person in the group have status in it, but the group itself has status in larger groups: the family in the neighborhood, the neighborhood in the community, the community in the state, or, in another way, the schoolboy in his class or gang, the school or gang in relation to other schools or gangs, or to the city, or the church, or to the police department, or, in still another way, a boy with the police department. This myriad of associations with other persons, especially persons within sympathetic boundaries, make the individual what he is. "The individual's conception of himself is based on his status

[1] Robert E. Park and Ernest W. Burgess, *Introduction to the Science of Sociology*, University of Chicago Press, Chicago, 1922, p. 55.
[2] *Ibid.*, page 55.

in the social group or groups of which he is a member."[3] And his rôle in these groups is determined by his own interpretation of his associates' interpretation of him, plus his own recognition of his status in other groups which give him an individual interpretation of himself as a totality. While men tend to play different rôles in varying group situations, after adulthood there seems to be, with exceptions, a tendency to maintain consistently a particular rôle within certain broad limits. The maintenance of anything like a consistent rôle, however, depends upon culture pressures, personal-social relations, and psycho-biologic factors, and the rôle may be changed completely by any unusual force in any of the three mentioned factors. This is not the place for a theoretical discussion and it is sufficient for us to know that ". . . the individual is influenced in differing degrees and in a specific manner by the different types of groups of which he is a member."[4]

Sociologists have emphasized the study of groups since it is through the influence of relationships in groups that individuals become persons. What we call personality is, in a large part, group bred. Groups are an important consideration in the explanation of personality, and knowledge of them is also important in coming to an understanding of a community. "The explanation of social groupings and their behavior as groups is generally regarded as the basic problem of sociology.[5] To understand a personality, and to understand a community, we need facts concerning social groups. There are various types of groups and they differ in their power to build social nature. It is often assumed that a type of group known as *primary* is the most influential in the molding of human nature. In the familiar words of Cooley, primary groups are those:

> . . . . characterized by intimate face-to-face association and coöperation. They are primary in several senses, but chiefly that they are fundamental in forming the social nature and ideals of the individual. The result of intimate association, psychologically, is a certain fusion of individualities into a common whole, so that one's very self, for many purposes at least, is the common life and purpose of the group. Perhaps the simplest way of describing this wholeness is by saying that it is a "we"; it involves the sort of sympathy and mutual identification for which "we" is the natural expression. . . . It is not to be supposed that the unity of the primary group is one of mere harmony and love. It is always a differentiated and usually a competitive unity, admitting of self-assertion, and various

[3] *Ibid.,* page 55.
[4] *Ibid.,* p. 56.
[5] George A. Lundberg and Margaret Lawsin, The Sociography of Some Community Relations, *American Sociological Review,* Vol. 2, No. 3, p. 318.

appropriative passions; but these passions are socialized by sympathy, and come, or tend to come, under the discipline of the common spirit. . . .[6]

Most families are primary groups, as are also boys' gangs, some adult organizations, as small neighborhood clubs, some church groups, and so forth.

Even though there is a tendency in recent years for relations of a primary nature to decrease, we are safe in saying that practically every human being has, at some time or another, been subjected to the influences of a primary group. When original ties with a primary group are broken, the great majority of people become affiliated with other groups, which, while not primary in every sense, approach that type of relationship. There are exceptions in the hoboes, some occupants of the areas of anonymity in great cities, the social "strangers," and some psychopaths. Whether or not prisoners should be included in this category we shall learn later. Primary relations do not depend upon propinquity, as it is rather the "warmth" of person to person relationships, regardless of proximity features, that determines the primary group.[7] Studying the men of one prison, as we are, we are not to be mainly interested in the prepenal primary group affiliations of our men unless we find that they compete with affiliations of a similar nature which may possibly exist in the penitentiary. It is our purpose in this chapter to ascertain if groups of a primary nature exist in the prison community, and we have searched for these facts in a special study which will be presented here.[8]

Informal Groups

That prisoners form highly integrated groups in which sentiment, morale, and solidarity exist is a fairly common observation. This aspect of penitentiary life has frequently been emphasized by the newspapers, the movies, and certain publications. Sanford Bates gives indication that prisoners are usually loyal to each other.[9] Warden Lawes makes some allusions to loyalty among inmates.[10] Higgins reports, in speaking of prisoners, ". . . these men cling to

[6] C. H. Cooley, *Social Organization,* Charles Scribner's Sons, New York, 1909, pp. 23–27.

[7] Ellsworth Faris, The Primary Group: Essence and Accident, *The American Journal of Sociology,* vol. 38, July, 1932, pp. 41–50.

[8] The writer presented a portion of this study before the Section on Criminology of the American Sociological Society at the summer meeting of the American Academy of Learned Sciences, The University of Chicago, July, 1933.

[9] Sanford Bates, *Prisons and Beyond,* The Macmillan Co., 1936, New York, p. 78 and p. 88.

[10] Lewis E. Lawes, *Twenty Thousand Years in Sing Sing,* Ray Long and Richard R. Smith, Inc., New York, 1932, pp. 112, 158, 160, and 199.

one another with a group loyalty not excelled in purity and inviolability by those fine emotions which animate and consolidate groups of human beings . . . in any relationship.[11] Similarly, Henry E. Field, in speaking of prison groups, records, ". . . gregariousness and an elemental sense of group loyalty sustains such a regularity" (of behavior).[12] Visitors in prison usually gain the impression that the inmates are closely affiliated when they observe small clusters of men intent upon each other's conversation. In conflict situations arising in a penitentiary such as riots or escapes, there is much evidence that a unity of thought and action exists. The assumption that social relationships among prisoners are intimate and more or less similar to the relations of primary groups in a free community, would seem plausible due to the like experiences the men have undergone, the mutual stigmatization that is upon them, and the fact that they are all in a subservient position. While some prison officials of many years' experience are not so definite in their opinion in reference to the strength and integration of informal groups, over half of such as were questioned were inclined to agree with the general assumption as stated.[13]

It is to test this rather widespread impression that the study included in this chapter was made. The objective has been to learn the nature and extent of informal group life. The specific questions to which answers are sought include: (1) What proportion of prisoners are members of informal groups? (2) How large are the groups? (3) What personality types have entered them and what types have not? (4) What is the nature of informal group life in prison, how "primary" are the groups, and what variations exist?

The data for this effort have been collected by three methods: Schedule, questionnaire, and individual case study. First, 190 men were interviewed with a schedule including six batteries of questions. With the exception of length of residence these men were selected at random. Of the men interviewed 99 had served between 11 and 15 months and 91 had been incarcerated between 3 and 4 years, with an average of 3 years and 7 months. Secondly, a questionnaire was given to 174 men, 93 of whom had been in residence not more than a year and 81 of whom had served at least 5 years. Distinction in

[11] L. A. Higgins, Prison Education, Massachusetts Prison Association Leaflet No. 67, Boston, 1920, quoted in E. H. Sutherland's *Criminology,* J. B. Lippincott Co., Philadelphia, 1924, p. 430.

[12] Henry E. Field, The Attitude of Prisoners as a Factor in Rehabilitation, *Annals of the Academy of Political and Social Science,* vol. 175, p. 151.

[13] During a period of three years the writer has asked various prison officials their opinion in reference to the strength of loyalties in prison cliques. Opinions were divided but about twelve of some twenty quesioned expressed the belief that most prisoners form closely knit collectivities.

length of residence between "short-timers" and "long-timers" was considered important in order to ascertain the significance of tenure on grouping tendencies. The other selective factor for the subjects of the questionnaire was intellectual capacity. Only those inmates who had average or superior intelligence were given the questionnaire since it was assumed that persons of duller intellect would find difficulty in understanding the thoughts presented. Thirdly, the writer studied the ramifications of group life among a number of inmates through interview and by observation. Many of these subjects prepared biographical or autobiographical accounts which lend knowledge to the subject. Very careful and detailed instructions were given to all who took part as to the purpose of the studies, emphasis being placed on the objectivity of approach, and especial insistence on the lack of effect on the prisoner's status or standing with officials. The 174 inmates given the questionnaire were not required to reveal their identity, although the other data collected were referred to the case history of each man which was at the disposal of the writer. It was necessary to cast out 13 of the schedules because of suspicioned irrelevancy.

Exploratory inquiries revealed certain general traits of informal group organization. Experienced inmates and officials with insight were consulted before a formulation of a group concept was made. From the information obtained in this manner it was possible to construct empirically a concept of a "prison primary group." Thus, such a group has been conceived as a collectivity of prisoners who possess a common body of knowledge and interest sufficient to produce an understanding and solidarity which is characterized by a we-feeling, sentimental attachment, and unanimity, and which allows, at the same time, elements of competition and resistance among members only to the extent that cohesion is not disrupted. These abstract values can be roughly measured in terms of behavior. The exchanges of confidences, the sharing of luxuries, the toleration of annoying conduct, the willingness to accept lowered status or punishment, one for the other, a frank admission to an outsider of these deeper feelings, a knowledge of the wishes of the other members—all give indication of a loyal attachment to a group. The concept we are employing does not simply refer to a number of persons, who, during a given time are in constant contacts with one another, but rather, the concept used agrees in meaning with that of the primary group of the general population.

The proportion of inmates affiliated with primary groups as defined, the size of the groups and certain aspects of their structure have been learned by interpreting responses to six batteries of questions. This, to be sure, is not a precision method. Pertinent and reliable data from inmates usually demand the technique of indirect questioning and mild-mannered cross examination (unless rapport exists), as answers to direct questions may involve highly complex motivations on the part of the man interviewed, especially if his identity is known. In presenting the schedule to 190 inmates there was no formality of questioning although the six types of information desired were clearly defined and will become clear in the following paragraph. If the inmate gave indication of affirmation for the six major questions he was then considered as being affiliated with a primary group.

After a friendly and most careful explanation of the investigation was given the interviewee, he was asked if he thought that gangs, cliques, groups, or bunches existed in the prison. He was asked to name their characteristics. Later he was asked if he happened to belong to such an aggregation. The concept of primary group was explained to him in vernacular and after he gave evidence of comprehension his reply was recorded. Men who denied affiliation were questioned intensively and if their denials were persistent and they were unable to give affirmative answers to the second battery of questions they were then tallied as being ungrouped. The second battery of questions required that the inmate being interviewed name the members of his group and tell something of their respective histories, traits, and ideas. Replies indicating a ready familiarity with this information was considered as a partial verification of the response to the first battery ,and the second battery was scored as affirmative. The third series of questions was directed towards learning the duration of the association. In what manner had he met the other men? Why did he "group up" with them? Why had the associations continued? If the answers indicated plausibility and there was some persistence of association with a minimum period of six months, the response was charted as positive. The fourth battery of questions dealt with the mutual experiences of the interviewee and his group associates. Did they exchange letters? Did they confide secrets? Did they defend one another from critics among other inmates? Did they frequently use the word "we"? Had they ever accepted punishments one for the other regardless of justice or cause, or, if not would the interviewee be willing to do so? After considerable questioning if the inmate persisted in giving affirmative answers the battery was scored as positive. The fifth and sixth batteries set up hypothetical questions. The fifth series was concerned with the interviewee's supposed reaction if he and his group members were paroled. Would he continue to be friendly with them? Would he share his living quarters, loan them money and in other ways continue the most friendly relations? Willingness to behave in this manner, as reported, was considered an affirmative score. The other hypothetical situation which composed the sixth battery intended to ascertain if the interviewee would allow his group members into the most intimate relationships if and when they were released. Would he object to a group member marrying his sister? Would he jeopardize his father's standing or reputation to protect a member of the group? Would he himself risk danger to save the life of the members of his clique? When affirmative answers were given to these questions the battery was scored as positive.

One hundred and ninety men were interviewed. After casting out 13 irrelevant cases it was found that 32, or 17 per cent, answered all six batteries of questions in the affirmative. They were then considered as members of primary groups. In instances in which the interviewee demonstrated by his remarks the essence of the primary-group idea and answered positively the first five batteries of questions but would not "go all the way" in the second hypothetical situation, he was considered as a member of a *semi-primary* group. Seventy-two, or 40 per cent, were included in this category. Thus, 73, or 41 per cent, of the total sample had to be considered as ungrouped in a "primary" sense and according to the empirical definition. In Table IX the three categories are shown distinguishing between short-term men (11 to 15 months of residence) and long-term men (3 to 7 years of residence).

TABLE IX

Type of Social Affiliation of 177 Prisoners as Interpreted from Their Responses to a Series of Questions Pertaining to Social Relationships

	Short-term Men		*Long-term Men*		*Total*	
	Number	*Per cent*	*Number*	*Per cent*	*Number*	*Per cent*
Primary Group	18	19.2	14	16.9	32	17.4
Semi-primary Group	45	47.9	27	32.5	72	40.7
"Ungrouped"	31	32.9	42	50.6	73	41.9
Total	94	100.0	83	100.0	177	100.0

It would appear from Table IX that continuing residence in prison decreases the likelihood of a primary group membership inasmuch as but 32 per cent of short-term men are ungrouped, while 50 per cent of long-term men have no primary group or semi-primary group affiliation.

An informal schedule method, emphasizing indirect questioning and cross-examination invites criticism especially when the replies are evaluated by only one observer. In order to test the reliability of this method and to collect other data as well, a totally different group of men were given a questionnaire under anonymous circumstances four months after the schedules described in the foregoing pages had been completed. The men were seen in groups of about

50 and the same explanations were given them collectively as were given to the inmates who replied to the schedule form. The degree of social affiliation was extended in the questionnaire method, but the concept of primary group was kept the same. The brief descriptions of four possible types of affiliation used on the questionnaire follows:

A. *The Complete "Clique Man"*: This is the man who is one of a group of three or more men who are all very close friends. They share each others' luxuries and secrets and have accepted, or are willing to accept, punishment one for the other. The "clique man" is so closely associated with this group that he thinks in terms of "we" rather than "I" and he acts as the group acts. The clique has some permanence.

B. *The "Group Man"*: This is the man who is friendly with a certain small group of men but who does not entirely subject himself to the wishes and acts of the group-as-a-whole. He would share his luxuries, tell some of his secrets, but would not go "all the way" for those with whom he is friendly. While he is particularly friendly with one group, he also mixes freely with a number of other men and is at least casually friendly with these others.

C. *The "Semi-solitary" Man*: This is the man who, while civil with other inmates, never really becomes intimate with them or shares with them any thoughts or acts except of the most casual nature. He is the man who is almost playing a "lone-hand."

D. *The "Complete-Solitary" Man*: This is the man who keeps almost constantly to himself and shares nothing with other inmates. While he may talk with other men, he is generally alone and seeks no one.

These four categories of possible rôles were carefully explained to the subjects so that the meaning of "A" agreed as closely as possible with the concept of primary group affiliation for the schedule subjects, and "B" agreed with the semi-primary conception. Rôles "C" and "D" were made to correspond with the ungrouped category in the schedule subjects, although the questionnaire was intended to refine the degree of "ungroupedness." Questions from the floor, illustrations by the writer, reading and rereading of the statements preceded the request that each inmate designate the type of situation that most closely fit his position in prison. The results are shown in Table X.

TABLE X

Responses of 174 Inmates to a Questionnaire Concerning Their Own Type of Affiliations in the Penal Community

	Short-term Men		Long-term Men		Total	
	Number	*Per cent*	*Number*	*Per cent*	*Number*	*Per cent*
Clique Members (Primary Group)	17	21.0	14	15.1	31	17.9
Group Members (Semi-primary Group)	23	28.4	39	41.9	62	35.6
Semi-solitary Men (Ungrouped)	28	34.5	31	33.3	59	33.9
Complete-Solitary Men (Ungrouped)	3	3.7	3	3.2	6	3.5
Questionable or Unsatisfactory Responses	10	12.3	6	6.5	16	9.1
Total	81	100.0	93	100.0	174	100.0

A comparison of Table IX with Table X shows strikingly similar results in spite of subjective methods obtained from two different samples at different times and thus lends reliability to the conclusion that about 18 per cent of inmates are affiliated with prison primary groups, as defined. Likewise, the semi-primary group affiliations are fairly constant, 40 per cent of the schedule subjects and 39 per cent (when corrected by eliminating unsatisfactory responses) of questionnaire subjects being included in that category. The semi-solitary and complete-solitary responses of the questionnaire total 37 per cent (or 41 per cent when corrected by eliminating the unsatisfactory responses) which is in surprisingly close agreement with the 41 per cent of the ungrouped men learned from the schedule method. (The almost exact results of the schedule and questionnaire methods are baffling, for the techniques employed would not ordinarily be expected to give such precise results. We are inclined to discount the exactness of the result except insofar as they indicate a trend: that about one-fifth of the subjects belong to primary groups, two-fifths to semi-primary groups, and that the other two-fifths are "ungrouped".) Considering the aspect of tenure the same tendency may be noticed in the questionnaire responses as was evident in the schedule results, namely that increasing residence seems to decrease the likelihood of primary group affiliation. In Table X, 21 per cent of short-term men as opposed to 15 per cent of long-term men indicated primary group affiliations.

Three additional types of data are somewhat suggestive of an absence of extensive primary group affiliations. Of 9 escapes in one year all were solitary except one. During a period of three months there were 128 men punished in solitary confinement for infractions of rules. Of these 87, or 67 per cent, were single offenders and 34 were in couples. One item included in a section of the questionnaire requested the opinion of the subjects as to the approximate number of inmates, thinking of the population as a whole, who became members of groups. The question was so phrased that the subjects had the choice of underlining one of the following words: "most," "half," "few." Slightly over 75 per cent underlined the word "few."

Knowledge of the size of the primary and semi-primary groups became known through the responses to the second battery of questions in the schedule method when the subjects were asked to name and characterize their affiliates. The average size of primary groups to which short-term men belonged was 4.4 members, the extremes being 2 and 7. The average size of primary groups made up of men of longer residence was 3.2 members per group structure, the largest collectivity having 5 members. The semi-primary groups were somewhat larger. For semi-primary groups in which one-year men are members, the average size was 7.8 and for semi-primary groups of the long-term men the average size was 9.3 with the extremes being not far removed from the average. Increasing length of residence not only tends to reduce the number of primary groups (Tables IX and X), but the groups themselves tend to become smaller as shown in the data here presented on the size of primary groups.

Appraisal of the personality traits of the primary, semi-primary and ungrouped men has been possible only for those inmates given the schedule, as the identity of the questionnaire subjects was unknown. Data needed for personality evaluation had already been gathered by the Mental Health Office in the form of social histories, psychometric tests, medical examinations, and psychiatric studies. The initial sorting and tabulation revealed that no observable or significant difference existed between the men considered as belonging to primary or semi-primary groups. Attention was then directed only to the distinctions evident between the grouped and ungrouped men. It has been found that those who enter groups have higher intellectual capacity than those who are not affiliated, although the differences are not pronounced. While the extremes range from inmates who are mentally defective, according to tests, to those of very superior intelligence, the average mental age of the grouped short-term men is 14 years and 3 months as opposed to 13 years and 4 months for those not affiliated. Among the long-term men, those who are grouped average 13 years and 9 months, while the ungrouped average 13 years and 6 months.[14] The chronological age of the affiliated and non-affiliated varies between 19 and 56,

[14] See Chapter II for the intelligence factor in the entire penal population.

the average of the affiliated being 25 years and 7 months, while the unaffiliated average 29 years and 1 month.[15]

In Table XI will be seen other relationships between the grouped and ungrouped men. It will be noted that inmates who have been married are grouped less frequently than men who have always been single. Among the "short-term" group the proportion is almost two to one, but no difference appears among the "long-term" men. The factor of siblings in the early home suggests that the association of brothers and sisters during youth is related with a capacity for membership in a prison primary group, although there is no marked distinction, except for the only child.

When the cases of men who were found to be affiliated and those not affiliated were evaluated criminologically, they fell into three broad classes: trivial offenders, serious offenders and very serious offenders. The diagnosis of criminality is the specific function of

TABLE XI

Comparison of Siblings in the Early Home and Marital Status between Inmates Who Have Become Socially Grouped and Those Who Have Not

	Short-term Men				*Long-term Men*			
	Grouped		*Ungrouped*		*Grouped*		*Ungrouped*	
	No.	*Per cent*	*No.*	*Per cent*	*No.*	*Per cent*	*No.*	*Per cent*
Marital Status								
Married	19	30.2	16	51.6	17	41.4	27	64.2
Single	38	60.2	12	38.8	16	39.0	6	14.3
Broken	6	9.6	3	9.6	8	19.6	9	21.5
Sibs in Home								
None	4	6.3	4	13.0	4	9.8	7	16.6
Few (2 or 3)	40	63.5	19	61.3	26	83.4	28	66.8
Several (4 or more)	10	30.2	8	25.7	11	26.8	7	16.6

the clinical sociologist and it is made on the basis of the amount of criminal experience an inmate has had, an evaluation of the criminal technique, the dangerousness to society of the pattern created, or continued, the harmfulness of the offense as related to the life adjustment of the offender, and the psycho-social ramifications of the crime on the family and affiliates of the offender. The relationship between the seriousness of the offenses and whether or not the inmates have become members of groups, as shown in Table XII, indicates that persons whose crimes have been serious or very serious become members of groups in prison considerably more frequently than do those men who have been incarcerated for trivial offenses.

[15] See Chapter II for the chronological age factor in the entire penal population.

TABLE XII

Comparison of Seriousness of Crime of 177 Inmates, 110 of Whom Are Affiliated With a Primary or Semi-primary Group

	Affiliated with Informal Groups		*Not Affiliated with Groups*	
	No.	*Per cent*	*No.*	*Per cent*
Trivial Offender	11	10.0	22	32.9
Serious Offender	79	71.9	36	53.7
Very Serious Offender	20	18.1	9	13.4
Total	110	100.0	67	100.0

The data were scrutinized for other variations between the grouped and ungrouped inmates, but no observable differences have become apparent. Height, weight, illnesses, venereal infection, schooling, occupation, and religious affiliation show no especial demonstrable differences. Ungrouped inmates tend to commit more infractions of the prison rules than do grouped inmates, although the differences are small. An item of probable importance which should have emphasis in determining the possible individual differences between grouped and ungrouped men is the previous conditioning among primary groups before incarceration. While such information has been difficult to secure because of lack of accessibility for first-hand study, some data in the form of letters from parents or wives have given valuable clues. In the early home of one inmate who has been considered a primary group member, the mother describes certain traits: "He was always a sticker at home . . . he liked to be with his family . . . he brought his friends here . . . once was arrested for beating up a man . . . who hurt his brother." In the history of one of the ungrouped men the following notations from the mother are found: "He never wanted to mix with no one and was always a good, quiet boy. . . . He had trouble at school because the other boys would not let him alone when he wanted to be." While these two examples are rather outstanding, the general data in regard to previous group life are not conclusive. In general, we find that the younger, more intelligent, single man who comes from an average-sized family and who has committed a serious offense enters primary-group structures more readily than do others.

The Nature of Prison Primary Groups

While about 18 per cent of the sample have given indications of a unanimity and a sentimental adherence for specified other inmates who make up their clique or primary group, it remains to be shown how deeply rooted and genuine are the bonds holding such a structure in combination. We should not expect to find that prison primary groups do not have some of the same functions of rivalry, competition, resistance, and opposition which are common to primary group structures among adults in a free community. While these wishes or "passions," as Cooley described them, exist in non-criminal primary groups, they are, at the same time, socialized and come under the discipline of the common spirit.[16] Determination of the integration of the prison groups, the unanimity and the "warmth" of the relationships has had to be determined largely by case study. However, the answers to certain true-false questions included in the questionnaire give some general opinions of the prisoners in this regard:

a. Seventy-two per cent of the subjects stated that friendships in prison are of short duration.
b. Seventy-seven per cent state that familiarity in prison breeds contempt.
c. Seventy per cent of the subjects conclude that the friendships in prison result from the mutual help which man can give man rather than because of some admired trait.
d. Ninety-five per cent of the subjects are of the opinion that most prisoners are more interested in themselves than in any other prisoner.

From this it would seem that the majority of inmates themselves do not share the rather common impression that consensus in groups is strong behind penitentiary walls.

One primary group of five men and one "hanger-on" were in close physical contact because of their work assignments, and were held together by a common understanding which arose out of a mutual interest in professional crime as well as from discussion of semi-academic subjects. In the schedule investigation they answered all six batteries of questions in the affirmative, yet more intensive study indicated that they had serious disagreements with periods of irritability lasting many days. In spite of this, however, they had never consciously violated any of the fundamental principles which held them intact. Inmate "Z" of this group was asked to write descriptions of his affiliates:

A.—A congenial companion, which means not too aggressive and with mind enough to appreciate and understand things. Very little formal education (sixth grade) but a rather wide acquaintance with books and modes of life. High principles, but no morals. (I'd have to write a book to explain that if you don't understand it now.) Interested in all sports but loses interest if he does not play well enough to keep up with the average. Golf, for instance. Studious: Bought a law course and went through it though he didn't intend to use it. Studies Spanish now. Has

[16] C. H. Cooley, *op. cit.*, p. 27.

a sense of responsibility toward debts and toward his friends. Doesn't intend to REFORM. Introvert.

B.—Has one of the nicest dispositions I ever noticed. Is very bright but has no serious interests. Went to high school but didn't finish, then went to business school where he learned to be a fairly competent book-keeper and stenographer. Has nice people. Plays ball rather well but doesn't go in for soccer or football, perhaps on account of small stature. Has a sense of responsibility toward debts and friends and doesn't intend to be a "hooky" (to steal) when he gets out. Studies a little in connection with his work and intends to use his knowledge in a business way when he gets out. No morals, but very high principles. Extrovert.

C.—Has a nice disposition but is sensitive and sometimes moody. Rather handsome. Predisposed to crime of a serious nature and his family are of the demi-mode, in this generation. Former generations were notably good citizens. Went to high school for a couple of years. Studies a very little here to prepare him for a job which he now holds. Is very generous (that goes for the former two subjects, too) and is very reliable. Plays baseball now, but was never athletic before, and is surprised when he finds that a natural physique enables him to do things well. Is introverted and has a slight trace of morals, but isn't intolerant. Has too much "time" to bother about reformation.

D.—Has a nice family with a good record in business. Is a good clerk, but isn't interested in anything except the privileges the job gets him. Is too wise to take chances, but is trustworthy and has good principles. Self-centered and shows very little responsibility about debts, and doesn't worry about anyone else. No morals. Has a low I. Q. because he didn't try to make a high grade, but could have done much better if he had been interested. Went to a small college and to business school. Never had a thought in his life not connected with himself. Good company and plays baseball and soccer well.

E.—Is a fair clerk and stenographer which enables him to hold a job which throws him with the rest of the bunch. Will go anywhere and do anything whole-heartedly *while he is with you.* Has no stability or character and has never been encumbered with a scruple or with principles. Has no morals and never had an abstract thought. Studies everything but never learns anything completely—and is just a cur dog.

Z.—(Inmate here refers to himself.) One of the brightest men that I ever met; handsome; a high moral character; deeply religious and completely REFORMED.

(It isn't actually correct to say that I have met this fellow, but I admire him very much. His main ambition is to decrease the opportunities for drunkenness among the citizens and to increase the population.)

The inmate indicated as *E* in the foregoing, when asked confidentially about the writer of the above descriptions, replied that *Z* is a "pig," and that he is "yellow in a pinch," and got along in prison simply because he was able to buy his way. When questioned more closely about his deeper feelings he restated his intention to "never let him down," although during the last few months he had become aware of how selfish Z really is.

A somewhat different situation is evident in another group, all of whom responded affirmatively to the schedule questions and who were considered as forming a primary aggregation. The inmate generally considered to be the leader of this group was asked to write a description of not only his clique but of the general grouping or ganging tendency as it exists in prison. The following inmate-writer classifies as a member of the élite. He may also be said to be integrated into the "prison culture." He thinks and writes in a way which is fairly representatives of the professionalized and fairly intelligent offender who has served many years in other prisons and who is acculturized.

Prison Friendships

I will tell you about some friendships I have known in prison that have been put to the acid test and have been found not lacking in those sterling qualities of honor, loyalty, esteem, affection, and unselfishness, the five component parts so necessary to lasting friendship. In speaking of my friends I shall discuss them as a group. First let me see if I can chronicle the different other groups in their respective order.

Group one: Composed of politicians, semi-politicians, and those aspiring to be politicians; *group two*: composed of trusties, semi-trusties, and those aspiring to be trusties; *group three*: composed of gang runners, water boys, tool boys, individual gang "stools," and their ilk; *group four*: composed of the fellatio boys and the homosexual girls; *group five*: composed of those who try to be neutral, mind their own business and do their own time; *group six*: for comparison's sake I am going to list my friends as group six, which is composed of fellows who have shown by action their friendships through loyalty, honor, mutual esteem, and unselfishness. More of a personal nature of group six later. Please bear in mind that there are exceptions to each of these groups.

Speaking of the groups, let's see in what qualifications *group one* is superior or better than group six. Are they more intelligent as intelligence is rated? Yes. Does their academic or educational intelligence better qualify them for a success in the chosen branch of the profession for which they were convicted and incarcerated here? I think not. I have seen college graduates starving to death trying to make a living stealing. I don't class embezzlement as stealing. In other words, it takes more than academic intelligence to make a successful thief—if there is such an animal.

Are the friendships of *group one* more binding than those of group six? For example, are they more honorable? Do they honor each other? No! emphatically, no! There is no honor among them; they hide behind a veneer and make a pretence of honoring each other for what they probably call friendship's sake. They cultivate this false pretense of friendship, not because they honor each other, but because they fear each other.

Hence, the cultivation of false friendships with the idea always in mind that their false friendships will keep their false friends from "stooling" on them individually.

Are they loyal? Hell, no! Neither to themselves, their own group, the officials who advance them, or to the other convicts whose good will they covet. They are like an unskilled harpist forever strumming his instrument trying to strike a chord that will better appease that little streak of vanity he probably calls his soul. Some are so egotistical they even think they have struck a perfect balance and so have pleased everyone. They "stool on," and pretend to despise the officials to the "cons," and likewise "stool" on the "cons" to the officials, figuring, of course, that they are deceiving both sides—what colossal ignorance—or is it intelligence? Of course there is no such thing as genuine affection or esteem among them. They are forced for falsity's sake to pretend affection and esteem merely to safeguard that subconscious fear that they will unleash their unethical machinery on each other. For they instinctively recognize in each the counterpart of the other. They are at least unique in one manner: they recognize no known standard of ethics, but each in his own individual way manufactures his own ethics to meet his own individual requirements. That is, at least something. Please remember, C., that when you are telling your attentive audience about the flourishing and beautiful friendships of the penitentiary politicians that I believe (granting you do tell them, or believe it yourself) you are telling them a lie about something that never existed. For how can there be friendship where there is no honor, loyalty, principle, or ethics?

Now for *group two,* composed of trusties, semi-trusties, and those aspiring to be trusties. First, have they honor? No! They sign away their honor, if they ever had any, when they sign the prison roll that pledges them to inform the authorities at once if they see anything untoward about their fellow "cons." They pledge their honor (my god what a sacrilege on the word) to the officials that if at any time they see any of their fellow cons escaping or preparing to escape they will immediately inform the proper authorities. They further pledge their word of "honor" that they will report any other "con" whom they observe committing an infraction of the prison regulations. Are they loyal? No! A man who sells his honor couldn't possibly be loyal even to himself. They stool on half of the cons and traffic in contraband articles smuggled in under the veneer of official loyalty, to the other half. Needless to say, there is very little true affection, no esteem, and very few friendships that are not pretended.

Group three: Composed of gang runners, water boys, tool boys, individual gang stools, and their ilk. There is no honor or loyalty among them. They each in their own individual way are trying to advance their own interests, and in order to do this they must find constant excuses for trampling on their fellow cons. Their aspirations, of course, are "politician" jobs. I think it is needless to say that there is no esteem, very little affection, and no true friendships among this group.

Group four: Composed of the fellatio boys and the homosexual girls.

Are they honorable? No! Not according to the recognized standards of honor. Is there honor among them? Yes. Are they loyal? I can't say. I should hate to bank too heavily on their loyalty, although I have seen them do some very loyal deeds. Are they affectionate? Yes, very. Are there any true friendships among them? Yes, according to their own standards. Have they a code of ethics which they recognize? Yes, more or less.

Group five: Composed of those who try to be neutral, mind their own business, and do their own time. Some of them have the qualifications necessary to form true friendships. This group is a minority group. (The Negro group I didn't mention because I think it unnecessary. They are all in the same category with possible exceptions interspersed here and there.)

Group six: Composed of fellows who were the best of friends, or who were the cleverest, most deceitful actors imaginable. Fellows I have known from four to twelve years; some are dead, some are out, and some are still in. (He names eight men, three of whom are no longer in prison.) The fellows mentioned had a very finely drawn code of ethics that they tried to live up to. I don't know how to begin chronicling the many friendly deeds I have seen the above mob do. I have seen them suffer the greatest indignities possible for each other. I have seen them do everything from risk their lives to splitting their last bag of "Durham" with each other. I have seen them stand and get their heads knocked in, in preference to being disloyal to each other. I have seen them go to the hole and do each others' "time." I have seen them take thousands of chances to help each other escape. In fact, I have seen them tested in every conceivable way and I can safely say I believe they always came up to standard. Just how many daily newspapers that mob read, I can't say for sure, but four daily would be a conservative estimate for an average in English. Then, there was an Italian, and a Spanish paper. Any unusual news feature or sensational piece of journalism was always commented upon and discussed. I have seen those guys willingly commit sacrifices that your ordinary man wouldn't do. I know of literally thousands of little and big unselfish things they have done and not talked about. If they weren't friends to each other I don't know the meaning of friendship. There is more or less of number six group in each department—kitchen, tailor shop, in each quarry gang, etc. The good, bad, indifferent are everywhere, I suppose. I don't imagine this is exactly what you wanted, but it is the best I can do.

A check-up with officials who had known the inmate-writer's clique for several years, and comparable statements from other members revealed that the statements concerning his own group were accurate. While there was occasionally much dissention among the five men, an underlying we-feeling and an ethnocentric orientation based largely on their notoriety as advanced criminals held them together.

The degree of close affiliation just described, however, has not been found to be typical of the majority of men considered as members of primary groups. In another group of four men, all of whom were serving long sentences, an escape had been planned. Circumstances were such that only two would be able to go. After much conflict as to whom the lucky persons would be, one of the two who were to be left behind informed an official and the plans were thwarted. Another group of four colored inmates were engaged in the manufacture of small quantities of intoxicating liquor made from potato peels. They had shared for some time in their product and before that had been on the most friendly terms. Three of them were considered as primary group members according to the schedule findings. Their "still" was finally discovered. When they were confronted with the evidence, all denied knowledge of participation, but under pressure three of the four independently admitted the charge and named all the others. Another collectivity of five men spent much of their leisure time in card playing. They had been closely affiliated for over a year and had demonstrated in critical situations strong loyalties, but two members conspired to cheat persistently the other three in the card games in which the wagers were made in tobacco, an item of great importance in prison. These very brief references are fairly representative of the situations existing in most of the groups that have been classed as having a primary nature, and it becomes evident that such groups are not generally comparable with primary groups in the free community. In most of the notorious instances in which men have demonstrated the essense of primary group affiliation and have clung together with the strongest loyalties the cohesion seems to have been largely the function of a situation in which the unanimity is a rapport such as occurs in the psychological mob. Upon analysis, the fidelity which appears to be a response to the primary group controls, is, in most instances, a response to the secondary group, or prison community mores, which have, to some extent, been assimilated through the interaction in the prison primary group. We will discuss this phase of prisoner activity in Chapter VII.

Another inmate, whom the author considers to have considerable insight, was asked to write his impressions of grouping tendencies in the prison. What he has to say has reference, not only to "groups," as we have used the term in this section, but also, to some extent, to class stratification as mentioned in the previous chapter.

Gangs and Inmate Groups Behind Prison Walls

Prisoners, when there is a chance to do so, divide naturally into groups of not more than four or five men, unless they are players or spectators at some game, and most of the groups are smaller—three men or four are accustomed to walk together or sit together in their spare time and they form a group which is not interrupted by other inmates. Others pair off and spend their spare time in walking and talking, pitching rings, quoits, or horseshoes, or sitting talkatively or silently together. There are, of course, prisoners in all gangs who do not mix with the others, by choice. Such prisoners are not obviously solitary; they meander to and fro, speaking with this man and that one, passing a joke with this group or joining momentarily in a discussion with another group, but avoiding familiar relations with all. These men are usually the old-timers who have lost their illusions and are no longer gregarious. New men are better mixers. A "fish" who has not done time before will generally show that he is green about prisons by seeking company and interrupting the groups of older prisoners until he is finally absorbed by some other element in the gang or shop where he works. Most pairs and trios, or larger groups are within a larger group; men pair off because of some mutual interest or liking, or form trios for the same reason, but a larger group is not as compact as the pairs or trios and the interest or liking is not so intense. The larger groups are usually formed of men who are to the same extent anti-social or who live in the same locality, but this is not the only element for consideration. It is a question to what extent the coal miners, who are a large class in this prison, are grouped, or what part the fact that the members of another group follow agriculture for a living, plays in their association. Most of the grouping seems to be inevitable: men of certain tastes, education, and interests congregate, and the group in which a man finds himself is almost always the only one in which he would be accepted. A certain amount of friendliness exists between the various groups, and a certain amount of contempt seems unavoidable. A city group will be on friendly terms with another group from a less densely populated district, and feel contempt—which is frequently put into words—for the agricultural group, and the latter group will resent the superior attitude of the city group and classify as hoodlums the ones who designate them as "yaps." Groups from the quarry gangs, and from the shops, are, in turn, part of an institutional stratus, formed, as in the gang and shop divisions, by common interests of culture or occupation. . . .

We may conclude this section by saying that the prison community is not largely made up of a great number of highly integrated groups similar to primary groups in the normal community. It has been found that about 40 per cent of prisoners are not in any way intimately integrated in groups in which strong social relationships exist. Another 42 per cent engage in some of the superficial practices of group life, but are not genuinely affiliated with specific groups. About 18 per cent of the inmates are associated with small numbers of other men in combinations which approach in structure and function the primary groups of the free society, but in many of these there is a lack of basic cohesion. These prison-primary groups are small in number and range between two and seven members. It appears that with increasing residence less men remain affiliated with such collectivities. By and large, those men who do enter the prison-primary groups are younger, somewhat more intelligent and more criminalistic than men who do not become affiliated with groups.

The "Ungrouped" Inmate and Symbiotic Relationships

We have seen that forty out of every hundred inmates are not closely affiliated with informal social groups. To call them "ungrouped," however, is almost an abstraction, as persons, unless insane, live only in association with other persons. Our meaning here, of course, is that 40 per cent of the inmates are ungrouped in the prison community by any direct or strongly positive relationships. While bonds of a primary group relationship do not exist for them, they are in association with other men: their cellmates, their work companions, their eating partners, and so forth. They converse with them and thereby share a situation. The "ungrouped" men, however, do not share their intimate selves with other prisoners, and in the section of this chapter devoted to a discussion of them we will bring to light, so far as possible, the reasons for their behavior, and what affiliation, if any, is substituted for the ones of the men who are affiliated in prison groups.

Our data show that the men not affiliated with primary or semi-primary prison groups are somewhat older, slightly less intelligent, more frequently married, and, in general, less criminalistic. If these tendencies were marked our deduction would be simple and direct. However, here, as in many of the data regarding prisoners, there are confusing and bewildering inconsistencies. For example, among the "ungrouped" men in the sample are three who are highly criminalistic. Likewise, while the general trend is for the "ungrouped" men to be older, a portion of them are younger. It is the general trend, of course, with which we are concerned, and for such our data are fairly satisfactory. To explain, however, the "nature" of the "ungrouped" men, we must search for more subtle influences than are shown in the ordinary case records.

More difficulty has been encountered in endeavoring to understand the "ungrouped" inmate, than in the interpretation of any other type of phenomenon. While such men are approachable and even friendly, they have treated this investigator, with some exceptions in the same way as they deal with inmates. When the confidence of a primary group member is once gained, he is frank, reasonably honest, and coöperative. Most of what we know about orientation and behavior of the groupally unaffiliated men comes from the behavior of the grouped men toward them. For understanding personalities this is one of the orthodox methods of the clinical sociologist. In the next to the last quotation by a primary-group prisoner, there is presented his attitude towards all the inmates whom he has classified. His fifth category (those inmates who try to be neutral, do their time quietly, and keep out of trouble, and who, he says are a minority) contains the only men for whom he has any respect except those of his own type which we classify as a primary group. Other members of primary groups, it appears, avoid, at least for a time, most other inmates than those in their clique. The men of the semi-primary group mix more freely and have communication with other inmates including the "ungrouped," but the "ungrouped" tend to avoid positive relation with all men. The unaffiliated inmates not only avoid group men but they generally avoid each other as well.

We have endeavored to determine the causes of "ungroupedness" and have come to the conclusion that there are three general types of causes. (We are not distinguishing here between the "semi-solitary man" and the "complete-solitary man," as the reader will remember the questionnaire subjects were assured of anonymity.) A goodly portion of the ungrouped men remain so because of strong positive relations with family or friends in the normal community. Their non-penal primary group thus controls their prison behavior. To them a riot in prison is not nearly so important as their two weekly letters and the bi-weekly visit. They do not become affiliated with prison groups because they feel no need. Their basic wishes are being satisfied at long range. They may have unconsciously become partially affiliated with an inmate collectivity only to find it lacking in the social satisfaction to which they were accustomed. As a supplementary cause these inmates also wish to keep out of all trouble in prison and believe that it can best be done by avoiding intimate contacts. Their wish to keep out of difficulty has direct reference to their bonds with persons outside and it is because of these persons outside that they endeavor to maintain good conduct.

Another cause for "ungroupedness" becomes evident in some men whom no group will accept. When these men first entered prison they may have been partially accepted in some form of group life only to be excluded later. Such men may have lacked personableness, or may have behaved in annoying ways so that the group which partially accepted them thereafter excluded them. Attempts to affiliate and build friendships with other groups would end in the same way. When a man learned of his "unwantedness" by several groups he would set up a defense mechanism which would find expression in such phrases as, "all 'cons' are alike; you can't trust them, and I don't want nothing to do with them; I'm serving my own time."

A third type of man who is frequently ungrouped is the so-called "stranger." The "stranger," as understood sociologically is a

> person . . . not . . . a wanderer who comes today and goes tomorrow, but rather the man who comes today and stays tomorrow, the potential wanderer, so to speak, who, although he has gone no further, has not quite got over the freedom of coming and going. He is fixed within a certain spatial circle, but his position within it peculiarly determined by the fact that he does not belong in it from the first, that he brings qualities into it that are not, and cannot be, native to it.
>
> The union of nearness and remoteness, which every relation between men comprehends, has here produced a system or relations or a constellation which may, in the fewest words, be thus formulated: The distance within the relation signifies that the near is far; the very fact of being alien, however, that the far is near. For the state of being a stranger is naturally a quite positive relation, a particular form of interaction. . . . Because he (the stranger) is not rooted in the peculiar attitude and biased tendencies of the group, he stands apart from these, with the peculiar attitude of the "objective," which does not indicate simply a separation and disinterestedness, but is a peculiar composition of nearness and remoteness, concern and indifference. . . . The relation with him (the stranger) is a non-relation. He is not a member of the group itself.[17]

We find among the "ungrouped" prisoners, the stranger. He is in the prison, but not of it. He associates with group men but does not affiliate with them. He is involved in processes, but does not participate. The prisoner-stranger deals with all persons in the same way. He seems not to have strong bonds with certain persons beyond the walls. Those with whom he is in communication and with whom he seems to have positive relations, constitute simply other contacts, no dearer, and no more intimate than the positive relations and direct communication with inmates by his side. Prisoner "X" is a stranger. He came to us for an eighty-dollar forgery. He neither liked nor disliked the men he defrauded, nor was there remorse for his crime, nor pity for himself. There was no concern as to reputation and he endeavored to continue his relationships with associates in the free community without explanation and without apology. Towards police and court officials his attitude was indifferent. When bargaining with them failed to reduce his sentence, he accepted the situation without anger or hate. Towards inmates he is friendly. When he is moved from cell to cell or from work-gang to work-gang, or from a comfortable situation to a less comfortable one, he accepts each change with equani-

---

[17] George Simmel, *Sociologie,* Dunker and Humblot, Leipzig, 1908, translated and included in *Introduction to the Science of Sociology* by Robert E. Park and Ernest W. Burgess, *op. cit.,* pp. 322–327.

mity. He seems steady and stable, and inmates confide in him. Advice is offered and words of encouragement are given, but the matter stops there. He is generally respected. The prisoner-stranger does not become acculturized. He has no conflicts and makes no essential accommodations. In short, the prisoner-stranger is basically socially cold.

The entire problem of group patterns in a community and the study of attractions and repulsions among individuals and groups is highly complicated. Interested readers will find that valuable studies have been made and are underway.[18]

---

[18] See George Lundberg and Margaret Lawsin, *op. cit.* See also, J. L. Moreno, *Application of the Group Method to Classification,* National Committee on Prisons and Prison Labor, New York, 1932, and his later study, *Who Shall Survive? A New Approach to the Problem of Human Interrelations,* Nervous and Mental Diseases Publishing Company, Washington, D. C., 1934.

CHAPTER VI

Leadership Phenomena

Wherever people live together there will be leaders and followers—some men dominating, and others submitting. The superordination of persons and groups and the subordination of other persons and groups are characteristic of communal life. In one sense the leaders in the prison community are the officials as they dominate and control the situation. But at this juncture we are interested in the phenomena of leadership among prisoners and not the despotic leadership of officialdom. Authorities in the penitentiary do not officially recognize any inmates as leaders. They are aware, of course, that certain personalities have leadership qualities and this knowledge is of value in executive dealings.

Leadership results from relationships among peoples. Various types of leadership exist according to the intensity of positive, personal relations and according to the structure of the society or community. Leaders, of course, are not isolated but exist only as the function of group life. It follows, therefore, that there will be leaders or potential leaders in every group that has some degree of integration. For example, each of the primary groups in the prison may be said to contain a person who is more or less of a leader, and it is our main purpose in this chapter to examine the leaders of these groups. In large aggregations such as the hundred men in a work unit, no one inmate may be said to be a leader under day by day conditions as there is only the slightest degree of integration among the one hundred men. Perhaps in a period of stress a leader might emerge in a large aggregation, but we are concerned here with the customary situation rather than with the unusual. Large aggregations, such as work units, or the entire population, are secondary groups. Such groups are less sympathetic and less integrated than primary groups, so the social relations among them are less positive and more impersonal than those of the primary groups. Thus, there is a difference between the leader whose rank is based on primary relations and the leader produced by secondary relations. We assign the term *leader* to the man who becomes the center of rapport in the primary and semi-primary groups and we use the term *popular* to designate the person who, through secondary relationships, has recognized status in larger groups.

Leadership Phenomena in Primary and Semi-Primary Groups[1]

Studies of leadership become exceedingly complex in the prison community because the overt behavior of the men is controlled by rules and regulations. Additional complexity is added by the changing population. The character of group life, as shown in the preceding chapter, also affects the type of leadership. Notwithstanding the difficulties involved, a knowledge of leadership is deemed important as a factor in the culture, and data have been collected which lend meaning to the following topics: (1) the personality traits of leaders, (2) the methods of gaining leader status, (3) the tenure of the leader, and (4) the general nature of leadership and its effect in the prison community.

For the purpose of this study the leader has been defined as a person who influences and directs the opinions and behavior of others and who shows the way by action or a reputation for action. He is the person who becomes the center of rapport.[2] He is the person about whom the informal, unregulated group life exists. It is evident that a precise definition of leadership cannot be drawn, due to the wide variety of situations in which leaders function. Although a concept of leadership has been assumed, it remains, paradoxically enough, one of the objectives of this chapter to gain a more refined understanding and a clearer definition of leaders and leadership in the prison community. In considering the four topics, we are to deal largely with the attitudes and behavior of inmates. To a prison official leaders do not exist unless they become trouble-makers and influence other men. While in some instances, as will be shown, leaders have also been trouble-makers, the duality does not frequently exist. This investigation does not intend to cover the leadership factor during periods of chaos such as riots or group escapes. It has been impossible to do so as no such situation occurred during the period of time covered by the inquiry. Reference is made to situations, however, in which such participation has proved to be important in the rise to leadership.

It was first necessary to learn the membership of primary groups, and through the study of them to ascertain which man in each group was considered the leader. From the schedules given, as reported in the last chapter, and as a result of the writer's association in the community, fourteen groups of a primary or semi-primary nature were considered. Eight of these groups existed in two work gangs, and six of them whose members were in various work units were studied. Over a period of some months, sixty inmates affiliated

---

[1] Donald Clemmer, "Leadership Phenomena in a Prison Community," *Journal of Criminal Law and Criminology,* vol. XXVIII, No. 6, March-April, 1938, pp. 851–872.

[2] E. T. Hiller, *op. cit.,* p. 560.

with the selected groups were interviewed concerning the nature of their affiliations, and in regard to leadership. Only passing attention has been given to small groups of twos and threes, not that leaders may not exist in them, but due to the lack of broad influence of these dyads and triads. It has been learned, however, that in these small groups one member is usually dominant and the others submissive, in varying degrees. Such affiliations are cemented by one or more of the following bonds: mutual home background, association in crime, expressed or unexpressed homosexual attraction, mutual toleration by a forced propinquity, the wish of a submissive personality to share in the prestige of a notorious and dominant one, and the close affiliation of two or three men who plan and plot for future crime.

After the development of various degrees of rapport, the writer learned the identity of the inmate in each group who was generally considered to be the leader. In Table I is shown the age, mental age, height, weight, and offense of each leader. The leaders "A" through "F" have headed those groups which have been described as having members not common to any particular work unit, and the balance have been leaders of groups assigned in definite, restricted work divisions. Leaders "I" and "M" are Negroes.

TABLE XIII

Age, Mental Age, Height, Weight, and Offense of 14 Selected Prison Leaders

Leader	*Age*	*Mental Age*	*Height*	*Weight*	*Offense*
A	46	18–0	6–0	165	Murder
B	26	17–10	5–7	140	Burglary
C	34	17–2	6–0	178	Robbery, Armed
D	35	15–2	5–5	155	Robbery, Armed
E	34	16–9	5–4	131	Robbery, Armed
F	31	12–1	5–8	148	Murder
G	26	14–7	5–10	167	Robbery, Armed
H	31	12–8	6–0	167	Murder
I	29	11–4	5–9	171	Robbery, Armed
J	35	11–11	6–3	145	Robbery, Armed
K	28	15–6	6–0	174	Robbery, Armed
L	29	17–2	5–7	147	Robbery, Armed
M	48	16–6	5–11	184	Robbery, Armed
N	26	9–6	5–6	144	Robbery, Armed
Average	32	15–0	5–9	158	

The average age of the leaders is shown to be 32. The average of the population as a whole is 34 years and 8 months.[3] The intelligence of leaders is above that of the general population which has been found to be 13 years and 7 months for white men, and 11 years and 5 months for Negroes.[4] Considered collectively, weight

[3] See Chapter II.
[4] See Chapter II.

and height seems to have little importance, yet it will be observed that none of the men are overweight. Of the 14 leaders, 9 have been in other prisons, reformatories, or workhouses for periods of 18 months or more. The case of each man has been carefully studied in reference to criminality, and every leader has been engaged in crime more or less professionally. An appraisal of the life history of the leaders reveals that they have all been reared in cities of 50,000 population or over, excepting "H" and "N" who have lived in large cities since adolescence. Half of them have been married. School achievement has not progressed beyond the eighth grade except in the cases of "E" and "L" who had two years of high school and "A" who quit college during the first year. It has become clear from a study of the history of the men that before incarceration none of them had been leaders in any sort of organization or group other than those which were held together by criminal activities. Thus "D" had no prestige as a school boy or in early employment until he became a dealer in whiskey during prohibition. Gradually, however, he rose from a hanger-on to the leadership of an organized mob of bootleggers and later, of robbers. "J" was a leader of a boy's gang which operated in a delinquency area of a large city. "A," who advanced in school farther than did the rest, held some prestige as an athlete, although he seems not to have been a leader. The leadership quality of "K" developed in a school for juvenile delinquents when he was twelve years old. Even as early leaders, however, there seems to have been frequent disassociation and fluctuation in rôle, varying between being an acknowledged leader, a quasi-leader, and a follower. For example, before coming to this prison "A" had no similar status in another prison. "M" had no following until he had been in residence for three years. While the social experience which the leaders have had has been important in conditioning them for the rank they hold as leaders, there seems to be no situation common to all unless it has reference to having engaged in delinquency at a relatively early age. Some of the following material will show that the attitude of followers toward leaders has pertinence only for the qualities demonstrated in the present or the immediate past.

The following passages seem to be representative of numerous statements obtained concerning the personality traits which the leaders appear to possess. An advanced offender who has completed twelve years on a life sentence for murder, noted in the table as leader "A," writes:

> I think that in a well-integrated group the man who is most trusted and has the most equable disposition is the chosen leader. . . . In sports, proficiency qualifies one's fitness for leadership only if he is square, too.

In anything else ingenuity in devising new pastimes or escapades qualifies it. Outstanding intellect is a liability since it is usually distrusted. In a group which is not integrated the aggressive organizer is the leader although he may not last long.

A forger who has been a member of a semi-primary group comments about his cellmate who is leader "F" of another group.

He arrived here about eight years ago without creating much excitement. Later he became interested in physical culture and built up his body. He is a proselyter and became a leader of certain men who were interested in that kind of thing. . . . He has a bull-dog face and a mild manner. His speech is better than one would suppose for a man with his appearance, and he possesses a gregariousness which makes him intimate with anyone he chooses to cultivate. . . . He has a good sense of humor and is . . . never running to officials.

"B" is recognized as a leader not only by the inmate population but by the administration as well. He has pronounced ideas as to the qualities with which leaders are endowed. In his statement one perceives some personalization and self reference.

Physically the leader is not small or large. I know of small leaders and I know of large leaders. Mentally they are above the average, although that does not mean much in here considering the low mental average of most prisoners. Temperamentally he is of the emotional type, the type who is quick to condemn the officials and anyone else. . . . Suggestions for this and that usually spring from him and he seems able to imbue his followers with enthusiasm. . . . I run over in my mind half a dozen leaders I know in here and the main trait that they all have in common is that they are absolutely "right."

A schedule was presented to 60 men who were members of groups in which the leaders operated. The men were asked to enumerate not only the major traits which appeared to be important in their ideas of leadership but the lesser traits as well. The data obtained are considered too subjective to quantify. The admirable traits assigned to leaders by members include first and most frequently the orientation known as "being right." [5] Other characteristics were described as courage, generosity, modesty, education, an interesting vocabulary, personal cleanliness, clever gambling, the ability to "con" (fool) officials, a reputation for holding liquor, possession of money with which luxuries could be dispensed, a large body of knowledge about a particular technique of crime, a fund of vulgar jokes or songs, the possession of attitudes against the judiciary, the

[5] See Dictionary, Appendix B.

prison administration, the parole board, and God, demonstrable sophistication in female companionship as evidenced by suggestive letters, the dignity and poise that come to some men after long years of prison life, participation in a spectacular crime, riot, or escape, a great capacity for eating, the ability to turn handsprings, seduce younger men, and play a guitar. Possession of a few of these traits is not sufficient to qualify a man for leadership. The essential trait is reported to be a concept of "rightness." Dishonesty of considerable proportions may be tolerated unless it involves group members or other prisoners in an unfavorable situation with officials. When such a condition becomes known the prestige of leadership is gone.

The acquiring of leader status in most cases is a gradual and unmeasurable process. In a few instances a change in group control is accomplished through conflict. When a man enters prison he is virtually ungrouped unless he has former associates already in prison. More often than not, friendly relations among associates are absent. A bank robber who has seen men enter prison for eleven years expresses the initiation process thus:

> When "fish" (new inmates) come in here they act lost, but I've never seen it to fail that the "hoosiers" (undesirable persons) group up with the "hoosiers," the "stools" (informers) with the "stools," and the prostitutes with their kind. The "right guys" don't group up for some time. You see them looking the guys over before they choose their friends.

Eventually, however, about 60 per cent of the men who come to prison, as shown in Chapter V, enter into or initiate some form of primary group life. If the group is already formed, a degree of consensus is reached before a new man shares in the full social life. He may, and frequently does, upset the equilibrium of established interaction. There may be many personal conflicts and much dis-association before a new balance is reached. It is as a result of such changes and interchanges in rôle that new leaders emerge. Not only does this condition apply when a new inmate enters prison but also when a hanger-on of one established group attempts to be included in, or to become a leader of, another group. The particular personality traits, notwithstanding, a person tends to become a leader when there has been some rift in the ordinary cohesion of group life. The traits of persons involved in the changes either accelerate or retard the speed with which the change takes place. To illustrate: An inmate was transferred from another prison in the same state because of conduct difficulties there. He was reputed to be courageous and to possess anti-administration feelings. After the transfer he was assigned to a work division in which there was much informal group life. One of the most prominent of these cliques had recently been disrupted by an unfaithful act of its leader. As a result the new inmate who was known to have the correct orientation soon came to be a member, and later the leader. The deposed leader mentioned several months later in explanation:

> He came from ——— with a tough reputation and his leadership is based on his reputation there. He has a punch and that gains prestige anywhere.

The new leader here referred to, lasted only six months when he was found to be inordinately selfish. He later led in a daring escape with a totally different group in which a guard was severely beaten. He was recaptured within a few months after having committed some professionalized robberies, returned to prison, and again became a leader of yet another group. After a total of about eleven years he was released and shortly after release again began stealing and apparently acting as a leader. Later, he was electrocuted.

Some inmates attempt to gain the leader's rôle and fail. This is due usually to two conditions: first, the character faults of the individual, and, second, the questionableness of the program as well as absence of need for a new leader. The following instance is revealed by leader "M" who describes an inmate with a poor reputation:

> He was long suspected of being a "rat" (informer) and he tried to get some petitions signed first in one shop or work gang and then another. Shop after shop and gang after gang was approached without getting results. To the inmate's question, "Who is handling this petition?" . . . The inmates when told, answered, "Why, that dirty fink (informer), he's got a lot of guts trying to get that petition signed." Among the hundred who refused to sign or having anything to do with the "dirty fink," there were scores of other finks who didn't have any confidence or trust in the first fink—who was like themselves.

Men sometimes become leaders by organization schemes. Leader "E" set up a round-robin tournament among seven baseball teams, appointed himself manager of one, and for weeks was distrusted by his ten close ball-player associates. Although they highly approved of the idea they thought he was seeking the warden's favor because of his activities in managing the softball league. In an argument with a prison official, however, "E" defended the players against the official and was then generally accepted as a real leader. By and large it seems that leaders gain their status by action or a reliable reputation for action that prompts admiration by the followers. This behavior always implies some of the values which the group holds in esteem as well as a possession of attitudes that they themselves lack, to some degree. However, the leader is seldom greatly different from the followers as he is more or less an epitome of them.

In conducting this study it soon became evident that there were frequent changes in leaders. Of the fourteen groups with whom the writer had the closest connection, three of the leaders had held their positions between a year and eighteen months. Six had been leaders between nine and thirteen months, and seven had been leaders between six and nine months. While these data are approximated from an appraisal of the followers, their complete accuracy is open to question. Even in the groups which seemed the most stable there were frequent quarrels. In three groups it was found that at one time two persons may have had about the same prestige. This does not indicate a constant striving for leadership, but is related to popularity which is considered as a different phenomenon.

An evaluation of leadership in a closed community is not, of course, comparable to that of a normal community. The main difference seems to be related to the leader's goal, objective, or program. Prison leaders, except in conflict situations, have no definite program. The only objective which the group and leader share is to make the time pass as agreeably and as comfortably as possible. When the group is made up of baseball players there is a goal, i.e., the championship, but this is transitory and never very important. Egocentricity or the tendency to oppose the wishes of others, while sometimes subjected to pressure of the group controls, still crops out and prohibits a common agreement as to objectives. Thus it follows that a leader without a program is not likely to have the permanence that a leader has who is fighting for a cause. Another prominent factor in the tenure of leadership is the surprising number of times that a leader thought to be "right" proves only too shortly to demonstrate some weakness. It is probable that many of the personality attributes that led to conflict with the larger social order and caused incarceration are operating to prohibit the leader from continuing in his rôle.

The general nature of leadership depends, of course, on the culture in which the leader operates. While we are not yet ready to attempt a portraiture of the prison culture, it has been implied that the prison is a highly complex community in which the social processes, to an extent, vary with those found in a free community. We shall see in a later chapter that the behavior patterns, which in a normal community would be social controls, actually have no strong social utility. It has already been indicated that impersonalization is the general rule among at least forty per cent of the men. Impersonalization, plus the individuation of most prisoners makes of the penitentiary an "atomized" society. It is little wonder, then, that in such a milieu we find prison leaders whose functions are minor and tenure uncertain, and it is not surprising that in the vast literature on leadership little similarity is found for leaders within and without the walls. In this connection one inmate remarks:

Leadership in Prisons

Historical heroes—leaders who have received the loudest acclaim from biographers—have been warriors who led their people to conquest or to freedom. Their dominant characteristics have been many—selfish Napoleon, ambitious Alexander, patriotic Washington, bigoted Cromwell.

Would any one of these men be recognized as a leader in one of our modern prisons? I think not. They would soon be known within the walls as "handshakers," "administration men," "rats," because of their ideals and ideas.

The "follower" in prison cannot be properly designated as a two-legged sheep, as sheep blindly follow a leader, stampede, pile up and smother, because of physical fear; the "follow-the-leader" prisoner riots and raises hell in general because of moral cowardice.

The average prison leader has no vision, little wisdom, an insatiable desire for notoriety, enlarged adrenal glands and only a trace of thyroids. He gathers a coterie of lesser lights who desire to shine with the reflected glory. This combination gradually saps the morale of others whose common sense tells them that stone walls cannot be beaten by force. (When the crisis arrives these easily-influenced chumps simply haven't the moral stamina to say, "Go to hell! I'm doing my own time.")

And when the show-down comes the crafty agitator squirms out of the mess leaving the sap to take the rap. The prison leader is never a "brave" man; he is merely totally lacking in fear.

In spite of the nature of the prison world, groups with leaders exist, and a few approach in structure and function the primary groups in a normal community. Before men come to prison they have been members of, and have shared in, various forms of group life. Official regulations notwithstanding, the pattern tends to continue. Before commitment some men were of the dominant type and some were submissive; this condition also tends to continue. The attitudes of new inmates have been modified during the arrest, detention, and trial process so that when they enter the penitentiary they have no strong affiliational drive because their attention rests so completely on the damage which has been done to their ego as well as on the great confusion of the first weeks of prison. They are highly self-centered. They think in terms of "me," "I," and "my case." Eventually, however, they become increasingly aware of the social life about them. Other personalities, usually leaders, become sources of interest. Gossip flourishes. By word of mouth they learn who is "right" and who is "wrong." Life comes to be dramatic, at least for a time. The primary group is the theatre and the leader manages the staging. The mechanism is an escape from the dull, deadening monotony of an impersonalized existence of which prison life otherwise consists. The leader, through consensus, keeps the group intact. By virtue of some outstanding trait he is able to provide and guide entertainment, thus providing a counter-irritant to the social stresses and strains which are inherent in prison life. He develops new subjects of conversation; he engenders new hates or rekindles old ones; he devises new forms of recreation and he may tentatively enliven hope. He may lead a protest or sponsor a riot. But there is no real permanency. After years of prison, conversation that was once stimulating becomes dull. Hopes and hates are likely to dwindle. In the readjustment after conflict, as in riot or protest, prisoners nearly always lose. Attitudes towards values fluctuate and personalities change. The bonds in a group, seldom very strong, weaken. Social lassitude leads to impersonalization and symbiotic contacts. It is this situation that accounts in part for the nature of group life in prison and the nature of the leaders.

In concluding this topic we may say that while a type of leadership phenomenon has been found to exist in a prison, it differs greatly from leadership as ordinarily conceived in an unrestricted society. The differences have reference to the particular structure of the informal group life, the absence of consensus for a common goal, the individualism of most prisoners' orientation, the official controls of discipline, the personality traits of those who become leaders, and the "atomization" of the prison community. For the purpose of furnishing a concept the prison group leader may be considered as a person who, for a relatively short period of time, guides and controls the less important opinions and behavior of his group in a minor way by behavior which they tentatively approve. The esteemed behavior consists of an anti-administration ideation and a complex of other traits which draws attention to the dramatic milieu which is the group, and away from the burdensomeness of an isolated existence. The leader holds prestige until there is disassociation in the group, usually brought about by conduct of his own which is inconsistent with the rôle the group expected him to play. A new leader achieves his status by action or a capacity for action plus certain personable traits approved by the group. He maintains his position until a change, either in his own behavior or in the values of the group, takes place. Such leaders as have been found to exist are somewhat more intelligent, slightly younger, and more criminalistic than the population in general.

Leadership Resulting from Secondary Relationships

It is possible for leadership of a sort to develop in primary and semi-primary groups, because the group members are in close enough contact with each other for certain men to develop prestige. The situation is different, however, when we think of leaders as leaders of the whole community. This is so because the men in one cellhouse and work gang, for example, are not in frequent or close enough communication with men in other work units and cellhouses. Real leaders of communities do not develop when portions within the community are isolated from one another. However, if isolation should break down, which it does in our prison under certain circumstances, then there is a possibility for a leader to develop.

Such leaders as exist as a result of secondary group relationships are those who are more or less in the public eye of the prisoners. They are the persons who have a large number of contacts with inmates of many or all work units and also have contacts and relationships with the sub-formal organization, that is, the members of various primary or semi-primary groups. Such a person is "Shorty." Shorty works in the hospital as a first-aid man and general helper to the physician. The hospital is open at all times to the sick, and every morning at least one hundred men gather there in line. While helping the doctor Shorty comes in contact over a period of months, with a large proportion of the population. Shorty is a distinctive personality; he is about five feet tall, very blond, Italian, quiet, smiling, friendly, and with an excellently developed musculature. He does what he can to make sick men comfortable and treats all inmates in a kindly way. Not only does he have direct and face-to-face relationship with the inmates but the population also sees him on the athletic field. He is the most skillful football player. In his position of quarterback he demonstrates athletic capacity equal to the better collegiate players. He also is the catcher of the baseball team, and performs with the same brilliance. Thus, for seven months of the year Shorty is seen in an athletic rôle by the entire population each Saturday afternoon, and during the week comes in personal contact with several hundred men. Everyone knows his name; most of the men like him. He does not assume the rôle of a leader, however, for the entire prison group. He is affiliated with a primary group and is the recognized leader of it. The football squad, numbering some thirty men, which might be thought of as a semi-primary group, more or less accept him as its leader. In whatever situation he choses to exert his influence it is possible for him to do so. His crime was a heinous one. With some companions he mildly tortured a woman in order to force her to reveal where a supposedly large amount of money was stored. While some inmates consider this crime unbecoming to a good thief, Shorty's explanations were sufficiently reasonable, according to the inmates' thinking, not to jeopardize his standing in the community. While Shorty constituted a center of attraction that drew prisoners to him, in terms of leadership in normal communities, he could hardly be called a leader type. In the hospital and on the athletic field men would do his bidding to a certain point, but had he ever attempted to become a dominant leader it is likely that the disassociation which characterizes much of the interaction among prisoners would have prevented his assuming the rôle of a genuine leader. Shorty was popular and an "expanded personality," [6] but not a real leader as we think of leaders in society. Leaders have programs and objectives. Shorty's only actual program was individualistic, i.e., to get out of prison as soon as possible. Shorty is known and even referred to as a leader by some inmates and a few officials, and according to our definition of *prison leader* he qualifies. From this description of him, however, it is evident that leadership among prisoners is vague, uncertain, indefinite and not comparable with leadership outside the walls.

In the groups of men who are interested in boxing or baseball, isolation is broken down. Men from several different work units who are interested in boxing occasionally gather at an appointed hour for practice. They constitute a rather large semi-primary group and one man among them is considered to be somewhat of a leader. One boxing affiliate described the leader thus:

> The leader of the boxing crowd is Jameson, whom you have on your list. He is not the best boxer in the gang, but he fought outside and is much better than most of us. He is thoroughly extraverted and has a nice disposition. He will box with anyone and let the other fellow hit him no matter how hard in order to teach him, or he will fight anyone with gloves. Not at all quarrelsome. He had a good reputation and is not a schemer. In contrast, the best fighter in the gang is a colored prisoner who is not equable. He is square enough, and is not a schemer, but he is temperamental. His temperament gets him into trouble and he is not popular.

A degree of leadership which develops through inter-action of a secondary group nature comes to the champion boxers. For an hour one noon each week boxing matches are held before the entire population. The man recognized as the champion in each weight

[6] Hornell Hart, *The Science of Social Relations,* Henry Holt and Co., New York, 1927, pp. 92–123.

class has considerable prestige and is a center of attraction because inmates hold physical prowess in high esteem. Most of the champion boxers are affiliated in small primary or semi-primary groups, but only one of them is a leader of such a group. Actually, these champions are only "popular," and not leaders, though it is possible that in a conflict involving a large number of men the inmates would rally around one of the boxers and let him assume leadership. Nothing like this has happened in our prison, but if it should, the champion boxers are potential leaders.

In the work gangs, usually composed of one hundred men, there are not only the informal primary and semi-primary groups which are held together by a general cohesion, but there are frequently other informal groups the members of which unite for a specific activity. Such groups are not closely cemented. Their specific activity may be baseball playing, gambling, discussion of literary topics, horseshoe playing, or what not. These loosely organized collectivities have persons who more or less direct the activities although conflict is frequent. The writer does not consider such men as leaders because none of them, to his knowledge, have been recognized as leaders of primary groups. Two such persons are described thus:

> In our work gang there are four men who lead certain groups, all of them concerned with athletics. Three lead ball teams, and one leads the boxers' group. The first, for the purpose of this essay, is W. whom we mentioned this morning and he leads one of the ball teams. He has a very high rating on the Alpha test, but the men in the gang do not give him credit for much intelligence, nor for good education. One reason, perhaps, is that he is obviously a member of a family which is, or was, in the lower brackets, economically. He has been a barber, and that strengthens the conviction in the gang that he is not exceptionally intelligent. Barbers, supposedly, are remarkable for their verbosity rather than for intelligence. Another reason is that he corrects the errors of the other men in the gang and that antagonizes them. His own errors of speech and pronunciation are the more glaring because of his habit of correcting others, and his errors are the ones common to members of the lower classes who are well-read, but who have not acquired from the parents and their environment habits and vocabularies to suit their present intellectual status. I would hesitate to say that he is liked for his personality and I doubt that he is trusted economically or admired for his principles. . . . So far, he does not seem much like a leader, does he? . . . One of the reasons why he is not trusted economically is that he is a schemer and that is precisely what makes him a leader of the team in question. He does not play exceptionally well; hardly well enough, in fact, to be chosen on a team managed by another man, but he is a good organizer and has chosen a team of his own. By doing that he may play where he pleases and he holds his players together by calling on their loyalty to the team and by bragging

about the aggregation rather than the individuals. He books their games and bets a stated sum on the game for the team as a whole instead of each player making a separate and personal wager. In addition to these things he is intensely jealous of his own prowess, and peaceful men hesitate to involve themselves in a quarrel which is inevitable if they criticize his playing, or to quit his team for another. . . . In this instance I would have to call him a pseudo-leader, a self-chosen leader who leads by virtue of his organizing ability and aggressiveness. . . .

Another team, predominantly colored, is led by a fellow named B. who is known as the best gambler among the colored prisoners. The "best gambler among the colored prisoners" is the crookedest gambler, but the colored men do not condemn a cheat. On the contrary they give him credit for shrewdness. He is a fairly good organizer and plays ball rather well. He is shrewd, unscrupulous, and aggressive. He acts as betting commissioner for his team and books the games.

It is probable that leadership phenomena are somewhat more orthodox and genuine in criminal groups before they have come to prison. "Loyalty to one's group is the basic law in the underworld," remarks Dr. Tannenbaum.[7] This is what the inmates say and to a degree it is true. We believe, however, that it is the exception rather than the rule. Too many men turn state's evidence. There are too many stool pigeons for loyalty to be widespread. Except for professional gangsters who comprise a relatively small but important part of the underworld, there is a question as to whether or not collectivities of thieves ever constitute integrated, informal groups. A professional thief, who was also leader of a small mob of criminals before incarceration, and a prison leader, as defined, makes this revealing statement:

If one of our mob got pinched by the coppers our efforts to get him released on bail or to "fix" his trial would depend on what sort of a person he was. If he was tight lipped and not given to squawking (an esteemed trait), we would not try so hard to "spring him," but if we felt he might squawk (a disesteemed trait), we would do everything we could to get him out.

In other words, the person with the better traits is treated with less consideration for his welfare than is a person with poorer traits. The motivation, of course, is not, as might appear, the continuance and integration of the group, but simply individual self protection. Behavior of this sort, characteristic of both pre-penal and penal groups and leaders, is not the sort to which we ordinarily ascribe the term "loyalty." There are evidences of real loyalties among groups and their leaders, but they are, we believe, the exceptions.

---

[7] Frank Tannenbaum, *Wall Shadows*, G. P. Putnam's Sons, New York, 1932, p. 64.

We are unable to report authentically on leadership such as occurs in occasional prison riots or group escapes. Descriptions of several of them which have occurred in other prisons by men who observed them or participated in them, lead one to believe, however, that the proportion of the men engaging in such collective behavior is always far less than that reported by the newspapers. The prison riot is caused usually by a long series of "abuses," which, over a period of time, are brought to the attention of the inmate body by leaders. Occasionally a riot will be planned and staged. More often than not, however, it is spontaneous, and the leaders that arise do so spontaneously. Their action, as that of their followers, results through contagious behavior in which the rioters constitute a psychological crowd, such as a lynching crowd. There is a transitory cohesion and an object of hate. The men who lead are the most active, the most resentful, and usually, we think, the most realistic of any of the prison leaders, but their tenure is short, and from our point of view they are important only as an atypical phenomenon.

CHAPTER VII

Social Controls

Social controls are complex forces resulting from the interactions among a people, forces which have grown up over a period of years and which have a utility. Social controls develop slowly from culturally established sources. In this and the following chapter we wish to discuss the configurations which are in the nature of social controls. Social control, as a topic in sociology, is exceedingly complicated and variagated. It may be approached and studied from several frames of reference. We will not here concern ourselves with abstruse theories, though in order to make comparisons the student of society should be familiar with social controls as they operate in a number of dissimilar communities. The sociological point of view is that of objective analysis and comparison.[1]

We have already looked into some forms of group life and the phenomena of leadership. The interactions resulting from the structure of groups limit and prescribe relationships and to this extent the very social structure of the prison community constitutes some social control. The existence of leaders in the informal groups also is a factor of social control. The greatest control, of course, is the penitentiary itself with its societal sanction, its walls, guns, rules, and regulations. This aspect of social control will be treated in the next chapter.

In a sense, our inmates are the persons in the normal community who did not channelize their behavior according to the broad social prescriptions. In committing crimes, they violated both laws and folkways which are social controls. But this does not mean that they were not, at the same time, influenced by still other social controls. Gossip in the gang, the code of the underworld, and the various dogmas of restricted groups, have all played a part in guiding their behavior.

We are to distinguish between the broader, more general and sanctioned social controls, which we will arbitrarily call the formal or compulsory controls, and the more subtle, less general types of mechanisms which tend to control our men in the prison community.

---

[1] Frank H. Hankins, *An Introduction to the Study of Society,* The Macmillan Co., New York, 1935, p. 479.

As we shall later see, it is in communities which are heterogeneous that a necessity exists for strong legal decrees, while any community of essentially a homogeneous character has less need for laws. The prison is essentially heterogeneous. We have pointed out before, and it is important enough to repeat, that, contrary to the opinion of some persons, the prison world is not a like-minded, highly integrated collectivity, but is, on the other hand, a diffuse aggregation wherein impersonal relations abound, and consensus of a high degree is absent due to the individuation of most of the personalities involved. This condition must be kept in mind as we examine the effectiveness of the behavior patterns we are calling social controls.

Social controls are supposed to have a utility, a utility which keeps people in line. From one point of view, everything that is social, that is, every type of interaction between and among human beings, comes under the subject of social controls. While we are not to ignore this greater interpretation we wish to think of social control more as social habits. Complimentary to social controls are the institutions which, because of their history, have set up established ways of doing things. It is the social controls which force the continuance of the established way of doing things. "By social control is ordinarily meant all those processes and instrumentalities by which the behavior of individuals is brought into conformity with social ideals and purposes. It is the means whereby the highly diverse action tendencies of numerous personalities are so integrated as to give unity and common direction to their activities. Integration implies capacity to work for common ends; it implies feelings of interdependence, a spirit of coöperation . . . and standardized modes of response. It requires the orderly functioning of the interacting individuals. . . . Social control is accomplished mainly through the processes of attitude formation. The individual is conditioned to respond in approved ways and is further filled with a desire for social approbation. These habits and this desire are supported by a scheme of ethical values, by mutual obligations or reciprocal relationships obtaining among members of the group (gang, family, club, etc.) and by the associated constraint upon the individual exerted by group opinion." [2]

We have stated that we are to discuss the mechanisms which are in the *nature* of social controls. By this we mean that the configuration of forces or mechanisms may not actually produce social control, but simply tendencies toward such control. We shall see if the prison types of social control agree with Professor Hankin's definition as quoted. While examining this subject we shall learn

---

[2] *Ibid.*, pp. 387–388.

what the attitudes and values of inmates are, the attitudes and values being direct or indirect resultants of all social controls.

Social ideals and purposes are different for prison inmates than for the man in the street. This statement is made generally, as some free men may possess ideals and purposes similar to those of the most criminalistic inmates, and vice versa. It is most difficult to say, when we restrict ideals and purposes to inmates and a penal environment, what they are. The greatest and the only universal purpose is for freedom. Freedom is the phase of the social purpose which emphasizes individuality. In the main we use freedom here as freedom from custody. This desire for freedom is universal among inmates and is peculiar to prisons, for in the general population the overwhelming social purpose is not freedom, but, to wit, security in a democracy. The social ideals and purposes of citizens are, in large proportion it seems, represented by such terms as security, success, service, truth, kindness, and so forth. There are exceptions according to strata and culture, but in general these ideals are aimed for, if not universally achieved. Such ideals are infrequently held by the residents of a penitentiary, at least during the major part of incarceration. With prisoners the wish for freedom is universal and comes first. Not universal, but fairly widespread, is the social ideal that no prisoner should cater to or be helpful to an official. This has been referred to before as an anti-administration mental-set. Even less widespread is the ideal that inmates should be loyal to one another. While feelings of interdependence and a spirit of coöperation among the men are not totally lacking, exceptions are frequent, yet, in general, loyalty would be considered as an ideal. Another social purpose is related to health. It is a fairly widespread collective purpose that inmates who are ill, either physically or mentally, are deserving of care and comfort. Self-reference enters into this pattern as the men never know when they will be in need of medical care. Much talked of is the loyalty to one's family. Other purposes and social ideals exist, but are not typical enough to be included in a community-wide appraisal. So we see that while social ideals and purposes are not entirely foreign to the inmate collectivity, there is neither the unanimity or breadth common to the non-penal social world, and we shall find that this situation influences the effectiveness of social controls. In so far as our inmates were members of normal communities before incarceration, most of the techniques of the social controls are those found in the normal culture.

The forms of social control are familiar under such titles as mores, folkways, dogma, legend, gossip, taboo, and we shall discuss them in that order.

Mores and the Prisoner's Code

By mores is meant, "the popular usages and traditions when they include a judgment that they are conducive to societal welfare, and when they exert a coercion on the individual to conform to them although they are not coördinated by any authority."[3] Mores are folkways which have become obligatory. "They imply a judgment as to the rightness or wrongness of the action of the group members, and, in a lesser degree, of outsiders."[4]

Prisoners, of course, do not speak of the mores. They do speak of a code which all prisoners learn by word of mouth. The code, like the mores, is not written down. It is simply in the culture as idea. Men unfamiliar with prison life soon learn what the code includes. It is not peculiar to our prison, but exists in all prisons as well as in the culture of the underworld. The code is not new. Forty years ago and more it was a phenomenon of communication among inmates and it includes the items (or values) which we have just mentioned while discussing ideals. The fundamental principle of the code may be stated thus: Inmates are to refrain from helping prison or government officials in matters of discipline, and should never give them information of any kind, and especially the kind which may work harm to a fellow prisoner. Supplementary to this, and following from it, is the value of loyalty among prisoners in their dealings with each other. This basic idea constitutes the prisoners' code. Other prescribed behavior has its roots in this principle. For example, it is prescribed that when an inmate is attempting an escape, other inmates should not only refrain from telling officials, but they should distract the attention of guards, for example, by noise-making while their companion sledge-hammers his way to freedom. This ramification, and numerous others which could be mentioned, refers to the basic item in the code. The code has been built up through many years and results, in part, from the conception of some law-breakers that society and the symbols that represent it (prison officials in this case) are natural enemies. The code is, and results from, an attitudinal configuration that a minority group to exist must have cohesiveness and be secure within itself. Emotionally, the attitudinal configuration is charged with hate, the hate that comes to persons who fail, and who have their failures "rubbed in" by the dominant group.

We say that the code is prescribed because every man in prison, without exception, knows it, and every inmate of our prison since its opening has known it. Its persistence, in spite of violation and the fact that it does control conduct in many instances and tends

[3] William Graham Sumner, ***Folkways,*** The Athenaeum Press, Ginn and Co., Boston, 1906, Preface, p. iii.

[4] E. T. Hiller, *op. cit.*, p. 46.

to control it in other instances, shows its vigor. The fact that most violations of it are hidden and secret is further emphasis of its controlling force. A ramification of the code, for instance, prescribes that inmates never talk to guards unless on business, or for other absolutely necessary reasons. A later chapter will show that communication with guards tends to conform with this prescription. When inmate "stool-pigeons" who violate the code wish to communicate with guards, they endeavor to do so without being seen. This further signifies the potency of the mores.

In a free community, as Middletown, there is a heavy taboo resting upon sexual relations between persons before marriage.[5] For years it has been a violation of the mores for such behavior to occur. This moral code is further supported by law and religion. But everybody knows that such relationships are common, even though not universal. The aspect of the general mores referring to sex experience before marriage is a social value in which the definition of the situation is probably in a process of changing, but at the present, sex relations before marriage are not prescribed, and the prohibition remains an item of the mores. And so does the code of prisoners still retain its function even though, as in sex relation before marriage, its violations are frequent. Nelson points out that prisoners ". . . with high ideals, men with a personal code which is vigorously lived up to, are infinitely more scarce in prison than anywhere else."[6] In some of the following quotations from our inmates there will be indication that a prison code does not exist, and the writer has already shown that violations are frequent, that informing officials is fairly common, and that loyalty among inmates is not by any means complete. But in spite of these instances, and as in our analogy of sex relations before marriage, can we say that the mores are destroyed or that new values have been created to replace the old simply because exceptions exist?

It would seem logical to expect that a code which exerts a coercion on the individual to conform to it, would not be effective in a community where impersonal relations abound, and where individualism in personalities is so common. We can only say, and it is controversial, that if the prison code was ineffective, the inmate portion of the prison community would be more woefully disorganized than it is, and that instead of impersonal relationships we would find open conflicts at all times, the absence of sympathy of any degree, and a community befuddled with its own uncertainties. It would seem that differences in response to the code by particular individuals and groups reflect the degree to which the different inmates and

[5] Robert and Helen Lynd, *op. cit.*, p. 112.

[6] Victor Nelson, *Prison Days and Nights,* Little Brown and Company, Boston, 1933, p. 118.

groups are retaining, and, or, mixing the mores of other communities in which they have lived. Culture conflict, resulting in haphazard, disintegrated, atypical behavior, more than likely comes from a person's membership in one group or community which sanctions mores, codes, and standards which are widely different from the mores, codes, and standards of another group or community of which he is also a member. We believe that those prisoners who have a double or triple allegiance in the matter of responding to the mores (the family primary group, the prison primary group, or entire penal community, or the group which includes one's wife or sweetheart) are the ones who violate the prison code most freely.

The subject of prison code is summed up by an inmate who ought to know; he has been twelve years in prison.

> Everyone knows the two lines Kipling wrote about Asia, but I'll quote them:
>
> > "Take me somewhere East of Suez, where the best is like the worst,
> > And there ain't no ten commandments, and a man can raise a thirst."
>
> He might have been writing about prisons as far as the ten commandments are concerned, and it is far easier to raise a thirst inside the prison walls than to satisfy it. Men are sent to prison for breaking laws, and most laws are based on the ten commandments, so it is obvious that the ten commandments cannot be the basis of the moral code subscribed to by prisoners. It should be obvious that murderers who do not steal, and thieves who do not kill, and sex offenders who do neither, can hardly be in accord where such things are concerned. Even among thieves there is no agreement: A banker who steals from his depositors looks with horror upon a bank robber who does his stealing violently, and the bank robber looks with disgust upon a banker who has betrayed persons who trusted him. Both call the minor thieves, petty, and the minor thieves call the banker a double crosser and the bank robber a hoodlum. In one group the code may hold it right to speculate with the depositor's money, in the next it may be held right to rob the loan-sharks who foreclose mortgages, or to steal automobiles, or chickens, but there is no rule elastic enough to cover all the forms of thievery. However, all thieves unite in condemning the rape fiends—that is invariably the term for rapists—and all rape fiends condemn the thieves. Thieves excuse, or sometimes, approve, murder when it is committed in the course of a crime, but a murderer who is not a thief is almost invariably a "rube." Murderers who are "rubes" condemn all other violations of the ten commandments. Most perjurers are looked upon as victims of misfortune, and most men convicted of arson ("fire bugs") are looked upon as victims of their own ignorance and stupidity. In short, there ain't no ten commandments—in prison. If the one common factor of all codes be hunted out, it is "Don't snitch." And that, to quote Kipling once more, is another story.

Even in such a simple and direct matter as the rule above, there is disagreement. The radical group—the hoodlums and professional thieves—hold that under no circumstances is it justifiable for a man to give information against another man. Others find exceptions to the rule, such as giving information against a man who has given it first, and trying to repay the snitching in kind, or using the law to get revenge against a man who has withheld a part of the spoils, or left his partner in the lurch. This seems to work in direct ratio with the strength of character of the prisoner: those with strong characters accept the rule and live up to it without exception, and those with weaker wills justify their lapses by casuistries. There are, of course, occasional exceptions who are selfish enough to seize any advantage, and whose only justification is, "I've got to look after myself." It is evident that there is no hard and fast code, even in this instance.

Another simple rule is that one prisoner shall not rob another, and this one is seldom violated. Tobacco and other articles of small intrinsic value are left in the cells and are rarely touched. If a prisoner is discovered taking things from another prisoner, he becomes an outcast. It is all right to steal from the state, but it is not all right to steal something to sell. The stolen articles must be given away. This rule, too, differs in different groups. In some groups it is all right to get a price for anything, even a small favor like carrying a note, or doing an errand, and in other groups the prejudice against "nickel grabbing" is so strong that it isn't considered right to sell one's personal belongings, such as shoes, or tobacco, etc. In some groups loaning money at interest is considered shrewd, and in other groups it is not right at all. What would the prisoner's code be, in the aggregate?

As I said before: There ain't no ten commandments and even the one which can be accepted as general is subject to different interpretations. It seems to be a personal matter and it must be taken individually, like honor among thieves. There is honor among thieves, but it is rare, and there are men in prison who live according to more or less rigid codes, but they, too, are rare. The only rule a sensible man could use in estimating prisoners is that they must be taken as they are found, individually.

Thus our informant tells us that stealing among the inmates is rare. But the following quotation by another man would indicate otherwise, and we have reason to believe that the opinion of the second writer is more nearly correct. The foregoing statement is correct insofar as the writer is speaking of his "class" and "primary group." The first paragraph in which he points out the existence of social distance between various types of criminals is in the nature of secondary relations, and it contributes to impersonalized relationships. The next statement portrays an incident of stealing between prisoners themselves, and shows the inmate-writer's attitude towards the prison code.

A convict dashes madly up the stairs out of the bath house and turns left toward the quarry. Another convict, weighing about 250 pounds, and stark naked, comes out a little to the rear of the first one, and he is wild eyed with anger as he shrieks, "Thief! Robber! If I had a gun I'd kill you! Stop him, somebody!"

What has happened is that the first prisoner who was fully dressed, saw a second, who was naked, had a roll of money in his hand, and figured that the man would not chase him while naked, so he took a chance and grabbed the roll and ran. He was caught, but rumor has it that he ditched the money before he was caught.

The act of stealing that money was not particularly interesting, but we will admit that the circumstances surrounding it were. Seldom a day passes that some prisoner does not lose something by theft. . . .

This brings up the subject of honor among prisoners—let's call it a Code of Honor. It is rather vaguely spoken of at times by the prisoners, but exactly what that code includes seems to be in the background so far that even the oldest prisoners cannot recite it.

From personal observation, I would say that any set Code of Honor among convicts is a huge piece of imagination used principally to give an atmosphere of romance to prisons in order that the movies may occasionally show a picture about a penitentiary and have the hero show the proper amount of "Honor among Thieves" to make a hit with the public.

Naturally, any convict hates another who would "squeal" on anybody, and there are many who will take a week in Solitary rather than tell who sold them a suit of Knit-Shop Underwear, or where they got an improvised razor, but it is mostly because they know that they will have to go to the "Hole" whether they tell or not, and telling on their "dealers" would not save them anything, so they assume the air of a martyr and bravely go to live on bread and water for a week.

There is one thing they all agree to, and that is if any convict goes out to testify against anyone for any reason, he needs to have a large rock dropped on him at the first opportunity. There are few men in the penitentiary who stood trial who have not realized that it "takes a crook to convict a crook," because nearly every state's attorney has a few "rats" hanging around who have committed some minor offense, and will do anything the state's attorney tells them to do, in order to keep out of jail themselves, and many is the man here, whose blood pressure has risen 20 points when they learned that the state had found witnesses who had heard him framing his alibi, or who had heard him brag that he had done so-and-so, or who had seen him distinctly around the corner when the defendant actually knew that it was a lie, but had no way to prove it a lie.

Therefore, about the only set rule the convicts live by, is, "Don't give the other guy a break, because he won't give you any." They trust practically no one, partially because they have learned that so very few can be trusted. There are, naturally, exceptions to this.

And, logically enough, the most conscientious followers of the rule, "Do unto others as you would have others do unto you," is a man whom the authorities claim "took the rap" in order to save his brother from prison, and his brother was guilty. However, in fairness to others, let me say that there are ex-bandits and other ex-outlaws, guilty as sin of the charges upon which they were convicted, who show real consideration for other inmates, and who do not stoop to stealing from other unfortunates. These few who show some inclination to live right within the prison walls, do not boast of a Code of Honor; they simply mind their own business, and treat others as they themselves want to be treated.

So I would say that the rumored "Code of Honor" among convicts is largely a myth, because the percentages of those who would strictly abide by it is so small as to be negligible. If such a thing were in existence and were observed, there would a much smaller percentage of prisoners in any state.

Personally I don't believe that nine-tenths of the prisoners of the penitentiary know the meaning of the word, "Honor."

One half is always watching the other half for something to tell the officials. Of course, a prisoner does this in the hopes of bettering himself, he may expect a better job, or think the warden will pass the word on to the Board and they will be lenient with him.

You can hear some one every day calling someone else a "dirty rat." You will be perfectly safe in watching that gentleman, for he is poison for any prisoner he can catch napping; his game is to do a great deal of talking, and some poor simple soul will fall for him and say, "He is a right guy, and I am tying to him."

Now we will talk about the fellow that uses his head for something besides to put a hat on; he doesn't have to be an overbright crook, he doesn't have very much to say to anyone, and especially to Mr. Loudmouth. He knows it is all done for effect. A man that makes a habit of running to the officials with little petty things on other prisoners will soon have to tell some lies because he can't find out enough truth to carry in order to keep up his reputation with the officials.

The way I would define the word "stool-pigeon" would be something like this: a man confined with several other men, that will voluntarily carry news on fellow prisoners is the most contemptible thing imaginable. Of course, I mean petty things. If one prisoner has intentions of murdering another, I don't call a man a stool-pigeon for informing the officials. Every man in this prison, I will be safe in saying, would tell on another if he thought he would help himself. . . .

This man tells us that the "rumored code of honor is a myth" yet in every sentence he shows that he himself is reacting to the code (the social control). That the author disagrees with the two prisoners over the presence of a code in penal life is unimportant, except to the extent that the mores in a prison are in a way characteristic of the mores in the free world; effectiveness is a matter of degree, and is not the only criterion. Other counterparts of the culture alter the effectiveness.

A situation involving the most complex tangle of the prisoner's code concerns a fifty-five-year-old inmate whom we shall call Ben.

Ben was a veteran of the war of 1898, and each month received a pension from the government. He was provident and saved his money and had a few hundred dollars in his commissary fund. Due to his crippled condition he was assigned to the crank gang. Idleness is the rule in the crank gang, and through the long day Ben managed to make a pet of one of the three or four cats in the prison. The best of food that his money could buy was none too good for Ben's cat. Two young inmates became aware of Ben's fondness for his pet and realizing that Ben had money, stole or kidnapped the cat and held it for ten dollars ransom! Ben loved the cat, and promised to pay the ten dollars for the cat's return. By telling the officials who had stolen the pet, Ben could have had the cat returned without paying, but he said, "I'm no fink, I wouldn't snitch on no one." Other inmates, however, who were known to be "right," and who, in any other situation would never inform officials, did so on this occasion, and Ben's pet was eventually returned. When questioned, one of the two men who stole the cat denied he had anything to do with it, and blamed his companion and another inmate who did not even know that the cat had been kidnapped. However, before the pet was returned, Ben had connived with an intermediary stool-pigeon who, in turn was to make some arrangement with an inmate clerk in the commissary, so that the two kidnappers would be able to draw from the commissary ten dollars' worth of food or tobacco, over a period of two weeks. Ben's stool-pigeon, if he were consistent, should have informed officials that Ben was, for some unknown reason, buying two young inmates ten dollars' worth of luxuries. The implication, of course, would be of a sex nature. His stool-pigeon, however, told the two kidnappers that he thought he could get Ben to pay off in cash rather than in commissary orders and he would do so if they would give him a share of the money. They promised the stool-pigeon they would do so, but confided to each other that they would stand him off. The inmate commissary clerk, who, by virtue of his position of trust would not be expected, because of his responsibility to officers who gave him the "good job," to engage in this sort of practice, nevertheless agreed to.

The inmate who traced this maze of interaction for the writer, was lied to by each party involved including the men who told the guard that Ben's cat had been stolen. There may be some slight inaccuracy as to what occurred, but the situation was essentially as reported here. The reader can well see the complexity of the relationships involved, and careful analysis will show that the code of the prisoners was lived up to as much as it was violated. This one isolated incident is also illustrative of the impersonalization so prominent in prison. The two men who acted most socially from the point of view of ethical standards in the normal community were the ones who anonymously informed the officials of the cat's theft. From the standpoint of the prison code, however, they behaved in such a way as to encourage community disintegration. This situation shows confusion in responses to the mores, but the responses are probably no more inconsistent than those in a free society.

That prisoners' relations with each other are frequently negative is shown by the facts which follow. In the quarry one day while the inmates were at work one man approached another with a drawn knife. The "chiv" had been fashioned from some scrap steel, sharpened to a fine point by rubbing it on the stone floor of the cells, and inserted in a piece of wood. He approached a man who carried money and, at the point of the knife, forced him behind a large rock and robbed him. The man who was robbed could not tell officials because he was not supposed to have the several dollars which were taken from his person. He did tell other inmates, but no effort was made to retrieve the money as the thief was dangerous and armed with a "chiv." The thief was not a member of an informal group, and was utterly oblivious of the fact that he was an outcast and avoided by other inmates. An informer eventually told the officers that so-and-so had a knife. He was punished in solitary confinement.

Additional evidence of the complexity of relationships is seen in another incident. The peddling and use of drugs in our prison has not been extensive. Like every other similar institution, however, some morphine or cocaine is occasionally used. The warden procured information that a particular inmate was selling cocaine. He accordingly set out to apprehend the individual and gave another inmate—a so-called stool-pigeon—fifty cents to purchase the drug. After a short time the stool-pigeon brought the warden some fine-grained white powder in a small envelope. The warden gave this to the physician for analysis, and the doctor said the material was a calcium compound and not cocaine at all. The inmate peddler was exploiting other inmates by false representation; he violated the rules and regulations of the prison and he violated the code of the prisoners. This is a close duplication of a frequent occurrence in the normal community!

"Conniving" is a word used to express specifically in our prison the type of relationships whose end purpose is to yield some benefit, material or otherwise, to the "conniver." It has its parallel in the free world. In prison it concerns the selling or trading of objects which may not necessarily be the property of the people involved. It is sometimes possible for a man who works in the knit shop to steal several pairs of hose. He steals from the state, and this is not considered by inmates as an infraction of law or mores any more, for example, than is the type of practical politics in which Boss Tweed and others have stolen from their government. Inmates, like the notorious Plunkett of Tammany Hall, say, "I seen my opportunities and I took 'em." The prisoner who steals the socks will sell them and pocket the money. One prisoner remarks:

> One of the rules of the prison that is unenforceable is that of "conniving," or buying, selling, and trading goods. Once each week one is allowed to trade at the prison store, or commissary, and the bills are settled by his account, if he has one, in the front office. Relatives or friends usually send many of the prisoners funds with which to buy a few luxuries and necessities. Most all the conniving is paid off in tobacco or candy. Food is stolen from the kitchen and sold; clothes and shoes are sold and a favor is usually considered worth a small fee. Some cash money is used for these sales as they get a reduction for cash.
>
> There is much thievery and a thief in prison respects nobody. I have seen them take the last sack of tobacco a man had, take pens and valuables from guards, and even as little as a box of matches. It just seemed they wish to acquire articles. Sometimes having no use for the same.
>
> Where there was a "task" (prescribed amount of work) to be done, I have seen some slow, mischief-making prisoners idle away the hours and then steal articles from others to make up the sum allotted to them.

In spite of what is frequently said, that prison officials demand that some inmates be informers, this is not common in our prison. As a matter of fact, the officials have little respect for the ordinary "finks," who run to them with gossipy information about the doings of other inmates. Such men are only tolerated. The writer has heard his warden remark that he wishes it were not necessary to deal with them. The one exception is, however, that officials must know if any concerted and serious disciplinary infractions such as escapes or riots are in the making. The stool-pigeon, in reporting such plans, is a valuable asset to the administration. But the informer who reports that so-and-so is gambling, or stealing food, or cursing the parole board, is held in contempt, even though officials will sometimes take action on his information.

I have stated that informers are predominantly those persons betwixt and between, and responding to the influences of two or more systems of mores. There seem to be five personality types who become stool-pigeons. First, is the man who has never before been in prison but whose dealings in the free world have been shady and unscrupulous, who is weak of character, desirous of personal comforts, socially immature, not closely affiliated with any adult groups, and generally dishonest. Such a type is frequently a forger or confidence man. Second, is the man of previous good standing in his own community, who is in prison for the first time, and who feels as one with officials, and identifies himself with them. Such a man is frequently a banker or business man who has come to prison for embezzlement or larceny. Third, is the man who has been criminalistic in an inadequate, non-professional way for years, who has served many terms in various prisons, who has reached the age when the glamor of life is gone, and who wants security and peace. Such a man may be any type of thief, but usually a burglar. Fourth, is the very young man who is not conditioned to criminality, but who finds himself in a prison, and is pretty overwhelmed by the whole thing; he yearns for home and mother. Such a man may be any type of thief, and is more frequently than not the boy who stole an automobile for a joy ride. Fifth, we have the man who considers that thieves and predatory criminals are the scum of the earth. He is the emotionally controlled, not very intelligent person who is not sure of his status in any group and knows only that he is better than the "real criminals." Such a man is the sex offender, or the man who has murdered during rage. Other general types may also exist. In citing these five general types of inmates who become informers, no reference has been made to motivations, but the reader can be sure that self-interest is basic.

The two following statements are fairly representative of some prisoners' attitudes towards the stool-pigeon system. A good portion of the inmates feel critically towards officials, and their emotions are likely to influence their objectiveness. The writer neither substantiates nor disagrees with the discussions which follow, but presents them simply to portray mental sets which are common.

It has been said by "Old Timers" that there are more stool-pigeons, rats, finks (or whatever name you wish to call them) in this prison than any of their knowledge.

Yes! they are here, and grow in numbers, and will continue just so long as the officials use them and praise them. There isn't a gang, a division or a gallery that hasn't a rat in its midst. When one has done most of his term and becomes a "short-timer," he is usually put outside the walls, but as sure as he does, he has signed the "Honor Sheet" professing henceforth to be a stool-pigeon.

Did I sign it? Yes! I did, but to study the conditions outside the wall. To myself, as some others, it is a mere scrap of paper, and I have signed my name to other things that were only formalities to me. If I felt I could better my conditions, that of lighter work or better eats, etc., that was my business.

In the first place, a prisoner is questioned when he arrives (his second trial). The officials gather from this interview if a fellow will "talk." If he lays blame of his crime on pals and shields himself or if he later goes out to testify in a trial of a pal, you can be assured the officials will soon have this man on a job where they desire inside information.

Many times a good prisoner, after months of incarceration, will try to lighten their work or shorten their term by "stooling."

One example or method is to listen and watch for some rule-breaking, or overhear talk of escapes, etc. They will tell their captain, who in turn informs higher officials, and the lawbreaker is punished. Sometimes a prisoner will interview the warden, or put in a request and get called to the deputy's office where they unfold their stories of some prisoner.

Many of the guards and deputies depend upon their rats for all managements of their gangs. I have heard the guards in groups discuss convicts who stooled and they would praise this man and that man and tell what could be expected of them.

There follow a few examples of "stooling" and the results:

A young man finishing a term of several years, interviews the warden and informs him if he will give him a good job he will clear up a murder case still unsolved by officials in his home city. Promise or no promise by the warden, the story was unraveled and this young man was taken back to the circuit court and there he "squealed," and he, with two other men, supposedly his pals in crime, came to the penitentiary sentenced to thirty years. Upon return the young man again interviewed the warden, and asked for the good job, and he was immediately told to leave the office. The officials had what they wanted—the conviction—now they were through. He was called a rat the prison over and several gave him sound beatings until at last he was afraid for his life in the prison yard and was transferred to another prison.

We have another rat who ran a "speak-easy" when in the streets, and one of the now officials was then a Federal agent, and a good friend of this rat's. When there was to be a raid the agent gave him the "tip-off." Now they meet under different circumstances. The rat is doing a ten-year stretch. He had only been here a short time and was on a good job when he found some civilian clothes hidden where convicts were planning an escape. The rat notified the officials, who lay in wait for the men. Of course they were trapped, caught, and punished. Later, when these men found who had "tipped off" their "plant," they hinted what they would do with the rat, and another rat, overhearing the conversation, warned the first squealer, and he went to solitary for protection and was accommodated with seven days on bread and water. When he was to be released from solitary he was told he had been transferred to another job.

Here he would have been in too much danger, so he refused to come out of solitary and tried to play insane. He was later released from the "hole" and placed as a clean-up man in a building that he never left. He often remarked, "I'll do what I please, and if Deputy ——— comes after me he will let me go." This he did, until he began having trouble with many convicts and was in several fights. Each time both went to solitary and the one man was always transferred, but never him.

At last he had a knifing affair and while in solitary he was told he had been transferred. He said, "Deputy, put that gun to my head and pull the trigger. I am afraid for my life in the yard."

Again he pleaded to be transferred to another prison but was refused. Today he walks about watching the shadows for fear of an assailant.

* * *

. . . The attitude of the average prisoner is illustrated in the following authentic anecdote: A deputy warden was holding "court" to hear reports on prisoners and was giving advice to a young lifer. The deputy was porcine and red-headed, and he used the red hair of the prisoner on trial as an excuse to give some counsel. He said, "If I were a prisoner here I'd keep all the rules. I'd work harder than I was required to work. I'd gain the good will of the guards; I'd shine their shoes if that would help, and I'D HELP THE OFFICIALS BY REPORTING TO MY OFFICER ANYONE WHO BROKE THE RULES. Now, will you promise me to do that?" The prisoner was well aware that he could be dismissed without punishment if he promised, but he merely said, "Deputy, I can't do that." "Why not?" the deputy yelled at him. "Because," said the red-headed lifer, "I'm a man." The inference, of course, is that the deputy was lacking in manhood and he did not fail to draw it.

From the standpoint of the penologists, and from the standpoint of all reasonable prisoners, the stool-pigeon system is necessary in prisons UNLESS some way is found to replace brawn with brains in prison employees. Even if that could be done the rats would still be in prisons, informing on their fellow men. There are tattle-tales in every class in every school, and in every prison there are men who have no scruples or ethical standards. There are many apparent motives for snitching, chief of which is desire for self-advancement at the price of someone else's well-being. Revenge, fear, jealousy, hatred, and nearly every ignoble emotion cause snitching, but the main reason, in my humble opinion is self-interest.

In various capacities within the prison I have had an opportunity to observe the methods of rats and nearly all of them try to adopt a highly moral attitude. This should not, and probably does not, fool the experienced prison official, but as long as stool-pigeon gets a better job, or has his case put before the parole board, or gets an enemy into trouble, or draws attention from his own violations of the rules, or gets immunity, he is not concerned. Even the officials who realize the necessity of using them despise them, but the system goes on, nourished by the weakness and selfishness of men. The most efficient prison official who has come within the scope of my observation never uses information given by stool-pigeons, and he enforces discipline fully as well as any user of such information. Also, he almost invariably warns the would-be informer that he need not expect immunity if he violates the rules.

Stealing from each other and informing officials about one another makes the inmate body look like a sorry situation from an ethical standpoint, and it truly is. In the ideas we have expressed so far, however, one sees evidence that some prisoners abide by the code and have some fidelity towards each other. A few more pointed examples will be helpful.

A few years ago while the lines were forming for supper an inmate named Charles fell into his accustomed place. He had been in conflict with a work associate over some trivial matter which had grown, the men thought, into a matter of great importance. While standing in a line of a hundred inmates, Charles' opponent stabbed him in the neck with a dull knife. The man was hurriedly overpowered by others standing nearby, and the knife taken from him. Charles bled profusely, but with several handkerchiefs the blood was held in check. He marched to the dining-room for supper, and, in spite of becoming faint, managed to get to his cell afterwards. Crude first-aid was administered by his cellmate. The next morning he went to the hospital where thirteen stitches were taken. He told the physician he had accidentally cut himself with a thick piece of glass. Neither Charles nor the inmates who witnessed the affair "squealed" to the officials.

When men have finished serving their punishment in solitary where the only food has been bread and water, the day they are released their group members, or even the most casual associates, will have food and delicacies ready for them as soon as they get out. The food may have been purchased or pilfered from the dining-room.

Cooking in the cell is against regulations but some ingenious electric "cookers" have been fashioned. With them the man may cook eggs, coffee, or anything they may happen to have. The electric lights in the cells at the best are weak. When an improvised electric cooker is being used it further dims the light. When the lights of a certain gallery become dim during the evening, men in adjacent cells do not make complaint, even though their own comfort is disturbed. One man explains, "Even the stool-pigeon will not snitch about other inmates' cooking. Food is that dear in prison."

Later chapters will present other facts which indicate that a type of loyalty exists, to some extent, and that a proportion of the inmates respond to the prison code. At least their behavior, by and large, does not violate the code. We cannot say how many of these men who do not violate the code, would, if the opportunity presented itself. Nor can we say for the free community how many men would, under certain conditions, steal another man's wife.

Some Folkways and Customs

"Folkways are the relatively durable, standardized usages prevailing in a group . . . they are the ways of a folk. Though apparently designed to fill a given need folkways usually arise without prior intention, in the process of living." [7] The folkways are a form of social control insofar as they, in a measure, effect the relations between people, as well as set up techniques of doing things, and show the correct way of behaving. "The folkways are the 'right' ways." [8] "They are made unconsciously." [9] When a folkway becomes more or less permanent, it becomes a custom.

The study of folkways has been most fruitful in the investigation of primitive and, or, isolated social groups. Because our prisoners are neither primitives, nor isolated, we should not expect to find their "ways" to be essentially different than the folkways of that part of America from whence most of them have come. It has been repeatedly pointed out that our prisoners are not a closely knit communal organization, that is, they are not ethnocentric. Groups in which ethnocentrism is strong tend to develop the most distinctive folkways because by so doing they are able to differentiate themselves from others.[10] The inmates, by and large, prefer to identify themselves as members of open communities and this is another reason we should not expect the development of folkways to be unique or peculiar. However, some of the usages give insight into the attitudes and values of the men, and we may discuss them here. The behavior itself, and not the etiology, is what concerns us. Those "ways" which are forced upon the men by the officials are considered in a different light than are the "ways" which spring up among them in what appears to be an automatic manner.

Eating, always important as an occurrence for social habits, is especially so in prison because of the rules and regulations which attend it. Prison food becomes monotonous so inmates endeavor to vary the monotony, and in so doing, both in the dining-room and unofficially in their cells, have developed a number of "ways" in reference to the eating functions. Men are not allowed to talk in the dining-room, although years ago they were allowed to converse with waiters about the food. When officials placed complete restriction on talking they also set up a system of symbols or gestures, the eaters could use when asking for food. In addition to the gestures, officially provided, the men themselves developed qualifying gestures which are supplemented by one-word expressions. Two fingers held aloft mean two slices of bread, but a moving fist means the heel or crust of the bread. Two fingers moved as blades of scissors mean more vegetables. The desire for gravy is represented

---

[7] E. T. Hiller, *op. cit.*, p. 46.
[8] William Graham Sumner, *op. cit.*, p. 28.
[9] *Ibid.*, p. 3.
[10] *Ibid.*, p. 13.

by a hand held flat; when a good portion is wanted, the hand moves downward and vice versa for a small portion, and so on.

Less common in the general dining-room than in smaller dining-rooms or in the cells, is the "poultice." This word is used very commonly and refers to a piece of bread on which two spreads appear: jam and peanut butter, or sugar and mustard, or any number of other amazing combinations. This usage has a utility. These combinations afford needed changes in taste sensations from the perpetually same bill-of-fare. Though this pattern is not unusual in the open community, it is in the nature of a folkway; prisoners learn of it from other prisoners and it suggests, and in a mild way "controls," one way of eating.

Inmates' "ways" of eating are little different than those of other Americans. Their table manners are probably more crude than most, and this is both a result of their pre-penal training and the influence of the immediate environment, and we are told frankly about it:

Table Manners of Inmates

This article can be, and should be, laconic. I suppose you want details, but I'd prefer to describe the manners of the population *en masse,* as Atrocious—with a capital A.

Manners, of course, are customs, but they are also rules to govern men's actions so that offense will not be given to others. Since prisoners are not allowed to talk in the mess-hall, it is hard to be mannerly; one cannot, for example, say "Please pass . . ." or "Excuse me," or "Would you like . . ." Waiters with large tin boxes full of bread pass along the aisles, and those who want it hold up their hands. A clenched fist means that a crust—which is called a "heel"—is desired. Other waiters pass with large pans (rather larger than dishpans, and slightly smaller than tubs) of beans, or cabbage, or "spuds," or very watery fruit, and one says "light" for small portions, "heavy" for large portions, "juice" for the liquid part of beans or spuds or fruit, or "dry" for the same things drained of the soup, or juice. Talking in the mess-hall is an offense which usually calls for a week or so in the "Hole" and that doesn't encourage men to be polite to one another.

Each man, when he goes to his place in the mess-hall, finds a cup, a knife, a fork, and spoon, and an aluminum plate. Six men eat at a table, all facing the front of the mess-hall and the backs of the men at the table in front of them and on each table there are two salt shakers, two pepper shakers, and a vinegar bottle. The aluminum plate must hold all that one eats, and some strange mixtures are the result. Molasses, or syrup, is usually passed for breakfast, and gravy is an invariable item. Many a plate has a lower layer of molasses and a top layer of gravy, with a "weeny" or a "meat ball" like an island in the middle of it all, and those who accept such conditions philosophically will tell you, "Hell!

It all mixes in your gut, anyway." Epicureanism??? Often one finds one's plate (How do you like the impersonal pronoun?) holding a portion of meat, or dressing, or spuds, and if it isn't wanted, the polite way to dispose of it is by pushing it neatly onto the table. Those with bad manners push it onto the floor. When I worked in the messhall I used to HATE those guys! Those who learned to show off their dexterity eat with their knife but few men care to practice the art enough to learn it. Bad manners seem unavoidable, but barbarous habits are unnecessary.

"Across the street"—The Officers' Kitchen—where the "Politicians" eat, the newcomers usually try to impress the regulars with their good manners. They say, "Please pass . . ." or "Do you care for . . . ?" and are very correct. A regular will come in and take his place at the family style table and look around to see what he wants. If anything is out of reach he will catch the eye of the man nearest the food he desires and say, "You blank, blank son of a blank, are you going to eat all that . . . ?" The other man will pass it, and grumble, "You lousy so and so, that's nine times I've passed that to you." If one of the regulars does happen to forget himself and asks a neighbor, "Would you like some of this . . . ?" he is instantly and inevitably told, "You dirty hoosier, don't you think I have eyes?" The words, but not the import of the retort will vary.

Not a folkway, but an amusing incident concerns inmate "X" who found the leg and foot of a mouse in his stew. He complained to a deputy who replied with great sympathy, "What in the hell do you expect, a whole mouse?" Truth or fiction, it is part of the fund of prison yarns.

Foods have different values. Least liked is gravy, and best loved is coffee. The man on the street who enjoys his four cups of coffee a day, and takes it as one of the pleasant little things in life, would be surprised to know the amount of lying, stealing, conniving, and doublecrossing that inmates engage in for "that jamoke." The prison coffee, the men say, is weak, but helpful. The type they like best is strong as lye, and almost as thick. With the aid of a "cooker" in the cells, or by a unique use of steam radiators in some shops, many gallons are "brewed" each day. Some of the coffee used is stolen from the general supply. Some is smuggled in. One man, recently killed by the police after an escape, said, "We'll get it one way or another." He told of fashioning a hollow tube one inch in diameter which he inserted into a burlap sack containing one hundred pounds of regular prison coffee, and by agitating the sack, he was able to siphon out a pound or so. This man was a semi-trustie and clerk who, through fair means or foul, gained access to the supply room. Some coffee is smuggled in by trusties who trade it in for a profit. A pound which would sell for fifteen cents outside will bring fifty cents in the prison.

We have already mentioned that the men construct ingenious

electric cookers. They also soak rags in the oil which collects around the machinery in the shops then place it in a can and in that way boil water. A few inmates will occasionally "connect" for eggs and bacon and fry them in their cells. Cold water can be boiled in a few minutes by using steam in the radiator, and eggs are hard boiled in this manner. Cooking, of course, is against the rules. The guards are watchful. A mirror system, similar in principle to the periscope, is sometimes used. The mirror is projected a few inches from the cell door so that the men can see the approach of the guard as he walks along the gallery. The occasional "shake-downs" of cells always yield a number of various kinds of "cookers." The officials punish violation of the food rules, but an unspoken understanding frequently exists. The cup of coffee in the cell provides for the inmates one of the more pleasant diversions of an otherwise dulling situation. Watchfulness, in order to avoid detection, arouses enough tenseness to make the situation interesting. The number of men who have a great desire for coffee is high, but the number who are able to prepare it individually is small. There is considerable generosity evidenced when two cellmates will divide their quart of coffee with two other men in an adjacent cell.

Where choices are limited we cannot expect a great diversity in folkways. The patterns which we label as folkways are also, sociologically, examples of communication, relationships, group interaction, responses to a dominating group, the playing of rôles by personalities, and so forth. If the subject-matter of each chapter is covered as comprehensively as our material permits, it is inevitable that there will be overlapping. Thus, in other chapters folkways become evident just as in this chapter on social control other phenomena enter.

In prison most inmates wear the same kind of clothes. A few trusties or "politicians" wear white shirts, which is allowed because visitors frequently see them. Fashions in clothes are revealing of the values and attitudes of a people. The cultural anthropologist in his study of primitive tribes gleans much insight from head-dress, etc. There is indication that the female's short skirt in post-war America was symptomatic of certain social ideations and changes. In the prison the casual observer sees 2,300 men dressed practically alike, yet some social habits in the nature of folkways exist. The caps which are furnished resemble those worn by railroad engineers except they are of heavier material. It is not in the folkways that these shall be worn straight upon the head. Nearly always the cap is tipped at a slight angle. This seems trivial and it probably is, but the writer has seen new men, who, when they enter the prison, stand for many minutes before the few mirrors which exist, and try on their caps in different ways. They have quickly observed the folkway and are being controlled by it. Also, the men prefer, and if possible obtain, pants that are reasonably tight in the buttock.

There seems to be a dichotomy in the matter of dress. About one-third of the inmates make efforts towards meticulousness, and the balance seem to make efforts towards shabbiness. There is some correlation here between meticulousness of dress and class assignment. As in Middletown, one of the uses of wearing apparel is to gain recognition.[11] To the few who dress well, clothes are compensatory. An inmate says:

The Well-Dressed Con

The well-dressed "con" may be thought of in two ways. First: If it were compulsory by the prison rules to keep neat and clean, shoes shined, etc., I believe it would work to the betterment of the institution, as well as the prisoner. The rules of a prison should conform as nearly as possible to the rules of the military. Military rules compel a soldier to keep a neat appearance and the soldier is furnished fatigue or work clothes to help him to do this, all of which creates greater respect for discipline and will instill in the young man a desire toward orderliness and cleanliness in his future life.

If a man is allowed to live in a slovenly or slip-shod manner, he may acquire the habit no matter what his early training may have been. Once acquiring this habit, he is very apt to look upon the laws of his country in a slip-shod manner, or with disrespect.

Secondly: The well-dressed con in an institution where the above-mentioned rules are not in effect often creates a feeling of jealousy in the prisoner who is unable to afford or manage to have clean clothes, outside underwear, and other things that are not furnished by the state, but are allowed by the prison officials. This feeling of jealousy will make the dressed-up con's time much harder, for there are men in these institutions who will stoop to anything to cause him trouble.

There are classes of the American who will keep neat and clean regardless of where they are or what trouble they incur in doing so.

Considering all phases of this question it is but a matter of living conditions and there are but few Americans who will not avail themselves of the best that the situation will allow, especially so if they have been taught cleanliness in their childhood.

There is much talk by the prisoners of the clothes they wore before coming to prison. Apparel is an item of considerable importance to the delinquent personality. A man who before incarceration was only moderately concerned with clothes soon becomes aware that if he is unable, in certain groups, to talk interestingly and knowingly about clothes, he will not be included. Thus the

[11] Robert and Helen Lynd, *op. cit.*, pp. 160–161.

ex-farm hand or the mechanic will spend hours pouring over fashion magazines or mail-order catalogues, in search of the exact width of the braid in full-dress trousers, the number of buttons on a dinner jacket, the shape of lapels on the business coat, and so forth. He familiarizes himself with such details because other men have knowledge of these facts and he is controlled by a pattern in the community.

Inmates, like everyone else, are interested in their bodies. Though they abuse them for pleasure, such as drinking, they take an interest in keeping as fit as possible in prison. The thirty-year-old whose hair is thinning or becoming gray is much concerned. "Lookit what this place is doing to me; I'll look like an old man when I get out." An effort to maintain health and growth of hair, for example, is seen in a type of folkway existent in some shops. Two inmates will coöperate in rubbing and massaging each other's scalps. Men whose scalps had never been massaged before see, when they come to the prison, the existence of this usage and fall into the practice quite naturally. Experiments in the treatment of the hair by oils and medicines is not uncommon. Men working on the farms experimented with a substance used for mange on hogs, and it was rumored that the treatment was successful. Knowledge of this spread outside the prison walls and a medical student wrote to the warden thus:

> Dear Sir:
> I am a friend of ——— of ———, and am studying medicine. It has come to my attention that a remedy for *mange on hogs* has been used in your institution to successfully grow human hair in certain cases of baldness among the inmates. I would like to buy a sample of this from you to test, or please send me the name of the company that makes this so I may buy a sample there.

Body interest is also shown by the desire to become suntanned during the summer. The aesthetic aspect is only slightly more important than the realization that sunlight contains vitamin *B* which is healthful. At one time inmates who worked in the quarry were allowed on warm summer days to remove their shirts. The sight of several hundred men stripped to the waist and with various shades of tan led the warden to say that the quarry was a regular summer resort. Body interest may also be shown by the non-laboring inmates who manicure their nails. Sometimes hours are spent with crudely fashioned wooden nail files. Before entering prison the majority of the men who engage in this activity were satisfied with an occasional nail cleaning, but when they came to prison they adopted the practice already existent.

Numerous other social habits exist arising among the men themselves or prescribed by the officials who, of course, are also controlled in a degree of folkways. It is unnecessary to go further into this topic now. We have not stated how completely or what proportion of the men are controlled, because we do not know. It seems, however, that there is much differentiation. Some work units have folkways and customs that others do not have. Among the informal groups, differences exist. The same man may behave in accordance with the folkways at one time, and not at another. It is these inconsistencies which prompted the earlier statement that our study in this chapter would be an inspection of patterns that were in the *nature of,* or similar to, social controls.

Dogma

We use this term not in a specific sociological sense but as a word to describe mental sets or attitudes held by a large proportion of the inmates. Dogmas are opinionated tenets. They are beliefs, unobjective and emotional. They exist in spite of the data from which they are supposed to arise. They are in the nature of social controls because they are influential in shaping attitudes. For example, the new inmate hears, during his first few months of incarceration, some twenty men denounce the parole board. The members are referred to as crooks, politicians, and dumbbells. The men who make such statements have no reliable data. They may make use of a single incident which, as they view it, gives evidence of unfairness, and enlarge upon the situation, coloring their statements with the emotion which arises over their own plight. Criticisms of the parole board are widespread, and the inmates who had no marked attitudes when they entered the community soon come to share in and possess the fairly common dogma. Another idea which may be termed dogma is the prevalent conception that all government officials are grafters and corrupt. A certain toleration may exist for grafting by police, prosecutors, and judges, but there is no toleration of anything approaching what the inmates think is graft among prison officials. When the newspapers report that a government official has been found to be dishonest, the inmates assume that all government officials are dishonest. This is in the nature of dogma; there is emotional belief but no analysis of the data. Common expressions by inmates are, "If I'd had two C's ($200) I'd never hit this can," or, "A grand ($1,000) in the right spot and I could have had the city hall, but I didn't have no fall-dough, and I couldn't get in touch with Johnny." The instances of corruption in the law enforcement agencies which the inmates know to have existed are *prima facie* evidence to them that all members of such agencies can be bought. "Every man has his price," they say.[12]

In the nature of dogma s the fairly prevalent attitude of hate and distrust for all penal officials. This phenomenon is tied up, of course, with the prisoners' code. Some guards will treat a new inmate in a kindly and friendly fashion. The new inmate responds, but when, at every hand, he hears other inmates curse and condemn the officials, he questions his own judgment and eventually, in a large number of cases, accepts the inmate doctrine. Thus he is controlled; hazy, indefinite opinions become attitudes.

The most important thing in the world is money, the inmates say, and they believe it. "Why, hell, with money you can do anything—live in the best flats, drive those low, racy cars, get yourself 'broad' after 'broad,' get into the best clubs, and clothes. You'd be surprised how an eighty-dollar suit makes me look, and a nice, gray, snap-brim hat. . . . You can take all your education and stick it in your sock—just give me the 'potatoes,' that's all I want. Let's see, just with fifty 'G's' a man can live pretty well." Money is the universal solvent, in the prisoners' thinking, money for luxuries, for comforts, for status. The unsophisticated inmates who never dreamt of wealth or luxuries and whose low financial standings were calmly accepted, become gradually accustomed to thinking of money as the most important thing in life. The acceptance of this attitudinal configuration is a step in the process of prisonization. The existence and prevalence of the configuration indicates that it is held as a dogma, and such dogma is influential as social control. We are not implying in this discussion that dogmas are common to prisoners alone. Prejudice which gives rise to dogmatic beliefs is widespread the world over, but some dogmas have a beneficial social utility. It seems, however, that the dogma of prisoners is harmful to themselves and to society. It tends to weld them together and to shape their behavior, but the unanimity which arises from sharing dogmas is broken down by more powerful forces, though the dogmas persist in individuals and upon release play havoc with stable adjustments.

Some Other Social Controls and Controlling Devices

Strictly speaking, the prison community has no folk lore. Basically, the prisoners are not a folk, nor are the tales and doggerel which have lived for years in the prison a lore. However, some of the data we present here are instrumentalities making for the control of behavior. A poem may have more effect on an inmate's personality, for example, than a speech by the warden. The legend of

---

[12] Victor Nelson, *op. cit.,* pp. 205–206. The same general phenomenon is reported for an eastern prison.

a "yegg man" may be more of a behavior determinant than the chaplain's Sunday sermon. The "folk-song" may make a greater impression on the prisoner than an eight-to-one decision by the Supreme Court. Songs and doggerel, rhymes and yarns, are a part of the culture; they are, as well, a carrier of culture. Compared with their influence in primitive tribes they are negligible, but many forms of folklore become negligible on the American scene. In a prison official restrictions retard their expansion. Impersonalization prohibits effectiveness. Nor must we think that the "folklore" of prison is unique, though it is frequently colored by prisoner influence. Most of the ideas passed from man to man, year through year, are crude and vulgar. That they remain, however, is evidence of their strength. A few examples will serve to represent the hundreds of items which are similar to folk-lore.

The Boston Burglar

I was born in Boston
A city you all know well.
Brot up by honest parents
The truth to you I'll tell.

Brot up by honest parents
And watched most tenderly
'Till I became a roving boy
At the age of twenty-three.

For Burglarizing I was taken
And then was sent to jail.
My friends they came to bail me out
But it was of no avail.

The judge then read my sentence
The clerk, he wrote it down,
And said, "For seven long, weary years
You're going to Charlestown."

To see my aged father
Come pleading at the bar!
To see my aged mother
A pulling at her hair!

Yes, pulling at those gray locks, my boy,
And the tears came streaming down.
Said she, "My son, my son, what have you done!
You're going to Charlestown."

They put me aboard an eastbound train
One cold December day.
And every station that we passed
I heard the people say:

There goes the Boston Burglar
In iron he is bound down!
For the robbing of the Boston Bank
He's going to Charlestown."

There is a girl in Boston,
I know she loves me well,
If ever I gain my liberty
'Tis with this girl I'll dwell.

If ever I gain my liberty,
Bad company I will shun.
I'll bid adieu to nite walking
And also drinking rum.

Come all you jolly fellows
A warning take of me
Never go night walking
And shun bad company.

For if you do you'll surely rue
And you'll be sent like me
For robbing of the Boston Bank
To the penitentiary.

Convict's Nite

While shades of nite came down ka-plunk,
A convict lay upon his bunk,
And wondered what made him so sore
Every time he turned his body o'er.
Excelsior!

His bed, it seemed was filled with rocks,
His pillow stuffed with concrete blocks,
His flesh was bruised, his limbs were bent,
But that damn mattress showed no dent.
Excelsior!

Oh, can it be the young man said
That they put scrap iron in my bed?
Now it was softer than I ween
He ripped the tick and there he seen
Excelsior!

They found him there one foggy day
All wrapped and twisted as he lay
Each lifeless hand still grasped a tuft
Of that with which his bed was stuffed—
Excelsior!

Many prisoners are familiar with the type of ballad of which "Frankie and Johnnie" is representative. A goodly number of items in Carl Sandburg's *Songbag* are known to the men. No less common is the doggerel, familiar in every bar-room.

Choose Your Company

It was early in September
Or perhaps it was in November
I was walking down the street
In drunken pride.
When my knees began to stutter
And I fell down in the gutter
And a pig came up
And laid down by my side.
A lady passed that way,
And I chanced to hear her say,
"You can tell a man that boozes
By the company he chooses,"
And the gol-darned pig
Got up and ran away.

A smiling Negro says that twenty variations of the following "poem" have been known for many years to gamblers in prison. It has a number of verses, a few of which we present here:

Gentlemans, do you see this here razor?
I had it sharpened just today.
I'm going to tell you some brand new rules,
Now follow them while we play.

Keep your hands above the table
While you're dealing, please.
And don't be sticking aces
Down between your knees.
Don't be dealing from the bottom
Because it looks too rough.
Remember, gentlemans, when playing poker
Five cards is enough.

Don't be makin' funny signs,
And tipping off your hands.
And don't be talkin' language here
That I don't understand.

"That Gal Lil," "The Face on the Barroom Floor," and "Parley Vous" are representative of other poems and songs. During the long hours in the cells, inmates attempt to write parodies on the better-known verses in which they include items of local significance. They also put words to familiar songs, as in the following which is sung to the tune of "Old Solomon Levi."

The Stranger

I'm a stranger in your city,
  My name is Paddy Flynn.
I got drunk the other nite,
  The coppers took me in
I had no friends to go my bond,
  No friends to pay my bail.
So they stuck me here for thirty days,
  In the county jail.

The only friend that I had there
  Was happy sailor Jack,
He told me of all the jobs he'd done
  And all the safes he'd cracked.
He cracked them in Nevada
  And he'd robbed the Western Mail.
Oh, I bless the day I got away
  From the ——— County jail.

Elsewhere in this book are further illustrations of the manner in which verse and doggerel tend to control the thinking, and subsequently the attitudes and behavior, of inmates.

The legends of prison concern both officials and felons, yet while they deal with persons they would not have persisted if they had not associated the persons with whom they deal with an important aspect of the culture. Legends are stories which illustrate a social process. The legendry of prison is probably less important as a factor of social control than is the legendry of a small town or a nation. George Washington cut down a cherry tree and bravely confessed when he was caught, has been an important educating substance for building character and patriotism in boyhood. "Slasher," a very criminalistic inmate of a decade or so ago, held one guard in one hand, kicked another down with his foot, grabbed a third in another hand, and bumped their heads together. We don't know, really, whether or not George Washington never told a lie, nor do we know for sure that "Slasher" man-handled three guards. Legends are not necessarily true to fact. They illustrate a principle: honesty, in the case of Washington; courage and anti-administration attitudes in the case of "Slasher." They serve as a means and a form of social control because they set up standards of behavior.

Most of the legends in the prison community deal with persons who have evidenced traits which are held in esteem by the majority of inmates. In the next chapter we will discuss escapes. We will learn that the stories surrounding a good many of the escapers are of a legendary character. Legends also deal with the pre-penal experiences of thieves. The "pete man" or "yegg man" is a vanishing type. Such thieves were the ones who opened small safes by glycerine, dynamite, or fingering. In the last ten years most safes have become tamper proof because of tool-proof steel, time locks, and so forth. "Yegg men" have no field of activity and their previous performances are becoming legendary. One legend deals with a pair of men who burrowed underground for eighty feet to gain access to a safe and procured several thousand dollars. They made their get-away safely, but within a week spent all the money in riotous living. Somehow or other, they were suspected of the crime and were arrested in the city near the small town where the theft had been committed. They were tried and acquitted and a large factor in convincing the jury of their purported innocence was their impoverished condition when arrested. Twelve true citizens could not conceive of two men spending several thousand dollars in a week. This legend points out the principle accepted by many thieves: Get it and spend it; easy come, easy go; a week of supreme pleasure is worth a few months of labor; let tomorrow take care of itself. Legends of similar nature concern bank robbers and confidence men.

Legends may also concern officials. In the case of "bad" officials the legends show what officers should not do, and in the case of "good" officials the legends show behavior of which the inmates approve. A "bad" official was "The Snake." The stories concerning him are alive with brutality and hypocrisy. A "good" official was "M" who was not a "pencil pusher," who walked away to avoid reporting a man, who defended the convicts before his superiors, and who, the legend says, would handle an "underground kite" occasionally if it did not threaten serious situations such as escapes or riots. Legends in prison also deal with small, informal groups. Stories are related which show how such-and-such men clung together under disintegrating situations. The unconscious utility of such stories is obvious.

Taboos are prohibitions which, in primitive tribes, carried a religious sanction. We wish to use the term less strictly here. It applies in prison generally to one phenomenon, only: syphilis. Except for syphilis almost nothing is taboo. Inmates, it seems, have an unreasoning fear of syphilis and persons who are infected with it are taboo. They are not to be touched and are frequently avoided completely, if infectious. About 10 per cent of our prisoners have the disease, but all are under treatment and not infectious. Men who are infected endeavor to keep it secret, but this is next to impossible because treatment demands a visit to the hospital and the patient's associates come to know why he makes the regular visits. The taboo of syphilitics is related to the health-ideal, noted earlier. The taboo affects relationships among prisoners and is important to us for that reason. A man with an acute gonorrhea is generally taboo, although less studiedly avoided than the syphilitic. As a matter of fact, he is much more likely to cause infection in others than is the luetic. Fear of syphilis exists also, of course in the general population. The reaction of the inmates is not surprising when one considers that a former colleague of the writer places a syphilitic inmate whom he is to interview four feet further from his desk than the man who is not infected.

Gossip is a device for controlling people. We shall discuss this topic later and will simply point out its essential factors here. It exists throughout the community but is effective, if at all, only in the informal groupings. A man who works in the quarry cares nothing for what the clerks in the front office say about him. He cares in a mild way what other quarry workers say about him, and most of all, what his primary group affiliates say about him. The situation in prison is similar to that of the city apartment house. Gossip may exist in a mild degree, but it doesn't control the subjects it concerns. Its substance is largely entertainment for the persons who use it. Gossip, of course always deals with personalities, and officials are not immune. If inmate gossip controls officials at all, it does so only occasionally. An official heard, through informers, how much he was disliked. He made some effort to increase the respect of the men and was, for a transitory period, successful. Gossip has been defined as, ". . . essentially a heterogeneous assortment of local facts and fancies about personal qualities and relations, largely vulgar and often vicious, communicated first of all through primary groups." [13] "Gossip is copious, and tends to occupy the mind without exertion; it is emotional and deals with personalities; it is untrustworthy." [14] These statements of Professor Lumley apply to the gossip which exists among prisoners.

Name-calling, flattery, praise, and superstition, especially among Negroes, are techniques of social control. They are effective in the main, however, only within the primary, semi-primary, or

[13] F. E. Lumley, *Means of Social Control,* The Century Co., New York, 1925, pp. 211–236.

[14] *Ibid.,* pp. 235–236.

interest groups, and differ only in degree as they are used in open communities. Name-calling, because so common, has not the same effectiveness among convicts as with other persons. Some of the names which inmates call one another, if used outside prison would be cause enough for fights, but in prison are for the most part passed off, or ignored, and only occasionally result in open conflict.

Though not a social control the weather is a factor which influences social relations. In an earlier chapter the reader was told how the morning fogs change the routine of the day and how on the occasion of a cloud burst and small flood, an uncommon degree of sympathetic relations developed. More important than these atypical incidents, because more frequent, are the dull, drab days of clouded skies. We are told about such an influence by an inmate observer:

Dull, Drab Days and Convict Temperament

"Misery loves company" may hold a world of truth for anybody—but not with your convict.

Living in a world of mental and, at times, physical misery, a prisoner's mind is easily influenced by any external phenomenon that will remind, and is reminiscent of his drab existence. Study a convict whenever Old Man Weather blankets the heavens with a depressing, slate--colored hue; a solid somberness that is broken only by sparsely scattered clouds that are thin, straggly, and sick-looking; clouds whose full-bodied and robust puffiness of a day, or an hour ago have wasted away and are now nothing but stringy streaks of whitish-grey vapor. The whole is a funeral sight. And this funeral view, a drab, chilled-looking and unfriendly-looking sky does work a depressing effect on prisoners. Ask one, on such a day, why he is looking so forlorn, so glum, and your answer will be something like this: "I dunno. I just ain't feelin' right."

Surrounded on all sides by architectural atrocities, unbroken ugliness, the mind directs the eyes to a more pleasing sight which is ever open for one's vision. And the only beautiful sight that tends to brighten up the drabness of their existence is an open expanse of sunny skies overhead, eye restful, soothing as a balm, and unlike an earthly view, seldom propelling the mind to longing flights of freedom. The sky is infinite space; no roads in sight, no gleaming rails to provoke a longing for New York, Chicago, Kansas City, or, for that matter, Oshkosh. But on the other hand, when drab, bleak, cheerless days blanket a prison, a kind of softening influence is gone. It is then that the drab day brings out for him and makes him fully consicous of the drabness that is evidenced on every side of him.

Misery loves company, but your convict does not want miserable days, days that will accentuate and remind him of the drab existence that he is ekeing out within shadows cast by penitentiary walls.

Some of the subjects we have discussed in this chapter are of negligible importance now, but a hundred years hence investigators might wish to look back at the quaint correctional institutions of the twentieth century to learn the standards which existed, the ways in which things were done and even the doggerel which occupied the minds of the people housed in the institutions. In another sense the processes under consideration here are important because they shape men's attitudes and affect relationships and suggest not only what is common in prison but what is common in at least certain strata of American life.

CHAPTER VIII

The Dominant Group and Social Control

A prisoner speaks: "In my opinion those inexpensive-looking solitary cells have, through overuse and abuse, cost the state more money than the new cellhouse. I know that the memory of one night spent in them and the 'throw-'em-in-the-hole' policy of this and other administrations has embittered me as no other prison experience has ever done. What, then, happens to the subject who was brutal before ever being in the hole?"

As indicated, this chapter is to deal with punishment, or the threat of punishment in its aspects of control. It is doubtful if we can offer anything new in this regard except to present the local situation. Since our compendium would be incomplete without references to disciplinary problems, we shall cite some and they will serve also to exhibit individual attitudees of selected prisoners. Punishment is as old as society. Our ancestors used it with as little lasting effect as we use it now. Its evolution from torture to the use of impersonal force has been slow.[1] The aim of the group which inflicts punishment is control, and they use punishment when there is evidence of a decided divergence and hostility on the part of members of a subordinate group.[2] A fight between two men may involve some of the ordinary objectives of punishment (expiation, retribution, deterrence, reformation) but such a conflict usually results from personal-social relationships. But when a policeman or prison guard in his official capacity as a representative of the governing body punishes a man, society itself is involved in its historical, political, economic, and sociological phases. We stress this fact to emphasize the complexity of a social relation which is seldom analyzed, but taken for granted.[3] The punishment of prison and the punishment within prison has become more impersonal and less vicious during the last two decades than formerly, although the first reforms in prisons themselves, that is, those that occurred in the latter part of the seventeenth century, were more progressive, considering the times, than most reforms since. And the *Zeitgeist*

---

[1] See F. E. Lumley, *op. cit.*, pp. 363–394.
[2] *Ibid.*, pp. 368–369.
[3] See Edwin H. Sutherland, *op. cit.*, Chapters XVI, XVII, pp. 298–348.

is important in considering prison conditions. Professor Sutherland points out:

> The methods of treatment of criminals have varied in content from time to time and place to place. They show a general tendency to be consistent with the culture. Two centuries ago, criminals were disembowled, quartered, hung in chains, branded, pilloried, ducked, and in other ways mutilated and shamed. That was a culture in which physical suffering was regarded as the natural lot of mankind, and in which the means of preventing pain were not well developed. Today, safeguards against physical suffering have been provided in other fields and a policy of physical torture of criminals cannot be harmonized with the general interest in the reduction of suffering.[4]

The fact that torture methods are used by police occasionally, and the fact that prison officials occasionally find it necessary to administer brutal punishment, does not destroy the general trend of "improved" methods of punishment. It is only a few years ago (1927) that, in our state, men sentenced to death were hung by the neck until dead—a barbaric method. Electrocution is the present method, and it will probably be another ten or twenty years before capital punishment is done away with altogether. So, in answer to the inmate who opened this chapter, we can only say that we admit to the awfulness of solitary confinement, and we admit that punishment heaped upon punishment is productive of further antisociality, expense, and tragedy, but conditions are better than they were, perhaps, and social inventions develop slowly. It is an unfortunate, but seemingly unavoidable thing, as our society and prison are organized, that inmates do not conduct themselves in such a way that punishment will be unnecessary. Inmates, being conditioned as they have, behave "naturally" when they attempt to escape or break the prison rules. Similarly, the attitudes and behavior of guards towards punishment is "natural" being conditioned as *they* have. We obviously cannot expect perfection in anything in which human material is involved. We must depend only on a slow, gradual, "improvement" in the relationships between convict and keeper, which will occur simultaneously and with the same rate of speed that honesty and socialization come to characterize the relations among people in a free community. It is unreasonable and illogical to expect guards to be more social in their thinking than the communities and interest-groups which produce them. The one hope is in the modifiability of human nature.

In our prison there is nothing unique in the manner of discipline

---

[4] *Ibid.*, p. 316.

or in the analysis we can make of it.[5] The occasional atavism is matched, no doubt, in other prisons and in the free world as well. Guards do not possess the reformer's zeal. They have their own lives to live; they have their own little frustrations, sorrows, and tragedies, and few people, guards included, have a "sense of state." The personality problems of employees in prison may be quite as serious as those of the inmates with whose care they are charged. The student of social science does not hate a stupid, brutal guard, just as he does not hate the feeble-minded rapist. For the betterment of society both need to be controlled, but the point of view must be kept objective. Perspective is everything.

In discussing the official social controls we will first inspect the rules and the relationships between the dominant group of officialdom and the subordinate group of inmates. Next we will consider the violation of rules, including the escape patterns, and follow with a description of punishment and point out other factors pertinent to the maintenance of discipline.

The Rules and the Dominant Group

With only slight changes the same body of rules have been in use for over fifteen years. Excepting those ordinances which deal with the cleanliness of the institution, the basic thought in every rule is to prevent riots and escapes. The attitude of the officials that the essential purpose of the prison is incapacitation is traditional. When new officials take office they are in communication for weeks or months with the employees they are to replace. This is sufficient time to indoctrinate the neophyte employee. Even if the tradition was not transferred from officer to officer, newly appointed workers would hold to the orientation that the purpose of prison is incapacitation and retribution, having assimilated these ideations from a society in which they are prevalent. In the book of special rules for employees the first words in Article I are, "Discipline is the first and highest consideration in the prison. . . ." Though the laws and the amendments to laws in our state which deal with the prison system include ideas indicating that reformation should be a policy of penal administrations, it is safe to say

[5] The reader who wishes a well-rounded knowledge of the history and policies of prison discipline will find valuable references in the following: Thorsten Sellin, *A Brief Guide to Penological Literature,* The Annals of the American Academy of Political and Social Sciences; *Prisons of Tomorrow,* edited by Edwin H. Sutherland and Thorsten Sellin, Philadelphia, 1931, pp. 225–232; selected bibliographies in the text books of Edwin H. Sutherland, *op. cit.,* John Gillin, *op. cit.,* and Fred E. Haynes, *op. cit.* Valuable insight may be gained from *Wall Shadows* and *Osborne of Sing Sing,* by Frank Tannenbaum, and *Society and Prisons* and *Within Prison Walls,* by T. M. Osborne, to mention only a few.

that less than five per cent of the employees ever consider the reformative aspect. The warden, perhaps, and a physician here and there may be concerned with means and methods of reformation, but the thought is utterly foreign to the average guard. A high official once said to the writer, "I want to break up the monotony of these men as much as possible." Decent as his attitude was, it is doubtful if the officer was thinking in terms of reformation. His probable thought was: the less monotony the less restlessness, and the less restlessness the less chance of attempted escapes. The writer does not disagree, of course, with the importance of incapacitation. We are simply endeavoring to show that it is the only consideration in the minds of most employees. The high officials naturally want their institution to show a profit from industries, and they want it to be clean and orderly. The better officials want the inmates to be as comfortable as possible, but basic to everything is discipline. Blind obedience is desired.

Discipline is maintained by the laws of the state and the rules of the institution. The statutes provide the skeleton framework for the operation of the penitentiary and set up as well, the machinery with which the laws are made effective. The rules of the institution are not laws, but have the same general controlling force because the administrative body which determines the rules is composed of public officials. Some disciplinary infractions by inmates are violations of both law and rule. An attempt to kill on the part of a prisoner calls for action by the state's attorney in the county wherein the prison is located, and such an offense also calls for action by prison officials. The inmates refer to this as "double trouble." If officials were so inclined, they might prefer larceny charges in a circuit court against the inmate who steals a ham from the kitchen.

The machinery of discipline includes not only the laws and rules and the dominant group who enforce them, but the material objects through which they are made effective: the walls, the guns, the bars, the uniform of the officials, and so on: At every hand the inmate is impressed with the power of official controls. The walls are high and strong. The gates and doors are heavily barred. When the walls are low and the exits poorly constructed, as is the case in some prisons, the inmates contemplate escape and plot to that end, and attitudes inimical to adjustment and reformation arise. The sight of a guard on a tower with a gun always clutched in one hand is a strong preventive of escapes.

The rigidity of prison discipline is traditional and is rooted in a number of historical, psychological, and politico-social conditions. An analysis of the major principles from which strict discipline has arisen is made by Sutherland.[6] We can do no better than summarize his analysis here, as it is apropos to our local situation.

First, rigid discipline was originally based, in part, on a psychology (which we no longer accept) which holds that when a habit is formed by compulsion it continues after the compulsory stimuli are removed. Thus, it was believed that if the prisoners were conditioned to do hard labor in prison, the motor habits established would continue upon release. Alas, human nature is not so simply changed.

Secondly, the type of work and the long hours of prison employees virtually preclude their forming many of the ordinary social relations so common in free communities. The rule which prescribes that officers should not become intimate with prisoners sets up a barrier in developing positive relationships and securing social satisfactions during the majority of their long work day. But by dominance over a helpless group, prison workers are able to tickle their egos and obtain some satisfaction through the power of authority. It is more than amusing to observe a few prison guards who, all through their lives, have been in a subordinate position, loudly command a cowed, helpless inmate to perform such and such an act. Prison life reveals conditioning.

Thirdly, a considerable proportion of employees have a spirit of retaliation towards inmates, and such an attitude has been bred in the personal-social interaction within their own personal group life, or results from broader culture pressures. Common remarks of guards are: "I hate those goddam niggers," or "You can never trust any of 'em; they'd cut your throat and never give it a second thought," or, "I seen the day when we'd take a con like that and whip him until there was no fight left in him." An assistant deputy once remarked before twenty other officials, "I tried to kill him (a rebellious inmate) but he wouldn't die; I didn't want him to be around here."[7] While such attitudes may seem horrible they are fairly common, and the student must realize that they are reflections of the attitudes of society which have become somewhat exaggerated as prison officials observe the conduct of inmates year after year. These sentiments are not a whit less understandable than the revenge-laden mouthings of public officials such as states's attorneys who hold office by the will of the majority.

The fourth general principle, and probably the most important one making for rigidity of discipline, refers to escapes. Whatever else it aims to be, a prison must be enough of a prison to keep men from running away.[8] Between most prisoners and their keepers

---

[6] Edwin H. Sutherland, *op. cit.*, pp. 412–415.
[7] Stated on March 17, 1933.
[8] Sanford Bates, *op. cit.*, p. 191.

there is basic conflict: the inmates "want out," and their warders want to keep them in. Escapes are important, not only because the public questions the strength of the state, or because felons who break loose are likely to engage in further crime, but escapes are important to officials because political prestige may be involved. The opposition newspapers point critical fingers at a state administration, including the governor, whose appointed warden allows escapes. It is frequently implied that graft and dishonesty exist, so officials keep rigid discipline to avoid escapes and maintain prestige. Prison scandals may mean loss of votes, and too many lost votes mean lost jobs. Incidentally, we have grave doubts if the press can sway many votes on account of prison scandals, but, even so, publishers keep pounding at the problem and are not always careful to stick to facts.

Three of the four principles we have cited which explain most of the strict disciplinary features in prison, refer to the personalities and attitudes of the officers. As we have said, the behavior of officers is a reflection of societal opinion, and as such, we cannot "blame" guards themselves for their orientation. Prisoners generally hate the officials, but, as a rule, the inmates see only one side of the officer's life. The guard who is an unbending, strict, and harsh disciplinarian during the long day, may be a sympathetic, understanding citizen among other citizens at night. The fact that relationships among guards themselves is as decent as most relationships among any people, is indicative of the dichotomy, or the dual rôle they play between their work life and non-work life. And there is no denying the fact, even though one takes the position of philosophical determinism, that inmates are not a gentle, easily-managed folk. The soft-voice-and-the-big-stick idea doesn't always work, as our penitentiaries are organized. Prisoners "want out." Many of them have nothing to lose. They will take desperate chances, and an understanding of determinism will not, in the situations as they exist, prevent occasional chaos. Our prisoners have not abided by the laws in a less restricted milieu than that of the prison, and it cannot be expected that they will conduct themselves peacefully in confinement. We must admit with Lawes that, "All prison administration savors of the nature of despotism. . . ."[9]

Some wardens and higher officials of penitentiaries have reasonably decent social motives. They are well paid in contrast to underlings and have prestige. Although they carry the responsibility, their work is essentially pleasing to them. The warden may have the responsibility, but he isn't discharged when an escape occurs. But some guard is. The guards do the hard work and in times of

[9] Lewes Lawes, *op. cit.*, p. 106.

trouble the buck is passed to them. A warden in another state, commenting upon the types of guards sent to him, said, "They have, instead of any elemental devotion to duty, the desire to know but three things—'When do we eat, when do we quit, and when do we get paid.' "[10] The same comments might well apply to the guards of our prison, but it is not an uncommon attitude among the uneducated workers in any field which offers a salary of around a hundred dollars a month in a job which lacks the means of satisfying basic social wishes. Let us observe the attitudes of some prisoners concerning their keepers:

The Worm Turns

I am not sure that any worm ever did really turn, but if you will take time out to follow me through these pages you shall be shown an imitation of the pure McCoy in worm turning.

I who have served sentence in three state prisons and am now whittling away on a fourteen-year jolt in a fourth, will assume the rôle of worm. You could play the part as convincingly as I, if you, too, had been finger-printed, questioned, psycho-analyzed, "case-stuffed," and impaled upon the scientific pin for microscopic examination as often. These processes serve to disrupt one's morale until he has a fellow feeling for worms in general.

To society, I and my fellow inmates are absorbing problems. Did it ever occur to you that you "outsiders" are even more perplexing propositions to us? Your servants, the prison officials, having told you all the inside stuff about convicts, this squishy old numbered worm will now crawl out of the bait-can and talk back, giving you some dope about individual, but typical "screws," then paint a word picture of "The Composite Screw." To save quotation marks and clarify my meaning: The screw to whom I refer is an alleged human who acts as guard in prison and whose vocation demands that he turn a key rapidly, with screw-like motion. Thus the moniker.

Before dealing with this lower form of animal life I must tell you about some "brass-collars" (wardens and their deputies) who have cost the American people many dollars. Incidentally, few people know that any warden's duties are largely administrative, while the second in command, the deputy handles the prisoners within the walls.

Case No. 1: A new, "fresh fish" con was hailed before a certain warden and told to "Get behind that wheelbarrow and push plenty, or I'll have you spread over a barrel."

The frightened retort was, "I hope not, sir."

"That be damned, you'd better have left hope behind."

True, this scene was enacted during the PPR era (pre-prison-reform), many years after our fanatical New England ancestors quit burning witches, but long before Michigan decreed that "life for a pint" was an accurate measure of justice.

---

[10] Statement of an inmate in *The Prisoner Speaks,* Annals of the Academy of Political and Social Sciences, *op. cit.,* p. 144.

But let's cut out ancient history and come on up several decades to the Right Now in this state.

Four convicted felons are brought from a county jail to the Big House. While awaiting trial they had talked the matter over and unanimously decided they were chumps to try to outsmart *The Law*. They wished only for a chance to do the square thing in prison, paying their debt to society and gaining freedom at the earliest possible moment.

They were lined up for inspection by the deputy warden who passed out some silly platitudes plagarized from an obsolete copy book. Then he said, sarcastically, "Well, you'll all do plenty time here." The writer knows that at least one of the quartet felt fairly poisoned with hatred and bitterness.

The officer under discussion greets many incoming prisoners with that bit of repartee. When I say it is wrong, there is no sentimentalism in my remark. I do mean that the taxpayers, a few years later, will have to dig up hard dollars for court costs—possibly undertaker's bills as well—because this stupid, incompetent servant made bad men worse.

Not long ago, between stretches, the writer investigated a prison for the benefit of a widely-read newspaper, the warden acting as "guide, philosopher, and friend." This officer indicated an elderly prisoner and remarked, "That man has been here thirty-three years; we shall try to get him a pardon soon."

In the name of God, WHY? The old bird was bound to be "stir simple," thoroughly institutionalized, misanthropic. Though probably incapable of again becoming a social menace he was sure to prove a social burden. When common sense is substituted for silly sentiment in penology, we will have better protection to life and property, at the same time salvaging much worth-while material from behind prison walls.

But now to plumb the social depths until we get the harpoon into a specimen of arrested development which we have called a "screw." In my opinion, some five thousand years hence some excavating geologist will uncover one of those quaint, stone-age places, formerly called "prisons," and expose to view the fossilized remains of an average screw. The anthropologist of the expedition will observe the peculiar feet, the head, almost solid bone, with low brow, the high cheek bones and brutal under jaw, and depart, muttering, "Old stuff. Merely an abnormal type of preglacial anthropoid ape."

The dumb screw who secures prison employment only because he has failed at all his other avocations, isn't the most dangerous and expensive member of the ilk. He arouses only contempt among the malefactors whom you have penned up for reformative purposes—at least your indeterminate sentence laws so declare.

Scorn seldom arouses the worst in a man, but hatred will lead inmates to burn and kill while in prison and to try and "get even" when released, and remember that more than ninety per cent of all prisoners are eventually freed.

The writer is day by day under the personal supervision of a most expensive member of the screw family. He would be a costly luxury even if he paid the state for the privilege of wearing a uniform, carrying a club, browbeating those under him, and cringing to those above. Instead of impressing a prisoner with the fact that the uniform represents inexorable social power, this man makes each command or reprimand a personal matter, his mere personality affecting the prisoners much as an infusion of acid does a mess of alkaloids.

It is stupidity of this type in those who may have become perverted by their mother's nightbarking, that fans the always present fuel of prison revolt into consuming flame. . . .

While our informant's comments are somewhat disorganized, the reader can have no doubts as to his attitudes.

I have tried on numerous occasions to get inmates with whom rapport existed to write a discussion with a title such as "Kindnesses of Guards." All but a few flatly refused. Their refusal is indicative of the code discussed in the last chapter. Not all guards are unsympathetic or vicious, just as not all inmates are criminalistic. Even those guards who seem to be persistently on the offensive have moments of kindliness, but it is almost impossible to get an inmate to admit this.[11] The only statement procured savoring of objectiveness is presented here:

Kindness of Guards

Kindness of guards is something to ponder over. The majority of the prison population consists of men lacking manly principle, who are ever ready to take advantage of a fellowman's weaknesses, and who think they are smart enough to dodge the law and its consequences. Such men are only too ready to take advantage of a guard's weakness—kindness.

By this I do not mean that a guard should be a hardboiled bully, or what may be termed a "sadist." He should be fair, treating all with the same consideration, show no favors to men because they help him "watch" the gang (as a rule they are the ones who most need watching) and will not reward kindness or confidence placed in them with deceit.

Most men are lovers of fair play and will respect the guard who shoots square with all, though they will have little respect for the guard who will let them openly violate the rules even if they themselves are the ones favored.

As an illustration I would like to refer to an incident that happened to me. I was caught violating the rule against smoking in the yard. Through the influence of one of the deputies the guard did not have me punished providing I promised not to do it again. I gave my promise and kept it for two years, even though this particular guard had left the service in the meantime. The guard who took his place proved to be a sadist, issuing many orders of his own making to certain men, and which he thought might act in some way as punishment for them, but which were inconsequential

[11] See the section on *Dogma,* Chapter VII.

to the interests of the institution and were utterly disregarded by other guards.

I was very careful not to violate any of his orders while he was on duty, but on his relief day I did violate one of them and took some bananas to the dining room to eat with cream (canned) for my supper. The next day he was on duty and one of his "helpers" (stool pigeon) told him what I had done. Immediately he threatened to send me to the solitary. He did not because he knew such an order would not be considered by the deputy warden. A few weeks later he caught some of the men smoking and though I was not with them he also placed the same charge against me, and I was punished for something I had not done. More than the punishment I hated the fact that the deputy who had used his influence on my behalf before thought I had broken my word. While I was in the solitary this guard told my cellmate that he knew I did not smoke in the yard, but I had taken some bananas to the dining-room against his orders.

The men in the gang did not respect this guard or like him, and all were glad to see him leave the service.

The above illustration is only one of many similar instances that I have witnessed or been the victim of in the seven years I have been here. I have always treated the guards just the same as I would like to be treated myself if our positions were reversed. I find that it does no good to get a change of work, or to be placed in a different gang after having been unfortunate enough to be placed under a sadist guard, for he will pass the word to the next guard, possibly expanding half-truths to the extent that the prisoner will have a hard way to go until the new guard gets acquainted and understands him, though there are few guards I have come in contact with who will take the trouble to try to understand the prisoner's nature.

As is known, the success of our industrial foreman depends entirely upon their ability to understand the nature of the men they have charge of. I doubt very much if many of the men employed as under-guards and given charge of shops or gangs of one hundred men or more, have ever held a foreman's position outside.

The gist of the whole question is fair dealing and the ability to understand men. Some men may wish to shirk their duties and have to be driven, others are willing to acknowledge their obligation to society and will do their time willingly.

I have seen the kindness of guards abused to the extent that the kind guard soon lost his position, but there is always a middle between the two ends.

There are several sides to rigid discipline and the attitudes of prison employees. It is not a simple problem. We cannot dismiss it with a word and simply report, as many investigators have done, that prison officials are incompetent. This writer, of course, favors a modification of discipline and is sure that reasonable, common-sense methods can be found. The entire problem of discipline and the problem of prisons themselves have wide sociological and philosophical ramifications. What, after all, is the purpose of society—what is the purpose of life?

Let us look at the "Rules for the Government of Convicts."

TO THE CONVICTS: YOUR ATTENTION IS DIRECTED TO THE FOLLOWING RULES FOR ONLY BY OBSERVING AND OBEYING THEM CAN YOU MAKE A GOOD RECORD AND SECURE THAT DIMINUTION OF YOUR SENTENCE WHICH THE LAW ALLOWS.

1. The first duty is strict obedience to all rules and regulations, and the orders of the officers under whose charge you may be placed.

2. In the evening, in your cell, you are permitted to converse in a low tone until the nine o'clock bell rings, when, if you have not previously done so, put out your light, undress, and retire.

3. You must not speak to any visitor, or give to or receive from a visitor anything except by permission of the Warden or Deputy. You must not gaze at visitors or strangers passing through the prison or on the visitors' gallery in the cellhouse but at all times, during working hours, give your undivided attention to your work. You are expected to apply yourself faithfully and diligently to whatever labor you are assigned, and after reasonable teaching to perform the same amount of labor as would be required of you outside.

4. At the ringing of the morning bell you must turn out, dress, make up your bed neatly, and be ready for marching out. At the signal, open the door, step out and close the same, without slamming, hold on until the bar is thrown, and remain standing with your hands upon the door until the count is made. In case of miscount, resume your place at the door until the count is correct.

5. On returning to the cellhouse, stand at cell with right hand on the door. At the signal, open the door, step in, and close the same without slamming, keep it firmly closed until the second signal is given, and the bar is thrown, and remain standing with your hands upon the door until the count is made. In case of miscount resume your place at the door until the count is correct.

6. You must not leave the line, or your place of employment, without permission. If sick, or unable to work, make it known to the officer in charge and act as he may direct.

7. You must keep your cell and furniture in good order. No marking, scratching the walls or spitting on the floor will be permitted. You must not make any alterations in your clothing or cell furniture. If your clothing needs repairs, report the fact to your keeper.

8. Singing, whistling, dancing, loud laughter, loud talking, or talking from one cell to another, or loud or boisterous conduct is strictly forbidden at all times, in cell or elsewhere in the prison.

9. You will not, under any circumstances, be allowed to "tinker" in shop or cell in any manner whatever, or trade, or give away, any article to another convict.

10. In going to and from your cell you will not be permitted to gaze

into cells, on the flag, or out of the window, but proceed in as quiet and unobserving a manner as possible.

11. You must not carry knives, tools of any kind, pencils, paper, or any material whatever, from your shop to your cell without permission in writing from the Warden or Deputy. The authorities furnish everything which is expected you to have and finding other articles in your possession, without the proper permit, will be taken as evidence that you have disobeyed this rule. Writing notes to other convicts, or carrying notes from one convict to another is strictly forbidden.

12. You must approach an officer in a respectful manner, always touching your cap or forehead before speaking. You must confine your conversation with him strictly to the business in hand. You must not address an officer on any matter outside the prison. Insolence in any form to an officer, foreman, or even to another convict, will not be tolerated.

13. When attending religious services, no loud talking will be permitted, the silence must be observed. No reading will be permitted, strict attention must be given to the services. Spitting on the floor shuffling of the feet, or any unnecessary noise, is strictly forbidden.

14. You are strictly forbidden spitting on the galleries of cellhouse floor.

15. You are required to bathe once a week, unless excused by the Physician, Warden, or Deputy.

16. On entering the prison you will receive three privilege tickets, which will entitle you, as long as you obey strictly the foregoing rules, to the following privileges, viz:

1) There are five (5) grades of prisoners established in this prison, known as A, B, C, D, and E.

2) The dress of grades A, B, and C will be blue, grades D and E will be stripes.

3) Those in grades A and B may see visitors once in two weeks and write a letter each week.

   Those in grade C can see visitors once in four weeks and write a letter every two weeks.

   Those in grades D and E can only see visitors by permission of the Warden and write a letter every four weeks.

   In addition to the above privileges, men in any grade, at the discretion of the Warden, may see visitors and write at any time in regard to their case or about important business or family matters. Men in grades D and E will be denied the use of the library books, newspapers and flag privileges on holidays and such other pleasures as the Warden may order enforced.

4) All prisoners received will be dressed in and remain in grade C for the period of three months without reports against them for infrac-

tion of prison rules, when they will be advanced to grade B. Those in grades D and E will be advanced in accordance with the rules of the Progressive Merit System.

5) No prisoner will be permitted an audience before the Parole Board, except those of grade A, unless by request of the Board of Parole.

6) The rules for the government of prisoners of this prison will work no hardships on any inmates and the authorities hope each and every one will so obey them that they will have the consciousness of knowing that they have done right and that they may refer to their record with pride.
You are permitted to receive such weekly papers as the Warden may approve. In case of special letters, written permission must be obtained from the Warden or Deputy. All letters, written or received, must first be examined at the office under the direction of the Warden, before being sent or delivered. All the above privileges depend upon your good behavior, and you will be deprived of one or all of them for bad conduct. The use of library books depend upon the care you take to keep them scrupulously neat and clean.

In these rules there are twenty-nine "should not's" and twenty "should's." An indication that our prison is fairly typical of all American prisons is found in the similarity in the rules and daily life of our institutions and the generalization which the National Commission on Law Observance and Enforcement makes for all American Prisons. In part, the Commission states—and it applies broadly to our penitentiary, "In most prisons the life of the inmate is controlled for him and he moves in obedience to numerous rules which leave him no chance for initiative or judgment. The treatment is *en masse*, not individual. Wardens and guards are usually more interested in ease of administration than in giving attention to the individual needs of offenders. This not only leads to a great variety of rules, but it results in a regimented life and a routine that tend to unfit the prisoner for life on the outside. . . . The fact that rules . . . are commonly disobeyed is one objection to them. Prisoners, in prison, are subjected to a regime of law enforcement which no one could live up to; this hardly promotes respect for law, nor does it send the prisoners out more law-abiding than when they entered. If the rules were actually enforced it would reduce the offenders to automatons. There is, however, a graver danger. The fact that they (the rules) exist and can be enforced gives officers and guards the opportunity to "ride" prisoners; that is, to overlook infringements of rules in some cases and to come down hard in others when the rules are violated." [12]

This statement sums up the situation fairly well, although our warden gives some individual attention through interviews and, when possible, changes men's work at their request. Furthermore, all contacts between officials and inmates are not distinctly impersonal. The rules notwithstanding, there is some kidding, and joking, and kindness, but the great majority of inmates lead a regimented, controlled life. In the Declaration of Principles of the American Prison Association, Article V states, "The prisoner's destiny should be placed measurably in his own hands; he must be put into circumstances where he will be able, through his own exertions to continually better his own condition. A regulated self-interest must be brought into play and made constantly operative." [13] This principle of socialized penology is still on paper and has not yet become a practice in the community.

Violations of the Rules

We do not know the amount of crime in the general population. We only know the number of commitments to various institutions and the "crimes known to the police." Similarly we have no accurate knowledge of the number of men who violate prison rules, but know only those who get caught. There are seldom less than fifteen men being punished in solitary confinement at one time, and rarely over fifty: Thus, between 1 and approximately 3 per cent of our populaton are caught violating rules of sufficient importance to demand solitary confinement. Slightly less than 1 per cent of the inmates have violated rules, the punishment for which is deprivation of a movie or ball game. While our prison has, on the average, about thirty men in punishment cells at all times, two federal prisons which the writer has visited, rarely have more than five inmates enduring solitary confinement. The difference refers mainly, we think, to the superior administration of federal prisons, but is related as well to the fact that most federal prisoners, except those at Alcatraz, are considerably less criminalistic than offenders in state penitentiaries.

The rules most frequently violated are eight and ten in the foregoing list. Many inmates will talk at all times regardless of restrictions. Loud talking from cell to cell is difficult to restrain in the

---

[12] National Commission on Law Observance and Enforcement: *Report on Penal Institutions, Probation and Parole,* United States Government Printing Office, Washington, D. C., 1931, pp. 215–220.

[13] From the Declaration of Principles of 1870 of the American Prison Association as Revised and Reaffirmed at the Sixtieth Annual Congress of the American Prison Association, Louisville, Ky., Oct. 10–16, 1930, included in Sanford Bates, *op. cit.*, p. 309, Appendix A.

cellhouse during the evenings because only two or three guards are on duty and they must watch over five hundred men. Talking in the dining-room and in line is common. It is not done openly, and if a guard is near, the men refrain, although some will talk out of the sides of their mouths, seeming to enjoy the risk. Tinkering (Rule 9), having contraband (Rule 11), mutilating property and clothing (Rule 7), leaving line or work (Rule 6), loafing at work (Rule 3), and smoking are the most frequent violations in addition to talking. Less often, but more serious, are fighting, refusing to work, sex misconduct, assaulting an officer, and escaping. In general, it may be said that the majority of inmates have no respect for the rules, as such, but obey them to avoid unpleasant punishments and to keep their record as clean as possible, hoping to gain recognition thereby from the parole board. Nelson's analysis of prisoners and the rules applies generally to our prison. He says, "The idea that a rule should be obeyed, not because it is sensible or pleasant, but because it is the rule, is utterly beyond his understanding. Such rules as forbid him to break out of prison, or to commit murder, he will generally concede to be obeyable; but all others he feels that he may break whenever he gets a chance, and thinks it outrageous that he should be punished when he is caught doing it. Especially is his anger aroused when he is punished for some offense at which the "screw" did not actually catch him, but was reported to the guard by an informer. At such times he feels himself a terribly abused person." [14]

Individuals who get in trouble in prison are usually the inexperienced and relatively non-criminal inmates. This point is well known among criminologists. We checked it, however, by inspecting, for six months, the conduct records of two hundred men, one hundred being recidivists of a fairly advanced type, and one hundred being essentially first offenders. The differentiation was made, not on criminal record alone, but on the diagnosis of criminality by the Mental Health Staff as well. It so happened that members of neither group had many conduct reports: two offenses totaling fourteen days for the recidivists, and 6 offenses totaling 22 days for the non-criminal group. The infractions of neither group were rebellious in nature. These data are not very conclusive, but we believe a laborious tabulation of a larger number unnecessary, as the fact is well recognized.

An executive with much experience in penology says, "Ordinarily speaking there are three classes of prisoners: the unadjustable, the adjustable, and the self-adjusting." [15] The first, he says, are purely custodial cases, and the last cause no trouble in prison and are of

---

[14] Victor Nelson, *op. cit.*, pp. 124–125.
[15] Sanford Bates, *op. cit.*, p. 224.

help to officials as school teachers, and so on. The larger number are the "adjustable" group with whom re-educative work must be done to reclaim them and prevent recidivous developments. While Mr. Bates refers to life-adjustment as well as adjustment under custody, these categories may well be applied to accommodation in the prison. Using his three-fold classification and applying it to our community, the "unadjustables" in prison are the psychopaths and unstable personalities, and those in poor physical health, age and criminality, notwithstanding. The self-adjusting are the eminently stable personalities who would adjust quickly to almost any situation, and the most of these have relatively short sentences. The "adjustables," who comprise the bulk of the population, are the common garden variety of prisoner, and age or criminality has little effect on conduct adjustment. The "unadjustables" are in constant trouble; the "self-adjusting" are almost never in trouble, and the manner of adapting in these two categories would seem to be largely intrinsic in the personality. But the "adjustables'" reactions are primarily reactions to situations, and their behavior reflects the situation more than it does the intrinsic personality make-up. Of course, any three-fold delineation of personalities is too simple. Strictly, a man might be adjustable one hour and unadjustable the next, but a classification of some sort helps us to grasp the situation. This three-fold classification is not in disagreement with the earlier stated dichotomy, namely, that the experienced prisoner, other things being equal, is not punished so frequently for misconduct as the inexperienced inmate.

Let us take three hypothetical but fairly orthodox incidents, and then depict one which does not fall into our three-fold classification. The population attends the ball game on Saturday afternoon and inmates "A," "B," and "C" are among them. The bleachers have roofs and the vertical uprights, spaced at ten feet intervals, make it very difficult for the man who happens to get a seat behind the upright to see the game, as each man must sit in his place as the single line marches in. Inmate "A" happens to get a position behind the post. He cannot see the ball diamond at all. Although he is much interested in the game, he sits quietly until, when the game is half over, a guard walks by. "Sir," he says, "I can't see the game here, and I wonder if you will let me move to the other side of the field where there are some empty seats?" The guard replies, "Someone has got to sit behind the posts; are you any better than anyone else?" and "A" answers, "No, of course not, sir, and if it is too much trouble, don't bother, I'll have better luck at the next game." "Well, go ahead," the guard says as he walks away. As "A" leaves his seat, he curses the guard loud enough for his inmate associates to hear. Inmate "A" treated the guard with respect and probably developed his good will. He did not lose standing with the inmates near him because he cursed the guard. "A" is self-adjusting; his reaction clearly reveals his insight and sheds light on his personality. He avoided trouble and achieved his aim.

"B" also gets a seat behind the post but as soon as he sees his plight he immediately gets up, and without permission, heads for some vacant seats on the other side of the field. He is hailed by a guard who inquires where he is going. "I got a seat behind the post and I can't see a thing. I don't see why I have to stay there when there are vacant seats over yonder." The guard asks, "Did you get permission? Do you want to go to the hole?" and the inmate answers, "No, but you know the warden wouldn't make a man sit where he can't see when other seats are vacant." The guard says, "No, and the warden wouldn't allow you to walk all over the yard, either. No, goddam you, get back to your seat and stay there." So, after some talk, "B" turns around and goes back to his seat and curses the guards for the rest of the afternoon. Though the methods were not very elegant, "B" did adjust. He maintained his prestige with his inmate companions around him who could observe that he was giving the guard an argument, and he did not become so aggressive with the guard that punishment resulted. If slightly rebellious, he had sense enough to know how far he could go, and that further "lip" would have called for a report.

"C" marches to the ball game with his gang, and his seat happens to fall behind a post. He jumps up at once, energetically waving his arms at the nearest official, and hollers, "I ain't going to sit behind no goddam post—now let me out of here; you can't push me around every goddam day." The official orders him back in his seat, but "C" persists in his objections with much activity and cursing, and when the guard comes up to lead him back to his seat, he says, "Take your dirty hands off of me you so-and-so." Well, "C" goes to solitary for eight days. His exaggerated reaction resulted not only from the post, but from the stored-up emotion and the instability of his personality.

To carry our hypothetical consideration one step further. It would be logical to assume that "A" was a forger or confidence man who had been in prison for several years, or long enough to make him wise, and also that he possessed average intelligence or better. "B" might be any type of offender, but possessing adequate intelligence, and being stable enough to realize the power of the dominant group. "C" might well have been of borderline intelligence and probably not an advanced thief, but one whose entire life had been primarily dominated by his affect. While these three incidents are hypothetical they are based on an actual case in which an inmate was placed behind a hogshead water barrel at a ball game.

The case of inmate "D" does not fall exactly into our classification. "D" was recognized as a good prisoner. He obeyed the rules and was polite to guards. He seemed trustworthy and was given a job on the farm outside the walls. He performed his work well and there was no suspicion of his misconduct. It was finally learned, however, that he was bootlegging whiskey and coffee to other inmates. The story goes that five pints of whiskey and twenty pounds of coffee were found adjacent to his trustie quarters. It has been said that the whiskey cost him seventy-five cents a pint, and that he sold it for two dollars. The fifteen-cent coffee brought fifty cents a pound, and the inmate had sixty dollars of cash on him. "D" might be said to be "self-adjusting," just as an entrepreneur is self-adjusting. Actually, he double-crossed the officials and overcharged the inmates.

Certain specific situations in the environment, the inmates say, are inimical to good conduct. Just as a low wall or poorly barred gate stimulates the formulation of plans for escape, so does the use of antiquated buildings incite dangerous attitudes. An inmate said:

> The chapel is a part of the oldest building on the reservation. It is finished in wood, nothing rare, just common everyday wood. Forty or fifty years have seasoned this material until it is as dry and almost as inflammable as tinder.
>
> Among the prisoners are many who are sufficiently radical actually to gloat over the scorched bodies of hundreds of fellow inmates IF THERE COULD ALSO BE A FEW OFFICIALS.
>
> Given those two conditions it doesn't require a particularly vivid imagination to picture a spot in the chapel, when it has been darkened for a movie, a spot where a convict sits, coat over his knees, with a handful of oiled shavings under his chair. Not even a whole match is necessary to complete the picture—just a split piece. The Columbus horror would be a mild incident in comparison.

In a less dangerous way the presence of rubbing alcohol in the hospital, even though it is guarded and kept in small quantities, and of hair tonic in the officer's barber shop, are invitations for a drunk. Other situations which are generally talked of by the men are not conducive to peaceful attitudes, respect for officialdom, and good conduct. Long before the period of this study a large sum of money was appropriated to rebuild and construct a wall on the south side of the prison yard. Some work was done and a wall constructed which gave rise to remarks like the following: "When we all know how crooked some of these officials are, how do they expect us to reform. Every time we look at that wall we think of how large a 'cut' some of the 'Big-Shots' got, and some of us get sent here for sticking up a gas station for fifty dollars." Another situation influencing attitudes to some extent refers to a previous administration which, before leaving office purchased large amounts of supplies for the industries. The inmates say, "Why, they got enough cloth there to last ten years. I guess they got their 'end' all right." Obviously the inmate body does not have accurate facts about, or complete understanding of, the construction of the wall, or of the purchase of what seems to them a large amount of supplies. Fact and accuracy are not necessary to influence their behavior; the belief alone is sufficient.

When the men march in line they are required to keep step, keep their hands out of their pockets, and be silent. The officials are reasonable, however, and do not expect military precision. Yet, whenever an inmate is commanded to take his hands from his pockets he recalls that when the warden or other high officials are in the yard on a chilly morning, they are likely to have their hands in their pockets, and the hue and cry of "injustice" rings loud. It is necessary in prison to have "shakedowns" occasionally. If the officers suspect trouble they will search every cell. The men who have no illicit possessions, and whose conduct is without question, take this as a personal insult, on occasion, and severe is the criticism of officialdom. In such situations attitudes are modified, misconduct may result, and usually, the nonconformist simply becomes more resourceful.

The violation of rules considered most hostile, of course, is escape or plan to escape. No one knows what proportion of the inmates spend their time in such contemplation. No doubt the rebellious man with a long sentence ponders the problem at length. Those men who fall into a mechanical and vegetable tempo of life raise their eyes to the wall, but seldom. Escapes at our prison have been few, especially since 1933, and the great majority of those who get away do so as trusties from the honor farm. Escapes from inside the wall are rare, but constitute a threat to law and order, and are usually followed by stricter discipline. Escapes are spectacular; they are the big gamble in an inmate's life. Let an old-time prisoner tell you about a few of them:

Betrayed by a Pattern

It was eleven o'clock at night and the regular eleven o'clock freight train was puffing and snorting its way into the penitentiary's yard. The powerful locomotive dragged the last of a string of eight cars into the prison and, as it wheezed to a stop, the heavy train gate creaked shut.

Fifteen minutes later a night guard on patrol duty in the prison yard thought he noticed a human form flit from one shadow to another in the prison quarry. Being a cautious fellow, he drew his revolver. His eyes had not deceived him. It *was* a human form that he saw skulking close to the rock piles stacked in the quarry.

To his cry of "Halt, or I'll shoot!" the shadow seeker came toward the guard with upraised hands. Questioned, the stockily-built stranger, dressed in a dark colored civilian suit, stated that he was on his way South, but that upon noticing that the freight had stopped, he had decided to look around a bit. He went on to say that he was still trying to figure out what fort, or sort of place he had stepped into. What lent plausibility to his story was the fact that this was not the first time that the prison officials had come across hobos asleep or awake in the freight cars which nightly entered the prison yard.

Marched to the Guard Hall, the stranger was questioned by an assistant warden who, phoned at his home about the stranger, got out of bed, dressed, and came right down. The prison count for that evening showed that all of the convicts were accounted for, and the assistant was convinced that the mild-mannered stranger was indeed an unwilling visitor of the prison. He was on the point of releasing the man when a veteran guard stepped up and whispered in the assistant's ear.

From twelve that night to six the next morning the stranger reclined on a long bench in the large Guard Hall. The morning shift came on. Each guard looked over the stranger. Not a single guard recalled ever having seen the man.

It was a good thing that the veteran guard had whispered to his superior. When the Bertillion man took the inoffensive-looking stranger's finger-prints, the would-be-hobo proved to be a convict who worked in the tailor shop!

The prison has a triple count system. The officials, finding no "dummy" in W. H.'s cell, are still mystified as to how three guards could have counted two heads in W. H.'s cell, when only one was in it. And if it wasn't for the veteran guard whose eye was attracted by the odd patterned shirt W. H. wore—the same pattern that, though dropped long ago, he recalled as having seen on a "trusty" about a year ago—the assistant would have been the laughing stock of the prison.

A Steam Showered Martyr

When the land site for a second prison was picked out back around 1870, the engineers were temporarily stumped as to what to do with a gully that ran right through the middle of the purchased site. The gully drained the accumulation of rainwater from the hollows along the hilly country that rose behind the bought site and emptied it into the nearby river. To fill in the natural drain would be damming up a spillway for the hill waters. And as the gully cut right through the selected prison site, they feared that a damming up or a filling in of nature's sluice would, besides endangering and undermining the proposed stone walls, force the rain-waters to flood the prison through the very spot where the east gate would be.

The engineering heads compromised by brickwalling the bed, sides, and the top of the gully. Besides solving the rainwater menace, they found themselves with a tunnel, which, in the future, would easily handle all of the finished prison's sewage. It is a very large tunnel.

Years later, four convicts took advantage of the solved problems of those post Civil War engineers.

One morning, under the very noses of two gun-towers, the four brazenly removed the heavy iron lid from a manhole. One by one they dropped into the gaping round hole. Ten feet down was a grating of iron bars. They were prepared. A bar was cut with a hacksaw. Singly, the first three disappeared head first through the downward-sloping, two-foot tile pipe, which took care of the kitchen sewage. The fourth prisoner, not liking the idea of sliding through that round opening with his head first, started down with his feet first.

About five feet down, a second tile pipe forked out and downward from the two-foot drain; a sort of overflow pipe for the larger one. Breaks of all breaks! Sliding downward, the fourth man felt one leg sliding into the smaller tile, and the other into the two-foot drain! Caught in that foul-smelling, treacherous trap, the convict was powerless to climb up the slimy kitchen drain or go down .

Although refuse, hot and cold water, and steam showered his face and body occasionally, the trapped convict did not yell for help. Thinking of his companions who would need at least a half hour to saw through the big, barred gate at the river's east bank, he covered his head with his arms and made the best of it.

An hour later, and after the four were missed, the fourth man was located and hauled out. Meanwhile, his companions had made good their escape.

Fog

The officials of the penitentiary have a fear of the freak fogs peculiar to the locality of the prison. And they have a good reason. Ordinary fogs, which hang for a time and then clear up, are bad enough. These can be guarded against. But the prison officials who run the Big House can recall fogs which have played them dirty tricks in the past.

One morning about twenty months ago, a thick fog blanketed the entire prison. The inmates that morning were kept locked up in their cells until the whitish mist had evaporated.

The country behind the east section of the prison is nothing but hills and hollows, and this gradually starts sloping away from the eighteen-foot board fence taking the place of a stone wall, which, showing signs of collapsing from the too powerful quarry blasts, was finally torn down. The half-circle board fence, with three machine-gun-manned towers straddling it, protects the highest point in the prison—a stone bluff.

The quarry gangs hadn't been out of their cells a half hour when the fog tricked the officials. It came down on the bluff like a suddenly-dropped curtain. Out of all the men who were working on the bluff, two men, notorious for their luck and daring on other escapes, eluded their gang guard. Crouching low, they ran for the wooden fence, never giving the machine-gun-manned towers a glance. With a pick they knocked out a fence board, and a few seconds later they were headed for the hills and hollows. Five minutes later a gust of wind blew the fog away.

All escapes are not successful. The following account is taken from the autobiography of an advanced and rebellious offender, and occurred over eight years ago. This man attempted five escapes, and was successful in one of them and was free for about eight months before being apprehended and returned. The statement below deals with one of the failures.

I had by now gained all my former strength back. I determined to put the plans I had figured out while in the hole into effect. Toward that end I began getting together all I needed: a change of clothes, blue overalls, outside cap, white shirt, and a light pair of shoes. The day of this escape was also to be on Saturday, but not of a night. I was going in daylight. I chose Saturday because it afforded me the best opportunity of walking away from the gang undetected. Because on Saturday evening while the rest of the gangs were out at the ball game we were forced, as a punitive measure for being in "brown," (brown clothes denoting poor conduct) to go to the clothing house for our weekly change of clothing. I intended, while the rest of the gang and the screw were in the clothing house, to walk away from the gang and make my attempt for freedom. When the following Saturday came, I was all ready to go. I had my blue overalls on under my brown pants and a white shirt under my con shirt and an outside cap in my shirt bosom. Up until the Brown Gang arrived at the clothing house on the Saturday scheduled for the break, I had mentioned to no one my intentions of trying to escape that day. On the way to the clothing house I decided to let one other of the fellows in the gang in on the "out," providing they wanted to go. When we arrived at the clothing house I asked them, including the whole gang, if anyone of them wanted to go over the wall with me. I explained that only one could go because the more that went, the less chance of escape we would have. I had spoken in a half sarcastic tone of voice, as if to say, who had got guts enough to go over the wall with me. *SM* was the first and only one who answered. "I'll go with you, *P*," he said. *S* had made grade and already had on blue overalls. "Come on," I said. On the way to the wall I told *S* what not to do. "See that cross piece with the wires on it running across the road to the kitchen? Whatever you do, don't step on it. If you do the wires will start jumping up and down and we're liable to get a rumble. And if we do get over, whatever you do, don't start running if the gun guards start shooting. Just walk off casual like as though you were a trusty working on the front lawn. If you run, they will kill us both from the main entrance." *S* said he wouldn't, and that everything was clear to him. When we reached the wall, I quickly pulled off my brown pants and con shirt, threw away my brown cap, replaced it with the outside cap, and started scaling the wall. *S* followed directly behind me. I reached the top first. When I looked down at *S* he was standing on the cross piece which held the wires and they were bouncing up and down like a wire with a monkey on it. Instead of jumping down on the other side, I hung and was trying to let myself down by holding on to the blocks of stone in the wall. I had just grasped the first stone when my grip broke and I fell. The fall knocked the wind out of me and skinned me from head to foot. *S* was on top of the wall, motioning frantically for me to move some pipes for him. I motioned that I was temporarily knocked out. He stood up and instead of jumping toward the ground, he jumped right up in the air. How he ever escaped breaking his ankles I don't know, but he did. We started walking away. I had *S* by the arm, cautioning him about running if the guards started shooting, when an old life-term convict who stays out in front in a ground tower and who had for the past three months been at the ball game at this particular time, started shouting, "There they go, Cap! There they go, Cap!" I said, "We're rumbled, *S*, for Christ's' sake whatever you do, don't run." Just as soon as the rat con started shouting, the two screws on the wall started shooting, and to make things worse, *S* wanted to run. Slugs were hitting all around us, between our legs, and just over our heads into the windows of the Administration Building toward us. Ten minutes from the time we left the Brown Gang at the clothing house we were coming back in the back door of the Administration Building. We had never been missed by the Brown Gang screw, and you should have seen the look of astonishment on his face when they led us past him on the way to the hole. We would have made a clean get-away but for the interference of the unpaid guard.

Though the inmates know that the life of an escaper is filled with fear of detection and other difficulties, and though they know that most escapers are caught sooner or later, these facts, like capital punishment as a supposed deterrent of murder, have no demonstrable influence. On the other hand, case studies of escapers by the writer have shown that some men have a wish to be pursued, a desire to be a "marked man." Psycho-social factors are operating in such instances and we cannot attempt an analysis here. Some escaped men remain free for ten or fifteen years. When they are returned they seem more crushed than those returned in a short time. Of course the matter of age is important in such instances. Some escapers are returned immediately. One strange case deals with an inmate, who, while incarcerated, pined for his relatives. He was lonesome, dejected, and unloved in prison, but he thought, "If I can only be with my family members again I can be happy." He made a successful escape, returned to his home, and was welcomed. When an aunt learned, however, that the prison would pay a fifty-dollar reward for his return, he was brought back after twenty-four days.

Punishment

Something must be done with the men who break the rules, officials say. Not so many years ago inmates were flogged. In our own prison some years ago, men in solitary confinement were handcuffed to the iron-barred door for some ten hours a day. Beating of inmates with clubs and fists was formerly common, but occurs now only rarely, and usually only with the men who assault officials. Our state has a law which prohibits officers from using physical force on prisoners unless they are assaultive or riotous. Formerly our prison also used the striped suits, such as cartoonists like to depict, for escapers who were returned, for sex offenders in prison, and for other dangerous men. This was discontinued about five years ago. Its purpose was ostensibly to make such men prominent so they could be more carefully watched, as well as to stigmatize them—which it seldom did. Formerly, a device known as the "screens" was used for habitually "bad actors." A man on the "screens" was kept in a separate tier in the cellhouse for months at a time. He was given regular food and had a bed in his cell, but was not allowed to work or to associate with other prisoners. A few years before the period considered in this study, the most ostensibly rebellious inmates were assigned to one work unit called the "brown gang," so-called because of the brown clothing issued.

When an inmate is apprehended breaking minor rules, the guard fills in a slip and sends it to the second assistant deputy warden. If the inmate is dangerous or an habitual rule breaker, he will be sent for the same day, but otherwise will be called to the guard office on a certain day to attend "court." The assistant warden will inquire into the trouble. If the inmate is guilty he usually lies, or blames some one else, although not always. The official will listen to his story, ask a few questions, and then give the sentence. "No movies for two weeks," is considered good luck. "Solitary for six days," is taken stoically by most men. The maximum amount of time the officials are allowed to make a man serve in solitary confinement is twenty-one days. This is a state law.

When the inmate is sent to solitary, his clothes are taken from him and he is given another pair of trousers, a shirt, and slippers. He is then assigned to a cell. While he is there he gets as much water as he wants, and bread twice a day. Men frequently lose five to fifteen pounds, depending upon their tenure in solitary. In solitary they have nothing to do. Smoking and reading are prohibited. The physician looks in once a day. "Thoughts come more clearly in solitary," one man says. Another remarks, "When a man is locked up like that, a bitterness of high degree develops towards society, but at the same time a devotion to one or a few persons develops." Daydreaming and reverie are common. Sex practices are frequent. If a man becomes seriously sick he is removed to the hospital, but upon recovery must finish his punishment. Solitary confinement brings psychosis and neurosis into view, and mental disturbances of less pronounced degrees, as well: "I'm not in prison —I'm walking with the masters. I'm living out of my time." After being released from a tour of punishment one man said, "It's a battle to keep level in here without trying to improve yourself."

We opened this chapter by saying that our prison presented the fairly typical systems of punishment. We have attempted to show certain individual responses and the utter futility of the methods used. But this has all been said many times before. Our penitentiary is by no means the most decadent, nor is it among the most progressive. A well-trained and carefully selected staff might correct some of the unnecessary abuses and construct a system of penology wherein punishment would be minimized. The Federal prisons are already showing the way in this respect. In general, however, there is a tendency for methods of punishment to be consistent, not only with the general culture, but with the culture of the region wherein the place of punishment is located.

CHAPTER IX

The Social Implications of Leisure Time

It is often said that human beings show a greater naturalness of expression, a greater spontaneity, and a more pronounced tendency to ignore conventions during their periods of recreation than they exhibit during the time spent in more serious pursuits.[1] This is also true of the inmates of prisons in spite of the restraints imposed upon them by the rules and regulations of the penitentiary. During leisure hours when the prisoners are literally "off guard," and when their attention need not be directed to required and specific duties, their personalities stand out more clearly. However, the distinction between leisure time and non-leisure time, which is clear in the normal community is less evident in the penitentiary where every hour, whether designated as leisure or not, is "time" in a very real sense.

Since the major objective of this book is to present a portrait of the culture of the prison community, to ignore leisure-time events and activities would be to disregard a most fruitful aid to the understanding of the influences reciprocal to the culture and the persons who contribute to, and share in, it.

Definition, Types, and Extent of Leisure Time

An orderly examination of leisure and its ramifications necessitates the defining and delimiting of the concept. In discussing this topic we are not concerned essentially with the pleasurable state of mind which persons in the free community experience when engaging in a leisure time activity, for, although the attitudes of prisoners toward spare or leisure time are of paramount importance, the prison environment prohibits the development of basically pleasant feeling states. Even though an inmate may attempt to give himself wholly to a pleasurable event, he is prevented by his awareness of his total situation from transposing himself completely into a leisure-time activity. We cannot, therefore, consider a study of leisure-time activity as a study of pleasant mental sets predominantly, but must adopt a more suitable and practical conception and define it as that

[1] M. H. and E. S. Neumeyer, *Leisure and Recreation*, A. S. Barnes and Co., New York, 1932, p. 74.

time when the prisoner is not engaged in the more formal and obvious duties which his status as an inmate demands. In this connection the Neymeyers[2] say: "Leisure is commonly thought of as the surplus time remaining after the formal duties and necessities of life have been attended to." The terms, "leisure," "leisure time," and "recreation," which are used somewhat interchangeably in this section and those following, always refer to an event or an activity (a pattern), together with the attitudes and behavior of the inmates towards the pattern.

Adoption of the definition as stated places the discussion of leisure into two general categories: the officially regulated leisure time, and the unregulated leisure time. In the first category we will inspect the several choices of activities in which the inmate may engage during those portions of the day in which there are no specific duties and when custody is less strict.

Before we undertake a discussion of the two categories mentioned, we shall consider in quantitative terms the amount of time given over to leisure in the prison. On week days there are four hours between five and nine P. M., an hour after the noon dinner, and two fifteen-minute periods before the noon and the evening meals. These hours and fractions of hours total 330 minutes, or five and one-half hours each week day. On Saturday and Sunday the schedule differs from that of the week days, and the men have at least eight and one-half hours of so-called leisure each day. Altogether there is a total of forty-four hours each week exclusive of the time given to sleeping, eating, and possible loafing when on work assignment. Of these hours twenty-seven come in the five week days and seventeen on Saturday and Sunday. The most protracted leisure is between noon on Sunday and the "wake-up" Monday—a span of eighteen and one-half hours. Excluding the nine hours given over to sleep each night, we find the average week has 100 waking hours, of which forty-four per cent may be labeled as leisure time.

The amount of leisure in a year totals ninety-five and one-fourth full twenty-four-hour days, or twenty-six per cent of the total time in prison. During the fairly common sentence of six years and three months of servitude, the inmate will have spent a total of 583½ full, twenty-four days of leisure. Similarly, a man who has served fifteen years has somehow disposed of 1,430 full twenty-four-hour days, or nearly four complete years. It is probably in reference to this excessive leisure time that Nelson reports an inmate, who had served over ten years, as saying, "About the only thing they can do for the likes of us is to take us out and shoot us."[3]

---

[2] *Ibid.*, page 163.
[3] Victor Nelson, *op. cit.*, p. 233.

Since it is pertinent to our study to compute the approximate number of hours which the prison administration attempts to fill with recreational activity, the following tabulation has been made.

Time, Type, and Length of Officially Sponsored Recreation

Month	*Event*	*Hours*
January	5 movies	9
February	5 movies	9
March	5 movies	9
April	4 movies	9
June	5 ball games	10
	3 boxing matches	2
July	6 baseball games	12
	3 boxing matches	2
August	5 ball games	10
	3 boxing matches	2
September	3 ball games	6
	1 movie	2
October	2 soccer games	4
	2 movies	3½
November	2 football games	4
	2 movies	3½
December	5 movies	9

From the foregoing table it is evident that 112 hours a year are provided for collective recreation. This amounts to 4 per cent of the total spare time, and two-tenths of one per cent of the hours a man spends in prison, excluding the time given over to sleep. Let those misanthropic individuals who cast charges of "coddling" at penal officials, become well aware of these facts. The table does not include the time spent with the radio, church, reading, or the like, as engagement in such activities depends upon the inmate's individual wish, his work assignment, and other factors.

Leisure-Time Heritages

Life in prison is dynamic. Prison is a going concern. Prison leisure and recreation are directly related to the contemporary leisure and recreation in the normal community, but are controlled by the administrative systems of the penitentiary, as well as by the customs built by the inmates themselves over a period of years. The similarity between the leisure practices of prison and the leisure practices of the normal community is dependent upon the constant admission of men fresh from the outside. The great scatter of ages, together with the varying lengths of residence explain the partial differences between the leisure-time ideations of men who entered prison during the nineteen-nineteens and early nineteen-twenties and those who entered during the early nineteen-thirties. The older residents have been conditioned to the post-war, jazz-age, boot-leg culture, whereas the newer men have felt the influence of the economic depression, prohibition repeal, and the humming technocracy epitomized in the fast car. The leisure-time ideations of prisoners do not vary widely, however, regardless of the socio-economic changes in the country. The differences which tend to persist are brought into at least overt conformity by the pressures of the penal environment.

Nothing more definite than some general statements can be offered regarding the leisure-time practices of our men before commitment. If it were possible to understand every cause and effect sequence on the recreational level of criminals' lives, we would be able to understand much more of criminality than we do now. But needed facts are missing and methodologies are imperfect for this understanding, and the same lacks prevail in the present analysis of leisure-time processes in the prison. From the two opening chapters of this book we have come to the general conclusion that our inmates, for the most part, have come from family situations which were far from socializing, and from neighborhoods whose conditions have been deleterious, and that they have had few opportunities for education and have not always taken those which were offered, and that their work has been predominantly of a menial nature. Therefore, it cannot be expected that the leisure pursuits of our subjects have contributed, except in rare instances, to the beautification of their lives, or to the welfare of their communities. The activities of the majority of the men have been of the adventurous and exciting sort which were pleasurable to them because of the thrills they offered, but which were of questionable value in moulding them into useful members of society. Leisure for another group has been largely a vegetablistic type of idleness in which recreational opportunities and facilities were absent. To the questions, "What do you do for a good time, for fun, for pleasure?" the answer frequently heard is, "I never had a good time." Better than the writer's generalizations are the words of the men themselves, or of their wives and their parents.

I. *Examples of Exaggerated Recreation: The Majority*

A fifty-five-year-old white inmate who has spent thirteen years in a prison says: "I would get myself two quarts of whiskey and a couple of pounds of cold meat and get a room in a hotel in a small town. I would lay up there alone for a couple of days until the whiskey ran out and then get some more. I would be drunk all the time but never noisy and never got into trouble. I guess that was the best pleasure I got out of my life after I was older."

A mother of a twenty-year old youth writes: ". . . . he was running around nights with his friends. . . . They led him on. . . . They would drive around the country like they were crazy. They had two auto accidents in two weeks and I think that one of L———'s friends would steal those cars. They would drink and gamble and go with those house women and L——— has never been the same since he met those other boys."

A forty-one-year-old white inmate from a wealthy home tells of his early leisure-time practices. "I started drinking when I was nineteen and I stayed drunk for about two years. The family had me take the Keeley cure, but I used to sneak gin up to my room in that hotel and place it in the water pitcher. It looked just like water and yet the attendants could smell it. Even when I was taking the cure I managed to stay drunk a good part of the time. . . ." Later this man used morphine. He gambled to excess, pursued unsavory feminine companionship, wrote fraudulent checks, and eventually shot a policeman.

A twenty-eight-year-old inmate with two years of prison residence comments: "When I won my first bet at the track, I wondered how long this had been going on. I played the horses for three years. When I would win I would spend the money carelessly and when I would lose I would sometimes get drunk, spend what I had left, then steal some more so I could lay more bets."

An inmate's wife writes: ". . . . It wasn't so much that he didn't love me or that he wasn't good to the children, or me, but he just seemed to have to go with other women. This broke up our home twice, but I came back to him each time. . . . I don't know what I will do now."

An advanced thief who entered prison during the latter part of 1929 remarks: "Those were the days . We would go from one speakeasy to another, and we were known all over the city. That liquor would kill you so we didn't drink too much very often. We went to the night spots with flasks. There were a lot of good musical shows in those days and we took them all in from the front rows. And I used to follow the football teams and make trips with them. . . ."

II. *Paucity of Recreation: Lack of Opportunity, Lack of Interest*

A twenty-year-old inmate says: "I never had a good time. Us kids had to work from the time we were old enough. Pa worked hard himself and he expected us to. I was shuckin' corn when I was nine, plowin' when I was twelve. I went to town once a month or so and it was fun to see the people, but we never did nothing. . . . I never saw a movie until I was over eighteen."

Another prisoner speaks: "There was nothing much to do in our town. I used to see the other guys down town but I never did nothing with them. . . . Yes, they played ball and went swimming, but I never went along. I could have, but I never cared for that."

A parent writes: ". . . his little sister goes to the library and belongs to some clubs and was in some plays at the school, but W——— never did anything like that. He was one to stay at home when he was a boy and when he got older he just went to the corner and he would just stay there with the other boys."

A wife writes: ". . . all the time I lived with him he never took me any place but to his relatives. He was never much for going out himself."

A young man reared in a large city which has a variety of recreational facilities and amusement places says: "We just never went to those places. Some of my friends followed baseball, but I would rather play "indoor" on the street there. I guess I just never went around much. . . . Some men tried to get me in a neighborhood club and I joined it, but none of the fellows stayed in it."

Suggestive of the leisure-time interests of inmates are the replies to forty-eight questions given to 200 men within a week of their admission to the penitentiary.[4] The subjects were unselected except that mental defectives were eliminated. A few of the more significant findings are presented here. Although 68 per cent of these men know that the 8-ball in a game of pool is colored black, only 17 per cent know that Frederick Stock is a veteran conductor of a symphony orchestra. More than 71 per cent know that a touchdown in football scores six points, but only 41 per cent are able to name even one favorite book. Likewise, 70 per cent know that in a dice game the numbers called "naturals" are seven and eleven, but only 24 per cent can identify Sinclair Lewis correctly. More than 60 per cent are able to name the winner of the World Series in 1934, but less than 18 per cent can name Sousa as "America's March King." Sixty per cent of the subjects are aware that in draw poker, five cards are dealt, but only 30 per cent can name three contemporary American writers.

Combining such findings as the above with the statements presented in our first two chapters, we are warranted in stating that a reflective or intellectual use of leisure time is almost non-existent, and that most of the leisure time of our men—if there has been leisure time—has been of the commercial, amusement and sporting type. To be sure, this conclusion is no startling revelation, yet it is well to keep in mind, as we examine the spare-time practices in the prison community.

Officially Regulated Leisure Time

Sports: America has been known as a nation which takes its exercise sitting down, and although this statement is less true now than it was ten years ago, yet at the present time "spectatoritis" is a term frequently used by investigators in recreational fields. This pattern of conduct is especially strong in prison. The one athletic pastime which for years has received the backing of the administra-

[4] From a recreational inventory prepared by the writer intended to measure the inmates' familiarity with various levels of recreation, interests, and leisure-time activities.

tion is baseball. Seldom, however, do more than twenty men participate, and the other 2,300 sit down and look on. During the years of this study an executive more enlightened than his predecessors made arrangements for allowing certain work groups, whose tasks kept them indoors, to have the freedom of the play field for baseball during the noon hour, but even this number is so small that the population in general still suffers from "spectatoritis." However, it is not the purpose here to evaluate the administrative facilities of the prison or the mechanics of the baseball program, but to point out certain of the social implications which accompany a baseball and sports program in the prison.

It is difficult to judge how much enjoyment the population obtains from the Saturday afternoon ball games with outside teams. In the early part of the season there is a mild enthusiasm. As the season wears on and the summer becomes hotter, the majority of the inmates lose what mild interest they had, and accept the march to the bleachers as just another duty imposed. It is probably only less unpleasant than many other things they are commanded to do. Those who actively dislike the baseball program are the older men who were not conditioned to be "fans" when they were boys. Much complaint arises over the hardness of the benches, the restrictions of movement, the heat, the watchfulness of the guards, and the "character" of convict baseball players. Such cheering as is offered is largely for the visiting team who represent some "free" community from a nearby city or town. This behavior seems to be derived from four conditions. First, the great majority of inmates dislike the "con" team because they think the players are prison politicians or stool pigeons. Second, the inmates are aware that the guards and officials enjoy the game and have a loyalty to "their" team and wish it to win, so the spectator-inmates, in order to be consistent, dislike the prison team because the officers support it, and adopt the visitors as their champions. At the best, however, it is a lukewarm partisanship. Third, the spectators like to identify themselves with persons other than their daily associates, at least impersonally, and for transitory periods. Fourth, the prison team has always been highly successful and victorious in games, and many inmates dislike to see prolonged success. Basic to these specific reasons the convicts have a deeply rooted dissatisfaction with their own status, and a rebellious attitude toward any factor or symbol which has caused or maintains it. If a member of a visiting team becomes officious and arrogant, the sympathies of the men revert to the home players, because the visitor is "acting like a guard!"

A few of the players have a following because they are known to be "right." When a player who has gone into a batting slump finally gets a hit, he is encouraged by the support of the inmates.

On the other hand, however, with the older, more sophisticated inmate spectators, there is no partisanship, and the game is simply an even on which they may gamble.

Although the spectators are likely to complain about the baseball games, the situation provides them with an opportunity for gossip and for contacts which otherwise they would not have. The men must sit in designated places but are allowed to converse with others near by, and are thus able to send messages to former associates to whom they rarely, if ever, get a chance to speak. This passing of information is accomplished by a device known as "passing the word." In the long lines of seated men one will say, "Pass the word to Morgan in 7-gang that O'Neill got pinched and is in the 'can' at Columbus." From man to man for a hundred yards this message is relayed until it reaches 7-gang and the Morgan for whom it was intended. The majority of the men who helped pass this message do not know the sender, the receiver, or the person involved. "Passing the word" is used only for fairly important topics, and messages have been started that never reached their destination because the men counted upon to relay them refused to do so because of the triviality of the news. The ball games not only provide a place for immediate social intercourse, but also furnish topics for conversation for days to come. Following a game there will be much discussion of the visiting players, the city or town they have represented, and the conduct of various personages at the game—all of which leads eventually to anecdotes in which the speaker plays the leading rôle. Not infrequently the events occurring at a game furnish the opening wedge for many hours of daydreaming and reverie. Such behavior is partially a response to a new situation—new situations stimulating, as they do, trains of thought, either in the form of memory or imagination, which deal with non-penal experiences. A new situation, for example, is the opening game of the year, or the fanfare which occurs on various holidays. At the opening game the prison imitates, so far as possible, the spectacle of baseball as it is known in the major leagues. The following news clipping from the prison paper is illustrative of this tendency:

> Due to cold weather it has been announced that the Cubs (the prison team) will not play until April 20th, at which time the inmates of this institution, led by the prison band, will march out to the Athletic Field and there witness the opening game of the baseball season. Guess we will have to dispense with the "flag raising" part of the usual opening game ceremony, for the very simple reason that there isn't any flag pole; however all the other salient features of the ritual will be observed. The warden will toss out the first ball; the usual animated pow-wow at the home plate between

> managers, captains and umpires, and then a stentorian announced, "Play Ball."
>
> The Cubs are ready. For the past month manager "Red" has been putting the boys through a most strenuous training program, bringing them up to the "barrier" in first-class playing condition. Not a sore arm or a "charley horse" among them. . .

The prison ball team and the games it plays with outside teams serves indirectly as an agency to stimulate interest in baseball in the major leagues. Some thirty or forty per cent of the inmates follow the sport. Each man will usually select a certain team as the New York Yankees, or the St. Louis Cardinals, and by means of the newspapers and sports broadcasts on the radio, follow it through the winter trades, spring training, and the 154-game season. The interested inmate comes to know the history of the major league ball players, the batting and fielding averages, the special skills and weaknesses of their favorites and the opponents. Such an interest with its accompanying knowledge supplies fuel for endless argument, small talk, and betting. The administration wisely allows radio broadcasts of games almost every afternoon, and during the World Series games in the autumn frequently allows the entire population to hear the broadcasts at the expense of the occupational program. Thus the activities of the Big Leagues combined with the schedule of the "home team" offer some emotional release for a considerable proportion of the community.

In 1933 the new warden soon became aware that the 370 men working indoors in the various shops were deprived of the exercise and fresh air which the men assigned to outdoor duties enjoyed. He then issued an order that during the clement weather of spring, summer, and autumn, men working in the shops might use the athletic field during the noon hour, an hour which they had previously spent in the cells. Supervision and baseball equipment were provided, but there was no leadership in organizing teams or schedules. Probably more than coincidence determined that soft or "kitten" ball should be selected as the type of sport, for only a few years before the warden's order an "epidemic" of kitten ball spread across America. Since prison life tends to imitate the free community life, the adoption of kitten ball was natural, although other factors, no doubt, operated in the choice.

Lacking official leadership the men from each work shop tended to keep together in certain sections of the recreation field when they first obtained the new freedom at the noon hour. Here they haphazardly "chose up sides" and played among themselves without manifesting any competitive spirit or any particular interest in the game. After several days of more or less disorganized play inmate

"J" perceived the possibility of inter-shop games. He launched the idea and it spread rapidly among the men in the various shops. After much talk and many arrangements among the various shop groups, a schedule was drawn up with dates for inter-shop games and the exchange of baseball diamonds, and provision made for a reward for the champions at the end of the season. The competitive plan inaugurated followed that used by the major leagues.

The organization of the "prison league" was largely due to the efforts of inmate "J" who drew up the schedules, had them approved by the officials, and directed the men on the field. We present one of the numerous bulletins "J" typed and posted to show how he adopted techniques to maintain interest.

Bulletin

A few months ago there were about 5 teams on the circuit that were capable of knocking off any good team that happened to be holding No. 1 diamond. But, the last few months has seen a change in the strength of the teams, as the chart will show. Today, what with teams breaking up every other day there are really only THREE strong clubs on the Circuit. OUGHT TO BE AT LEAST FIVE, considering that there are 8 teams on the Circuit. It's up to you managers. You can either have a team that can give out some pretty stiff competition, or you can have just a so-so team. WHICH DO YOU WANT?

Take the Knit Shop Team, for instance. They had a rotten ball team at one time. But—they reorganized, and now they have a pretty strong club, which has climbed from the so-so class to 2nd position. Yet—the only team left on the diamond that can give them any kind of battle is the Clothing House Team. IT SHOULDN'T BE THAT WAY! There should be other teams, at least 5 out of the 8, capable of giving them stiff competition. The fault lies with the managers. They're satisfied to go along in the same old rut day in and day out, not caring whether the team loses or wins. (Do I hear, " 'Taint so, 'taint so!")

Monday—Clothing House Team vs. Colored Giants. The Giants, at least, have no scruples against playing with good, hard balls; something that the Knit Shop refused to do.

Was that Mendenhall's newly organized team that lost to Rhone's Team on No. 3 diamond yesterday? If so, let me know. . . .

Rivalry, competition, and occasionally open conflict marked the inter-shop games. But as each season wore on, the teams cared less and less whether they won or not. It seemed, however, that a certain duality existed. A team's collective behavior might become listless and purposeless at one time, and later, regardless of success or failure, show unified purpose and collective initiative. The causes of such cyclic group behavior are related not only to the psycho-social aspects of monotony and variations in leadership ability, but also to the simple factors of temperature, humidity, as well as to the "heaviness" of the dinner which immediately precedes this play hour. The eight teams varied in their cohesiveness, although none of them may be said to have been closely integrated. This is probably due to the relatively large number of players on each team and the necessity for frequently substituting one player for another. Bickering—much of it good natured—flourished and there was ample opportunity to blame fellow players for errors. Through long experience prisoners have become adept at placing the blame on others, and their criticisms, even in a ball game, sometimes become very irritating to the recipient made doubly sensitive by long prison residence. This discord and wrangling among the players together with the realization of their total situation, and the fact that baseball victories are not very important so far as they individually, are concerned, prevented close harmony among team members. The men sharing the play field during the noon hour, regardless of the fortunes of their shop team, find that hour the most pleasant of the day. Custody is relaxed. Freedom of movement is allowed. Baseball playing is not obligatory and the inmate may walk leisurely up and down the edge of the field and gaze off into the distant hills—and many of them do so.

Football was first played in the autumn of 1933. The reaction of the spectators to football was not dissimilar to the response to baseball. Football spectatorship proved to be a new experience for a large proportion of the men and they found the first half of the first game interesting. The majority of the inmate spectators had no knowledge of the rules or objectives of the game, however, and eventually lost interest because of its technical and legalistic aspects. Generally the sympathies of the inmates, as in baseball, were for the visitors. One game in early November occurred on a cold day and the warden gave the population their choice of attending the game or remaining in their cells. About 1,000 men came out to the game. For the first time in the history of sports at the prison these 1,000 men cheered for the convict team, as the prisoners held a small normal college team to a zero to zero score. This almost paradoxical behavior on the part of the rooters can be explained first by the fact that the spectators were a selected group—they came to the game by choice—but more important, in all probability, was a feeling of aversion towards the opponents because they were "college boys." In our investigation of the almost paradoxical vocal support given the home team, attitudes were discovered inimical to the college players because they held such status. The half of the population which did not choose to attend the football game, the older, or more provincial men, developed strong anti-football feelings because the weekly games with outside teams took the place of movies. Their objections, however, came to naught, because they were made individually and had no corporate expression.

The writer coached the football team. This meant about two hours a day of intimate contact with the twenty-eight men who made up the squad. The response to coaching was good and the relationship between players and coach was harmonious. The men were physically large, somewhat more intelligent than the population in general (average M. A., 13 years and 9 months) and were, for the most part, occasional or accidental offenders rather than habitual criminals. Also, many of them had had some high school training. They varied in age between nineteen and twenty-seven years, and had been in prison for periods varying from five months to eight years, with an average residence of three years and one month. In general, the squad would be considered somewhat above the average or "better" than the ordinary inmate, socially speaking.

As on any athletic team, competition for positions was keen and often broke out into open conflict. However, a strict leadership kept the conflicts from becoming too damaging. Football, being essentially a team game, demands the utmost in collective action, therefore the most difficult coaching task was to develop coöperation and team feeling in the players. Unlike the students in a school where there is a tradition and loyalty to be maintained, the prison players had little but contempt for their "school" and it was necessary for the coach to arouse in them an appreciation of what value the game, properly played, would have for them as individuals. To this end he stressed the advantage to them in physical improvement, in training for the world of hard knocks which they would face when paroled, and an attempt was made to develop a sense of status which would be applicable to the social organization in the penitentiary. An effort was also made to build up a we-feeling and a morale and with some success, except that when the players became physically weary and when the misfortunes of the game buffeted them, they behaved like eleven separate individuals rather than like a coöperating unit of eleven men. It was possible to develop the men into hard, vicious, and effective tacklers. Tackling is spectacular, observable by the spectators, and demonstrates courage and agility. Tackling is an essentially individualistic aspect of football; the inmates did it well. Blocking, equally as essential as tackling, was never effectively done by the men. Blocking is not individualistic, but demands the coöperation of two or three men. It is not, usually, a spectacular aspect of the game and blockers receive little of the applause. The coach considered that the difference in effectiveness between blocking and tackling to be directly related to the individualized orientation of the men and not to athletic skills. Taking into consideration the great difference between the inmate team and the visiting teams in personalities and type of living, we found the actual athletic behavior was quite similar. During the first season the prison team won one game, lost one, and tied four against teams of approximately their own age and size.

Boxing has made up part of the sports program since the summer of 1933. For a period of nearly an hour each Wednesday noon the entire population marched to the bleachers. A regulation-sized boxing ring was utilized for the eight or ten bouts held. Three types of encounters took place: grudge fights between two inmate "enemies," boxing contests in which no grudge motive existed, and free-for-alls, in which six or eight men fought to see who could remain standing longest, the winner receiving a prize, usually tobacco. The interest of the spectators at the "fights" was keener than at any other sports event. This is probably because the desire for combat and the physical courage and stamina it requires are qualities held in high esteem by all inmates except the older men and a portion of the "con" men and embezzlers. Other reasons for the interest and enjoyment of the boxing program by the inmate spectators seem to be: (a) attendance at the boxing match relieved the men from spending the Wednesday noon hour in their cells; (b) the show presented some aspects of new experience sufficient to provide material for later associative speculation or daydreams; (c) the performance lasted less than an hour and was thus not long enough to become boring, and (d) certain unmeasurable and only barely perceptible emotional releases occur for many of the spectators bringing a feeling of relaxation.

Of the three types of encounters the grudge fights have the most significance. Angry inmates who start bare-knuckle fights during the daily life, if observed by officials, are stopped and made to "fight it out with gloves" under regular boxing rules at the Wednesday noon shows. Grudge fights are announced as such and excite considerable gossip among the spectators concerning the cause of the grudge. The work associates of the men involved usually know the grounds for the ill-will and relay the information by word of mouth so that within a short time the news has spread to the entire community of 2,400 persons assembled in the grandstand. Some of the grudge fights are concerned with delicate matters. Sex is often a basic motive. Injustices, real or imagined, among "rap-buddies" are frequent causes. Some causes of grudge fights are trivial, such as an argument over a card game, but the fights may assume a vicious character due to the tenseness always present in restrained individuals. Status also becomes at least mildly important for a fighter when he is ranked by the spectators for his courage, or lack of it, in the ring. The regular boxing contests which are promoted by an inmate "promoter" are exhibitions of skill and strength and have no great social significance except that the champion of each weight division becomes a person of as much importance as can be achieved in a social organization in which impersonalization flourishes.

A few other sports are fostered by the officials. Horse-shoe games are allowed for the quarry gangs and farm workers. Some men play the game at least fifteen minutes a day, year in and year out, and become experts. Some fifty or sixty men who achieve real skill in the game use their status, or what they believe to be their status as "champs" to compensate for their failures in life, notably their immediate situation of prison residence. An occasional soccer game presented by two visiting teams arouses little interest and supplies no further social implications than do other sport programs. The first game, however, furnished source material for conversation, as soccer was a new form of sport to almost the entire population.

Movies: The movies are enjoyed more than any other recreation fostered by the administration. While about one-half of the inmate population have only the mildest interest in the sport program, everyone, excluding the blind and some mental cases obtains at least transitory entertainment from the moving pictures. The formal baseball or football seasons are the only periods when movies are not held once a week. On some occasions, for example, a holiday like July 4th, there will be a movie in the morning and a ball game in the afternoon. In general, there are between 30 and 35 movies per year. Blumer [5] has found in his Payne Fund studies that a large proportion of the prison population have the opportunity to witness movies about as frequently as the non-penal population. In our prison the chapel serves as the theatre and the productions usually consist of a news reel, a comedy, an educational short, and a feature. Three showing are held, one on Friday evening for trusties, other select inmates, and officials, and two on Saturday. The prisoners are marched to the movies as they are to the ball games. Talking is not permitted officially although no trouble is caused for conversers who maintain reasonable quiet.

The features which are shown in the prison are the same that will be seen in any first-rate theatre, although the prison, of course, presents them some months after their release in large cities. Gangster and highly emotional love stories are not permitted, but otherwise the main pictures are typical Hollywood productions. Such actors as Clark Gable, Eddie Cantor, Grace Moore, Claudette Colbert, and others are the featured players.

[5] Herbert Blumer and P. M. Hauser, *Movies, Delinquency and Crime,* Payne Fund Studies, The Macmillan Company, New York, 1933, p. 164.

The exact effect of the movies on the prisoners is unknown. Of course reactions vary with varying personalities. Blumer found that with reformatory men who are younger than our men, 67 per cent declared that movies made them feel more cheerful and contented, 61 per cent said that the movies they saw made them feel to some extent like going straight, and 68 per cent admitted that the movies aroused them sexually.[6] No comparable data are offered here, although the following frank statements by inmates give some insight:

Advanced offender, age 31, says: "Movies don't have any effect in reforming me. They might make some sap cry, but tears are no sign of reform, and, anyway, those guys that cry in the show don't know what it's all about, or are stir-bugs."

First offender, ex-banker, age 50: "I like the comedies best . . . they make you forget the place . . . the big picture (feature) makes me think of where I am. . . . No, I don't think the movies make men do sex things . . . but I've heard them talk and joke about it. . . . Yes, I think I can understand how a certain kind of picture might reform a man if it caught him just right."

Inmate "P" says: "You can take this or leave it, but I know it to be a fact. Those cinemas which offer a love theme are directly and inseparably the cause of heightened sex longings on the part of the men. Masturbation and . . . perversions both by individuals and couples . . . occur more frequently after movies where beautiful women are shown."

Inmate "X" reports: "I believe the shows do more harm than good. . . . I always get lonesome afterwards, but of course I stay to myself quite a bit anyway."

There is much evidence to the effect that the movies provide material for ideas which the men use in initiating subsequent daydreams and reverie. This principle has been mentioned before in relationship to baseball, but it is more prominent following movies. Similarly, the movies supply topics of conversation usually leading to sex talk or heated, but feeble, argument over ethical points raised by the story. Snatches of conversation following a movie: "How'd you like to take that baby to bed?" "The guy was a chump to give up his dough for the girl." "You notice the way the man's clothes fit—smooth, all right, and that hat. I had one of those when I was pinched." "Living in a joint like that (luxurious) and me in these cells!"

A few inmates have imaginative and retentive minds and place themselves in the rôle of a certain screen actor, remember his traits, mannerisms, oddities of speech and many of the lines he spoke, and partially play that rôle as they plod through a daily prison routine.

[6] *Ibid.*, p. 195.

In such instances the effect of the movies on personality is extreme. In some 20 or 30 per cent of the prison population (the intellectually dull, the unimaginative, the socially cold, and the preoccupied) the movies probably have no marked effect of any lasting kind. As they file from the chapel the perceptions of the past ninety minutes are largely blotted out. The majority of the men are affected by the cinema no differently than are non-prisoners who see movies in the normal community, except for this possible important exception (and this point is raised as hypothesis) that the total complex of perception obtained from the picture tends to strengthen whatever psycho-social configuration is most prominent in the personality. The customary picture will have a love interest, a hero who overcomes obstacles, and so on. Our inmates seem to identify themselves with the hero of the movie or with some other member of the cast, but transpose the pictorial setting of the picture into their own sphere. Thus, the lonely man becomes more lonely. Men whose sexual starvation is overwhelming feel that situation more deeply. The man who has strong urges for legitimate success in business, trade, athletics, or the arts finds his urges somewhat increased. The person whose predominant psycho-social configuration is for luxury and comforts, if he possesses basic preditory attitudes finds his desires more crystalized, and he becomes more zealous for unlawful gain. But like most other feeling states which men develop in prison, these urges, with the exception of the sex urge, tend to be leveled off by the heavy, day-to-day dreariness and monotony, and the socially useful feeling states seem to wilt before the socially harmful ones do.

Radio: Radio programs bring to the semi-isolated prison community the life of the normal world. There is no gainsaying the importance of the radio as an agent contributing to the culture of the penitentiary. What radio means to the isolated farm family twenty miles from town, it means to the convict inside tall walls. Crooners and comedians from New York become as well known as prominent political candidates, football stars, toothpastes, and automobiles.

Except during the major league baseball season, the prison radio offers programs for one-half hour at noon, and usually from seven until nine in the evening. Occasional afternoon programs may be offered, but not frequently except during the summer when the ball games are broadcast. A typical day's program would include organ or dance music at noon, commercials and a sports review in the evening, incidental music and a chain program at seven when a comedian with dance orchestra is heard, and perhaps a half hour of hill-billy music and fifteen minutes of news by a commentator. During political campaigns speeches predominate. Only infrequently will there be heard the more substantial offerings such as symphonic music, "Town Meeting of the Air," "March of Time," or similar programs. News flashes are never emphasized if they tend to specialize on world or national events, but such programs as deal with local news, especially of a political nature, are offered. Censorship of crime dramas, or actual crime news is strict.

In all of the cellhouses there are several loudspeakers. The size of the cellhouses demands that the radio be loud. Those who dislike the programs have no choice, although they may attempt to turn their attention to other things. The constant programs become almost unbearable to the men with an active dislike for radio. Situational reactions, a temporary form of psychosis, have had their immediate causes in the blatant blare of radio. To men with no interest in baseball, the drone of the broadcaster describing for two hours a day, over a period of six months, the minute doings of eighteen ball players becomes almost insufferable. Many men have schooled themselves to ignore the radio entirely. Even though a loud speaker may be only a few feet from them offering music, jokes, drama, and commercials for two hours at a time, they have no knowledge of the content, and when the power is cut off they are aware only of a change. Other men follow the radio programs avidly. The sports fans and gamblers count the fifteen-minute sport review as of considerable importance. Game scores, race results, and interesting tid-bits of knowledge about celebrities provide many minutes of speculation and conversation for such addicts. Those men who follow, sponsor and champion particular teams or athletes, are always eager for the sport news. In this the prisoners are no different than many non-prisoners, for being a "fan" of something or other is almost an American folkway. Steiner comments, "Following the fortunes of favorite teams and players is an important leisure-time pursuit for large numbers of people." [7] It is probable that a proportion of prisoners become greater fans and develop greater emotional loyalty than do non-prisoners, due, largely, to the absence of other interests. Besides sport enthusiasts the radio provides amusement for comedy fans. The broadcasted jokes are told and retold. Mimicry of Gracie Allen, Ed Wynn, Eddie Cantor, Stoopnagle and Bud becomes common. The dance music fans come to know the history, compositions, currently popular tunes, and music styles of such orchestras as those of Guy Lombardo, Wayne King, Abe Lyman, Waring's Pennsylvanians, Ben Bernie. The "hoe-down" or hill-billy music fans thrive on the minstrel shows and the country dances. Among the many radio programs offered during a week there usually are a few that appeal to each

---

[7] Jessie Steiner, Recent Social Trends, *op. cit.*, p. 929.

individual inmate, and the balance of the renditions are simply something to be endured.

By and large, the men listen to the radio in their cells, usually lying down and undressed. They may read, converse, eat, play cards, sleep, or daydream during the program. They may listen attentively, partially, or not at all. Precise knowledge of the affect of the radio on the mass is unknown, but the following statements, considered fairly representative of various types impart some evaluation:

"I would like the radio if there wasn't so much damn much of it . . . all the time it goes until you get almost nuts."

"About all I listen to is the scores. I'm a 'Card' fan, see, and . . ."

"Ed Wynn is so screwy he's funny . . . me and my cell partner get a lot of laughs out of him."

"I go in for dance music pretty much because the new tunes, if you know 'em you can whistle and hum them during the day and the time passes faster. I used to play the sax, you know. . . ."

"Those torch singers are my dish. They get in my hair, like before. . . ."

"Radio, no. I never listen to it 'cause I've got my books and home-town newspaper, and besides I go to sleep early every night."

Letters and Visits: Classifying letter writing, the receiving of letters and visits from home folks as part of a leisure-time program may be debatable. Letters may be partially justified in so far as they are written and read during spare, or leisure, time. While visits occur during the working part of the day, they provide a change of scene and associates for the inmate, and are sometimes, but not always, occasions for pleasant feeling states, and to this extent visits may be thought of as leisure-time activities.

Letters are routinely written on Sunday afternoon. One sheet of letterhead paper, ruled on each side and a pencil are given to the inmate, if he needs one. Ninety minutes after the blank paper is passed the finished letters are collected, read by the censors in the following thirty-six hours, and mailed. The rules pertaining to letter writing are as follows:

All inmates in Grades A and B may write weekly. All inmates in Grade C are permitted to write every other week. All inmates in Grades D and E are only permitted to write the first Sunday of each month.

Name, number, and serial letter must be given at bottom of letter.

Use of other inmate's writing privilege is strictly forbidden and subject to punishment, with writing privileges suspended indefinitely.

Acquaintance letters: Inmates are forbidden to correspond with persons where no previous acquaintance has been established.

Letters not to be addressed to General Delivery. Letters not to be addressed to newspapers. Two letters not to be written on one sheet.

Officials not to be criticized. Institution not to be criticized. Do not mention other inmates by name or number.

Letters may be written to or received from a foreign country, if written in other than English, otherwise not admitted or sent.

Friendly letters to friends must be of a friendly nature. Business letters are to be confined to business.

It is often said that prisoners are not articulate, but judging from the letters shown in Chapter VI, and taking into consideration the fact that the intelligence of prisoners does not vary greatly from that of the normal population, one can only conclude that their written expression is fairly adequate. Of course the illiterate and intellectually dull cannot write letters, but they prevail on other men to help them. The contents of the letters are personalized and deal almost always with the private lives of the sender and the addressee. (See Chapter VI.)

Real ingenuity is developed in manufacturing phrases and words which have ambiguous meanings, ambiguous to the extent that the ostensible meaning is innocent yet the hidden meaning, if known, would be censored. The following examples will illustrate. Innocent enough is the sentence, "John S. was released from the hospital although he is not well yet, and I am afraid he will have a relapse awfully soon. If his sickness clears up he promises to give me some money for tobacco." It means: "John was paroled; he is going to steal right away, and if he makes a 'score' will send the writer a lawyer." Similarly, a well-known "junker" (morphine user) wrote to his sister, formerly a user, "I am feeling awful, can't eat or sleep. If you could send me some more money for food at the commissary I could get back on my feet," which means: "I am awfully 'low' without the 'stuff.' Put money on my account and by bargaining, I can pick up a quarter grain in the yard." Many symbols are used which are agreed upon during visits. Thus, the phrase, "The mosquitoes are getting worse," may mean that the inmate's associates in the offense are becoming more threatening; or an innocent word like "weather" may mean "escape," as in the phrase, "Can't figure out the weather," means "I can't beat this joint." How much of this duality comes into the letters is unknown, although probably such devices are used only by the most advanced offenders.

The writing of letters constitutes an essentially pleasant diversion compared with many other aspects of prison life because of the opportunity for expansion of the ego. Sacrifice, self-righteousness, strength in adversity, hope for the future, and self-pity are prominent themes in the letters. Some letters, of course, are completely defeatist in theme, and many consist solely of pleas for money.

Receiving letters is less pleasurable than writing them except in those instances when the letters bear good news pertaining to the inmate's status. Usually letters from home or friends include thoughts which cause lonesomeness, shame, vindictiveness, feelings of being unwanted, feelings of being misunderstood, and sorrow or remorse in other forms. It is only the rare letter received by an inmate which contains humor, non-personal abstractions, or subtle encouragement.

Visits are complex hedonistic experiences. Especially trying to both the inmate and his visitors are the first few visits after a new man is admitted. Most frequently the relatives had last seen the prisoner in court, dressed neatly in civilian clothes. They find it shocking when they next see him in prison dressed in drab dungarees, with a number emblazoned on his shirt. In their full view he is searched by a guard. He is allowed to kiss wife or mother, but a keeper with a hard eye watches the proceeding. On opposite sides of a broad table, visitors and prisoner are allowed a full hour. An inmate tells it better:

> The gong at the double gate clangs twice when visitors appear, as a signal to the Usher, who comes to the gate and takes the names and addresses of would-be visitors. A "visit slip" is made out at the door, and after that is O. K.'d by the assistant warden, the Usher's runner goes to the gang or shop or department in which the prisoner works and brings him back to the administration building. The slip passes him through the back gate, and he stands beside the door while the guard bawls his name to the turnkey at the front gate. The turnkey repeats the name loudly enough for the visitors in the Reception Room to hear, and they come through the double gate into the Guard Hall which contains the visitors' table—an odd piece of furniture, sixty feet long and four wide, with a partition underneath it which reaches from the floor to the bottom of the table and makes it impossible for visitors to pass anything to, or receive anything from, prisoners. The visitors walk the length of the table, and greetings, handshakes, and caresses are exchanged under the watchful eyes of the guard. Then the prisoner and his visitor or visitors separate at the end of the table and take chairs opposite one another. They are at liberty to say anything they care to say, without restriction or censorship, but nothing is allowed to be passed across the table and a guard keeps his eye on the polished surface of the table from a chair set above the level of the table top at one end of the hall, and another guard stands alertly at the other end. Written messages or material of any description must pass through the Usher's office, and any other articles must be inspected there, also, before passing into the possession of the prisoner. Money for the accounts of prisoners, like money received by mail, is received at the Usher's office, and turned over to the cashier. The prisoner does not receive the cash, but is given credit for it, and can spend it at the commissary.
>
> Most visitors at this out-of-the-way spot come in automobiles, and the

cars are as varied as the visitors. New, high-priced cars are parked here occasionally, and the scale of cars descends to battered, antiquated, Model T's which are barely able to run. Visitors and cars, alike, run the scale of appearances, but appearances are not the only thing to be considered in visitors. The old lady who comes in the Model T to visit an erring son may be a great deal finer in comparison with the modish and exotic female who shows silken limbs as she steps gracefully from a Cadillac, than is the Cadillac above the old lady's decrepit Ford. On the other hand, thoroughly nice people come in high-class cars, and thoroughly bad ones. . . . Not all mothers—song writers to the contrary—are good, though most sons think that the woman who gave them birth is faultless. Poverty is not proof of honesty or goodness—nor is wealth proof of wickedness.

Sometimes the garish young women who step out of the classy motors leave a bored male escort to spend weary hours outside, alone, while they enter and exchange caresses and gossip with some prisoner who accepts the caresses at face value and pretends to believe everything he hears. The general attitude is, "A gal's gotta live," and few questions are asked.

The visitors are predominantly female, as are the correspondents, and they range from mothers, sisters, wives, and daughters, to common-law wives, pseudo-cousins, who claim relationship to obtain permission to visit or write to prisoners, down to those morbid and senseless females who seek a thrill or a dubious romance with some prisoner whose name they have obtained. There are more of the latter than an uninformed person would believe possible.

Some women bring five or six children of varying ages and states of cleanliness—cleanliness seems to be in inverse ratio to the number—to see the husband and father. Such meetings are pitiful: almost always the children seem to be too heavy a load on the woman who is, at best, inefficient and inadequate. Nearly all visits here have pitiful aspects, even the meetings of the wild gals and their erstwhile lovers, since they, too, have feelings. Probably the most pitiful are those meetings of parents who have led unqualifiedly decent lives and are forced to make sacrifices and endure privations to pay occasional visits to sons . . . powerless to help the old folks or prevent them from spending their money on visits.

If visits are regular every two weeks, the worst horrors wear off after the first year and wife or mother with their loved one become more accustomed to the social gracelessness of the visiting hour. The temper and tempo of the visit depend, of course, on the nature of the personalities involved. From much inquiry and observation the most usual topics of conversation in the order of their importance are as follows: (1) release of the prisoner: parole, pardon, parole arrangements, job, petition, sponsor, escape; (2) experiences of prisoner: food, cellmate, guards, punishment, work, leisure; (3) condition of visitors: health, finances, troubles, neighbors, relatives; (4) prisoner's crime: trial, judge, police, jail, offense, and rationale; (5) the future: reform, vengeance, more crime, luxuries, and compensations. If the visitor is a young wife or sweetheart, sex longings are implied. Frequently the young husband is plagued by jealousies and doubts as to his wife's fidelity. Often the inmate begs, unashamed, for tobacco and candy money.

While the radio, the newspapers, incoming new prisoners, and the keepers, to some extent, bring into the prison the contemporary life of normal society, the patterns thus disseminated are distinctly impersonal, but when the visitors have been previously affiliated with the prisoner in the primary-group bonds, every word and gesture of the visitor becomes personal and is memorized and relived. Some effects of visits can be seen in the following observations:

> "I cry when they come and I cry when they leave."
>
> ". . . and I said, 'Here, mamma, it won't always be like this. . . . God, she is looking old. . . . I've got to do something . . . she's out there all alone."
>
> "My wife plays me for a sucker. She had a kid by the sheriff that sent me here . . . and I hate that son-of-a-bitch, and I hate her, and they'll get theirs when my turn comes."
>
> "Rose, my sister, was here. She's just out of the 'can' at Aldersen. She looks swell; the time did her good and she's off the stuff (morphine). She's going to see Joe who can get one of these small-time judges to spring me on a writ, she says."
>
> "That's what worries me. I can't expect her to wait for me. If I get less than four years, I'm lucky. She's only 20. I told her to get a divorce, but she's trying to stand by me. I haven't got a chance."

While visits are essentially tragedies for the persons involved, the constant visitor, the wife or mother who comes to see her loved one year after year, comes to feel almost at ease in the visiting room. The tragedy remains, but through a bond with the inmate visited a type of assimilation occurs. The visitor may learn to like a certain guard and to hate another. The visitor will carry away the argot of the prison community, and in some instances the visitor will gain a new appreciation of the problems which a prison administration faces in discharging its duty.

Mothers with children who visit the husband and father are beset with the difficulty of protecting their children from harmful influences and impressions. A loyal wife, always accompanied by her five-year-old son, visited her husband regularly. Little Jim came to be well known in the visiting room and was petted and made much of by the trusties and guards. The mother related to her inmate husband that the little girl next door to their home in the city had tattled to her mother that little Jim had teased her. Jim's mother punished him and the little boy took it stoically. When Jim next saw the little girl, the story goes, he walked up to her, and in slugger fashion hit her on the jaw, saying, "You will 'fink' on me, will you, you son-of-a-bitch." Five years old!

Reading: Such reading and study as is done occurs during the leisure-time periods. The newspapers receive the widest attention because of their daily appearance, the brevity of articles, and the fact that one paper is read by many persons since it is "passed along." Every day about 300 newspapers come in. In addition to the daily sheets to which many prisoners subscribe, there are the local, small-town papers which may be weeklies. Altogether, about 90 different papers come in each week. Censorship of newspapers exists in name only, and very rarely have papers been withheld because of censorship.

In general, inmate interests in the newspaper topics in the order of importance are (1) crime: police, parole, prison riots; (2) sports: baseball, football, horses, auto races; (3) home and local news; (4) comics and cartoons; (5) columnists such as O. O. McIntyre and Winchell; (6) political and national news; (7) international news. Very little attention is paid to topic 6, unless an election is in the offing in which case the prisoners follow the campaign closely, hoping that the current political party of office holders will be defeated and the official family of the prison thus be changed. Topic 7 attracts attention only if war appears in the offing, arousing the hope that a national emergency may lead to outright release of inmates to do army service.

The most avid newspaper readers are the small number of men who religiously, month after month, and in some instances year after year, "follow the ponies." From the entries of horse races in the sport sheets these men pick winners and bet mythical dollars, keeping elaborate records of their wagers. The followers of baseball also depend on the papers for statistical data such as batting averages. Certain features of newspapers as jigsaw puzzles (in 1932-33), crossword puzzles, "How much do you know?" columns, and especially health columns, provide leisure-time pursuits for the men. Editorials are almost never given attention, but the continued stories appearing in many sheets have numerous followers. The effects of newspapers on the prison population defies analysis except in the broadest terms. In general, the newspaper supplies diversion. It causes some readers to forget, temporarily, their woefully sad life, yet for others it emphasizes the unhappiness of their lot. It adds knowledge and facts to the lives of inmates, but seldom wisdom. The newspapers, emphasizing as they do, either subtly or directly, the profit system, play a part in increasing the capitalistic orientation among prisoners. Advertisement and news, or feature articles emphasize travel, fine clothes, expensive cars, and wealth in general, and imply that possession of, or experience with, such things makes for status and prestige in our society. Such an attitude has been part of every prisoner's orientation, and the newspapers read in prison tend to reinforce such a perspective.

Magazines offer the same diversions as do the newspapers. The magazines most read are: *The Saturday Evening Post, Colliers,* the *Red Book,* and *Film Fun.* Purchased in lesser number are: *Adventure, American Mercury, All Western, Astounding Stories, Ballyhoo, Baseball Magazine, Black Mask, Breezy Stories, Camera Craft, Clues, Cowboy Stories, Current Psychology and Psychoanalysis, Esquire, Etude Music Magazine, Farm Journal, Field and Stream, G-Men, Harpers, Hunting and Fishing, Mechanics and Handicraft, Modern Romances, Motion Picture Magazine, Modern Screen, Popular Mechanics, Popular Western, Poultry Item, Radio Stars, Railroad Stories, Romantic Range, Screen Romances, Silver Screen, The Stage, Sweetheart Stories, Texas Rangers, Thrilling Mystery Stories, Thrilling Ranch Stories, Thrilling Western Stories, True Confessions, Weird Tales, Readers' Digest, The Billboard, Literary Digest, Time, News-Week, Who's Who in Baseball,* 1000 *New Jokes,* and so on. A survey of the reading tastes of the men will indicate the diversity of interests and give some insight into the personalities with which we deal. The pulp magazines have more readers, of course, than *Etude* or *Time, Time* having but four subscribers on a selected week. Like newspapers, the magazines are much read and passed from cell to cell.

The book reading of inmates can best be illustrated by quoting brief passages from a special "Survey" of the library by an inmate who worked in it. The inmate quoted has very superior intelligence and a general familiarity with library systems, in so far as he had attended a large university for some years. After formulation of a plan and general instructions by the writer, the inmate-researcher proceded independently, and the passages which follow are taken verbatim from his twenty-page report.

In making a survey of the prison library one is impressed with the lack of personal direction. "Father buys the books, mother keeps the key to to the bookcase; and hands the boys a volume from time to time upon request." The collection is under the control of the chaplain who uses the book room as an office. His duties as the prison preacher and as the overseer of the spiritual welfare of the convicts take up most of his time, and he has little to do with the conduct of the library with the exception of acting guard during working hours. There is no intensive routine and with the exception of a transitory record made at the time of issue, no one knows to whom a book has been issued, when it was issued, nor its present location. Based upon the theory that since the borrower cannot possibly get away, the book must certainly remain, and a skip in numeral sequence on a shelf is the mute and only testimony to a missing volume. Continually there are being returned to the shelves what are known as "stolen books." Since there are no checks on borrowers, a book may be withdrawn, the identifying numbers erased, and the volume sold for tobacco money to another who may not be aware that he could borrow it from the library freely. So the book is lost indefinitely until the purchaser is paroled, or until the hidden identification—always on page 27—is discovered and the book is claimed and returned to the book room.

* * *

The only contact which the prisoner has with the library is through the medium of a mimeographed catalog which is loaned to him for a day or two. There are four inmate assistants in the book room, each of whom has a definite number of cells to serve. Upon request, the assistant delivers a catalog with an issue ticket which has space for sixty accession numbers. On the reverse of this ticket are printed the library rules:

1. Do not loan your library book.
2. Do not deface library book or cover.
3. Always return book charged to you.
4. Do not keep book longer than two weeks unless you have had it renewed by the librarian.
5. Do not take library books from cell unless you are changing quarters.
6. For infraction of the above rules you will be denied library privilege for one month.

When the issue ticket is filled and the catalog returned, the prisoner is constituted a patron. Among these sixty numbers, representing titles, it is expected that at least one of the volumes will be available, and the book will be delivered during the same day, and if not available, the withdrawal slip is returned to the borrower until the next day appointed for his particular group.

* * *

Accessions: On the shelves are some three hundred volumes in German text. Included in this lot are numerous German Bibles. There is so little call for books written in the German language that these books have never been catalogued. The state library has at times presented volumes, duplicates on its shelves. Much of this material is comprised of government reports and quite valueless in this collection. Many books have been accepted as gifts from private owners. Very valuable, indeed, to some studious prisoners are the International Correspondence School reference texts, especially to those learning the cement, metal, or wood working trades. So also there has been acquired a number of secondary school textbooks on several scientific subjects. Most of these are obsolete; however, there is some call for them from persons whose imaginations have been quickened by an attractive news story. There is no chance to exchange books with other libraries hence these accessions have accumulated for years and remain dead timber.

* * *

The Catalog: Upon accession, the books are catalogued in two general divisions of *Fiction* and *Non-Fiction*. There is no "system" of cataloging. The new accession numbers, in sequence, are used merely to designate the volume's place on the shelf. The fiction class begins wth numeral one, the non-fiction class begins with numeral five thousand. The non-fiction class is further differentiated in the catalog by arbitrary divisions such as Religion, Science, Philosophy, Biography, and the like. Since accessions in the non-fiction class are very rare, no recent change has been made in the catalog save as "Unclassified" in an appendix.

As a guide to the reader, fiction has been divided into subdivisions based upon pertinent subject matter. Since there is no chance for the general borrower either to inspect the books desired, or even to ask advice of the librarian concerning the subject matter of these books, a custom has developed by which subject matter may be indicated by symbols which may cover an extended range of subjects and still be closely identified as of one group. Thus the symbol has come to stand for "type" and is depended upon by the average borrower exclusive of either title or author. Roughly, the symbols used are the following:

W Western stories.
N-W Tales of the Northwest.
M Mystery or detective tales.
U Tales of gangsters and the underworld.
L Love stories.

This classification, in the main, is a true one, but there are shades of meaning which are reserved in the cataloguer's mind and which are quickly acquired by the borrower. The letter "W" is generic, in that it applies not so much to locale as to character—the rancho, the cow-puncher, the six-shooter, the outlaw. Time and geography enter not so much the borrower's mind as the lure of ACTION—the broncho, the sombrero, schapps, and poncho. So, too, on the other hand, there has grown up a custom of combining tales of the Northwest, where flows the Oregon, the mines, the wheat ranches, the mountains and trout streams, the bob-cat and the grouse and quail, irrespective of character or plot, under the purely geographical symbol "N-W." In like fashion, letter "M" immediately announces the detective and mystery tales while symbol "U" narrows this class more closely to the "underworld," the "Me-Gangster" type.

These are rough-hewn classifications, but they serve the purpose fully as well to the mind of the borrower as would more elaborate media. The love motif must come in every tale, and yet the romances are symbolized by "L" as "love stories" or left unmarked in the catalog as being too unwieldy for simple classification. Hence it is that "classic" romances—Dickens, Galsworthy, Hugo—not easily classified, remain unaccented in the lists, and remain unknown to the mass of prisoners.

* * *

This is the greatest weakness of the catalog, for the tendency of the unaided reader prone to follow the line of least resistance, orders his books exhaustively to type, and allows the fuller, richer expression of romance lie idle on the shelves. *Les Miserables,* in two volumes, a good translation, and in excellent print has probably not been withdrawn in years. Recently it has been in the hands of an unusual and bright young man, who, because of his delighted interest has developed a "vogue" among his friends. Just now there is a demand for it from a number of persons. And so was *The Forsyte Saga* unknown and unsought until it was discovered recently on the shelves and made a "book of the month" among the better trained clerks. Since no records are kept of transmissions, it is quite impossible to formulate any statistical study of book issues, except as based upon the memories of the assistants, but it is very probable that a Dickens or a Thackery are not withdrawn once a year. If it were possible for the borrower to enter the book room, if only once a month, to spend a few minutes in earnest conversation with the librarian on a vigorous reading schedule, the use of the library would become more vital, more aggressive and more helpful.

* * *

In the catalog are listed two thousand and forty-two titles, but under the popular fiction titles are from three to ten additional copies. The total number of classified volumes is four thousand, sixty-two, and with certain as yet unclassified books, the total is somewhat over five thousand.

* * *

Why men order the books they do has as many answers as there are men.

"Please give me a book on psychology." "None in just now." "Well, if you haven't any, give me a Western."

A certain Negro has always asked for texts on electricity. He cannot read a word but obtains some sense of gratification in being able to impress his companions who are as ignorant as he.

One man, by design, received the same book for three months and did not know the difference. Each week he would put in his order, the book would be gathered up and then returned to him, and each week he would be asked how he liked the book. Invariably he replied that he "liked it fine."

Many men order books and then never read them because

1. They wish to impress the parole board by claims of studiousness.
2. They desire to cause as much trouble as possible to any person whom they consider has a soft job.
3. Some never receive letters from the outside, hence the delivery of a book tends to break the monotony and gives them something to look forward to.

* * *

Statistics: . . . On a certain day a study was made of number 4 gallery, chosen because it represented a fair cross-section of the prison population, men who were neither highly, nor poorly, trained; neither all young nor all middle-aged men, with a representative degree of culture, attention, and industry. From these ninety-eight men were received forty-six issue tickets which would indicate that fifty-three per cent of the convicts do not make any use whatever of library facilities. At once we realize, however, that this is not a true conclusion for without doubt some men had returned their tickets three days previously and were not finished with their withdrawal, and then, on the other hand, there is no proof that these present withdrawals were not occasioned by errors made in enumeration, or in filling the call itself. Other questions and objections arise as well, but the fact remains that on that day forty-seven per cent of the entire gallery requested books.

Now let us learn what they wanted. Of the forty-six issue tickets examined, twenty-seven men, or fifty-nine per cent of the total, asked exclusively for "Wild Westerns." This brooks no comment, but is illuminating to consider what was desired by the remaining nineteen men who asked for partial non-fiction.

Devotional		3
Poetry and Shakespeare		2
Educational		10
Texts	6	
Trade Manuals	4	
Belles Lettres		2
Travel and Biography		2

* * *

Gallery 4 is a fine, average group of reading men. It must be remembered that galleries which house the clerks, teachers, and other educated prisoners must needs show a higher average; on the other hand, there are galleries on which are housed the illiterate and wholly non-reading inmates. So, working on a fair estimate we find:

1. Only about one-half of the prison population is constantly interested in books.
2. Of these "interested persons" we find that more than half have only a diversional interest. That emotional stimuli are desired, and that the thrill of the six-shooter and of the broncho-buster is chosen to engender that craved for stimulation, is evident.
3. That in all of this survey in no case was there found any single trend toward eroticism. (doubtful)
4. In no case was there any attempt to lessen the tedium by means of the study of games such as chess, bridge, checkers.
5. That of the smaller number, about forty per cent showing interest other than emotional, nearly all were found to have a very sincere desire to better themselves or their condition as indicated by their choice of helpful non-fiction.

Within the population are two or three groups of literati: men who are familiar, and intelligently familiar, with past and present novelists, philosophers, and the poets. They are able to give quotations from a variety of authors from Dickens and Carlyle to Sinclair Lewis and Hergesheimer. Byron and Oscar Wilde are as well known as are Carl Sandburg and Samuel Hoffenstein. One inmate had memorized Sandburg's long epic, "Good Morning, America."

Among the philosophers Nietzche is most prized by one small group. Will Durant's popularized books aroused much philosophic interest among the literati. James Branch Cabell, Mencken, Michael Arlen, Emil Ludwig, Richard Halliburten, T. E. Lawrence, Margaret Ayres Barnes, Thornton Wilder, Charles Merz, Maxim Gorki, and Upton Sinclair are some of the writers with whom the prison intelligentsia are conversant.

The writings of such authors came to the penitentiary direct from the publishers through the efforts of a few men—perhaps three or four—who had sufficient funds in their prison accounts to purchase them. I have had a long acquaintance with these men and in listening to their discussions have been impressed by the rather profound knowledge of some, and by the excellent memories of all of them. Even though the number of men concerned with literary pursuits is small, the effects of such reading has its minimal influence upon the general culture.

Church: Church and religion, topics of considerable importance to at least a portion of the population, are little understood and therefore not given the emphasis in this study which they no doubt deserve. Church is considered in this chapter as a leisure-time activity because the inmate has his choice of attending, or not, and because many inmates view it, inquiry reveals, more as entertainment than as religious experience. Like the movies and other official leisure-time events, it provides new, or somewhat different experiences and is thus used for subsequent conversation or possibly daydreams. Church, the Protestant Church, that is, serves this function for at least a portion of the population. No facts are at hand to reveal how many of the congregation find in the services religious aid. That some do there is no denying. It is the opinion of numerous inmates that those who attend because of a religious drive are usually the intellectually dull, the emotional, the provincial, and the aged. Criminologically, these same observers report that sex offenders, murderers, and embezzlers are in attendance at the service in a much greater proportion than their share of the total population.

The character of the service depends upon the leadership of the chaplain. During the period of this study two chaplains held office successively, and both conducted fairly conservative meetings although the latter was inclined somewhat towards the "old-time-religion" techniques. The usual type of program consisted of an opening hymn, a prayer, a Scripture reading, another hymn, special music by civilian musicians, general announcements by the preacher, a sermon, a closing hymn, and a benediction. In all, the services are straight-forward and simple and organized to make a direct appeal to those who have religious inclinations. The sermon is customarily based on a biblical text, but leaves it at once and plunges into the forgiveness-of-sins theme, and points out that no one (implying that even you inmates, miserable sinners that you are) will be deprived of the Kingdom of Heaven. "Repent and be saved. . . . Go and sin no more. . . . For the Father so loved his only begotten son. . . . Suffer little children to come unto me" The poetry of the Bible, the pleading of the chaplain, the heaviness of Sunday morning in prison brings tears to the eyes of many men. Others look grave, sardonic, derisive. While a logician might riddle the sermon, inmates are not logicians. The three following prepared statements by inmates are revealing.

Religious Attitudes of Prisoners

(The Functions of the Chaplain)

"Gonna go to church?"

"Yep," shouts back another convict, locked in his cell on a Sunday morning. "I hear there's gonna be a pretty good entertainment this Sunday."

An odd answer? Not a bit. Such an answer coming from a man who desires an hour's escape from the close confinement of his cell plus the added attraction of a bit of entertainment, is quite natural. If the last vestiges of an earlier religious training has long ago been discarded by these youngsters just out of their teens, what chance has a prison minister of working a right-about-face, or what would be the equivalent of a miracle? The answer is, "None." The good that is accomplished by a prison minister (usually obtaining his position through politics) is nothing to brag about, if it even equals that. In the first place, convicts know that what he preaches hardly, if ever, dovetails with what he practices, or even attempts to put into practice.

Which brings us to the question of, "In what way doesn't he live up to what he preaches?"

He utterly fails to put into effect, nor does he even make a half-sincere attempt to couple the prettily phrased spirit of righteousnes that flows from his lips when addressing his flock, with action. And if the truth were known, his flock is vastly more interested in the charms of some female entertainer whose presence on the stage of the prison chapel is good for a song or two, a piano recital, or anything that will enliven an otherwise dull service. His congregation knows that he is insincere and lackadaisical in his efforts to reclaim, brighten up, or lighten the onerous burden that is theirs. However, there are a few who gravitate to him, and finally ingratiate themselves into the good graces of the chaplain. But, for the most part, these are prisoners who are serving time for crimes of sexual degeneracy: rape fiends, perverts, crime against nature, and incest. Why this particular type of prisoner invariably turns religious, sometimes with a fervor that is disgusting, is beyond my understanding.

Your prison parson daily comes in contact with men struggling to rise out of the mire of a past environment, but does he extend them a helping hand, does he interest himself to the extent of swaying the prison officials in favor of the convict who is trying to better himself? He does not. In an apologetic manner he will tell you, "I will see what I can do," —a time-worn expression of prison officials—and there the matter drops. His job is political, and like all political appointees he "passes the buck" to the other man, who usually passes it on to the next one. Convicts know a prison "Holy Joe" for what he is: one who, although garbed in clerical cloth is without the guts to stand behind the fire of his spoken convictions; one who, if an eye witness to some of the brutalities that are a part of every prison, would hastily turn away, and would not even let out a whimper of protest for fear of incurring the displeasure of the lazy official staff. Still, he calls himself a disciple of Christ one who preaches, and is supposed to believe in justice, mercy, and kindness.

What part does he really play in the miserable drama of prison life? None. He could be dispensed with and there would be not the slightest chance of any calamity befalling a prison or to anyone of the hundreds of social lepers. But that would never do. The chaplain is placed there by the state and he receives his pay from the state. And although the chaplain is, in nine cases out of ten, merely a figurehead, although he is a representative of the church, he has his usefulness—to the state! The religious welfare of the state's wards is provided for. This precaution of installing a state-paid chaplain prevents other religious organizations, that may have the backbone to expose, from coming in personal contact with inmates; a move that circumvents any effort by these organizations to get first-hand facts concerning corruption, mistreatment, etc.

And the prisoner, knowing that the average chaplain is a fraud, an inoffensive creature who is only too ready to side with the administration officials, whether right or wrong, does not inspire the whole-hearted confidence of his criminal flock. He may be gratified, upon looking over the swelling attendance each Sunday, and murmur a prayer of thanks. But—I wonder if he has ever given such a problem a thought. If the convicts were given the preference of either attending church or a Sunday morning yard privilege where they could sop up a bit of salubrious sunshine, would bare pews be the only hearers of the chaplain's sermon, and would he be looking for another job?

You answer it. I already know the answer.

Church Has Helped Me

Going to church always helps me. The chaplain has talked to me and I am taking courses from the Moody Bible Institute. The church service is really beautiful. It is the music I like and the Scripture reading. The Bible is God's word. God meant His word for everyone. Being here has made me better. God has forgiven me and I give the chaplain credit for showing me the way. He has led me to see the right. . . . The church brings the spirit of God to our lives. I watch the men during the service. They listen to all that is said. God's spirit is with them and He comforts them. He makes them clean. Some of the boys cry when they hear the old hymns because they remember their mother singing the songs to them when they were little. . . . The service doesn't last long. We have hymns, prayers, and a sermon. The sermon is about the Bible, but the chaplain makes it plain and fits it into our lives. He tells us that there will be a place in heaven even for the least if we repent our sins. . . ."

Sunday Services in a Prison Chapel

The audience is seated and the preacher rises,
He chooses a text from his Bible and elaborates, wasting his breath.
And a "Fish" soliloquizes—
"That 'pie in the sky' may be tempting but why should our pleasures all come after death?
He promises great things in Heaven, and scoffs at the pleasures of earth.
I wonder how much that Rube's pay is—it's certainly more than he's worth!

Yeah! That'll be great when the last shall be first,
But what is it worth, while I hunger and thirst?
Is he last if his heart held a prayer while he cursed?
Is he first if he prayed while he secretly nursed
A desire for revenge? Are the best and the worst
So easy to pick that the man at the gate
Of the orthodox heaven can tell each his fate
Without making us wait?

"The dumb hoosier labors. The clever guy shirks
Bank robbers break rocks, and embezzlers are clerks.
The forger's a waiter. The burglar's a tailor,
And some ignorant rube is both foreman and jailor.
The preacher takes pay for extolling the Lord,
But prisoners pray to, and curse at, the Board (Parole Board).

(The preacher stops. A woman plays and a moron rises and sings.)

"If that's what they call ENTERTAINMENT
I'd rather just think about things.

"Hey, Hey! How is this for a racket?
I can slide through my minimum sentence
And go up with a tale of repentance
If I get the Sky Pilot to back it.
I'll try that scheme, and if my story sticks,
I'll drop religion when I hit the bricks.

"I'll have to act the dunce. No convict with a brain
Falls for religion. Ask one to explain
Some abstruse point, and listen to his lies!
I'll tell old Holy Joe that I believe
His 'line'—and snicker up my sleeve.

"This ought to put me over with the Board;
All politicians claim to love the Lord.
I'll talk about my soul
And make an awful bluff.
If it works strong enough
I'll get a quick parole."

So Brown, Wellington, and Bones in dignity and glory
Omnipotent, omniscient, will listen to his story.
And, giving him credit for early repentance,
Will turn this guy loose in the minimum sentence.

The Catholic church services are the same as those of the normal community, lacking only the dignity of the cathedral atmosphere. The sermons are made practical and deal with hope, reform, penitence, and immortality. The priest, familiarly, and not disrespectfully called "The Buck," hears confessions at stated times and performs all the ordinary rites of the Catholic church. It is the writer's impression that the majority of both Catholic and Protestant inmates are religiously insincere.

Unregulated Leisure Time

The foregoing enumeration of leisure-time activities as sponsored or countenanced by the administration may conceivably give the impression that the inmates' leisure hours are filled pleasantly enough. It is true that if all the men were interested in everything which is offered there would be enough events to occupy the time. Such men would be avid fans of baseball, football, racing, as well as radio enthusiasts, with definite interest in several programs each week. They would follow world and local events in the press and read a goodly number of stories in books and magazines. Church, card games, kitten-ball and a lively correspondence would shorten their days. But men who commit crimes and come to prison are not temperamentally so constituted. One of their greatest social weaknesses is a paucity of interests. But few inmates are able to keep a steady, persistent interest in even one activity over a period of years. So the reader should recall that for every activity, save the movies, there are probably more men who find the activities either boring or exasperating than who find them interesting. To help fill the leisure hours in some way some men have developed other pastimes which will be discussed in the following paragraphs.

Gambling: By gambling is meant an unqualified promise to give money, or other valuables, or services to the winner of an unascertained event. Two or more parties may be involved and a common definition exists as to what constitutes winning, either because of well-established rules, or by verbal agreement. The old-timers in the penitentiary say there has been gambling ever since they can remember, and it is safe to say, by deduction, that some forms of gaming have always occurred in every prison. The reasons for this assumption are: (1) The types of men who come to prison are generally already familiar with games of chance, and (2) idleness, especially of the earliest prisons was conducive to gambling. In investigating the history of betting it appears that the methods have always been similar to the methods of gambling in the normal community except that prisoners have, in a number of ways, refined or complicated games or betting methods. Legends of gambling exist in the culture, and some of the most popular men in prison have been gamblers. Like physical courage, gambling skill is a value held in considerable esteem. A prisoner from Kentucky expressed his preferments in life as fast horses, strong whiskey, wild women, and stud poker, a somewhat less elegant modification of a well-known Kentucky adage. As new forms of gambling become used in the free society they are soon after adopted in the prison. The chance game of "numbers" or "policy," largely a post-prohibition development, patronized by Negroes, was introduced into the prison on a small scale during 1933 by a group of three inmate "promoters." While it was not a successful method because of the restraints placed on the betters, it lasted two months. Another imitation was a lottery based on the Irish Sweep Stakes.

While newer forms of gaming are occasionally introduced as they become popular in Americana, the most extensive betting is done with, and through, the established methods. Stud poker, draw poker, coon-can (a card game especially suited for two players, usually cellmates), seven-card-peet, rummy, and other card games are always popular. The poker games which demand three or more players are usually played in dormitories or in the hospital where cells do not isolate two men. Of gambling on baseball there is no end. Every type of wager conceivable is made on major league games. There are bets on individual games, the number of games won per week, per month, or during the entire season. Bets are made on batting averages, the number of games a pitcher will win during the year, or on the strikes and balls of each inning in a particular game. Wagers are also made on or against the prison team. Fewer men are acquainted with football, but considerable betting is done on intersectional games. Auto races, especially the Indianapolis classic in May, get attention. For the Kentucky Derby or the Preakness groups of 15 to 20 men will draw the name of a horse from a cap, each person paying the same fee, the winner taking all. Dice games are likely to start quickly when a keeper is far enough away to permit it, and the players are able to keep out of view behind a rock in the quarry. Dice are not allowed, but are smuggled in or ingeniously fashioned out of various materials. Bets on the weather, on the number of new admissions per month, on the weight of an inmate, points of knowledge such as the date of Lincoln's death or who discovered Alaska, are much less frequent, but occur often enough to warrant recording here.

Betting, of course, is against the prison rules, but it is difficult to detect and prove because all wagers are agreed upon verbally, or stakes are held by a third party. Card games are allowed and while the keepers know that the men gamble on them, proof of it is difficult to secure, and it is frequently "too much bother, anyway," as one guard commented. Dice players or "crap shooters" are most frequently caught and punished because such games are so noticeable. The wagers are frequently made in money, usually from a nickle to five dollars, except for a small number of moneyed inmates who gamble up to twenty dollars. Tobacco is also used as a stake. So many sacks of "Bull Durham" or so many packages of "tailor-mades" are bet against similar amounts, unless odds are involved. Matches are frequent stakes, and have high utilitarian value. Wagers between cellmates are so organized that the loser has to clean the cell so many days in succession. The stakes in other gambling may be food, either the type purchasable at the commissary, or regular dining-room food. A loser, for example, may give up his Sunday pie for a month because he picked the Giants instead of the Cubs or Sun Beau instead of Cavalcade. Betting takes other forms and in at least one case a passive homosexual was wagered against a twenty-dollar bill, the story goes.

Gambling is a function of certain traditions in the prison culture, and the personality attributes of the inmates as well. In a sense, gambling is an escape mechanism, like drinking. Gambling, whether the player wins or loses, is a means of keeping the personality keyed up; it serves as a hypodermic with an emotional kick. Betting also provides the winners with commodities in the form of luxuries which have great worth for the prisoners. Men gain status, to some extent, by being known as shrewd gamblers. The ethical practices are probably no worse than those of real gamblers in large cities. Among most players cheating at cards or dice is condoned. Detection in cheating does not necessarily mean ostracism; it simply means more careful scrutiny in the future. Many renege on debts, and if they do so against enough people, soon no one will bet with them, not because the reneger is despised, but because betting with him is bad business. How many men gamble is not known. Estimates by inmates who should know show that 15 to 20 per cent of the population gamble regularly, and that another 20 per cent gamble fairly often—a few times a month, perhaps. For the purpose of this study, however, it is not so important to know how many men gamble as it is to know how widely disseminated are the ideations about gambling. Inquiries reveal that gambling causes much talk. Because the talk deals with competition it is interesting and catches the ear of persons nearby. Thus, it is that many men who knew little or nothing about gambling acquire the ideations and in many cases, to counteract ennui, make bets.

There follow some general observations on gambling and the experiences of an inmate who indulged in it.

Pawning, Gambling, Conniving, and Thievery

Not long after I had become accustomed to the ways of the prison than I began to gamble and as the old saying goes, "A young fool pays to learn." Every cent and every dollar was used in wager or put across the table to play poker or to shoot dice. When no longer money came from home, I began to pawn everything of my possession: shoes, handkerchiefs, underwear, socks, rings, and every necessity was put in pawn, or, as we said, "soaked" to some prisoner of means.

Well I remember having received a fine pair of shoes that my dear, old grandmother had labored to get for me, but on the afternoon of their arrival I pawned them for the sum of two dollars. In one week I must pay two dollars and fifty cents for their return, but gambling being a new racket to me I readily lost, and there was no way to secure the cash by the end of seven days, so in that way my broker became the possessor of my shoes, and I either had to lie to my dear old grandmother, or do without a Sunday pair of out-size shoes. The former being the easiest way out, I chose to write her explaining the shoes were too small and I could not use them, and could not return them, so please send me a half size larger. After a few days I received another package containing shoes, but in the meantime a "friend" had given me a dollar and to this I had added a few more by betting on ball games, so this time I mentally thanked my dear old "ace in the hole" (my grandmother) and went on wearing my new shoes and betting at random until funds again ran short. Again I pawned, but this time my other clothing, and I managed to win a small sum, but not using tobacco I only had to buy such articles as toothpaste and occasionally a few bars of candy, and sometimes I would loan without security for 25 per cent for one week.

There were men who loaned many dollars each week, and I have seen them pay as high as 100 per cent interest. The authorities did not allow cash money to be admitted by letter, but by the "grapevine" system, or by having a friend or relative slip money to them while visiting, much money got into the pockets of the prisoners.

There was always one thing I could not understand about cash in prison. The authorities would not allow it to come to the prisoner, yet when the prisoner mailed a special letter or bought ice cream at the ball games in summer, he must have cash.

Many of the young boys wrote love letters to men of means and on a day when a gang went to the store you could see the boy receiving groceries, candies, and tobacco, for the services they were to render, or had already rendered along the way of perversion and love. Of course there were the "gold-diggers" among the "boys" who played their little game like the sisters of the streets. For a mere kiss, with promises of other relationships, they would make a man of loving disposition spend his money on them, never realizing satisfaction of the boy's promise.

The crapshooters would gather in some out-of-the-way place or out in the open with enough "good guys" surrounding them to shut off the view of the "screw," then they would proceed until one or two men had monopoly of the money, hardly ever more than one hundred dollars.

One incident I recall of having seen a stool-pigeon point the finger on a game, and the "screw" shook the bunch down and put *one* man in solitary for shooting craps. The question I always wanted to know was how one man could shoot craps alone. Another was a shake down of a game when there was about five dollars on the ground when the deputy came up, but no one would claim the money, so the official said, "Well, this will buy me cigars for some time to come," and walked away. Another time a young "fish" was caught shooting craps with some old timers and they left him holding the dice, but when the deputy was going to take him to solitary, he said, "I could not shoot by myself," and the deputy said, "Well, who was shooting?" The fish said, "Him, him, and him," and finally five men went to solitary and like a lone blackberry in a bucket of milk, it was a Negro and four white men.

In the old dormitory, or the "Bore's Nest," as it was known among the convicts, much of the gambling was done. A bed was used as a table and when the gang was in the hall you could see a group gathered around, and always a bunch of sight-seeing ones. Not very often, but occasionally, a fight arose over one of these games, but considering the type of prisoners involved, everything was on the Q. T. Now and then I have seen a guard take a hand in a game, but seldom, because they could not trust the stool-pigeons nestled among the crowd awaiting news to carry to higher officials. Men would pawn everything they possessed and would write home to relatives for money. It was a pastime, and I have seen men so interested in a game that they were seemingly in a state of coma, nothing would attract their attention. . . .

Drinking: From the standpoint of the number of men who manufacture, or connive to obtain liquor, the problem of drinking is not important, but from the standpoint of interest of inmates and consternation of officials, the drinking problem is of some consequence.

Alcoholic liquors are procured in two ways: manufactured by inmates, or brought into the prison, either bootleg or (since repeal) legitimate whiskey, by trusties or guards. Prison-made whiskey is foul stuff. Known as "boiler-house rum" or "potato brandy" the concoctions are usually made of fruit juices, yeast, and sugar, obtained from the dining-room by theft. Other drinks have been made by using potato peelings. So far as is known no regular still has been found in the institution in which this study was made, such as was discovered in a sister institution The home-made whiskey has a strong alcoholic content, a dreadful taste, and is reported to make the few men who use it very sick. Before becoming ill, however, they have a few hours of emotional release during intoxication. Because of the watchfulness of the officials, prison-made whiskey has become rare. On the prison farm where custody is less strict home-made spirits are produced in more abundance and used with greater safety. Inmate gossip has it that one prisoner stayed quietly intoxicated for several months, yet went about his duties without suspicion. Most of the men who drink over-indulge and become noticeable because of drunken behavior or sickness. The attitude of officers toward men apprehended drinking is more rational than towards other disciplinary infractions. While the offenders are punished by a long stay in solitary, the guards do not abuse them but take the position, as one keeper expressed it, "Oh, well, what can you expect of the poor bastards, I don't blame them for getting drunk, but it's our job to keep them from making the stuff."

Bringing liquor into the prison is considered a far more serious offense than the local manufacture of it, because, by the very act, there is evidence of breaking trust, either by a guard or a trustie. How much smuggling goes on is unknown, but it is probably not widespread. The motive of the carriers is financial. A pint of whiskey retailing at one dollar will bring four dollars inside the walls. Some few guards who wish to bolster their one-hundred-dollar monthly salary have engaged in this practice. Detection brings dismissal. The prisoners who drink were alcohol users before incarceration, and remembering the oblivion that whiskey brought, realize that nowhere could a temporary oblivion be more desirable than in prison. This attitude leads to plans and conniving. The opinion of the body of inmates towards liquor traffic is largely one of amusement. Detection of a jug of "boilerhouse rum" becomes an immediate subject of conversation. In general, liquor usage in the prison is of minor significance in a broad sense, although it tends to disintegrate further the personalities involved. If guards traffic in liquor and are apprehended, the knowledge of such a situation further convinces some inmates that graft exists in places both high and low and this idea reinforces the anti-official attitude.

Reverie-plus: In some of the foregoing sections reference has been made to daydreams and reverie which have been initiated during a recreational activity and which brings to the isolated inmate some new perceptional experience. Reverie is placed in the chapter on leisure time because most reverie occurs during spare or leisure time and often as not produces an emotional tone that has some aspects of pleasantness. Yet reverie is individualized, and does not classify as recreation because it is passive and non-social.

Reverie is not an abnormal phenomenon, and all persons engage in it to some extent. It is not the reverie of the normal, non-isolated person who has a relatively broad number of interests and activities that concerns us here, but rather a deeper, more complete type of implicit mental activity. Reverie is perhaps not the proper term, yet we hesitate to apply other, more exact labels. While the term reverie will be applied to this phenomenon, it will be more proper to think of it as a reverie-plus. The condition is akin to what Nelson calls "prison stupor." Reverie-plus, as the writer has come to understand it from a number of years of observation, seems to be the function of two conditions: a personality which tends more towards introversion than extraversion, and which is interacting in a restricted and more or less monotonous and static environment. The concept of introversion is well known and needs no elaboration. A monotonous environment, as here used, refers to a situation which does not change greatly from day to day, and in which symbols representing lack of change cover up such changes as do occur. Thus the cells, the food, the walls, the daily routine, the long lines of marching men go on year after year. When, for example, there may be a change in associates or in some daily duty or in some recreational activity, such modifications are insufficient to break the perception of sameness because too many other factors remain unmodified. To the person whose extraverted trends are greater than the introverted trends, the monotony of the total situation does not weigh so heavily. But add to the environment of those individuals whose orientation is introverted, the other factor of monotony, and the condition of reverie-plus develops. About the prison yard and the shops one sees inmates for whom smiles, small talk, alertness, and attention to the environment come easily. One also sees about half as many men who seldom smile, who seldom talk, who stumble as they walk in lines, whose errors in their tasks cause small concern, and who respond normally to social stimuli only when a stimulus is strong or different. Status or social approbation is as nothing. It is reverie-plus that controls them. The following examples, greatly abbreviated and simplified, have been reconstructed by the writer from conversations of many hours, and serve to give only a general idea of the content of one type of reverie-plus. This first account resulted from an impression obtained at a movie.

I (the inmate) am captain of a brigade. I have two hundred men in my charge. We are a portion of the United States Army. Under my command are three lieutenants several sergeants, and a corporal for every squad. Some of the men are radio operators, expert riflemen, and some are electricians. Over three-quarters of them are ordinary infantrymen, but made up of the best-skilled men in the service. The War Department in Washington has sent me to Alaska. I have my men encamped on a high hill overlooking a bay near a city. We are at war with Japan. It is expected Japan will attempt to invade Alaska in order to stop the gold supply. Our camp is on a small mountain overlooking a bay and in the bay are planted mines which are controlled by electricity from a control board in my headquarters. We have also some small artillery. I am in constant radio communication with Washington, and advise the War Department there concerning the situation. . . . I refused to let my men go to the town nearby for I wish to keep the townspeople as ignorant as possible of my doings. I go to the town myself, but take off my uniform before going. I have become acquainted with the mayor and the chief of police. I have thought that there might be Japanese spies in this small city and I have had every suspicious character arrested. One Japanese boy of eighteen was acting as a house boy for the superintendent of a gold mine. I had his quarters searched and found a high-powered radio which he was using to send messages to the Imperial Japanese government. I had this boy executed. I demolished the radio. He had a sister of seventeen years, beautiful and yellow. I put her in boy's clothing and took her back to my camp to act as house boy. She was so slim that my men did not know she was a female. I made love to her. She began to love me. She told me secrets of the greatest importance. Because she loved me she was willing that I advise my government of the plans of the Japanese Army. For this I was promoted to the position of Major, and was recalled from my post in Alaska. I took my "house boy" with me and went to Washington where they put me in charge of a secret service department, etc."

The reverie presented in the following paragraph gives evidence of more definite plan than is often found in the reverie of inmates.

Down in Kentucky I (the inmate) own a large plantation. There are thousands of acres and I am the master of the plantation. My wife is a beautiful woman and my five children play around me when my day's supervising duties are done. I ride around my plantation on my big, black horse. We do not have slaves, but I pay my help well. I have 300 employees, most of whom are farm hands who live in a little village of their own more than a mile from my house. My house is a big, white building with high pillars. We have a huge porch on which, during the summer, I entertain the people of the countryside. I am called "Colonel."

We serve long, cold drinks, juleps, but none of my guests nor I ever become intoxicated. We drink as gentlemen should. On the plantation I have a stable for jumping and riding horses and also for race horses. We breed horses there and though I myself do not train race horses I sell them at auction. Around the broad acres are white fences. The approach to my mansion is a long driveway over which tower massive elm trees. Though we have automobiles, most of my plantation neighborhood friends prefer to ride horses as they would in the olden days. I myself prefer my horses and am teaching my children to ride and jump. We have twelve servants in the house, and an old Negro butler who has been in my family for years. My plantation grows cotton and I am fabulously rich. I pay my hired hands well and they respect me like the old slaves used to respect the plantation owners. We have dances in our big living-room when the entire countryside comes, etc.[8]

An exposition of reverie of a different type is well shown in the following verse, written by a prisoner:

Escape

When the long day is done and twilight reaches
The windows crossed by grim, disheartening bars,
My cell is locked, but I, in dreams, am free
To roam at will—to splash through surf, or lie
In lazy ease on clean, wave-beaten beaches
In the sweet-scented night beneath low-hanging stars
Till the night gong recalls reality.

The spell is broken. Beauty fades. The musty cells
Break back into my consciousness.
The bars obscure the pale, cold, northern moonlight,
All that remains of this night's dream. Yet I am sure
That as the slow, relentless days go past
I still shall have my dreams, till, at the last
Of all my days, when days and dreams are done,
My sorrows vanish in oblivion.

The mental content of reverie-plus is as varied as life itself. Full understanding would demand extensive study over a long period of time. The essential aspect, however, is self-reference. Sex coloring is common, but is different than the ordinary sex yearnings, and bizarre items may be included. Almost never does the content contain ideas relating to criminal or penal life. In some reverie-plus

[8] Both of these accounts over-simplify the mental phenomena they are intended to portray. They were contributed by two semi-neurotic inmates for whom the writer was more or less a "father confessor." It is interesting to note that the reverie concerning the armed conflict with Japan was described in 1933, long before the Japanese invasion of China.

a fantastic world is built. The inmate lives in this world, illogically adding on or lopping off situations which are not conducive to the implicit development of the ego. The mechanism producing this phenomena is escape from the intolerable situations in which the man finds himself. The condition has all degrees of intensity and the intensity varies in the same man sometimes in cyclic form. Seldom do men develop the condition during the first year of residence. Seldom also do men with physical illnesses engage in reverie-plus because, apparently, their pain keeps them too close to reality. In those persons in whom the condition becomes intense, psychoses are likely to develop. For the most part, they can cling to their reverie in idle hours, drop it partially at the bark of a guard, and take it up again when attention to the immediate is not demanded. By saying that it furnishes aspects of pleasantness is meant that by use of the escape, the person is so socially out of touch with the instant environment that it causes little pain. While being little more than a guess, perhaps 15 to 20 per cent of the population exist under varying degrees of this phenomena.

This section is included to point out the existence of the condition rather than to add much to its explanation. We also wish to substantiate the observation of Nelson[9] and others, with the exception that in the present study the phenomenon we are calling reverie-plus does not seem to affect so large a proportion of the prison population as Nelson implies, and that the psychological attributes are not essentially phlegmatic.

Character Study: By "character study" is meant that type of interest which one human being has in another human being, an interest which is not based on motives of competition or for a utilitarian purpose. It is the interest that like have for like. In the sewing-circle, in the chatter of fraternity brothers, and in the buzz of the country club porch on a summer's afternoon, this phenomenon exists. It is different from gossip, because it is not malicious, and it is not a means of control. The theme of it becomes evident in the often spoken words, "People are so interesting." "It takes every kind to make a world," or, by inmates, "I know human nature. . . . I can tell what a man is by looking at him. . . . When you are around these places for a few years you get to understand your fellow man pretty well." It is surprising how many inmates feel that they have an unusual ability to read character, considering that their residence in prison indicates, at least a gross lack of putting such knowledge into practice. The inmates believe they possess this talent as a result of having "been around" or because they have had many idle hours in which to observe their fellow man. This interest

[9] Victor Nelson, *op. cit.*, Chapter X, pp. 219–242.

is one of the reasons that men tolerate the telling and retelling of other prisoners' "cases." The motive for listening to the long recitals of an inmate's crime, detention, and commitment include, in part, the listener's desire to analyze the speaker. The trait, of course, is not universal, but it is common enough to deserve mention as a leisure-time activity, as it affords a release from the tedium of prison life. Not all the responses elicited by listeners, qualify as "character study" as we are using the term here, for in earlier chapters different significances have been given to the interplay of conversation between inmates. Yet in some conversations character analysis prevails.

* * *

In the officially sponsored recreation and in the unregulated leisure-time activities, we see a series of patterns and activities that stimulate a diversity of reactions. If we had methods fine enough to measure the responses of the men to the life which is going on about them, we should probably find as many variations, as many effects, that is, as there are men. In one thing, however, there might be consensus. No matter how interesting, or how exciting a leisure pastime might be, there always exists that deadening sense of confinement which prohibits the complete release of the personality to the activity at hand.

CHAPTER X

Sexual Patterns in the Prison Culture

Interest in sex topics is universal. The prison, like any other isolated community made up of but one sex, is a fertile field for the development of sex abnormalities. Among homeless men, in the armies and navies of the world, on an expanding frontier, and in prisons, sex phenomena with various shades of abnormality develop. In discussing the phenomena as they exist in the prison where this study was made, one should keep in mind that the facts presented are not peculiar to any time or place. While the subject will be treated briefly, its importance cannot be overemphasized. Possibly no other influence in prison life is so conducive to the disorganization of particular persons as are the sex ideations which develop. Not only are single personalities made socially unstable by stimuli from the sex level of culture, but everyone in the prison environment is affected in varying degrees by the influence it contains.

When abnormal sex behavior is considered as a natural phenomenon it can be treated in the same objective fashion with which causes and effects are sought in the scientific examination of any other social and biologic subject. Abnormal sex conduct is referred to here as a natural phenomenon because it has appeared not in any one time or place but has existed since the facts of man's behavior have been recorded by man. The Bible is not without reference to "abnormal" sex behavior. Anthropologists record its existence among the earliest civilizations. Historians state that homosexuality flourished in ancient Athens and Rome, and had, to some extent, social approval.

It may prove helpful to those not familiar with the psychology of sex to review briefly here the processes in the normal development of the love life, and then to show the processes by which abnormalities are likely to occur.[1] When the baby is born into the world he knows nothing of life. Some things give him satisfaction, and some do not. He responds and tends to force continuance of the things which give him satisfaction. The things which give him satisfaction are first organic, and are definitely tied up with the inherent

[1] John J. B. Morgan, *The Psychology of Abnormal People,* Longmans Green and Co., New York, 1928, pp. 223–267.

sex impulses. This stage of the individual is known as the self-love stage because the infant is concerned only with himself. The mother nurses him and contributes to his comfort by caring for him and caressing him. Thus the mother comes to be an object of love because she contributes to his self-gratification. The baby may learn that some of the satisfactions which come through the mother can also result from his own efforts. Thus, if it is pleasant to suckle the mother it also becomes pleasant to suck his thumb. As he grows older he learns that satisfactions may come to him from other persons besides his mother and other close associates. The baby, as he grows to childhood, gradually learns that if he persists in his demands for attention and instant satisfactions the agencies which give or contribute to them may withdraw them. Thus he learns to postpone his desire for satisfactions and makes sacrifices so that in the end he may get the pleasures he seeks. If, during this process of learning he becomes aware that his sacrifices give pleasure to others, he will continue such behavior because pleasure to others increases their regard for him. He develops loyalties and he acquires sentiments from his experiences in group life. As the child grows he is acquiring human nature. He learns first to play alone, then with other people. By the time he is six or so, he does not yet distinguish between companions as to sex, but by the time he is eleven or twelve years old he begins to prefer companions of his own age and sex. This is the "chum" age during which normal boys and girls develop strong friendships with others of their own sex. By the time he is sixteen he has begun to "like the girls," and from that age to sometime during the twenties he has feelings of love, usually for several girls, singly, or at the same time. In the normal course of development he will learn that one particular girl can give him more happiness than can any other person. He learns to love her in a mature way and she becomes his wife. In the regular development of married life the young husband, if he has learned his lessons properly and has been well socialized, comes to the higheset stage in the love development in which he finds that his greatest satisfactions come from seeing his mate happy. Her happiness will frequently depend upon having children in the home. The love between husband and wife towards the child of their union constitutes the climax of the love development.

This theme of the love development applies especially to more advanced civilizations, and is presented here to represent what is customary among American peoples. We have very briefly summarized the normal development of the love life which presents the following stages: first, the self-love stage; second, the love for the persons in the immediate environment, as members of the family; third, the affection for persons of the same age and sex, i.e., the chum stage; fourth, the immature, exploratory heterosexual stage in which a number of girls may be the objects of youth's desire; fifth, the mature stage of married life; and sixth, the love of the parents for their child. Throughout all this development, until the highest stage is reached, there is always some self-love. This is not abnormal because it is universal. This self-love, however, is frequently not expressed, as items of the culture prescribe otherwise.

Since love is the most intricate and complicated of human emotions, it is not surprising that many persons do not develop in the normal way, but, through some cause or other, remain at one of the lower stages of development. Some never advance beyond the first stage, the infant stage of self-gratification. They may masturbate or gratify themselves in other sensual ways. Others, who reach the second level, that of love of mother, and remain there, may manifest the so-called "Oedipus complex" which so often disrupts their entire lives. Adults who remain at the third stage of development, the chum stage, may show homosexual tendencies, and those who advance to the fourth level, but no further, are the lovers of many women, the Don Juans, the promiscuous, who cause untold troubles. But not all those who develop to complete maturity remain at that level, for through rebuff, or failure, or some other cause, they may regress to a lower level where satisfactions are more easily obtained.

The causes of these irregularities in development are as complicated as are the irregularities themselves, and causes may be due to inherited traits or the result of faulty learning, or both.

These processes which have been outlined here apply to the inmates of prisons as well as to other persons. Not only have many of our inmates not developed their love life in the normal manner, but the problem is further complicated by their living in an all-male environment. Some abnormalities are not related to irregularities in the sex development, but are almost completely the function of the prison environment. Regression may occur. Human nature is modifiable, and the learning process which continues throughout life is essentially psychological, but the kind of knowledge obtained through the process is of sociological importance because what shall and can be learned is determined by the content of the culture. Let us look to the prison culture to determine what sex stimuli exist.

The Committed Sex Offender

If the men who have been convicted and sentenced for sex offenses had been sent to another institution so that our prison would hold no sex offenders as such, this probably would not greatly decrease the interest in sex, although the overt behavior would be lessened. Years of observation have led to the opinion that the inmates most active in abnormal sex behavior are not those generally committed for such acts. The men sent to prison for sex crimes are an important influence, however, because they are the occasion for much talk among the convicts as a whole. As shown in Chapter II, about 6 per cent of the total population are sex offenders. Of this group 62 per cent were committed for rape or assault to rape, 17 per cent for indecent liberties, 11 per cent for incest, and 10 per cent for crime versus children or nature. While about 15 per cent of the total prison population are mentally defective, 29 per cent of the sex offenders are in that intellectual category, and another 22 per cent are of borderline intellectual capacity; also, sex offenders have had somewhat less schooling than have other offenders. The Negro-white distribution for sex cases is typical of all kinds of offenders. However, in proportion to the total population for each race, fewer Negroes than whites are committed for indecent liberties, incest, and crime versus nature or children, the more abnormal offenses. In one sample of 173 cases, 39 were Negroes, but 36 of these Negroes had been sentenced for rape or assault to rape, and but 3 for the more pathological sex offenses.

For sex crimes other than rape the average chronological age is higher than for non-sex crimes. The percentage of recidivists for the entire prison is about 42, while 37 per cent of the sex cases have been in difficulty previously. The predominant residence of sex offenders before incarceration is as follows: metropolitan areas, 10 per cent; cities with populations less than 75,000, 40 per cent; towns and villages, 44 per cent; and open country, 6 per cent. According to the inmates' statements at the time of admission, 32 per cent of the 173 sex cases were single, 52 married, 8 per cent separated or divorced, and 8 per cent widowed. For the penal population as a whole, the percentages for these categories as shown in Chapter II were 37, 38, 14, and 6 per cent, respectively. These figures, however, give no indication of the nature or stability of the marital relationships, although it is interesting to note that 20 per cent more of the sex offenders than of the prisoners as a whole have been married. This can be explained partly by the fact that sex offenders, on the average, are somewhat older. Also, it is quite possible that the statements of sex offenders concerning their marriage are less reliable than are the statements of other prisoners.

The following excerpts from case studies of sex offenders reveal some of the experiences they have had and the patterns they bring to the penitentiary.

An inmate denies he is guilty of rape and says:

It was a woman that I had been going with for a long time. She got mad because I quit her and she had me arrested on a charge of raping her, but I beat that rap. The next day she had a girl friend of hers say that I had raped her. Both of them were "hustling" women and I was convicted on this second charge. She had her girl say that she saw me with this woman. She is supposed to be a married woman, but her husband makes her get out and hustle, and has hustling girls at the house. I was in G——— at the time this girl said I raped her. I went up for trial four times. The first time my witnesses were there and the fourth time they were not. After I beat the first charge the woman called me up and said she would "trick me yet" if I did not get out of G———. This second girl said I grabbed her and carried her on the sidewalk for six blocks before I raped her.

The following is from the case history of a twenty-nine-year-old, married white man, sentenced for rape:

On the evening of July 23, 1933, our inmate asked permission of his mother-in-law to take the two little girls (who were staying with her as summer boarders) along with him in his truck to the city where he was to dispose of cattle. Permission was given and the inmate and the two girls, sisters, aged twelve and thirteen, left in the large truck for the city. When they approached the suburb of ———, the inmate took one of the little girls into a woods, undressed her, and forced coitus upon her. He immediately did the same thing with the other child. He then drove to the city, disposed of the cattle, and on the way back to the home town stopped at a tourist camp, rented a cabin and took both girls with him to bed.

Portions of a letter from an official describe an atrocious and abnormal type of rape:

The girl, clad only in bloomers, was sleeping in her room when her assailant entered the house, went to her room and carried her to an automobile outside, muffling her cries with a handkerchief. Mrs. Y———, however, was awakened and rushed out of the house in time to see the car disappear down the road. She identified it as one driven by M———. The sheriff was called immediately and posses were sent out in pursuit. One group of men, including the girl's father finally located the M——— car about three miles east of ———. M——— was in the car while the girl, beaten and bleeding from many wounds, had been thrown out onto the ground. Mr. Y——— and his party rushed the girl to the Y——— home where she received medical treatment. Apparently she had been struck five times with a car crank. The end of one finger on the left hand had been bitten off, and teeth marks of the human attacker were found at other places on her body. The girl was unconscious when found and remained so for some time, but later in the day rallied and is expected to recover, though she is still suffering greatly from her terrible experience.

Older men not infrequently are guilty of abnormal sex behavior. The following excerpts from a case is that of a man who, prior to his sentence for indecent liberties had not been in any serious difficulty.

> X——— is a seventy-year-old white man who pleaded guilty to indecent liberties. He was pasturing his cow at T———, in the city park, and induced two little girls to handle his genitalia. The man tells us that, due to kidney troubles, he had frequently to urinate suddenly, and that the little girl went home and told her mother of this exposure. This is his only record of difficulty.
>
> *Classification*: We are dealing definitely with an inadequate personality reaction with senile deterioration which accounts for the low results on the psychometric test. This man will be unable to adjust on the outside and his crime was probably associated with his senile deterioration. This is an old man with a physical ailment caused from an injury in early childhood. At that time his father accidentally let a log fall on his head fracturing his skull. Later in life this caused a paralytic stroke. The doctors at that time informed him that he would go insane. Since that time he has frequently suffered from loss of memory and would often have to go from house to house asking where he lived. Since being in prison he has suffered loss of memory several times, and during the interview his mind once left him. . . .

Another type of sex offender is presented in the following portion of a case:

> The inmate is a forty-four-year-old, native-born white man who pleaded guilty to Crime against Nature. He was found at 3:30 in the morning in a barn near ———. He had broken the locks on the doors and was found in the act of having intercourse with a female goat. Other offenses of a similar nature had occurred in the community.

The admission to the prison of a man guilty of this type of crime gives rise to an unusual amount of conversation among the prisoners. This particular prisoner was greeted in the prison humorously at every turn by the salutation of "Ba-a-a, B-a-a-a."

The attitudes of prisoners toward these different types of sex offenders varies considerably. Men who have raped little girls are universally viewed with disgust, while men who have raped adult females are tolerated. Abnormal behavior with boys is condoned by many inmates. For the most part, sex offenders claim they are innocent of the crime for which they have been sentenced, and spend a great share of their conversation in an explanation of how they were "framed." This tends to focus attention not only on themselves as individuals, but on the topic of sex as well.

Attitudes Toward Sex as Phase of the Culture

We know that in normal communities there are certain restrictions upon sex activity. The culture, through customs, mores, and laws, prescribes that a man shall have no more than one wife at a time, or that persons shall not seek sex gratification in any but private places. Reasonable modesty about sex relations is the expected behavior in the normal community and is the result of the prohibitions which the culture places on individuals. On the other hand, the normal culture contains many sex stimulants in the form of pictorial art, popular songs and dances, movies, areas of vice in large cities, and the like, but the impulses which these culture items stimulate are canalized by most of the individuals in socially approved forms of behavior. In the prison culture there are similar items of sex stimuli.

The 2,300 men who form the prison population live in an area of thirteen acres. A thousand men are incarcerated in a cellhouse. Cellmates spend thirteen hours of each day never more than six feet apart. Toilet duties are of necessity performed openly. Bathing under the showers is done openly, eighty men at a time. Over the radio come dance tunes and songs alive with love themes and suggestive sex implications. The magazines and newspapers in their advertisements portray women in all forms of undress. Magazines, especially those of the cheaper type, are filled with love stories and sex topics. Letters from sweethearts, girl friends, and wives carry the love motif. None of these stimuli, taken separately, are strong enough to cause the average, normal man to engage in abnormal sex behavior, but combined with the all-important factor of a womanless environment, they give rise to sex yearnings, attitudes, and behavior which assume great importance to the men behind bars. For the most part our prisoners have been sexually promiscuous before incarceration. They have known as much as any other particular group of men, the physical charms of women. As stated in Chapter II, 64 per cent of the men have been married and there is no reason to believe that their sex lives were less normal than that of the non-delinquent population. Employees in the prison are frequently impressed with the physical attractiveness of the women who visit inmates, and it remains a paradox to the guards "how such swell-looking women go for these lousy 'cons.'" Considering, then, that the sex life of the inmates has probably been normal in amount, it is little wonder that a high degree of yearning exists.

Victor Nelson,[2] in a chapter entitled "Men without Women,"

[2] Victor Nelson, *op. cit.*, p. 143.

expressed the longing for feminine contact which is experienced by the man in prison. "For of all the possible forms of starvation surely none is more demoralizing than sexual deprivation . . . to be starved month after month, year after endless year where 'every day is like a year, a year whose days are long,' for sexual satisfaction which, in the case of a lifer, may never come, this is the secret quintessence of human misery. . . . (Prisoners have) a hunger not only for sexual intercourse, but a hunger for the voice, the touch, the laugh, the tears of Woman; a hunger for Woman Herself."

A young married man in prison, yearning for his bride, said, "If I could only have her with me, no matter if we had to live in a place like this, I could be happy. If she will only wait, I'll never leave her again—I'll never leave her." An older man, convicted of a double murder, a man who had never married, remarked, "If I could only hear the laugh of a child, or see a woman bustling around a kitchen, I would know what life is again." Many expressions of loneliness are less socialized and more directly sexual than the examples given. Without further elaboration it may be stated categorically that sex yearning and lonesomeness for feminine companionship is for the great majority of prisoners the most painful phase of incarceration.

The prison community is not without its constitutional sex psychopaths, who exhibit abnormal sexual traits. In addition, there are those men whose homosexual behavior is a frank and genuine expression of their regression from a more mature stage of sex development, a regression which antedated their entrance into the penitentiary. A third type of prisoner who manifests abnormal sexual behavior is the "prostitute" who engages in sex abnormalities for money or favors. There are those who maintain that these last-mentioned men are not abnormal, but that they engage in abnormal sexual practices only because of economic desire.

The presence of these three types of sex psychopaths in the prison multiplies the interest in, and conversation about, sex topics. Such persons have numerous contacts with other prisoners who, in turn, relay their influence to still other inmates, so that a virtual honeycombing of sex ideations spreads in all directions with these three psychopathic types as the cores.

Abnormal sex practices have probably always existed within prison walls. The new man coming into the prison may hear of some particularly scandalous sex behavior which occurred many years before. Such gossip is passed on from year to year and is in the nature of a tradition. While traditions ordinarily have a wholesome social utility, legends of this sort charge the atmosphere with sex stimuli.

As has been stated earlier, the community does not have a high degree of consensus. Almost nothing is taboo. A great share of the contacts among men are impersonal or symbiotic. Individuation is the general rule. Status or rank is important only for a relatively few inmates. Disregard for personal reputation is common. Men are possessed with the idea that nothing they do in prison is important so long as they are not caught. The prison world is, by and large, an aggregation of self-centered individuals whose accommodation, one with another, is partly coercive, and only in a minimal way sympathetic.

To summarize, we have a population of adult males whose previous sex experiences have been wide and generally not restricted. They are unhappy for many reasons. A high degree of yearning for the body of woman engulfs them. They are living together in cramped quarters and are bombarded on every hand by stimuli of a sex nature in newspapers, radio, magazines, and books. In their communication with each other sex topics become an important subject. They are in contact with individuals who are sexually abnormal and were sexually abnormal before they came to prison. Also, about 6 per cent of the population have been sentenced for sex crimes and each of these personalities is an occasion for focusing attention on sex. A consideration of all these factors indicates that the prison culture fosters abnormal sex behavior and tolerates it.

Three Levels of Sex Adjustment

Data concerning sex behavior are difficult to secure. The information included in this chapter has been obtained primarily from a few inmates and officials who were aware of the writer's objective interest. Our information suggests three general levels of adjustment: the abnormal, the quasi-abnormal (those on the fringe of abnormality), and the normal. "Normal" is used here in a general non-scientific sense, and does not apply to phenomena beyond the prison walls. Of the three levels mentioned the so-called normal comprises the largest category. A summarization of the estimates of the inmate advisers indicates that possibly 60 per cent of the prison population may be included in this category, 30 per cent in the quasi-abnormal group, and about 10 per cent in the frankly abnormal group.

The inmate who is making a "normal" adjustment in relation to the sex drive is the individual who has experienced an orderly development of his love life from the self-love stage of infancy, through the autoerotic stage of boyhood, to the level of mature, adult love for one woman. Even though his love development may have been essentially orderly, his sex adjustment in prison hinges on two factors: first, a reasonably short sentence, and second, the existence of one or more love objects in the free community. If he loses his love objects and has long years of imprisonment he may, unless his will is stronger than that of the average prisoner, engage in abnormal sex activities, but only in an active, masculine rôle. The men in the normal category are more beset by sex starvation, yearning, and loneliness than are the men in the other groups, and unless they have built up a staunch philosophy in which they can take refuge they are the most unhappy men in the prison community. They can understand and tolerate the depravity of other men, but they want none of it for themselves. For the adult male in the free community, masturbation is an abnormal act, but men in prison whom we are inclined to include in the "normal" level, masturbate occasionally and explain their behavior on a strictly biologic basis. Their masturbatory act is accompanied by heterosexual ideations. At first they worry about the act. They do not find it satisfying, but as the months pass it is accepted as a means of relieving tension. They do not engage in the practice frequently and some of them develop, intelligently, all manner of occupations and devices to consume as much of their energy as possible. One man developed bulging muscles by exercising on his cell door and frankly stated that after an hour of such work he was tired enough to sleep. Those who, overcome with ennui, have given themselves over almost completely to reverie-plus, are sometimes sufficiently out of contact with reality that the sex drive is not an overwhelming problem. Reading and study are a transitory refuge. It is probable that this level of sex adjustment has somewhat less than the expected proportion of mental defectives, since those whom the inmates term the "dumbbells" (those who behave in a mentally defective way) commonly engage in masturbation.

There are all degrees of responses to the sex urge among this "normal" group. Frequency of masturbation varies with age, with opportunity for privacy, with years of residence, with the extent of assimilation into the prison culture, and with the frequency and degree of manifestation of affection by those outside the prison. It also depends, of course, upon the character traits of the individual. A study of the men in this level of adjustment brings to light an important principle: that while they are subjected to the ideations of the abnormal and quasi-abnormal patterns they do not themselves initiate abnormal sex patterns, though they may be catalytic agents in the dissemination of such patterns. They may behave as agents because of the toleration which the greater number of them have for the abnormal sex practices. They talk and joke freely about sex and are not averse to posing humorously as homosexuals if they can thereby produce a laugh.

Tentative satisfactions as well as stimulation may come from the movies, reading, poetry, and writing. Inmates will memorize vulgar poems and doggerel until they can recite them by the hour. In a sense this activity is a substitute for sex experience and as such serves some purpose. The appeal which verse makes to men striving to make a normal adjustment is exemplified by the following:

I Gave a Little Kiss

I wished for just one hour of bliss,
That you might love me well.
And so I gave a little kiss,
And cast a little spell.

And this, alone, was my intent
To share, when we should part,
A memory, but I never meant
That it should break my heart.

Through the Night

Stars, all the sky is keeping, but not for me.
Somewhere my love lies sleeping, so peacefully
Somewhere her hair is gleaming on pillows white,
While in the distance, dreaming, I walk the night.

Sometimes, perhaps, she'll waken and think of me.
Sometimes she may be shaken, so lovingly.
But when the dawn is breaking and I seek rest,
My heart will be sadly aching for the one I love best.

Ode to the Girl

Little girl, you are so small
Don't U wear no clothes at all?
Don't U wear no shimmy shirt?
Don't U wear no pettiskirt?

Just your corset and your hose,
Are those all your underclothes?
Aren't U afraid to show your calf?
It must make the fellows laugh.

Little girl, what is the cause
Why your clothes are made of gauze?
Don't U wear no undervest,
When U go out fully dressed?

And so on. This particular doggerel goes on for twenty verses, and like the strip tease acts of burlesque, becomes franker as it progresses.

Interest in verse in which sex and love are the theme is matched by anecdotes about sex experiences, gossip concerning prison scandal, and frank expressions of plans for sex experience upon release. The writer gave an article, printed in a scientific journal, to four or five inmates to read. It concerned the grouping tendencies and sex activities of a girls' reform school. They relished the reading of it and pointed out in long conversations and in writing, what they thought were inaccuracies in the paper. Men in this "normal" level manifest considerable interest in women's prisons and girls' reformatories, and humorously express the wish to be transferred to them by some such statement as, "They could probably use a good janitor up there." The important point in the consideration of the interest the men at this level manifest in verse, anecdotes, scandal, gossip, and the like, is that these are, with them, a substitute for the abnormal behavior of the other levels.

The length of time a man may continue to live at his present normal level of adjustment cannot be predicted with certainty. A man who is now in the normal level may, as times goes on, come to behave in a quasi-abnormal way, and eventually sink to frank abnormalities. His adjustment to sex urges depends upon numerous factors: his prenatal conditioning; his ability to withstand the pressures of prison culture; and the nature of the relations he has been able to maintain with persons and primary groups beyond the prison walls.

In the 30 per cent which comprise the quasi-abnormal category are those men who have either developed normally, and regressed during imprisonment, or who have become fixated at one of the earlier stages of development and never progressed further. Those who have reached the mature stage of sex development and regressed may, upon release, again achieve the mature stage. But since during incarceration they have dropped back into an immature stage of development they will fall into the category under discussion, the quasi-abnormal group.

In the 30 per cent who compose the quasi-abnormal group are likely to be found the older men, men between thirty-five and forty-five years of age, and, as well, the very youngest men. Inmates in this group are more likely to be recidivists, a fact which accounts in a large measure for their being in this classification. They are usually more "prison wise" than first offenders, and less likely to have positive relationships with persons in the free community. Lacking such ties, their interests, such as they are, lie largely in the prison community. As explained earlier, most of them are unable to occupy themselves with definite interests of a wholesome nature. Contrary to their insistent denials, these men have a keen sense of failure, and while they may not always admit it even to themselves, this feeling of failure prompts a variety of conduct which they would not countenance outside the prison. The realization of their failure to adapt in the free social world has so reduced the threshold of resistance that they are quite easily assimilated into the prison culture.

The occasional sodomist who plays the masculine rôle is placed in this category only if his abnormal behavior is accompanied by ideations of sex contact with a female, and no love reactions exist between him and the person who plays the passive rôle. These men, who are known by such appellations as "wolf," "jocker," or "daddy," do not lose the respect of their associates through their activities, but may even gain some status. According to our criteria these men would be behaving in a quasi-abnormal manner rather than in a frankly abnormal way until sodomy becomes an end in itself and is no longer looked upon as a substitute type of activity. Most of the abnormal behavior in which two men are involved is of this type. However, frequently the act is not actual sodomy, but what the inmates call "leggins." Also, in this category should be placed that portion of the prostitutes who do not actually engage in sodomy, but who simulate the female rôle for "leggins," only when they can't avoid it, or for money. These are the younger sophisticated men, attractive in appearance, and who are, in the main, heterosexual. By clever innuendoes and coquetry they play up to a "wolf," and give indication that if he treats them right he may sometime in the future be favored. By "treating them right" the prostitutes mean that they are to be furnished with such luxuries as tobacco and candy. The prostitute will use every trick at his command to avoid actual sex contact, but sometimes gets "snared," for a "wolf" may become insistent when he learns that he is being played for a "chump," and demand that the "kid" keep his promise. The basis for distinction between such behavior and the frankly abnormal is not great, and it is probable that the young men involved would not even attempt such overtures had there not been some obstacle in the way of the orderly development of their sex and love life.

Among two younger men in prison an intense type of friendship may develop. They are likely as not heterosexual, in the main, and resort, for example, to mutual masturbation simply as a substitute measure during which the ideations are essentially toward the female. Mutual hugging and kissing may precede such an act, but their behavior would not likely regress to sodomy. Whether or not behavior of this kind is wholly the result of sex starvation in a prison environment it is difficult to say. It is reasonable to suppose that fixation on an immature level in the love development is an added factor. An older prisoner describes such young men in his autobiography:

> Of course the younger fellows get the most kick out of them (the movies), especially the sex shows. I have seen them grab each other and squeal and take on as though they were the stars featured in the show. And I have no doubt that many of them have long distance intercourse with the feminine stars featured in the cast. I guess it is merely following the old custom of, "If you can't get a loaf, take a half a loaf." Being unable to get half a loaf they make believe they are getting the whole loaf.

Among the estimated 30 per cent of the quasi-abnormal men are those who occasionally subject themselves to fellatio, but these should be included only when the act is allowed as a substitute and is accompanied by heterosexual ideations. The pervert most scorned but none the less used, is the fellator. The inmates who subject themselves and come to prefer this type of sexual gratification are considered definitely abnormal.

Since it is a controversial matter as to whether or not the habitual masturbator should be classed in the frankly abnormal level or the quasi-abnormal, it is sufficient to point out the existence of the phenomenon. It is said that some men masturbate at least twice daily, year after year. One feeble-minded prisoner confided to the writer that he had been a habitual masturbator for twenty years. On two occasions an inmate attempted to emasculate himself and, according to report, was taken to the hospital with his testes bleeding and hanging down his legs. It was the consensus of opinion of the inmate advisers for this chapter that masturbation, even of the habitual type, should not be classed as definitely abnormal since it is too prevalent in prison, and those addicted to the habit are not otherwise abnormal as judged by prison standards. However it may be classified, the fact remains that it represents an arrested stage in the libido stream, and when excessive, is conducive to disintegration of the personality. A letter to an official, a copy of which was given to the writer by the inmate himself, indicates the desperation of such men:

> To ———
>
> I am still rational enough to see that you have done all you could for me FROM YOUR STANDPOINT. But I believe you will see differently when you know the facts.
>
> I have been a masturbate for twenty-one years; that is, a sexual habit started at the age of six grew into masturbation when I matured at fourteen. For the last eight years I have known nothing but a terrible fatigue; the

life is sapped out of me; ambition and even the desire to live are leaving me. I have struggled desperately against it; twice for five months at a time I fought down the desire. ALWAYS a losing fight in the end. I tried to get a woman. I was to be married once; engaged to a little girl who really loved me. But she couldn't understand the need of my body and would not get married quickly, so that failed. Religion is a mockery so far as I am concerned; the promised "help" was not forthcoming.

I know I have not done my part. I am ashamed. But I COULD NOT. It will do me no good to go out to the world again if I stay here much longer. My only hope now is to get a woman and live with her or marry her—live with her until I can change this abnormal desire into a normal, healthy desire and build up some strength.

Keep me in here much longer and I will not have strength to fight the little battles of everyday; I will go mad and end on the hill. That's not foolishness; it is inevitable. I came in here to escape the world; I did not know how to settle my problem then. I believe I do now. This is a last chance. If you must deny me, then forget me entirely or consign me to the limbo of forgotten cases.

I have tried to tell this to doctors; they either cannot see the fact or they will not see it. Maybe there is nothing these doctors can do here. They will not castrate me. I cannot work out my own salvation. Take these facts to the Board and let them decide. They can very easily lose one worthless life by deciding against my release. This has gone so far now that castration would not help. I pin my hopes to this last chance. It rests with you, gentlemen.

It is evident that this prisoner's problem preceded his commitment. Such a phenomenon is, none the less, important to us in understanding the patterns which men bring to prison.

In the third, or definitely abnormal level, we include the inverts and those other inmates who are habituated to homosexual practice as an end in itself. The inmate advisers believe that 10 per cent, or about 230 men in a population of 2,300 are in this category. Physicians and psychiatrists in the prison are of the opinion that there are no more than ten or twelve pronounced sexual inverts among the prisoners. The invert is an individual who presents some feminine characteristics in the bone formation, the deposits of fat, the high voice, absence of beard, or other physical traits common to the female. Some inverts may be masculine in biologic equipment, but simulate the female in traits and mannerisms. Inverts are not always homosexual, but generally are so. The physicians are probably correct in their statement that the number of true inverts in the prison is very small, but no one knows how large a proportion of the men are inverted in the sense that since an early age they have been conditioned to behave like members of the opposite sex. So far as the writer knows there are none, but some inmates report that their associates are interested in sewing, needle work, cosmetics, cooking, silk clothing, and other items essentially feminine. However, whatever the proportion is, it is small. The important point here is that most of the 230 men who are habitually abnormal in sex behavior have become so through contacts with a culture which contained such items. These contacts may have been made before incarceration or since. Perversion is a learned reaction just as normal sex behavior in the conventional group is a learned reaction.

It is evident, then, from the foregoing section that some levels in the prison culture are conducive to sexual degeneracy, and from studies of the conditions in large cities we know there are certain areas which condone and even encourage sexual perversion. It is not surprising that those individuals who have not had the benefit of training in the mores and customs of the larger group of conventional society should, when subjected to the influences of sex perversion, respond in kind. The general subject of sex in prison is not a pleasant topic, but neither is graft in government, and both must be faced with a calm objectivity. Sufficient understanding may eventually lead to control.

The all-male environment, the absence of strong social controls, the impersonalization of social relationships, and, most of all, the existence of centers of infection in the penal culture, stimulate abnormal sex conduct. The most important of the infectious foci are the definite homosexual psychopaths who spread perversion throughout the community. The inmate whose story is presented here in part was a sex psychopath before he came to prison. After his first year of residence he was recognized as an abnormal sex case by a large number of the men and by some officials. The number of lives he influenced either directly or indirectly, is unknown. He mentions some of them in the following description of his life in prison:

. . . Time moved swiftly and peaceably enough until we moved to a dormitory. Although we still bunked together, life was different. Two hundred men in one room that resembled a barn loft, mingling as one, caused much excitement, confusion, and dissatisfaction, but due to self-control and good will power we managed to stay together until his release.

He was not of the hoodlum type as had been my lot to catch. He was not hard at heart or deceitful and in my opinion better morally than the average prisoner. We had planned who my next bunk mate should be ere he left on that morning train, and night found our new pal in his place. The summer dragged on, and although hot and weary from a day in the quarry we always found pleasure in playing cards at night and oftentimes sunk on into the pleasures of sexual relation as the hours waned into early morning—always alert for stool-pigeons and guards. We lived that summer in a mad reign of jealous hearts. We quarreled about our friends and those we mingled with, both jealous of the acts of the other. These were my first prison "love affairs." My last buddy and I had played the game, but on the Q. T., not even being suspicioned by our fellow men. But now—well, nobody was blind and they could see for themselves, and those long, lingering kisses were not shielded by shadows, and as always among American People, a scandal started, but he swore he loved me and I bestowed my affections upon him. We never grew weary of sinning, though we did not call it so, and only the truest of lovers, knew and showed the love that we two knew. We loved with a passion strong and true, swearing we could not live without each other.

There is always a day approaching when love must end, and so it came. He received his notice of freedom. How could we stand the days of parting? He must go and possibly out there in a free world he would sit in the moonlight and bestow those burning kisses upon another, and if the other should be his wife, perhaps a babe on her knee!

But it was only natural, and although we had loved with all our hearts, we could not stand at the altar, neither could play the part. So, with tear-wet eyes we made our plans and made ready for his departure. We had been happy although under a cloud of sin, and now all must come to an end. Sin furrows the fairest brow but now I gazed on his handsome face as he bent with tear-wet eyes to steal that last farewell kiss. Then, turning my head, I found my way back to my bunk, the tears trickling down my flushed cheeks. Here I longed for night to come so I could bury my grief in slumber.

Long, dull, dreary days followed and each mail I waited for news of him, but none came. At last I saw no hope and wandered about for weeks until I fancied I had met another "heart-breaker," but just when we planned to move together I was given a clerical job. But only a few days kept us apart, for I managed, and I got him with me. I seemed his teacher, then, and he readily learned the ways of prison lovers, and I soon had him in my power. He was, as the other former cellmates, of strong stature, good-looking, and in the late thirties.

It seemed that all I wished was to be loved, and as I lay gazing up into his large brown eyes he seized me almost savagely and crushed me to his breast, raining kisses upon me. I lay like a little child in his arms, never tiring of his love and kisses, a burning sense of sin surged up within me and I started up with a pert demand "to put some pep into life," and in a few moments I was lost in that memory of pleasurable sin.

When morning dawned I arose and cheerily called to my pal, but he wore a gruesome frown; he looked worried. In his innocence he thought of the worst, and of home. But after a few days when he was assured that no trouble would come of our pleasure, the poor fellow turned upon me almost beast-like, again crushing me to him and with one long, lingering kiss, he said, "You good little Devil. Until death do us part," and he acted as though he had been starved of love, and so another one of those "wild crushes" started.

Seldom were we found apart, and we cared not what others had to say about the affair. We loved with a love that was more than love, my pal and me. We even dreamed of our love and planned great things we would do some day. I've known the thrill that mad dreams bring, and I've lived afar from the things that are, never seeming to care. The things people made with their hands were as dust to me, but the years of struggle and playing the game just breaks the heart of a man, and in a short time I began to think I'd become a nervous wreck, and to save myself from complete exposure and downfall, my pal and I agreed to live apart until times were better. And so he moved a possible twenty feet from me. We were still great pals, but no one understood the change.

Possibly once a week, or every ten days we planned so we could be together. We stole a few lingering kisses and occasionally a sexual pleasure.

Suddenly, as if a storm from the sky, a "framed-up lie" pulled me from my job, and I was removed to another part of the institution. By writing notes, my pal and I kept in constant communication until at last the day came for him to go home. He was granted permission to come to the gang to see me, and there were tears rolling down his cheek as we said farewell. I had become accustomed to such partings and only dismissed the matter casually, saying to myself that I'd pick up another soon. But this was a mistake, for in this new gang of 97 men I found none to my measurements of a man. So in two months I had moved again, this time amid a bunch of young men, boys, and wolfish old men. It was difficult to make a choice, but finally I chose another, and by a bit of bribery we soon found ourselves celling together. This was yet a different type of man, although in his early forties. He was not very passionate and time only brought me to dislike him. At last the "break" again, although my fault, as I had fully made up my mind to quit my foolishness and pleasure and be ready to leave the prison soon, as a good prisoner. I moved with a boyhood friend from my own home town, and although we both had played the game it had been for my own satisfaction and now we set our minds to go straight and to help each other to do so. And, as the months wore on he was given different work and soon I, too, was given a very good job.

This time I was to cell with a habitual liar, and a pervert of the worst type, and so I fell back into my old practices. With little work and plenty of food I gained until I weighed more than I had ever weighed in my life of thirty years.

We were both hot tempered and many arguments arose, although usually I would threaten to move and he would decide everything in my favor. In this case there was no love on my part, but it seemed he went jealously insane, and often he would lie and cry and talk at random by the hour, usually at night. He had a good pull with the officials, and that alone kept him on the job which he had held for years.

Because of jealousy he had friends of mine moved from my sight, and even arranged that I take over his work at times. Eight months of this life had made me many enemies as well as many, many friends among the convicts. Oftentimes his troubles were laid to me. He took much authority upon himself and bossed other convicts until they resented it to the extent that they framed lies and told some truths which featured the undoing of both of us, and soon we found ourselves on different jobs.

I have now moved back to the Dormitory or the "Bores' Nest"; my term is now measured in months. In three weeks I have changed my bunking place twice and I have found another man, who, by his good looks and gentle manners has enticed me into the old path. So it seems life must be just one thing after another and I must turn my life to that of being a "Homosexual" type of mankind.

Sometimes as in a state of coma I picture in mental dreams my future. Although the world does not know it, or admit it, many and many of its populace are of this same type. It is only a delusion to think that the society type of men and women are perfect and that their relations are as God created them.

It seems there is just an innate feeling among some people to look down upon the poorer element with a masked face. Only God knows what is hidden behind that mask, and year by year some stagger into the ways of crime and eventually they unfold their life history; and it is shocking to their friends if they told all the happenings during their span of years in life among society.

Gambling again took its hold upon me, and from that day until this I have never found time to read a book or magazine, and I have dropped farther and farther into that dismal abyss of sinful path of love for man.

In nearly all my affairs the love and pleasure is on a 50-50 basis and both souls are going down that never endless trail to hell on earth, that of a prison life and a nameless grave. Mr. Psychologist says to forget and start life over again. "Forget, hell," when two-thirds of the mob around me are of the same kind, enticing me onward. That was my crime, the cause of my spending six years isolated from the same kind out there behind prison walls, among the same type of men, only worse. And yet a man is told to forget.

There are those behind bars who know that if they were free they would not even know where their next meal and a night's lodging would be, and so just linger on in a jovial mood, day after day, knowing now that they have clothes, a bite to eat, and a place to "flop."

It is evident that this man is a passive sodomist and while not the only one, a decidedly harmful influence.

Not only do individuals as solitary units spread a wave of abnormal sex influences throughout the community, but a situation made up of many men, dominated by several who are frankly in this abnormal level, can cast an influence which touches hundreds of lives.

The situation described in the following quoted material existed a few years before observations for this study were begun. The inmate describes a particular shop, a vice spot, where, in his own words, "things were wide open." A few sentences will give a sufficient understanding.

When I arrived at the Shop I was met by a committee of cons. My job was to consist of piece work. There were ten of us on the job and we received among us not over two jobs a week which took from ten to twenty minutes.

After talking to Jack, Joe, and the boys and looking the joint over for a few days, I concluded that this was, if there was such a thing, truly the convict's paradise. There was everything to delight the heart of the convict on pleasure bent. Kids were openly hustling their wares as harlots in a house of prostitution. From fifty cents to five dollars was the price demanded and paid for their sexual coöperation. The kids were the best looking ones in the joint. The fish line was watched very diligently, and when a pretty young kid was discovered he was surveyed in the bathroom and if he was found to be featherless as well as beautiful there was a mad scramble. The poor, ignorant kid was showered with money and personal service, regaled with lies of the greatness and influence of the big shot.

Communication by sexually abnormal inmates is sometimes carried on by "kites," samples of which follow:

Dear Buddy:

"Honey" tonight I'm lonely and yet I don't know why, unless it's because I miss you so; your love, your kisses, your everything was my life. Now we are apart and I never knew I loved you until now. Isn't love a funny thing? And what won't a guy do when he is in prison and in love? Gee! I only have 8 months and then I'll be free and we by chance may meet where there are no guards to watch us. And then, oh, Boy! Do you need tobacco or anyhing? Guess I'll eat a little lunch and go to bed. Wish you were here tonight. Answer tonight or in the morning, Babe.

"The Vamp."

Buddy Mine:

You little devil! If I was over there you wouldn't be lonesome. Say, kid, if you can spare it bring me 3 or 4 sacks of tobacco and some matches out to the game Sat. I'll pay you back when sis sends me some money. Your time is so short, be careful. I wish I had only 8 months, but I have over 2 years yet. Well, shorty, I'll see you Sat. I never did like to write.

Your old side kick.

One of the writer's advisers agreed to write his impressions of homosexuality in prison. He would seem to be qualified as a competent observer inasmuch as he has spent eleven years in prison or reformatory. He is articulate and has superior intelligence. The reader is left to interpret the statement for himself:

In places such as boy's correctional schools the taint of pederasty touches more youths than the officials care to admit. Hot-blooded youths of fourteen, fifteen, and sixteen years of age seduce, if you may call it that, the younger boys. In turn, these boys, when they have graduated to a state reformatory are seduced by still older boys, who, in turn, are seduced by still older men in the penitentiaries. It is a common belief in a penitentiary that anyone who has served a term in either a boys' correctional school or a reformatory are seduceable. . . . Of course the latter opinion is far from being one hundred per cent correct. Undoubtedly there are hundreds of youngsters who have served terms in such schools whose bodies came out of those hotbeds of pederasty untainted.

Although boys' correctional schools and reformatories contribute some "punks" to the penitentiaries, the penitentiaries make pederasts out of quite a few youngsters who have never seen such a school. Many a youngster's manhood is sullied in a man's prison. This sullying of young manhood is as much the youngster's fault as it is the fault of the one who "makes" the kid. Except in an isolated case or so no physical violence is used in influencing a youngster to the ignominy of homosexuality. Sometimes the boy succumbs to offers of tidbits of food unobtainable at the prison table; sometimes he succumbs to the offer of money; sometimes he succumbs because some abnormality in his make-up causes him "to get to liking it after the first time." Sometimes he succumbs to an offer of ——— which should leave no doubt as to the meaning, and sometimes he succumbs because he is "talked into it."

From time immemorial man has, regardless of social taboos, gratified his animal appetites as often and as frequently as he had a desire to do so. This appetite is a force whose cry for gratification, when checked by social taboos, drives some individuals into committing atrocious crimes that shock a whole community, such as the rape of children anywhere from six to fourteen years, and drives others suffering from repressions into practicing acts of perversion between female and male, female and female, and male and male.

On every side can be seen Nature's law of procreation and propagation of the species: males and females paired off for this. Nature's main purpose. But it did not take man, with his vivid imagination, long to find out that besides resulting in procreation and propagation, copulation was the quintessence of sensual pleasure. Now sensual pleasure, after one has had one's first taste of the joys of the flesh, soon saturates every fibre of the human body with a sort of crave to experience many many more of the same kind of fleshly joys. (The promiscuousness of the present generation is an example.) In this he is helped by the human imagination, capable of making one see and feel erotic sensations with a vividness that inflames the senses and, if repressions have already set in, intensifies sexual repressions.

Now let us consider the sexual repressions of a prisoner. Because he is in a penitentiary does he forget the many, many pleasures he found in the fleshpots of another day? Ridiculous. He is made of flesh and blood, has an imagination and is beset with carnal desires, even though some prisons mix plenty of saltpetre with his food!

For example, take the prisoner who knows nothing about homosexuality, but whose mind is beginning to be warped by sexual repressions. His chances of turning to the ancient "Greek love," for gratification are excellent. His repressions, his inflamed thoughts of past moments of pleasure with women, slowly, but surely begin to warp his mind after he has been in prison anywhere from six months, upward. Women are denied him. Science has yet to find a harmless drug which will palliate man's animal appetites. The prisoner's craving for sexual gratification will not leave him, but torments him; at times lashes him into a frenzy. What is he to do? He is among a world of men and it may not be long before his repressions make him turn to the only fleshpots around him—men!

Just as women is prison turn to their own sex for unnatural gratification, so do men in prisons turn to the unavoidable, the inevitable—homosexuality. The calls of the flesh are stronger than those of the spirit, and your prisoner is not very strong in the spirit or he wouldn't be where he is. Usually your homosexualist-in-the-making craves the feel of soft flesh. He has embraced the soft, warm bodies of women in the past, but having no women to embrace, his erotic nature cries out for the close contact of soft, warm flesh.

The inevitable happens.

He may be in the bathroom, or he may be celling with some youngster who has made a favorable impression on him, when he makes the discovery. His eye rests upon, and is attracted by, the blemishless skin and supple body of some stripling. His inflamed mind, suffering from sex repression, begins to speculate.

Funny he hadn't noticed what a lovely, soft-looking body that kid had. Wonder how it would feel to snuggle against such a soft-looking body. The sensation couldn't be very different from that of lying close to the body of a woman, rubbin' against her, feelin' her soft, warm body pulsatin' against his. Wonder if anyone's got a chance of "snarin' " him. Got a long time to do, an' sure as hell got to do something or go bughouse. Wonder how a guy could approach the kid. He sure is a dream stripped off. Curvin' body just like a woman's and what a smooth-lookin' skin!

From the time he starts to speculate as to what pleasures are in store for him once he "snares" the kid, your homosexualist-in-the-making finds himself going about making a conquest with the same glib-tongued tactics he would employ with a woman. If the kid works in some other shop than his own, the would-be "jocker" begins writing "kites" to his new-found love. These kites, when there are signs that the kid is "susceptible," sometimes attain a passionate tone that really puts them on an equal with the "scorching" letters received by a woman from some Don Juan type of suitor. Once the kid has been won over, nothing, whether it be rare tidbits of food, money, or tailor-made prison clothes, are too good for him. However, the kid's "jocker" in time may tire of his male love and proceed to transfer his perverted affections to others, and then still to others.

Distasteful as it may seem to some persons, jealousy, infidelity, and other notes of discord which usually play a great part in the married life of men and women on the outside, also play a part in the unnatural union between male and male. If a "kid" possesses more than his share of fair looks, the jocker is jealous of the least sign of encroachment upon what he considers his personal property. Many a knife "scrape" in prison can be laid at the door of some fair-haired lad. Usually the wielders of "shivs" are fighting over an affair of amour, while not a few onlookers are hoping that both duelists send each other to the hospital so they can have a "chance" at the lad. I have seen some serious knife slashing—over what? Over the affections of some "punk."

Just as a woman is kissed and petted, in like manner do some of the more confirmed homosexualists play with their "kids," especially if the kid happens to be exceptionally fair-looking for a male. I have heard prisoners state that if they could only fondle, kiss, and pet some particularly handsome stripling they wouldn't care if it "went any further than that." The old saying, "every woman has a little man in her, and every man has a little woman in him," must contain a germ of truth, for I have known of cases where "kids" kissed, petted, and "loved up" as a woman would be, were known to respond with a fire and passion that must have warmed the heart of the kid's lover.

In every prison in the country there is another type of prisoner who can be called a professional homosexualist, and who, instead of waiting to be "snared," goes about making conquests just as any woman of the streets would do. These, as a rule, sell their bodies for what they can get, whether it be a nickel, dime, quarter, or dollar. To them it is not so much the money as it is the pleasure they get out of sexual intercourse with another male. These "professionals," however, form only a small, very small percentage of the male prostitutes in a prison. They went in for that sort of thing before they ever entered prison, and undoubtedly will resume practicing their perversion when released. These so-called professionals have an instinct for "spotting" others of their kind, and the bond of their profession seems to draw them together, and it doesn't take much imagination to guess what they're talking about: the "men" they enjoyed all last week, and their new conquests! I have known of several cases where this type of homosexualist were caught in the act of selling their bodies, were segregated, and made to cell by themselves. Deprived of a cellmate they have been known to employ a phallus fashioned out of wood upon themselves. To such a low level had they degenerated that they were shameless in admitting the use of a wooden phallus.

Once in a while prisoners, possessing a sort of effeminate beauty both as to body and face, enter a prison. The havoc they raise is incalculable. I have a certain youth in mind who, when it came to the prison . . . could have boasted of being a male Helen of Troy.

A brief history of this lad would prove interesting. An orphan, he was committed to an orphanage. His boyhood, from the time he was taken out of the orphanage, was spent in a correctional school, a reformatory, jails, etc. At the age of twenty-two, being somewhat of a roamer, or "bum kid," as the hobos call his type, he drifted about and soon found himself in another institution—a penitentiary.

To say that this lad was handsome, judged by masculine standards of beauty, would be putting it mildly. His was a sort of full-blown effeminate beauty, which made not a few cons just stare and stare in wonder. He stood about five feet, nine. His eyes, large, clear, and expressive, were of a violet blue, a color rare in a male. His blond countenance, radiating a glow that had a womanly appeal, made those staring cons just a bit dizzy.

And it didn't take the more curious cons very long to find out "how he stripped down." They made the most of the opportunity presented on bath day. One look was enough. They stared and stared at the nude figure of this lad and raved about him from that time on.

Not only did the lad have the looks and the swelling curving body of a female but he had long ago been "snared" in one of the institutions mentioned. Furthermore he possessed quite a few feminine traits. A goitre operation left the usual scar, and this disfigurement caused the effeminate lad not a little concern. He had a habit of slyly hinting about the number of his past "daddies." He also had a habit of "falling head over heels in love" with whatever con chanced to appeal to him. Many a convict friendship was broken through the unstable whims and fancies of this male siren; not to mention fist fights and cutting scrapes.

I was once given the opportunity to read a note of love which this boy had sent to a con, a close friend of mine. Now the general tone of this note was not unlike that of a love-sick woman timidly "sounding out" the susceptibility of some man who had caught her fancy. Unknown to the young man, the con who received the note chanced to be one who happened to be one of his most ardent, but silent admirers. In answering the note the con suggested that the lad "let himself loose" when answering the note. The apple of the prison's eye did! If ever a note read like one written by a hyperpassionate woman to a man, this answer was it. In due time the whole thing developed, or I should say, was rushed into a prison "affair d'amour."

Cons who consummated their sexual desires with this boy usually went into ecstacies whenever they launched into a glowing account of his woman-like qualities. According to them he was a sort of nymphomaniac; no woman ever responded with such fire and ardor to kissing, fondling, and caresses. Of course, one must allow for a certain amount of exaggeration, especially when anything is told by one whose erotic nature finds a stimulus in the telling of a past sexual episode. However, I do recall that, to those who were favored the lad was this, was that, and was the other. It is doubtful if any woman, regardless of the degree to which she had refined the art of eroticism was raved over as much as he. They were indeed bewitched by the prison siren's charms.

Perhaps within the next couple of hundred years a more tolerant society will take steps to decrease to a negligible degree the "making of homosexualists" in prisons by permitting inmates with wives "private visits." The state has often stressed the importance of preserving the family ties of a prisoner so that when he is released his chances of making good are greatly bettered by a united family who can help him to stay on the "straight and narrow." The sexual angle of married life plays a more important part in the life of two married persons than most persons think. The much used "incompatability" used as grounds for divorce, if the full truth were known, often springs from sexual incompatibility, either on the woman's part or on the man's. With a prisoner's wife suddenly deprived of "legal" intercourse—and she may have scruples against illicit intercourse—it is only natural that the majority of such wives turn to divorce and remarriage. Such a step on the woman's part means a broken home for the prisoner, who, when he does re-enter the outside world goes out with much bitterness in his heart and a "don't-give-a-damn" attitude. The one thing that may have worked out as his salvation, his reformation, that is, preserved family ties, is lacking, and if he fails to "make good" who can say how much of this failure can be laid at the door of his broken home. . . .

We may close this chapter as we opened it. Abnormal sex behavior is not unique to any age or locality. Our prison is no worse in this regard than others. When an environment contains patterns such as we have described here, the reader can judge for himself the impropriety of sending any but the most criminalistic men to prison. Since these data have been collected, the conditions in our prison have been improved, but culture changes slowly and more is needed than a careful discipline to uproot patterns which are so firmly fixed.[3]

[3] For an exhaustive study of sex behavior in the prison environment, see Joseph E. Fishman, *Sex in Prison*, The Commonwealth Fund, 1930, New York.

CHAPTER XI

THE SOCIAL SIGNIFICANCE OF LABOR

The bulk of penological literature is made up of essays, studies, and reports concerning prison labor and its ramifications. Prison labor has assumed importance because it is tied up with the profit motive. Such interest-groups as manufacturers' associations and labor unions, as well as government and prison officials have been attentive to the problem because it contains the most difficult ethical involvements. Is it just, the labor unions say, to allow prisoners to make goods which deprive union men of work? Is it fair, ask the manufacturers, for the prison to produce commodities which compete with our products? Though generally unconcerned, the taxpayer sometimes asks, Why shouldn't those convicts pay for their keep? On the other hand, say the wardens, Would you have us keep our prisoners idle so that they become more criminalistic and less capable of adjusting when they are released? These problems go deep into penology, and deeper still into the American culture. Adjustments have been made, as mentioned in Chapter III, but in the penitentiaries of the nation idleness abounds. We are not to be concerned here with the larger problems of prison labor, but with some of the processes involved. Those readers who are not familiar with the general history of prison labor in this country from 1682 to the present, will find the topic a fascinating one.[1]

Although legislation concerning inmate labor has always included statements, sometimes platitudinous, about reforming the criminal by teaching habits of industry, the basic emphasis has been concerned with the financial aspects. And while attention to the financial aspects is not particularly unholy, the important factor in prison labor is the *laborer*. It is the writer's opinion that the work function in prison is less important than the leisure-time function, if one considers the inmate! It is only an assumption that education of the prisoner in habits of work will tend to reform him. In a quantitative sense work is less important than leisure, because there is less of it. However, from our frame of reference, labor is important as social phenomena and not as an economic function.

[1] Louis N. Robinson, *Should Prisoners Work?*, John C. Winston Company, Philadelphia, 1931.

Through the work duties in the prison inmates come in contact with each other, and so far as we can tell, the social processes which operate in the work life are those described in Chapters IV, V, VI, and VII. Such exceptions and variations as we have knowledge of will be offered here.

A Community and Its Work

In an earlier chapter the work functions have been classified as industrial production and maintenance work. In a normal community of 2,400 people, about 40 per cent of the population, or some 960 persons, would be the expected number who would engage in productive occupations. The Lynds found in Middletown that 40 per cent of the population were gainfully employed.[2] The balance were housewives, or children and other dependents. If a normal community with an open market employs but 40 per cent of its people in gainful labor outside the home, we can hardly expect that an abnormal community with a restricted market should gainfully employ its entire population! Idleness in prison is to be expected. It is a natural phenomenon. The blame for it does not rest on officials or legislatures, or any particular decade of peoples, but on a national economy whose system of distribution is so absurdly disorganized.

In our prison idleness has not been the great problem that it has been in some others. While every man, excluding a hundred or so who are infirm or ill, is assigned to a job, there are not enough duties to occupy all. Twenty-six inmates who are representative of the important work units of the prison,[3] were queried as to the amount of idleness and loafing in which they engaged. It was found that one-third of the time they spent in shop and work gang, they loafed. Loafing is not primarily a function of laziness, as the officials have the authority to make men work. The idleness results from the lack of an industrial market, and from overstaffing the existing jobs. The men who are employed in the quarry loaf between 5 and 10 per cent of the time, while the workers in the important shops are idle between 50 and 60 per cent of the time. Among the twenty-six men, only two claimed a full day's work: a plasterer's helper, and a clerk. To the excessive amount of spare time cited in Chapter IX we must add another thirteen hours a week

---

[2] Robert and Helen Lynd, *op. cit.,* Chapters II, III, and IV.

[3] An informal schedule method was used (See Appendix A). Eight of the men were workers in the two largest shops. Four of them were assigned to the quarry units. The balance were assigned to various other work units inside the walls, no more than two being from any one occupational group. The average amount of servitude was four years and nine months. The range extended from fourteen months to thirteen years. The mode was in the two-year frequency.

of sheer idleness for the average inmate. The work-week officially amounts to five eight-hour days. Saturday afternoons are given over to recreation, and one-half day a week is used for bathing and barbering. One-third of the work-week is spent in idleness, and of the total time the men spend in prison, only 16 per cent is given over to work. The non-criminal in the normal community who works the customary forty-four hours each week is occupationally engaged for the 25 per cent of his total time. Serious as this disparity is, the important factor is the way the non-working hours are spent. Persons in a free community may spend them more or less pleasantly in profitable, or recreative activities. For prisoners there is no surcease. And this, I contend, is the most important penological problem as penitentiaries are now organized.

Sanford Bates says, "The greatest single obligation on a prison is to establish in its inmates the habit of diligence." [4] The strong implication in his thought is that diligence must be established through work and occupational duties or vocational training. True as this is in theory, experience has shown that it is practically impossible to develop diligence in most prisoners by methods of work. The greatest single obligation of a prison, it seems to this writer, is to stimulate and provide interests of a wholesome nature in spare-time activities. This is not impossible. One of the big problems in the future of America, as technocracy increases, will be the problem of leisure time. If we can teach our inmates enjoyable and socialized methods of spending their leisure time, it is possible that, as new values replace the old, ex-convicts will less frequently engage in crime. As for work placement in this machine age, we must inculcate a doctrine in prisoners that most of them cannot expect to be highly successful as workers. They must be taught to be satisfied with running a machine, tilling the soil, or like work which any person of low average intelligence and a decently healthy body can do. Most of them must be taught that their basic satisfactions of life are not to be found in the field of work, but in the field of leisure-time activities. If we can improve by re-education the constellation of attitudes which are associated with the usage of leisure intervals, we may make progress in reducing crime, as industrial training in prison never has. A well-adjusted life is a life where the basic wishes are satisfied, or approach satisfaction. Let us not imagine that habits of industry give ex-prisoners the major basic satisfactions. If we teach the men habits of play (a much easier thing to do) habits of reading, the development of hobbies, and the thousand and one other pleasant things which may occupy men's non-working hours, there is at least a chance for progress. Thus,

[4] Sanford Bates, *op. cit.*, p. 92.

in my hypothetical prison the most important employee is the director of recreation and activities. More important is he than the industrial superintendents, than the chaplains, than the teachers, than the doctors. He must be trained, highly skilled, a leader, and an executive. But this is for the future. We must, of necessity, return to the ugly present.

As we have seen there is a wide variety in the work which our men do in prison. Half of them are in the industries. Half of them maintain the plant. The kind of work the inmates do may be thought of as a horizontal distribution, as shown in Chapter III. We may classify the workers in yet another way. The prestige that the workers hold in the eyes of officialdom may be thought of as a vertical distribution. On this vertical scale is (1) the ordinary convict worker; (2) the semi-trustie or "politician"; and (3) the trustie. Such reward for work as exists in the prison is advancement on this vertical scale. The distinctions in prestige and the manner in which it is achieved are well set forth in the following statement by one of the men:

Prison "Politicians"

Caesar wrote "Omnia Gallia in tres partes divisa est," to start a book which has caused untold grief for youngsters the world over, and I must begin this essay by using the same arbitrary division, but I am dividing the population of a prison and not an empire. Thus, for the purpose of this essay I shall have to call the bulk of the prisoners by one name—"cons"—and the remainder will be classed as "trusties" and "politicians."

The cons work in the quarry gangs, the shops, brick yard, boiler-house, barber shop, laundry, rock crusher, or various other jobs. It isn't the job, but the privileges attached to the job which makes it a "political" assignment, and cons are the prisoners who have only the ordinary privileges and eat in the convict dining-room.

Trusties are those who work outside the walls, with the exception of the "outside" quarry gangs. The "outside" quarry is fenced in and the gangs are guarded by armed men so the opportunities for escape are not frequent or easy. Trusties are usually chosen from the gangs who work in the outside quarry, and are picked because of certain qualifications such as short time, tractibility, responsibility, or ties of property, or family, outside. The trusties do necessary, and often hard, work outside the walls, without close supervision. It may be farm labor, milking, caring for hogs or sheep, driving a team or truck, or work around the Farm dormitory. They have certain privileges and a measure of freedom greater than that given to men inside the walls, and better living conditions in the way of food and quarters. The cons feel that the trustie is nine kinds of a damned fool for not running away, but he feels that the trustie works for his better food and greater privileges.

A politician may be a lifer or a long or short term man, and he may be a man who would not be trusted for a moment as far as escape is concerned. He is a politician because he holds a job which is of sufficient importance to call for a "meal ticket"—the right to eat in the officers' kitchen, and other liberties such as the privilege of wearing white instead of "hicory" shirts, and the spending of an hour or so at the ball diamond for exercise. Clerks are politicians, so are butchers, and the men who work in the officers' barber shop, and in the hospital. The prisoners who prepare and serve the officers' food are politicians. Warden house-servants are in the privileged class and so are the warden's runners, chauffeurs, and stenographers. A few skilled workmen have privileges and "meal-tickets." The name goes with the privileges and not with the job, since so many different occupations are "political."

In view of the average con, those who are politicians got their jobs by the use of outside influence, or by "handshaking" tactics, or by snitching, but never because of the possession or use of more than the average ability. The sorting and recording of in-coming and out-going mail is viewed as a sinecure, by the uninformed. The man in the quarry or the shops thinks that clerical work, involving the keeping of long and intricate sets of accounts, is a "snap" job, just "pushing a pen." It is easy to "peck at a typewriter" or cook, or wait on table, in their opinion, and it doesn't call for brains or ability—fortunately! Cons say that there are just as good barbers in the con barber shop as can be found in the officers' barber shop, but, strangely, no con ever got a good shave or hair-cut in the con shop, and admit it!

The men in the shops and quarry gangs say that anyone can cut meat, or nurse, or be a librarian, or keep books, or cook, or be a waiter, or peck at a typewriter. All that is needed is a "drag" from some source or another.

There are politicians who obtained their jobs by the use of influence from the outside, and there are others who got jobs by "handshaking" or by snitching. What of it? The con in the quarry or the shops, if he could, would use influence from the outside, if he had it, or could get it. The "handshaker" who tries to gain the friendship of the guards and officials goes only a little further than the con, since there are few of the prisoners who are not more or less amiable to their guards when the circumstances seem to call for amiability. The only ones who deserve condemnation are the snitchers, and they are more deserving of pity since, when all is said and done, they have paid for a job with one of the few worth-while things left in this lousy world—self-respect. And despite the opinions to the contrary, there are certain men who hold politician jobs by ability, and got them by ability. Getting a job is one thing and holding it is another. A job, even if given as a reward for snitching activities, must be held by work, and responsibility cannot be dodged. Work in the quarry and in the shops can be dodged, and is avoided, and I know from personal experience. I've dodged it, and, when necessary, I've done the work.

To close this discussion I want to say that there are men in the shops and in the gangs who could fill certain jobs now held by politicians, and I feel sure that a man could be found among the cons to fill any job in the place. That doesn't mean that I agree that any man among the cons could fill any job, though that is the thought behind their envy, and the justification for the envy. Many of the men now in the shops and gangs will succeed to the jobs now held by politicians, as those now holding them go out, or lose their jobs, and I wonder how many of them will feel, as I do, that their privileges are, perhaps, insufficient pay for the extra hours of labor and the extra responsibilities demanded by a politician job.

The writer of the statements just quoted classifies as a "politician." His own elevation on the vertical scale resulted both from "handshaking" and the possession of real ability. Some months, incidentally, after he wrote this description, he was "busted" (demoted) and sent to the quarry to toil with the rocks. He wrote a ditty describing the work, which started thus:

Bend down and grab it,
Stand up and swing.
Every damn day
It's the same goddam thing.

Discretion dictates that the rest be omitted.

The Problem of Inmate Efficiency

It has become apparent in the opening chapters that our prisoners are predominantly unskilled workers. They have engaged largely in menial work and have worked irregularly. It would not be surprising then if the work which they do in prison is not of the highest quality. One of the authorities on prison labor states, "Taking the prison population as a whole, it is apparent to even the casual observer that there is a goodly percentage of whom no sane employer would hire on any terms." [5] Robinson refers mainly to the mental defectives and psychopaths. We would probably be surprised if we knew the number of men who have a mental age under eleven years, and yet capably handle factory jobs in the normal community. Many jobs are, in our machine-age culture, suitable for persons with limited intelligence. Most of our prisoners may seem to be inefficient as workers, though the shop superintendents say that they can be trained to do almost any kind of work. The difficulty is, however, that the teaching process is time consuming, and a superintendent never knows how long an inmate will be with him. The inmate may be sent to solitary. He may be ready for parole as soon as he is trained. He may escape. After learning a technique he may tire of the job, and refuse to work. He may

[5] L. N. Robinson, *op. cit.*, p. 137.

become ill. He may adjust well with one inmate worker and not with another, so the superintendents and guards give training not with the idea of developing skilled employees or craftsmen, but simply well enough to keep up production. It is doubtful if a guard ever thinks of endeavoring to rehabilitate a man through improved work technique. Those few men who obtain trade knowledge do so primarily by their own initiative.

Among the twenty-six anonymous inmates who were interviewed concerning occupational duties, twenty stated that their prison duties were dissimilar to their previous line of work. For three men some relationship existed, and for the remaining three, prison work was identical with pre-prison employment. When asked if they thought it would be possible upon release to put to use anything in work technique, which they had learned in prison, fifteen said, "No," four said, "To some extent," and seven said, "Yes." Incidentally, a large proportion were of the opinion that the knowledge they had gained of "human nature" would be useful to them.

The same inmates were queried as to pride in their work. They were asked outright if they took pride in the things they made, or in the cleaning, cooking, or repairing they did. Further questioning to evaluate the sincerity of their remarks led to the conclusion that sixteen had some, or considerable, pride; ten would not admit pride.

Among those scored as possessing no feeling of pride, some brief remarks were: "No one can have any pride in sewing socks." "I would like to see some one take pride in breaking those rocks." "I have no pride in sweeping the walks. I do it good so I don't have to do it over." "You get pride when you're paid, and the more pay you get, the more pride you have." "No, I loop socks." The larger proportion of the men made such remarks as the following: "I can follow the barber trade when I get out, so I do my best here." "I always like to do a good job." "I take pride because I like to see them (completed suits of underwear) pile up." "I like to satisfy." "Yes, even when working for nothing." "Yes, I have pride in myself." "I want to please the captain." "Having pride keeps you from worrying." A dining-room waiter says, "I don't like to sling hash, but I do the job the best I can 'cause I want to help the boys."

Why do prisoners work? Why does anyone work? We do not know the complete answer to the last question, but we do know the answer to the first. Prisoners work because they want to, and the reason is simple. Most inmates know that idleness is not only boring and conducive to greater unhappiness, but they also know that unless they keep busy mentally and physically they are possibly headed for a breakdown. They have seen an idle companion answering unreal voices, and they have been awakened at night by the psychotic's scream. They do not know the psychiatrist's term for a situational psychosis, but they know such exist. Even when they have a job, there is more than ample time, they know, to go "stir-bugs." So work is an agent, an agent to help keep the personality balanced. Also, by means of a job they are able to have contacts and develop some interests.

The problem of work efficiency of prisoners is really not settled. Though some authorities say that inmates are slow workers[6] and woefully inefficient, the charge may well be made that it is the total administrative situation that is inefficient. With improved administration it is logical to suppose that the quality of work would improve. It is logical because the biologic equipment of prisoners (intelligence, coördination, health) does not vary greatly with the equipment of the ordinary worker in the normal community. With an improved total administration would come shorter sentences for many men, adequately trained civilian trade instructors, wages for workers, a socially emphasized leisure-time program, and other values that have not yet been tried out thoroughly, if at all. Mass treatment (to increase occupational efficiency and habits of industry) should be supplanted not especially by methods of individualized treatment, but more particularly by treatment directed at small, carefully selected groups. Only after such methods and experiments have been tried, can we come to a fair evaluation of the efficiency of prison labor and laborers.

Workers' Attitudes and Perspective

Attitudes result largely from interaction with other persons and contacts with the material culture. In this section we will give our attention to the attitudes of inmates toward their work, toward the broader aspects of work, and such other attitudes as may appear or develop while they are assigned to an occupational unit.

If attitudes result from social contact, then it is our business to know something of the extent and type of such contact. The twenty-six men who compose our sample were interviewed on this subject. On the average each inmate talks to eleven other inmates during a fairly typical work-day. Varying from a shopman, who talks to three, to a waiter who talks with 125, or a runner who talks with fifty, the median number of persons talked with was seventeen. However, the runners' and waiters' conversations are not typical, and have been excluded, and by so doing the average of eleven has been calculated. The length of conversation extends from a continuous, all-day dialogue, to short, two- or three-minute periods.

[6] *Ibid.*, p. 279.

The men who are able to engage in continuous conversation are those working shoulder to shoulder. In the shortest conversations they may be working together but not given to much talk. Usually the participants gather in small clusters which disintegrate quickly. The most typical conversations are between eight and ten minutes in duration, and include two to five participants, and may occur during work, or loafing periods.

The number of topics discussed during working hours is large and cannot be completely enumerated here. The four topics most commonly spoken of in the order of their interest to the men are: Cases, sports, the outside, prison scandals, and the daily work. In discussing cases the men relate the story of their crime, arrest, detention, trial, chances for parole, length of remaining sentence, and so forth. Sport talk is of baseball, horses, and especially of gambling. "The outside" conversations usually deal with, and are meant to mean, any anecdotes or references pertaining to family, occupation, and knowledge gained through reading, or visits, and none of which pertains to crime. Prison scandal includes any conversations dealing with inmates and officials. It is usually acrimonious, vulgar, and colored with sex references. Prisoners talk of their work least of all, and such comments as are made are usually necessary, or critical.

The frequency of conversation of inmates with guards varies from twenty-seven times a week to none. The twenty-six inmates speak with their guards about 240 times a work-week, or thirty-four times a day. Most of such talk is confined strictly to business, as the rules forbid indiscriminate conversation with keepers. In the smaller work units there is some "kidding" between guards and inmates. Speech contacts with foreman or superintendents are even fewer. Over half the men had never spoken with their superintendent; the balance spoke to him less than five times a week. Practically all conversations that were held, dealt wholly with work.

The 60 per cent of our sample who had pride in their work are also the ones, excepting two men, who "like their work." By "like" we mean that they are adjusting to it without great personal distress. They do not enjoy their work as do some persons not confined. They "like" it in terms of the other possible job placements they might have. Some few men whose work gives them status and authority probably actually enjoy the work they do, but the number is small, and as the years pass, what enjoyment they had vanishes with the pain of restraint.

In an attempt to test the inmate attitudes towards freedom of association, the men composing our sample were questioned thus: If you had your choice between two general plans of work in prison would you prefer working under a completely silent system and receive a wage each month, as they do at ———, or would you prefer to have the liberty of talking to other men and a reasonable freedom during work hours as you have here, and not get paid— Of the two systems which would you prefer If further explanation was needed it was given. Seventeen of the men declared for freedom of association as against nine who would rather receive wages. From a small sample we cannot draw definite evaluation, though at least one suggestion appears. It would seem that social contacts are definitely important. Other and subsequent inquiries tend to verify this tentative conclusion.

In a further investigation of attitudes related to work the following questions were asked: Ignoring your own case, and thinking only of the inmates you have known, do you think that it is the *work* which they do in prison that aids some men to reform? Is it the work itself, or does prison scare men? In other words, do you think that there is any connection between reformation and prison labor? In nearly every interview it was necessary to rephrase the question so that the meaning was clear. Seventeen of the men stated that there was no connection between prison labor and reformation. It was the opinion of nine that such a relationship existed. Once again we have no conclusive answer though the weight of opinion seems to be that the type of prison labor these men have known is not related to a reformative process.

In search of the socio-occupational perspective of the sample of twenty-six prisoners, several questions were asked. Definitions of "machine-age," "profit system," and "socialism" were requested. The men were asked if they believed in labor unions, if they admired Henry Ford, and the late John D. Rockefeller. Their opinion as to whether or not it is the responsibility of a government to provide employment for unemployed persons in the normal community, was solicited. The nature of these questions prompted answers which are difficult to tabulate, though an effort was made to do so. Seventeen of the men believed that the unemployed in a normal community should "dig in" and get their own jobs, while nine thought the government should provide work. Half of them were against all labor unions. Twelve gave a reasonably good definition of "machine-age," but "profit system" and "socialism" were satisfactorily defined by only four and three, respectively. Nearly all of them admired Henry Ford and John D. Rockefeller. It is difficult to analyze the meaning of these findings. Controversial as the subjects may be, it would seem in general that the perspective of the men is limited. They are simply not concerned with the broader problems. They are illiterate in the sense that they are unread. Yet, in all probability their knowledge may be no more meagre than that of many citizens who vote.

In a few paragraphs here I have tried to hint at some aspects of the prison labor problem which are uncharted. Further study is needed, and social repairs should follow valid findings. Let us see what a sixty-three-year-old inmate philosopher with four prisons behind him, but no more ahead—he died shortly after this was written—has to say about the labor problem:

Prison Labor

While the state moves well out in the van in the segregation of mental incompetents, delinquents, and the common or garden variety of felons, one fails to see just where the movement will lead to without coöperation from other departments.

Why waste time in an effort to discover that a prison inmate is mentally and morally off color; that his life's history shows him to be "work-shy"; that his home life during his adolescent years was of such a nature as to have wrecked the morals of the apostle Paul; that he is erratic and unsocial; that his idea of clean indoor sport is a game of Kelly pool at the corner joint; but, all in all, that he possesses a trace of manhood upon which to build a better future, IF something constructive isn't done about it.

After all of this circumlocutory and apparently irrelevant bit of bombastic oratory, we find ourselves squarely up against that puzzling penal proposition "PRISON LABOR." There are but two classes of people interested in this question—prison officials and organized labor. Those to whom it is most vital, know little and care less. I refer to the taxpayers and the prisoners themselves.

Because proper employment for convicts is a "long pull" investment, the citizens who pay the bills for good government lack sufficient vision to realize the eventual large returns.

Organized laborers are but a class whose numbers are not enough to make their interests overshadow those of society in general; at best, unionism has degenerated into one of the major rackets. When their leaders raise the old cry, "Useful employment for prison inmates will take bread and butter from free men," it would be well to remember that if convicts are NOT usefully employed they will eventually take something more precious than bread and butter from society.

In another penitentiary idleness is the rule, the only work being that of actual prison maintenance. When the warden proposed installing machinery with which his charges might manufacture their own clothes and shoes and enough for other state dependents, certain politicians insisted that those supplies could be purchased more cheaply on the open market. True, they can. But if those prisoners are kept for years in idleness the people in that state and surrounding states are going to need protection to life and property in wholesale lots, AND PROTECTION TO LIFE AND PROPERTY CANNOT BE PURCHASED IN ANY OPEN MARKET. Far better to keep the men usefully busy, even if the first cost of the articles produced seems excessive.

The answer to all of this would also solve another major problem—GOOD ROADS.

About 50 per cent of the population of any prison can be usefully employed within the walls in the kitchen and dining-room, the cellhouses, the bakery, tailor shop, and shoe shop. Those activities absorb the element of inmates who can never be classed as "trusty."

Another warden quite conclusively proved that one-half of the inmates of any northern prison might be safely worked outside of the prison walls with less than 2 per cent of escapes. In doing so he learned some things which few wardens know. When he instituted the first comprehensive movement of using penitentiary inmates on road work, many of them in camps far from the institution, he "trusted" no man who lacked a family. After a year or so of this policy he found that his loss by "walk-aways" was nearly 10 per cent. To his business-trained mind this seemed too great an "overhead" or "underfoot" or whatever one might call it, so he interviewed some of the recaptured escapees. He then went into a huddle with his deputy warden and said something like this,

"Mr. Smith we haven't been really trusting any of these men. We merely hoped that their families would betray them in case they left. I find that a majority of these fellows ran away TO SEE THEIR FAMILY. It would seem that the floater who has no place to run to, would be a better risk. In the future, if *any* prisoner shows an inclination to put out a fair day's work and meet us half way, GIVE HIM A CHANCE."

Soon his percentage of escapes dwindled to less than 2 per cent.

Nearly every one of these United States has years of "backroad" building to do work which cannot be done by free labor because of overtaxation. Why not put groups of our prisoners out where some of them who have never done a real, honest day's labor can learn the sheer joy of doing constructive work on something that will endure and be a benefit to society?

Here is one case illustrative of how the thing works out: When the state of ——— was building the new prison at Jonesville, all men whose time for parole had been definitely indicated, were put out to work on the project. While the writer was so employed, many of his friends and acquaintances came out with later gangs. Among them was Jimmy X, a gangster who had never done a hard bit of labor during any of his 25 years.

We were digging tile ditches, grubbing stumps, and the like. Bright and early the boss handed Jimmy a collection of tools and indicated a large oak stump which was to be removed from the bosom of Mother Earth. Any thief is a good worker if you can get him started. The boy was no exception. He gave them the best he had all day with the result that he could hardly crawl out of the hole when evening came. As we walked to camp he limped up beside me and said, "Old Timer, I can't make it. This graft will kill me. I'm goin' to beat it tonight."

I said something about the stupidity of letting an oak stump make a lifelong outlaw out of a man. The kid was still with us in the morning—too tired to run, I guess.

A couple of weeks later as we walked in someone came galloping up behind me, stepping high, wide, and handsome. 'Twas Jimmy. Slapping me on the back, he said, "Hell, old Kid, this graft hain't got me buffaloed a-tall. Believe I could make it stick on the outside."

Far be it from me to claim that the boy was actually a better man or that he did go to work when he was released. I don't know. But this I do know: The hands of society were clean in the matter. Jimmy had been given a real chance to learn something about himself that he had never known.

Seven Daily Workers

1. Guzumback goes to the quarry—the laborer. Every day except Sunday for five years Guzumback has marched silently to the quarry. Every day, that is, except about fifty when he was in solitary confinement for one thing or another. He was there twenty-one days once because he tried to escape. The officials never liked him. He "came down" with a bad record, and after he tried to escape he never had a chance of getting out of the rock hole and to an easier job. So every day he wielded the pick and the thirty-pound sledge. At times he is talkative and aggressive. "The dirty bastards keep me in this water hole year after year; they expect me to reform. I'll show the dirty bastards what a crime wave is when I get out of here. Look at Lobby up in that filthy hospital spittin' blood out his lungs. He got his right here in this hole. And that goddam doctor doesn't care whether Lobby lives or dies."

Guzumback talks for days. Every thought is expressed; every expression is loaded with oaths. Then he turns silent. For days at a time he will speak only occasionally. But he sledges the rock with the thirty-pound maul and heaves the crumbled rock into the carts. His body is strong. He has great power in his arms. He knows he is strong and he silently yearns to crush in his big arms the necks of the screws and the heads of the parole board. Guzumback is really "tough." He was a professional thief for years and has taken the good with the bad, but this "set" the board gave him is the last straw. He will be forty-four when he gets out. There are some grey hairs now in his temples, and his face is weather beaten and hard with stern lines. Not for him this two-bit gambling. He will take a "kid" now and then, but he doesn't "play the boys." And as the years pass he becomes sterner and more silent. His prayers, both morning and evening: ". . . the dirty bastards, . . . the dirty, lousy, rotten bastards."

2. A "politician" goes to lunch—the clerk. Penrose "came down" for embezzlement. He was a cashier in a small-town bank which flopped in 1932. There were others mixed up in the deal, but when the bank examiners came the books were eleven thousand dollars short, so Penrose was sent to the penitentiary. He goes about his duties in an office in a quiet, capable manner. He learned

the routine quickly. For seven hours a day he sits at his own desk with his long columns of figures, and the onion-skin vouchers which he checks and rechecks. His balance sheets are always right and neat. He talks affably with his inmate colleagues, and more than respectfully to the chief clerk, but he never tells them much. When his plump, gray-haired wife comes to see him they sit in tears across the broad visiting table. He is a trustie and he wears a white shirt and he eats in the officers' kitchen. When his trustie companions tell wild and vulgar stories he laughs quietly, but does not add to the talk. He has been only a few times in the "back yard" where the "real criminals" are and prefers to spend his leisure time with books. He is interested in his work. Every figure he places on the ledger sheets is tidy and he knows what they mean. He isn't a "snitcher," or a "handshaker," but just a capable clerk who once was a banker. And he cries at night.

3. Durkon helps the carpenter—the man with a trade. Durkon is an occasional thief. He has worked as a carpenter most of his life, and while he has done good work he never became quite proficient enough to figure jobs or lay out plans. He has always worked for someone else except for repair jobs. When work was slack and when his wife and three small children didn't have what he thought they should, he went out and got it. They found a two-hundred-dollar radio in his home, and that's why he is in prison. Every morning after breakfast he goes to the Master Mechanic's shop. The carpenter chief, a civilian, gives him exact instruction on how to repair a staircase. Durkon takes his tools and the needed lumber to the worn stairs and slowly, but meticulously, makes them new again. He is friendly and smiling, and talks with everyone, cusses a little, but avoids the vulgarities. Since he came to the prison he has learned quite a bit of carpentry that he didn't know before. He has also learned some things about stealing which he is remembering. He more or less respects the big-shot criminals—men like Guzumback, and he likes to hang around and hear what they say. He isn't going to steal any more, he says, but he would like to live in a bigger city and have a big new car when he gets out. Being a carpenter in prison is not such a bad job. He has the freedom of the yard, and doesn't have to march in line. He usually has a hammer and a ruler with him, and struts a little. "Most of these ordinary 'cons' can't drive a nail," he thinks to himself. When the chief carpenter put him on a job which demanded that seven window frames be made in quick order, he worked tirelessly, and when he got through felt proud of himself, and felt he was a part of the plan of things. He is only serving two and a half years. The nights in the cell are pretty awful, he says, but the days aren't

so bad, and he will go home now in eleven months, fifteen days, and about three hours.

4. Sam does the washing—the laundryman. Sam was born deep in Georgia, but came north when he was five. He is not an ordinary "dumb nigger." He has been around quite a bit and has made some "good scores," as he tells his companions in the laundry. All day long he wears boots because the water on the laundry floor in an inch deep until they clean it up at night. Sam stands over one of the big motor-driven wash tubs, where he talks all day as he throws the soiled, smelly clothes into the hot water. He doesn't like the stooping and lifting, but he mildly enjoys turning those polished faucets and watching the dials. He sure enough doesn't like prison, but he talks, and he laughs through the long, hot days. Sam is a little vulgar and profane and he gambles. The food is lousy, he says, but he eats quite a lot. He has a few more years to go, but there'll be lots of stuff out there yet, and he won't work in no laundry, by God.

5. Curly knits the socks—the shopman. Only twenty-one and with brown wavy hair, everyone got to calling him Curly. He is slender and boyish and hasn't much beard. He had stolen quite a few cars for joyrides before he smashed up one night and they caught him. The first few months of prison were not half bad. Everyone liked him, especially the older fellows. They gave him tailor-mades and candy, and he wondered for a while what it was all about. He works in the knit-shop where the machines buzz and rattle all day, when the orders are good. His machine is a looper. He has to feed it yarn and then watch to see there are no jams. It isn't very absorbing work and he has time to think a lot. Curly is distractable, though, and he never thinks about one thing very long. He has served ten months and will see the parole board soon. He wants to get out and be free again, but he hates to leave Steve. Steve is his cellmate, older and wiser, and they get along fine. But Curly has been worrying a little lately. He doesn't completely understand things. Well, anyway, the work in the knit-shop isn't so bad. He won ten "sacks" the other day on a horse in the fifth race at Belmont, and the Yankees were leading the league. . . . Curly will see the parole board all right, but he won't get out. He will keep celling with Steve and he hasn't got a chance.

6. Joe goes on errands—the runner. Joe has been sitting for more than fourteen years on this one, and had two others before. He killed a guy one night when he was drunk. People think the deceased got what he deserved. Joe has been a runner for years. He has been a good prisoner, quiet, polite, obedient. His job takes him all over the yard, and he knows most of the guards and hundreds of inmates. He hears all the news because he gets around. He and

his other runner colleagues make up the grapevine. Joe doesn't tell all he hears, though, because he is prison wise, and such news as he tells is calculated to be harmless. In the mornings Joe will sweep out his workquarters and empty the cuspidors. When his boss wants something in another gang, Joe will go for it without delay. He is interested mildly in everything which occurs in the prison and has no strong hates, unless it is against the young, rowdy inmates who make all the trouble. Coffee and chow are his only real pleasures, but he likes to play poker, which he does with some skill, but he never has yet learned to turn down two pair. He is kindly. He has suffered for years, and his one tenacious thought is—Will I ever get out?

7. Blatoni makes the gravy—the cook. Tony was in the World War. He enlisted when only seventeen and fought for the States in the trences in France. He was wounded by shrapnel. Upon recovery he became assigned to the quartermaster corps and learned cooking. When the war was over he returned home a hero. Never having had a job he couldn't find one. Soon he got into petty bootlegging in his neighborhood. When twenty he was one of the less important members of a mob. By the time he was twenty-five he was in the big money, and bootlegging was no longer a racket but a business. He wasn't the chief, but an important lieutenant. He was pinched a few times and paid some big fines. After the repeal of prohibition, Tony's income was gone. Eventually, to continue his accustomed scale of luxurious living, he went on the "heist." Several robberies netted large returns until he and his companions were caught. He came to prison, a gangster by reputation and code. Tony has had several jobs but for several months has been standing over a range in the kitchen where the meats are roasted and the gravies made. Tony knows the angles of prison life; he knows them so well that he doesn't attempt to become integrated in any cliques. He is respected by keepers and prisoners alike. He "wants out." Tony figures that officials and inmates can't help him, so he leaves them alone. He is working through lawyers. Different than Guzumback, Tony doesn't curse the officials or the parole board. That he hates the board members there is not the slightest doubt, but he accepts them philosophically as an obstacle which he must overcome. Tony is, of course, very unhappy in prison. He hates the nights worst of all. There is that difference between the yellow gloom of his cellhouse and the amber duskiness of a night club. And in the day time when he thinks of his plans for release he stands patiently over the stoves preparing meals for the mouths of the prisoners. "Some day I'll get sprung," he says, "and be out there on my own."

We see in these brief character sketches that during the work life of the men the thing which concerns them least is the work. Guzumback has revenge and hate in his heart. Penrose, the clerk, plays a rôle of the well-adjusted inmate during the work hours, but he cries himself to sleep at night. Durkon, the carpenter, thinks that prison is a convention, and when he leaves he will do bigger and better things. And Sam in the laundry is always thinking of girls and cars and lots of spending money for the good times that remain when he is released. Curly is becoming homosexual and isn't interested in looping hosiery. Tony cooks the food automatically and ninety-eight per cent of his conscious thoughs deal with a method for beating his rap, one way or another.

The work is not absorbing. Most work in the free world is not absorbing, but the thoughts the workers think as they do their daily tasks are not distinctly antisocial or conducive to the disintegration of the personality as is the case with prisoners. The grudges and the brooding, the illicit plans and the wishful thinking of men confined, will probably never be obliterated completely, but a step in that direction would be accomplished by the development of a well-rounded leisure-time program. This is the important problem, as our prisons are now organized.

Collective Behavior in Protest

Except for occasional riots, collective action is rare in prison. There is even some question if riots can be thought of as the collective behavior of a prison population. In most riots of which the writer has information through prisoners who participated in them, the rebellious and destructive behavior was participated in by a small proportion of the prisoners only. This would seem logical if the thesis set forth in Chapter V and VII is correct. Bates [7] points out that in every major prison disturbance there are both remote and immediate causes. In the minor disturbance which will be reported here, this two-fold view of causation applies.

First, it should be clearly stated that the prison we are studying has never had a major riot, and it is doubtful if any of the little disturbances which have occurred approach the riot stage. Certainly none of them did during the period of our study. Considering the two facts, that there are over 400,000 men incarcerated in prisons throughout the country, and that the administration of all is stringent, the wonder is that riots are not much more frequent than they are. This inability, or unwillingness to protest actively is probably related to certain items in the prison culture, which operate with, and on, the personalities of the inmates. Because collective

[7] Sanford Bates, *op. cit.*, p. 79.

action is so rare, we feel warranted in describing briefly the following situation which may be tentatively thought of as a "strike."

Assigned to a certain work gang are about ninety men whose duties are of a laboring nature. The gang is really a utility unit and does such work as unloading flour, and other foodstuffs, and lumber from freight cars which are run into the prison yard. They also unload coal cars. It was in connection with this activity that the strike developed. On the day of the trouble the men went to work in the usual way. Several got into the two coal cars and shoveled the coal to the ground. Here it was shoveled by the other crews into wheelbarrows. Still other men wheeled it to the boiler-house, where others scooped it into assorted bins. The work went along in orderly fashion, although on this particular day the guards urged greater speed than usual. When the whistle blew for lunch the two guards instructed the men to keep on working. No explanation was given to them as to why it would be necessary to miss the noon meal, nor were they told that they would be fed later. Because the ninety some workers were spread out in an area of 6,000 square feet, there was no immediate stoppage. Within a few minutes, however, cries of "Don't work! Don't work!" filled the yard. The cries spread within the gang and soon about seventy men stood idle. The other members of the gang idled some but gave indication of willingness by continuing slowly with their duties. A captain soon gathered all the men together. He used threatening tones and words but explained that it was necessary to work through the noon hour and that they probably would be fed later. Of the seventy who had stopped work about half returned, and thirty-four were marched to solitary. Those who returned to work were booed by those who rebelled, before the line for the march to solitary was formed.

Subsequent questioning of the men in the work unit brought out these points: (1) This gang had considerable idleness, because there was not enough work to keep them busy. The keepers resented seeing the men loaf, and when an opportunity came to make them work, the keepers enjoyed driving them. (2) The first three men to yell, "Don't work!" had long sentences and previous records. (3) A few months before, the gang had been kept steadily busy for six consecutive days during which they unloaded four to five carloads of coal a day, the coal having to be handled twice. Some men were concerned lest this same thing be repeated and lest they miss their noon meal. (4) An unmeasurable feeling of unrest pervaded the prison population. A new group of officials were taking charge. There was anxiety about the expected new parole board. The food had been somewhat below standard. The weather was muggy during the early spring day and the previous night had been stuffy. (5)

The week before, two members of the work unit had been placed in punishment for reasons some inmates considered unreasonable. (6) There was something of a cleavage between the more advanced prison-wise inmates and the newer and less criminalistic prisoners in the gang itself, the first-mentioned having a strong antipathy towards one of the guards, and the latter having less bitter feelings.

Other probable causative factors were also mentioned. We cannot stop here for an exhaustive analysis. The most frequently cited factors indicated that, first, the strikers were tired of the semi-tyranny of one guard and of his driving methods which they had been made to accept for some months, and, secondly, they were physically tired, dirty, and hot, and in no mood for the prolonged work of coal heaving, while the balance of the population went to dinner. The strike was unsuccessful because the leadership was weak; no essential unanimity existed in the gang; no definite goal was in sight; and, among the thirty-four men who persisted in refusing to work, there was even some disagreement as to the causes for the action they took. It appears that with a great many of those who started to strike but did not continue, an imitation process prompted their action more than a cognitive weighing of the factors involved. The threat by officials caused a more complete consideration by many of the men of the hopelessness of any gain. Strictly speaking, the stoppage of work cannot be called a strike.[8] The event approached strike behavior only for the men who persisted and were punished. They had a we-feeling of sufficient degree, though for somewhat diverse reasons, to prompt spontaneous, corporate action in the face of obstacles.

One more example of collective behavior may be cited. On three occasions during the period of study, large groups of men protested by loud booing, about having to work during a cold winter day when they were made to leave the comparative warmth of the cellhouses and march to the quarry. Though they hollered and booed, they none the less marched in orderly files to their duties without other resistance.

An occasion when the prisoners might have voiced protest by booing, pertains to electrocutions. Our prison is designed as one of three localities in the state where men convicted of the death penalty should be put to death. Fortunately, the occasions when this must be done are rare. Three times during the period of our study convicted men were electrocuted. The fact that the prison population voiced no protest over the *idea* of capital punishment, which they easily might have done by booing and catcalls at mid-

[8] E. T. Hiller, *The Strike,* University of Chicago Press, Chicago, 1928, pp. 12–15.

night when the condemned men were to die, indicates the individuation of most prisoners, and suggests that such collective action of protest as does arise, comes out of an immediate situation in which they themselves are involved, and not as protest to an idea.

CHAPTER XII

Culture and the Determination of Attitudes

In the foregoing chapters we have been dealing with numerous items, traits, and levels of culture. We have shown to some extent how these various aspects of culture influence relationships and shape the attitudes of the men. We have broken the social life into segments in order that study might be easier, but we must be careful not to over-simplify. The interdependence and interrelationships of these segments which we have observed weld themselves together and make of penal life a continual ongoing process. In this final chapter we wish to summarize and categorize, if possible, the manner in which attitudes of prisoners are modified as the men spend month after month in the penal milieu. The inmates are adults before they come to prison. There is much behind them. Attitudes and philosophy of life may or may not be developed. Regardless which of many conditions exist, the detection, detention, and trial procedures tend to raise questions and to disrupt philosophic equanimity. No matter the state of mind, men who enter prison are subject to the pressures of the environment. There can be no accounting for the miniscule differences in the assimilation process, and we must be satisfied, at the present stage of social science, to learn of the major trends. We will first try to weave together the predominant factors which make up the prison culture as viewed in a structural sense, then to point out the possible extremes of assimilation which may take place, and finally, to illustrate the relationship existing between various stages or degrees of assimilation and the possession of certain attitudes.

The Prison Culture

What do we mean by the totality of the prison culture? In the most complete sense the prison culture is the social organization of the penitentiary, both formal and informal, plus the interactions among the 2,300 men and 200 officers living in the prison's thirteen acres. The culture consists of the habits, behavior systems, traditions, history, customs, folkways, codes, the laws and rules which guide the inmates, and their ideas, opinions and attitudes toward or against homes, family, education, work, recreation, government, prisons, police, judges, other inmates, wardens, ministers, doctors, guards, ball-players, clubs, guns, cells, buckets, gravy, beans, walls, lamps, rain, clouds, clothes, machinery, hammers, rocks, caps, bibles, books, radio, monies, stealing, murder, rape, sex, love, honesty, martyrdom, and so on. Such an answer does not tell us exactly what the prison culture is, but it does suggest its extreme complexity, especially when one considers the multitudinous shades of attitude and opinion which may exist. As a matter of fact, throughout this book we have been delineating phases of the prison culture, and at this point we wish to integrate our previous findings and to suggest the significance of them in the determination of attitudes.

In attempting to answer the question, "What is the prison culture?" it will be helpful to think of the social structure and of the social processes operating reciprocally as a force in the formation of attitudes in individuals.

If we may accept as reliable the data presented in Chapter V (they would seem reliable because two distinct samples yielded essentially the same results), we can extend the findings for the entire population. We learned that about 18 per cent of the inmates were affiliated with what was called prison-primary groups, and that each group had about four members. From this finding we are able to compute that about 400 of all our prisoners are rather intimately associated in some 103 different informal groups. The interaction in and about these groups, and the social life that exists is part of the "unseen environment" and has much greater influence on individual personalities, we are inclined to believe, than all the rules, official admonishments, sermons, or other factors intended to guide lives. In Chapter V we also learned that 40 per cent of the men were affiliated to some extent with larger collectivities which we called semi-primary groups. The average size of these was eight members, and from this we are able to compute that some 920 of the total inmates are loosely affiliated in about 115 different groups. Slightly over 40 per cent of the sample, as shown in Chapter V, were found to be more or less "ungrouped." If this is so, about 960 men in our prison have no definite or intimate social relationships with other prisoners. Such data as these are important in comprehending the structure of the prison society.

The structure may be viewed in other ways. First, of the 2,500 men in the community the 200 officers are dominant and the 2,300 inmates subordinate, and this stratification tends to be rigid. Secondly, there seems to be a distinction between the "elite class," the middle class, and the "hoosiers," and while this demarcation is not strictly rigid, the members of the elite class seem also to be those men affiliated with primary groups. A third view of the social structure refers to the various work gangs and cellhouse groups, but these stratifications are administrative and not spontaneous, though they are important because they cause isolation and preclude to some degree spontaneity in the development of social relations. A fourth structural factor refers to Negro and white aggregations. A fifth point of view will interpret the social structure according to similarity of criminal types: the confidence men and embezzlers constitute one class of the total structure; the bank robbers and advanced thieves comprise another segment; the abnormal sex offenders are a type; the aggravated assaulters are another, and so on. Sixth, the "politicians" and trusties compose a part of the structure, while the ordinary working convicts comprise another segment. A seventh viewpoint might structurally categorize the population according to those whose sex behavior in prison is normal, quasi-abnormal, or abnormal. Yet another categorization might place recidivists in one stratum and the non-criminalistic offenders in another. And still another structural delineation might refer to the personality differences resulting from the regional influences of pre-penal conditioning.

To view the prison population in this structural sense is important because the framework of a society sets up and limits the social processes. "What distinguishes societies and individuals is the predominance of certain attitudes over others, and this predominance depends . . . on the type of organization which the group has developed to regulate the expression of the wishes of its members." [1] "In other words, attitudes correspond in the main to the established social structure. The lines of cleavage among groups, whether of superordination or subordination or of amity, hostility, etc., are marked by distinctive attitudes; and this is true also of the relations between the members within each group." [2]

Of the nine structural aspects of the prison community two seem to be of outstanding importance in the determination of attitudes. Greatest is the fairly definite cleavage between officials and inmates. This structural stratification gives rise to conflict (a function or social process) which is of great importance in developing attitudes. Next in importance in a structural sense is the existence of spontaneously formed primary and semi-primary groups, which, as structures, provide an opportunity for the operation of social processes. The processes in operation for group members and the unaffiliated as well, as detailed in previous chapters, are competition for inclusion in the group, occasional conflict, followed by accommodation and assimilation, and, in some cases, a subsequent conflict

---

[1] Robert E. Park and Herbert A. Miller, *Old World Traits Transplanted,* Harper and Brothers, New York, 1921, p. 25.

[2] E. T. Hiller, *op. cit.,* pp. 70, 71.

and a new accommodation to another primary or semi-primary group. Thus, the existence of groups is an occasion for social processes. Social processes are an occasion for attitudes which result from values which make for positive or negative personal relations and cause associations or disassociations.

Our problem of determining the origin, development, and types of attitudes which exist would be relatively simple if in the prison community we had an *established social structure,* because then the attitudes which develop would in the main correspond to it. But, as has been shown throughout the study, cleavages are by no means absolute. Even the stratification between officialdom and inmates is not definite, as witness the "stool pigeons," the prisoners who identify themselves with the officials, or even the occasional official who identifies himself with the prisoners, as well as the "marginal men" who are "two ways," and the "social strangers" who are of no strata. While the primary groups tend to set up cleavages, there are no definite or absolute structural demarcations. Disassociation abounds in the population in general, and only less so in the spontaneous groups. There is no absolute definition of situations nor is there, except in a few instances, even a majority of the men who agree as to a common definition of a situation. Our discussion of group life, leadership, and the mores indicates this. Yet, in spite of the opposition, conflict, and disassociation which comprise a goodly portion of the personal relationships within the prison world, the men tend to adjust among one another even though sympathy and other-regarding attitudes may be more the exception than the rule. Such adaptation can be explained by the relation known as symbiosis, by which is meant a living together so that a benefit exists which is mutual for the parties involved. This occurs in spite of the ruggedness of individualism among the inmates, and, while symbiosis does not rule out impersonalization, the need for a degree of coöperation in coping with an unfriendly environment, keeps individualism from becoming too rampant. Let us now try to characterize the social world of the prison.

The prisoner's world is an atomized world. Its people are atoms interacting in confusion. It is dominated and it submits. Its own community is without a well-established social structure. Recognized values produce a myriad of conflicting attitudes. There are no definite communal objectives. There is no consensus for a common goal. The inmates' conflict with officialdom and opposition toward society is only slightly greater in degree than conflict and opposition among themselves. Trickery and dishonesty overshadow sympathy and coöperation. Such coöperation as exists is largely symbiotic in nature. Social controls are only partially effective. It is a world of individuals whose daily relationships are impersonalized. It is a world of "I," "me," and "mine," rather than "ours," "theirs," and "his." Its people are thwarted, unhappy, yearning, resigned, bitter, hating, revengeful. Its people are improvident, inefficient, and socially illiterate. The prison world is a graceless world. There is filth, stink, and drabness; there is monotony and stupor. There is disinterest in work. There is desire for love and hunger for sex. There is pain in punishment. Except for the few, there is bewilderment. No one knows, the dogmas and codes notwithstanding, exactly what is important.

This picturization is not an epitome. The situation is too complex to epitomize. While the description applies in general, it does not sum up. The variations and exceptions have been shown in the foregoing chapters, and while no effort has been made to compare the prison world with a non-penal community, certain broad similarities become evident. In a sense the prison culture reflects the American culture, for it is a culture within it

It is into this complex maze of the prison world that the newly-committed inmate comes. Most all of the men who enter prison are confused and uncertain about the social world they have left. They are preoccupied with self and their philosophies are frequently in a state of flux. They have anxiety over the future. What the prison does to them depends upon the degree to which they become assimilated.

Assimilation or Prisonization

When a person or group of ingress penetrates and fuses with another group, assimilation may be said to have taken place. The concept is most profitably applied to immigrant groups and perhaps it is not the best term by which to designate similar processes which occur in prison. Assimilation implies that a process of acculturation occurs in one group whose members originally were quite different from those of the group with whom they mix. It implies that the assimilated come to share the sentiments, memories, and traditions of the static group. It is evident that the men who come to prison are not greatly different from the ones already there so far as broad culture influences are concerned: All speak the same language, all have a similar national heritage, all have been stigmatized, and so on. While the differences of regional conditioning are not to be overlooked, it is doubtful if the interactions which lead the professional offender to have a "we-feeling" with the naive offender from Coalville can be referred to as assimilation—although the processes furnishing the development of such an understanding are similar to it. As briefly defined in Chapter IV, the term assimilation describes a slow, gradual, more or less unconscious process during which a person learns enough of the culture of a social unit into which he is placed to make him characteristic of it. While we shall continue to use this general meaning, we recognize that in the strictest sense assimilation is not the correct term. So as we use the term Americanization to describe a greater or less degree of the immigrant's integration into the American scheme of life, we may use the term *prisonization* to indicate the taking on in greater or less degree of the folkways, mores, customs, and general culture of the penitentiary. Prisonization is similar to assimilation, and its meaning will become clearer as we proceed.

Every man who enters the penitentiary undergoes prisonization to some extent. The first and most obvious integrative step concerns his status. He becomes at once an anonymous figure in a subordinate group. A number replaces a name. He wears the clothes of the other members of the subordinate group. He is questioned and admonished. He soon learns that the warden is all-powerful. He soon learns the ranks, titles, and authority of various officials. And whether he uses the prison slang and argot or not, he comes to know its meanings. Even though a new man may hold himself aloof from other inmates and remain a solitary figure, he finds himself within a few months referring to or thinking of keepers as "screws," the physician as the "croaker" and using the local nicknames to designate persons. He follows the examples already set in wearing his cap. He learns to eat in haste and in obtaining food he imitates the tricks of those near him.

After the new arrival recovers from the effects of the swallowing-up process, he assigns a new meaning to conditions he had previously taken for granted. The fact that food, shelter, clothing, and a work activity had been given him originally made no especial impression. It is only after some weeks or months that there comes to him a new interpretation of these necessities of life. This new conception results from mingling with other men and it places emphasis on the fact that the environment *should* administer to him. This point is intangible and difficult to describe in so far as it is only a subtle and minute change in attitude from the taken-for-granted perception. Exhaustive questioning of hundreds of men reveals that this slight change in attitude is a fundamental step in the process we are calling prisonization. Supplemental to it is the almost universal desire on the part of the man, after a period of some months, to get a good job so, as he says, "I can do my time without any trouble and get out of here." A good job usually means a comfortable job of a more or less isolated kind in which conflicts with other men are not likely to develop. The desire for a comfortable job is not peculiar to the prison community, to be sure, but it seems to be a phase of prisonization in the following way. When men have served time before entering the penitentiary they look the situation over and almost immediately express a desire for a certain kind of work. When strictly first offenders come to prison, however, they seldom express a desire for a particular kind of work, but are willing to do anything and frequently say, "I'll do any kind of work they put me at and you won't have any trouble from me." Within a period of a few months, however, these same men, who had no choice of work, develop preferences and make their desires known. They "wise up," as the inmates say, or in other words, by association they become prisonized.

In various other ways men new to prison slip into the existing patterns. They learn to gamble or learn new ways to gamble. Some, for the first time in their lives, take to abnormal sex behavior. Many of them learn to distrust and hate the officers, the parole board, and sometimes each other, and they become acquainted with the dogmas and mores existing in the community. But these changes do not occur in every man. However, every man is subject to certain influences which we may call the *universal factors of prisonization.*

Acceptance of an inferior rôle, accumulation of facts concerning the organization of the prison, the development of somewhat new habits of eating, dressing, working, sleeping, the adoption of local language, the recognition that nothing is owed to the environment for the supplying of needs, and the eventual desire for a good job are aspects of prisonization which are operative for all inmates. It is not these aspects, however, which concern us most but they are important because of their universality, especially among men who have served many years. That is, even if no other factor of the prison culture touches the personality of an inmate of many years residence, the influences of these universal factors are sufficient to make a man characteristic of the penal community and probably so disrupt his personality that a happy adjustment in any community becomes next to impossible. On the other hand, if inmates who are incarcerated for only short periods, such as a year or so, do not become integrated into the culture except in so far as these universal factors of prisonization are concerned, they do not seem to be so characteristic of the penal community and are able when released to take up a new mode of life without much difficulty.

The phases of prisonization which concern us most are the influences which breed or deepen criminality and antisociality and make the inmate characteristic of the criminalistic ideology in the prison community. As has been said, every man feels the influences of what we have called the universal factors, but not every man becomes prisonized in and by other phases of the culture. Whether or not complete prisonization takes place depends first on the man himself, that is, his susceptibility to a culture which depends, we think, primarily on the type of relationships he had before imprisonment, i.e., his personality. A second determinant effecting complete prisonization refers to the kind and extent of relationships which an inmate has with persons outside the walls. A third determinant refers to whether or not a man becomes affiliated in prison primary or semi-primary groups and this is related to the two points already mentioned. Yet a fourth determinant depends simply on chance, a chance placement in work gang, cellhouse, and with cellmate. A fifth determinant pertains to whether or not a man accepts the dogmas or codes of the prison culture. Other determinants depend on age, criminality, nationality, race, regional conditioning, and every determinant is more or less interrelated with every other one.

With knowledge of these determinants we can hypothetically construct schemata of prisonization which may serve to illustrate its extremes. In the least or lowest degree of prisonization the following factors may be enumerated:

1. A short sentence, thus a brief subjection to the universal factors of prisonization.
2. A fairly stable personality made stable by an adequacy of positive and "socialized" relationships during pre-penal life.
3. The continuance of positive relationships with persons outside the walls.
4. Refusal or inability to integrate into a prison primary group or semi-primary group, while yet maintaining a symbiotic balance in relations with other men.
5. Refusal to accept blindly the dogmas and codes of the population, and a willingness, under certain situations, to aid officials, thus making for identification with the free community.
6. A chance placement with a cellmate and workmates who do not possess leadership qualities and who are also not completely integrated into the prison culture.
7. Refraining from abnormal sex behavior, and excessive gambling, and a ready willingness to engage seriously in work and recreative activities.

Other factors no doubt have an influencing force in obstructing the process of prisonization, but the seven points mentioned seem outstanding.

In the highest or greatest degree of prisonization the following factors may be enumerated:

1. A sentence of many years, thus a long subjection to the universal factors of prisonization.
2. A somewhat unstable personality made unstable by an inadequacy of "socialized" relations before commitment, but possessing, none the less, a capacity for strong convictions and a particular kind of loyalty.

3. A dearth of positive relations with persons outside the walls.
4. A readiness and a capacity for integration into a prison-primary group.
5. A blind, or almost blind, acceptance of the dogmas and mores of the primary group and the general penal population.
6. A chance placement with other persons of a similar orientation.
7. A readiness to participate in gambling and abnormal sex behavior.

We can see in these two extremes the degrees with which the prisonization process operates. No suggestion is intended that a high correlation exists between either extreme of prisonization and criminality. It is quite possible that the inmate who fails to integrate in the prison culture may be and may continue to be much more criminalistic than the inmate who becomes completely prisonized. The trends are probably otherwise, however, as our study of group life suggests. To determine prisonization, every case must be appraised for itself. Of the two degrees presented in the schemas it is probable that more men approach the complete degree than the least degree of prisonization, but it is also probable that the majority of inmates become prisonized in some respects and not in others. It is the varying degrees of prisonization among the 2,300 men that contribute to the disassociation which is so common. The culture is made complex, not only by the constantly changing population, but by these differences in the tempo and degree of prisonization.

Assimilation, as the concept is customarily applied, is always a slow, gradual process, but prisonization, as we use the term here is usually slow, but not necessarily so. The speed with which prisonization occurs depends on the personality of the man involved, his crime, age, home neighborhood, intelligence, the situation into which he is placed in prison and other less obvious influences. The process does not necessarily proceed in an orderly or measured fashion but tends to be irregular. In some cases we have found the process working in a cycle. The amount and speed of prisonization can be judged only by the behavior and attitudes of the men, and these vary from man to man and in the same man from time to time. It is the excessive number of changes in orientation which the men undergo which makes generalizations about the process so difficult.

In the free communities where the daily life of the inhabitants is not controlled in every detail, some authors have reported a natural gravitation to social levels. The matter of chance still remains a factor, of course, in open society but not nearly so much so as in the prison. For example, two associates in a particular crime may enter the prison at the same time. Let us say that their criminality, their intelligence, and their background are more or less the same.

Each is interviewed by the deputy warden and assigned to a job. It so happens that a certain office is in need of a porter. Of the two associates the man whom the deputy warden happens to see first may be assigned to that job while the one he interviews last is assigned to the quarry. The inmate who becomes the office porter associates with but four or five other men, none of whom, let us suppose, are basically prisonized. The new porter adapts himself to them and takes up their interests. His speed of prisonization will be slow and he may never become completely integrated into the prison culture. His associate, on the other hand, works in the quarry and mingles with a hundred men. The odds are three to five that he will become integrated into a primary or semi-primary group. When he is admitted into the competitive and personal relationships of informal group life we can be sure that, in spite of some disassociation, he is becoming prisonized and will approach the complete degree.

Even if the two associates were assigned to the same work unit, differences in the tempo of prisonization might result if one, for example, worked shoulder to shoulder with a "complete solitary man," or a "hoosier." Whatever else may be said of the tempo of the process, it is always faster when the contacts are primary, providing the persons contacted in a primary way are themselves integrated beyond the minimal into the prison culture. Other factors, of course, influence the speed of integration. The inmate whose wife divorces him may turn for response and recognition to his immediate associates. When the memories of pre-penal experience cease to be satisfying or practically useful, a barrier to prisonization has been removed.

Some men become prisonized to the highest degree, or to a degree approaching it, but then reject their entire orientation and show, neither by behavior nor attitudes, that any sort of integration has taken place. They slip out of group life. They ignore the codes and dogmas and they fall into a reverie or stupor or become "solitary men." After some months or even years of playing this rôle they may again affiliate with a group and behave as other prisonized inmates do.

Determination of the degree of prisonization and the speed with which it occurs can be learned best through the study of specific cases. The innumerable variables and the methodological difficulties which arise in learning what particular stage of prisonization a man has reached, prohibit the use of quantitative methods. It would be a great help to penology and to parole boards in particular, if the student of prisons could say that inmate so-and-so was prisonized to x^3+9y degrees, and such a degree was highly correlated with a specific type of criminality. The day will no doubt come when phenomena of this kind can be measured, but it is not yet here. For the present we must bend our efforts to systems of actuarial prediction, and work for refinements in this line. Actuarial procedures do not ignore criteria of attitudes, but they make no effort as yet to conjure with such abstruse phenomena as prisonization. It is the contention of this writer that parole prediction methods which do not give as much study and attention to a man's rôle in the prison community as is given to his adjustment in the free community cannot be of much utility. Indeed, earnest belief in this idea has been a propelling force in preparing the present volume which, it is hoped, will bring some aspects of the prisoner's world into clearer relief.

For the present it is of some value to recognize that prison life affects the attitudes of men in varying ways depending on the many factors already set forth, and we will give closer attention to the prisonization process now.

Attitudes and Adjustment Reflecting Prisonization

The study of individual cases is probably the most fruitful source of information concerning the relationship between prisonization and the determination of attitudes. In the last chapter brief character sketches were presented of "Seven Daily Workers," in which occupational adjustment was emphasized. As a first step in making specific the meaning of the concept of prisonization, we will take these same seven men and interpret their rôles as inmates in terms of the prisonization process.

1. Guzumback has worked in the quarry for five years. He had been in prison before and when he first came to us he was already "prison wise." His reputation as a good thief preceded him and gave him an entree into personal relationships with the prisoners, but it also made him a marked man with the officials. He was assigned to the quarry and was satisfied to be there for the first year or two. He did not at once "group up" but after a few months he became integrated with three other men and they formed a clique. Guzumback shared his past experiences with these men telling them in detail of his thefts and encounters with the law. In turn he learned of his associates' experiences and in time they all came to think of each other as "right guys." All four of the group hated the officials and the parole board, and despised stool-pigeons. For the "hoosiers" they felt a pitying contempt, but they mingled with other convicts in a friendly and congenial way. They had some strife among themselves but it was always patched up until a day came when *X*, who was more or less the leader, was suspicioned of talking too much in the wrong places, that is, where stool-pigeons

could hear him. Gradually *X* was excluded and Guzumback became more or less the leader. He gambled occasionally, made some plays for "kids," told endless yarns and continued to express his hate for officialdom. He kept his clothes as clean as he could, "made connections" for food which he cooked in his cell, wore his cap at the correct angle, and conducted himself as a right guy should. He boasted a little, but in a tactful way, and not too frequently. He was sent to solitary a time or two for insolence and when he returned to the gang his prestige rose. His few contacts with persons outside dwindled until he received not more than one letter a month and very infrequent visits.

By the end of the first year Guzumback was prisonized to a high degree. He saw the parole committee and got his set, a fifteen-year final. He became hypomanic when he learned of the long time the board had given him; he became completely prisonized. He soon started plans to escape but his attempt was discovered and he was sent to solitary for twenty-one days. As the second and third year passed Guzumback remained more or less a primary-group man, but with his unending days of labor in the quarry he became more and more self-centered and less interested in those about him. Finally one of his associates developed a cough which was soon diagnosed as due to tuberculosis. The friend was sent to the hospital and stories leaked out that he was having hemorrhages. This frightened Guzumback. Some inmates say that he was so frightened at the possibility of his contracting the disease that he turned "rat" to his keeper hoping to get transferred to another job. True or false, his prestige ebbed, but Guzumback did not care a great deal. Though frightened about his health he was physically strong and could take care of himself. He fell silent and for days at a time would talk very little. Reverie-plus controlled him. In the early part of his fifth year he was transferred to another quarry gang. There were new faces and he made new friends, eventually becoming integrated into another primary group. He took up his old denouncements of officialdom. He was insolent and threatening to his keeper. Again he gave indication of a high degree of prisonization.

In Guzumback we see the cycle of prisonization. In the later part of his first year and in the two succeeding years he was probably completely prisonized, but in his fourth and early in his fifth year his behavior gave less evidence of prisonization as he became more introverted. He violated the mores for his own gain and was indifferent to his loss of prestige. During the later part of the fifth year, through an assignment to a different work gang he again demonstrated a fairly complete degree of integration.

2. While Guzumback represents one of the higher degrees of

prisonization, Penrose, the clerk, represents the least. Penrose entered prison in late middle life, dignified, polite, and outwardly calm. A small bank of which he was cashier was eleven thousand dollars short when the examiner came. In terms of social consequence his crime may have been much worse, for example, than of a man who held up a filling station, but at any rate the officials liked him. Penrose was capable, too. He was a good bookkeeper and was assigned to an office at once. The officers felt sure he would never escape and he was made a trustie. He got to wear a white shirt and to eat with the other inmate "politicians." While he had to sleep in a cell, his cellmate was also an older man and both were new to prison. He was friendly with all inmates in a quiet way and listened to their stories with astonishment. His wife wrote him a letter every day and his daughters at least once a week. He heard about stool-pigeons and abnormal sex behavior. He heard typical rumors of graft and that the parole board could be bought but none of these things penetrated deeply into his inner thinking.

Penrose served about two years. When he left he knew but little more of the unseen environment in prison than when he came. He was first of all not susceptible to acculturation. He was isolated from the penal community proper by his trustie job as a clerk; most of his daily associates were either people like himself, and those who were integrated in the culture did not attempt to include him in their circles. His cellmate was as isolated as he. While he learned about some phases of prison life and found them interesting, they did not seem important as compared with his daughter's baby, his wife's health, and his own fallen prestige in the home town.

3. After a few months in the quarry Durken was assigned to the carpenter shop where he did reasonably good work if the instructions were clear. He had been married at the age of nineteen and by the time he was twenty-eight, at the time he was incarcerated, he had three children. Before marriage he had done some petty stealing without being detected, but never stole again until a few months before he came to prison. "Christ, almighty!" he would say, "a man can't go on and on and on and never have nothing." Durken is extraverted and makes friends easily. After the swallowing-up process, during which he was glum, and after he got a good job in the carpenter shop, he began to blossom out and to find the penitentiary life quite interesting. Due to his job he had considerable freedom of movement and more or less freedom in his selection of associates. He finally fell in with seven or eight other fellows who worked next door to the carpenter shop and spent such time as he could with them. They were a good mob, he said, and were always finding something funny in a bad world. All of his relationships were not jocular, however, and he learned about

"rats," "punks," escapes, and stealing methods. He also liked to listen to the real big-shots talk and felt quite flattered when Blatoni once called him by name. Durken never squealed on anyone and had only contempt for anyone who would. He didn't hate the officials or the parole board because they had treated him very well. He gambled occasionally on the ball games, and for the first time in his life he learned why, in some cigar stores he had seen, there was always a big crowd hanging around the back door. He learned that such places were "bookies" and if you were lucky you could make lots of money there, and he kept this in mind. He bet a few sacks of tobacco on the horses and learned how to read the entry lists. Durken has never engaged in abnormal sex behavior, but he has heard quite a bit about it and it has set him wondering sometimes.

We see in Durken an inmate who is prisonized in some respects and not in others. His boyhood delinquencies, his early marriage causing some lack of freedom, his extraverted personality, and similar factors make him susceptible to acculturation. Combining to aid these factors are the type of work given him, the slow but distinct integration into a loosely organized semi-primary group, his aptitude for remembering devices for making easy money, and his amused respect for big-shots, all of which indicates that he is prisonized to some extent. Had it not been for the short time the parole board gave him and the fact that his wife writes frequently telling him in great detail of his children, Durken might have become affiliated in a primary group and more completely prisonized.

4. Sam is the Negro laundryman. He was twenty-four years old when he came to prison. Sam is healthy, energetic, extraverted. Being used to Hicky-Freeman clothes and Florsheim shoes, he didn't like the old clothes they gave him and he resented it when they clipped his greased, straight black hair. But he soon got used to these things as well as to the food, the marching lines, the hard beds, the bad odors, and the regular hours. Because he laughed and cussed a lot he made many friends. The other Negro laundrymen liked Sam and he was soon included as one of them. They realized that Sam had been around and that he had "scored" on many occasions that the law didn't know anything about. Sam put some new ideas into the heads of his coworkers and he was a center of interest. He didn't learn much about prison life that he didn't already know in a greater or less degree, because he had been in a correctional school when only fourteen years old and later in a workhouse or two. He picked up some new terms, however, and also disseminated some. He gambled constantly on everything and bet his tobacco, his Sunday pie, and the small allowance that one

of his girl friends in the city sent him regularly. Sam won quite consistently because he cheated, which he laughingly admitted. Sam learned to be suspicious of stool-pigeons, but he never actually learned to hate the officers because he considered that they had treated him fairly well. He didn't like the work in the laundry and had tried a few times to get a better job but the officials kidded him and he continued on in the laundry not too regretfully. He didn't indulge in mutual sex play but masturbated on occasions without compunction. Sam was a sort of leader among the eight or nine men he most frequently contacted, but neither he nor they thought of him as such. He had a few fights and usually came out victorious. He seemed to live every day for itself and while he yearned to be outside again he endured the rigors of prison life and planned for the future. His aunt and a girl friend or two sent him letters on ruled paper and a dollar or so now and then. He had enough to eat; he liked the movies; he played ball quite well, and he had friends to talk to. Prison was bad, sure enough, Sam would say, but he could do his time standing on his head if he had to.

This inmate exemplifies the ease of acculturation when acculturation has previously occurred in a similar type of environment. We cannot say that Sam is prisonized to the highest degree, however. He would seem to be a rather self-sufficient type of person in whom some items in the culture find receptiveness and others do not. He accepts the semi-primary group life as natural. He is influenced to some extent by his associates in the group but there are some mores, such as hate of officialdom, which have no immediate significance for him and he does not, therefore, share the common attitude. Sam is a quasi-leader because he is an interesting person and can provide and guide amusing pastimes. It is reasonable to suppose that if Sam had a longer sentence and a paucity of outside relationships he might become prisonized to the greatest degree.

5. Curly was distinctly boyish when he came to prison after he had just turned twenty-one. For the first few weeks everything astonished him and he felt lost and alone even though he celled with another youth only slightly older than he. Curly had stolen several cars for joyrides, but had never made any money from thefts except once when he took a radio from a car and sold it to a friend. Curly was just getting interested in girls when he was arrested, but he was still bashful and shy, even though he could do a number of courageous things such as turning a sharp corner at fifty miles an hour. In prison he didn't have the prestige that he did with the lads in his neighborhood, because so many men in prison had done much more than he had. He was assigned to the knit shop and after he had been there a while it seemed that a lot of the older fellows liked him. They talked to him, these older fellows, in a quiet way and

boasted modestly of what they had done. Occasionally they gave him smokes or candy rather casually, and he appreciated the gifts because he had no money and no kin folks except his father who paid no attention to him. During his idle hours in the shop he heard talk of past exploits, denouncements of "screws," pungent descriptions of past love affairs, and so on. He heard talk of gambling and saw some of it. He learned who, among the convicts, were "right" and who were "wrong." In a few months he began to talk like the other fellows and began to feel a part of things. He had lots of friends, he thought, upon whom he could rely for help. Among these was Steve, who was about thirty, and who had already served six years. Steve was a big-shot and his few closest friends were big-shots. It was from Steve that he learned about betting on horses. At night in his cell instead of reading the funny pages he took to watching the entry lists for the tracks and following the ball teams.

After Curly had been in prison about five months, all of a sudden, he was told to change his cell. He was told to go to number so-and-so, and when he got there with his few belongings he found Steve. He and Steve became fast friends. They played coon-can and occasionally made coffee in their cell at night. Weeks passed and finally Steve tried to do something which angered Curly. They didn't speak for a few days, but the difficulty was finally ironed out. Steve said he was sorry but explained about the Greeks and the Romans. Other attempts at sex play by Steve were repulsed, but by the time Curly had been in the prison ten months he was engaging in "leggins," the last step before sodomy.

At the end of ten months Curly had become fairly prisonized, but not completely so. However, his prisonization was of such a nature that his personality was definitely damaged. Lacking home connections, being distractible, feeling lost and immature, Curly was susceptible to prisonization. The level at which prisonization took place to the greatest extent, the sex level, has biologic as well as social significance. Comely, youthful, and shy, Curly was considered fair game by the prison "wolves." He learned to gamble and he learned the prison argot. He developed a feeling of contempt for stool-pigeons but never learned to hate the officers although he made no efforts to be of assistance to them. He was a member of a semi-primary group as a hanger-on, and, being Steve's "boy" was on the fringe of a primary group. All in all, Curly's acculturation was rapid and it could reasonably be predicted that after the three or four years of his sentence he would be completely prisonized.

6. Joe has been a runner for nine of his fourteen years of servitude. Having been in two prisons before he came to us, the swallow-

up process had little effect on him. He quickly accustomed himself to the daily routine and the lack of variety in the diet; he expected the environment to administer to him; he wanted a good job. Joe got several good jobs because he was polite to officers, efficient in his work, and quiet. After five years Joe was assigned to the job of runner and porter, finally getting a spot that he liked. His duties were not so great but that he had time to tinker with and repair watches which he did with some skill. Because his working quarters were isolated, he was able to brew himself an occasional cup of coffee. As a runner he had the freedom of the yard, a privilege which he never abused. While outwardly friendly toward all inmates, Joe never actually grouped up. His three closest friends were members of three different groups. Every day he had contacts with hundreds of inmates but these contacts were all of the touch-and-go variety. To his close friends and his cellmate Joe would unburden himself and listen in turn. Except for occasional letters from old buddies of the Spanish War days he had no relationships with persons beyond the walls. While he would gossip about officials, he never developed hatred towards them. For the pardon board which had twice refused his petition for pardon he held a burning distrust, however. No one ever knew him to "fink" to officials, but on the other hand he did not avoid or hate the men who did; he was simply careful of his speech when he was around them. He gambled at poker and counted the occasions when he won as the most pleasant to be had in prison. He avoided abnormal sex behavior though he probably masturbated when necessary.

In Joe we see the type of man in whom prisonization advances to a middle degree. Prisonization has become most pronounced in the acculturation to the universal factors. Officials refer to men such as Joe, men who go along year after year without causing trouble or showing any particular change in orientation, as "institutionalized." His general avoidance of close confidences in group life and his only partial acceptance of the mores are indicative that even long years of residence may not make for complete prisonization. Differing from Guzumback whose prisonization was cyclic, Joe advanced to a certain stage from which he did not waver.

7. Blatoni came to prison as a notorious gangster. He was known to be a "right guy" who never double-crossed a friend. Almost at once he was hailed as a big-shot. His quiet manners contradicted the expectations of some scoffing inmates who believed he was overrated. Jails and prisons were new to him and it was many months before he could get used to the coarse clothes, the unpalatable food, and the daily routine. Many prisoners wanted to know Tony and to shine in his reflected glory. During the first year he was friendly to all and in a measure enjoyed his prestige.

He even affiliated in a mild way with a semi-primary group. He despised stool-pigeons but never expressed a hatred of officials. Occasionally he gambled on the ball games for small stakes. He had as many visits as the rules allowed and received numerous letters. He was not so apt to talk of his past criminal exploits as he was of his family and friends and his arrangements for seeing the parole board after the first eleven months. By the time he saw the board, however, he had become somewhat prisonized. When the fateful day came, the day he was to receive his set, Tony learned that the parole board had "blasted" him. They had commanded that he serve many years in prison. He was infuriated. For the first time his few close associates saw a display of the temper and heard the strong language which they had expected from a thief of his reputation. For days he was in a rage, but he kept his emotions concealed from officers and from most of the inmates. As the months passed by he grew less sociable. His contacts with persons outside the walls continued and it was on such relationships that his attention was turned. He avoided affiliation with groups. He silently cursed the early morning rising and the long dull evenings. He played up to officials just enough to get a fairly good job. He showed no hate towards them and probably felt none. Towards the parole board he was deeply bitter but few knew of his feelings. He was so immersed in his own plans and schemes to "beat his rap" and spent so much time thinking of it or expounding it to a few others that acculturation could not be completed. As the second year turned into the third, however, the subtle forces of the prison culture began to evidence their influence on him, and while he was still hopeful that he wouldn't have to serve the sentence that had been given to him, yet he became less active in fighting for release and slipped into a state of reverie-plus, taking each day as it came and becoming more and more resigned. However, when some unusual incident occurred, such as an unexpected pardon for some man whom he knew, or some change in the official family of law enforcement, Tony's interest would revive and he would snap out of his reverie only to lapse again into a lethargic type of existence.

With the exception of Penrose, the clerk, prisonization has advanced to a fairly high degree in the seven cases just sketched. While complete data are not shown here, success on parole would be considered unlikely for Guzumback, the quarryman, Sam, the laundry worker, Curly, the shop boy, and Blotini, the gangster. Durken, the carpenter, and Joe, the runner, would seem somewhat better risks on parole, but their adjustment in the free community would have to be considered as questionable. While no one criterion can be an adequate determinant for predicting parole success, the degree of prisonization must always be given the attention of a major determining factor by parole authorities. Other things being equal, the inmate who has become prisonized to advanced degrees would be a poorer risk on parole than others who had not. This would seem so because a high degree of prisonization involves so many "unfavorable" factors. The most important of these, we think, is affiliation with a prison primary group. It has been shown that forty per cent of the inmates belong to primary or semi-primary groups. From studies made quite independently of this present investigation we know that about 17 per cent of the men violate parole. (This figure is the ratio of men violating parole in a selected year considering all men on parole, and is the most common measure of violation.) Who knows but what the 17 per cent of men who become parole violators are the same men who in prison were affiliated with primary groups? It is an interesting speculation and mentioned here simply as hypothesis.

As a further effort to understand the workings of the prisonization process, and to illustrate the relationships existing between its various degrees and the possession of certain attitudes, the considered judgement of ten inmate advisors was obtained. These advisors were given detailed explanation of the prisonization concept, and were then queried, not concerning their own status of prisonization, but of the population in general, and then of their four closest associates. Obviously, data so subjective are difficult to tabulate and analyze, but the impressions and comments of these men are suggestive.

All ten advisors agreed that a process which might well be called "prisonization" existed. They were in essential agreement that the writer's hypothetical schema, showing the lowest and highest degree of prisonization, was as suitable and practical a measuring rod as could be devised but they frankly admitted that their judgements were impressionistic to a large extent.

Concernng the inmate population in general, the ten inmates offer the following judgements in regard to prisonization. First, more of the 2,300 inmates approach the higher degrees of prisonization than the lower. Second, averaging the ten answers to the question, "What per cent of all the inmates are *completely* prisonized?" the result was 20 per cent, and the respective answers, in terms of per cent, were: 40, 10, 15, 5, 30, 25, 5, 45, 5, 25. The reader can see the wide divergence in opinion, and we can come to no definite conclusion but it is interesting to note that none of the ten advisors considered that a full half of the penitentiary population to be completely prisonized. Third, it was the collective judgement of the advisors that those inmates who became prisonized to high degrees were much more likely to return to crime upon release than those whose prisonization did not advance, but that there were exceptions. Fourth, of the seven factors in the writer's hypothetical schema to show the most extreme degree of prisonization, eight of the ten advisors agreed that the strongest determinant making for a high degree of prisonization was a long sentence, but the judgements on this topic were not clear cut due to the inter-dependence of the six other factors.

When the ten advisors were questioned about their four closest associates in regard to prisonization the following impressions resulted. Of the 40 men under appraisal by the ten advisors, 11 were considered completely prisonized and only 2 were thought to be prisonized in the least degree. Of the remaining 27, the degree of prisonization varied but the judgement of the advisors was to the effect that of the respective men whom they were evaluating, more approached the higher degrees than the lower degrees. Other questions put to the advisors about their four closest associates yielded such a jumble of opinions, that analysis is almost impossible.

From the case-sketches illustrating the various ways in which prisonization occurs and from the judgements of the ten inmate advisors, we have enough knowledge, imperfect and inexact as it is, to suggest that most men in penitentiaries have no chance of being salvaged if they become prisonized to any appreciable extent.

The apparent rehabilitating effect which prison life has on some men occurs in spite of the harmful influences of the prison culture. Among the writer's wide acquaintanceship with hundreds of inmates those who were improved or rehabilitated were men who, in the first place, should never have been committed to prison at all, and who, in the second place, were engulfed by the culture, or prisonized in only the slightest degree. While sometimes the so-called real criminals are rehabilitated, the occasions are so rare that the total effect is neglible. Such "rehabilitation" as occurs with the actual criminals refers to the type of "treatment" which keeps them in prison until they reach such an age that they no longer have sufficient physical nor mental vigor to commit further crimes. In a cold, objective sense this means of "rehabilitation" has some societal utility, but, at the same time if other methods had been used the waste of human resources might have been avoided and the dignity of human personalities maintained.

To a few men the pressure and unpleasantness of prison life is such a shock that they are literally "scared out of" further adventures in crime and thus become prisonized to a lesser degree. The same fright phenomena are frequently found in persons who at one time became highly prisonized but who later rejected the influences of the prison culture and remained at a low level of prisonization. "I don't want any part of it," such men say, "this is the low spot in my life and I'm all done with it—I'm all washed up." Their sincerity is demonstrated by their behavior as shown when they slip out of group life, avoid close contacts with other men, take up new studies, and lay plans for a legitimate life when released.

To a few of the inmates whose prisonization has not progressed to the higher levels, a new sense of loyalty and responsibility towards their home folks seems to develop. Prison life serves as an agent to reveal to them the faults which they consider lie within their own natures. Demonstration of such changes in perspective becomes evident mostly by what they say, but many concrete examples are known where subsequent behavior proved the genuineness of their declaration.

The adoption of religion usually occurs among a few men who are relatively unprisonized. They take up religious teachings because they are prisonized only to a mild degree and the adoption of religion, in turn, prevents further prisonization. We have no information to offer as to the permanence after release of the religious influence, although it is important in the penal community because it reflects the attitude and adjustment of men in reference to prisonization.

For the most part, it is among the men who do not become deeply integrated into the prison culture that reform takes place. (1) Inmate *A* came to us for a petty house burglary. His previous life had been without criminal blemish. He had worked about machines in factories and had always had an intense interest in things mechanical. The deputy warden assigned him to the machine shop where he assisted the acetylene welder. As months passed the inmate welder taught him the trade. *A* avoided close relationship with inmates and developed a friendship with the master mechanic. His family remained loyal. When time came for his parole he was a thoroughly competent welder capable of passing the regular examination. He left the prison with a specialized trade. (2) Inmate *B* was incarcerated for a murder resulting from a love triangle. He was given the minimum sentence. His first three years were spent in the prison proper where he held a number of ordinary jobs. He was civil and friendly with his inmate companions but did not affiliate with any cliques. He was polite to officers, a hard worker, and maintained excellent conduct. After three years he was made a trustie and sent to the farm where he was assigned to care for the poultry. As months passed he became interested in poultry raising and sent for government literature which he studied carefully. During his five years on the prison farm he amassed a fund of detailed information about egg production and poultry raising sufficient to enable him, upon release, to make a comfortable living. (3) Inmate *C* came to prison for robbery, armed. Earlier he had been in a reformatory. During his first six years he lived and worked in the yard and became prisonized to a high degree. He became the heavyweight boxing champion and was a prestige bearer. An employee encouraged him to continue his boxing career and assisted him with it. The warden aided his progress by making him a trustie and by placing him on the farm. The development of boxing skill, the change of environment, the friendship and guidance of the employee facilitated a reduction of attitudes and inmate *C* became less characteristic of the criminological ideation of the prison culture. After a total of eight years he was paroled. In the first six months he made a hundred dollars as a boxer but gave up fighting for marriage. He has lived steadily with his wife and has had two children. He has worked quite regularly in a factory and as a truck driver while his four years in the free community has been, in general, non-criminal. On one occasion, at least, he purchased two articles of property which he suspected were stolen. It is probable that the attitudes allowing the purchase of stolen goods reflect the six years during which he was prisonized to a fairly advanced degree. (4) Inmate *D* came to prison for forgery. During his forty months of servitude he maintained close bonds with his family and avoided intimate relations with prisoners. After his first year he was assigned to the hospital as a nurse. With the encouragement and help of the physician he studied medical textbooks and nursing manuals and became a competent surgical nurse. He would never have developed this competence had he accepted the anti-administration ideations and other dogmas of the inmates who were highly prisonized.

Many other examples might be given to illustrate how men who are not imbedded in the prison culture are aided by some influences of life in prison. However, even men who seem to improve themselves as a result of incarceration face problems and obstacles, tangible and intangible, the rest of their lives. The problems they face are, in part, the problem of prisons themselves, and in our closing pages let us consider some of the broader aspects.

Conclusion

We have looked into the unseen environment in the penal community. We have weighed data impartially and with objectivity. Where data were inconclusive, we have not hesitated to say how little understood are some of the processes and problems. We conclude our studies by presenting some observations and comments, comments which are not based on specific data, but which are intended to reflect one investigator's speculation on the problem of prison as related to the totality of society.

It has not been the special purpose of this study to foster recommendations. The literature of penology is alive with practical and intelligent recommendations as to methods by which the penitentiaries could be improved. We leave as recommendation only the broad principle set forth in Chapter XI, i.e., that the socialized instruction in the use of leisure time is more important than formal education and trade training and the other customary apparatus of reform. But we would be amiss unless an effort were made to view in perspective the penitentiary as a part of the total social life of which it is made.

It is becoming to be a common practice for those persons who observe the human scene, and find in it nothing but chaos, to conclude their comments by slyly hinting or openly suggesting that there can be no basic correction of the problem which they have appraised, other than a social revolution. Such suggestions are too complex to admit of analysis here. Few will deny, however, that no matter how idealistic the revolutionary idea may be, the revolutionary ideology in practice is apt to be frightfully hard, psychologically and materially on contemporary generations. For the student who specializes in one particular field which is closely related with all other human activity, the tendency to spread responsibility for the chaos in his own field, is well known. This writer fits into such a pattern and has confidence that the amelioration of the prison evils depends upon amelioration of the ills in many other institutions and agencies out of which crime arises. But in the consideration of present day problems your writer is confused along with others. He is not sure, for example, exactly *what is important* in the totality of life and society. He is sure, of course, that prisons are awful. He is sure that the protection they claim for society is generally exaggerated, from the long-term point of view. He is sure that the prisons work immeasurable harm on the men held in them as well as the employees that care for them. But, he is not sure that these facts of which he is sure about prisons, are very important in the great totality of society. In the United States, for instance, we seldom have more than a half million men and women in durance vile. A half million persons in a nation of one hundred and thirty million comprise a negligible percentage if the hypothesis is adopted that the greatest "good" for the greatest number of people is the most important value in life. If we could blindly follow this hypothetical ethic, our problem would be simple: we could simply liquidate or comfortably but permanently segregate all criminals and other undesirables. At once, however, we would run into a snag. The obstacle is related to the concept of responsibility.

These half million or so people in prison are not yellow dogs; they are not the public rats that they have been called. They were born into this world, utterly innocent. They may have been handicapped with physical anomolies, but that is certainly no fault of the little biologic organism we call the baby. Most of the half million in durance vile, did not come into the world under great constitutional handicaps, however, but, in early years were no different than others who grew to become respected citizens. What then makes them, thirty years later, the double-crossing, dishonest, unfaithful, unaffectionate people they so frequently turn out to be? Is it not true that they have *learned* to be that way? And have they not learned to be that way in a society in which patterns stimulating dishonesty exists? These half million people have not assimilated the mental sets or attitudes which make them what they are in a vacuum. In the sense that our inmates have learned to be what they are, they themselves are not to blame; the attitudes and ideas which they have learned exist in the super-organic phenomena of society, and, more tangibly, the systems of thought and habits they develop are part and parcel of the social group in which they have had relationships.

When the question of criminal responsibility or blame is under consideration, attention must be given to the causes of crime. It is trite to say that causation is intricately complex, though it is only in the last decade or so that the understanding of divided responsibility has developed. We no longer assign criminal causation to the individual offender. Dr. Tannenbaum develops the point and, ". . . rejects all assumptions that would impute crime to the individual in the sense that a personal shortcoming of the offender is the cause of the unsocial behavior." [3] He goes on to say, "The assumption that crime is caused by any sort of inferiority, physiological or psychological, is here completely and unequivocally repudiated." [4] Dr. Tannenbaum has special reference, of course, to the eighty-five or ninety per cent of offenders who more or less persistently pursue a predatory criminal career, and not especially to those pathological few who become involved in crimes of passion. The outstanding studies of criminal causation, in recent years, emphasize and deal largely with the social factors involved as causes of crime.[5] And while complete understanding of the forces making for crime still elude us, it can be said that the field is now becoming demarcated. So, even if the hypothesis of the greatest good for the greatest number of people, is held as socially useful, we cannot accept it, if it refers to liquidation of the criminal, because it raises

[3] Frank Tannenbaum, *Crime and the Community*, Ginn and Co., Boston, 1938, p. 22.
[4] *Ibid.*, p. 22.
[5] Clifford Shaw and Henry D. McKay, "Social Factors in Juvenile Delinquency," *National Commission on Law Observance and Enforcement*, Report No. 13 on "The Causes of Crime," Vol. II., Government Printing Office, Washington, D. C., 1931.
Frank Tannenbaum, *op. cit.*, pp. 3–218.
James S. Plant, *Personality and the Culture Pattern*, The Commonwealth Fund, 1937.

strong conflicts with another ethical hypothesis just as socially valid, and that ethic we know under the abstract term of *justice*. The ideology of justice is written into our constitution and into part of our laws, and more important, is deeply rooted in the mores of the people. A sense of justice is one of the foundations of social life.[6] To hold the criminal responsible for his acts when we know from our studies of causation that he is not wholly responsible, violates the precepts of justice, and in so doing, utilizes the doctrine of freewill, and ignores the doctrine of determinism. Though we postulate a sense of justice as a foundation of social life, there is much evidence to indicate that the public, lacking understanding and interest in the causes of crime, still clings to the idea of individual responsibility. "Individual responsibility for misconduct is still a point of departure between expert and popular opinion."[7] In complex problems of criminal responsibility, expert opinion must guide, educating public opinion as it leads the way.

Even if one were to hold, for the sake of argument, that the inmate is what he is because he deliberately, of his own free will has chosen to be that way, and consequently should be punished for it, what then should be the attitude in terms of justice towards the so-called respected citizens who year after weary year, plunder and steal? Everyone knows that in high places there is graft and waste, dishonesty and greed.[8] Some newspapers, claiming to be public benefactors, twist and distort news for their selfish interests. Some people in government make of their public trust, a seething scandal. In some business and industry, and occasionally in the church, we find the same philosophy, the same attitudinal structures in individuals that exist in the men who come to prison. Remembering these facts, and considering our principle of justice, we must forever refute the concept of individual responsibility, of the "mad-dog school of penology," of strong retributive measures. To be sure, and to be consistent, we can no more completely blame or hold individually responsible the non-incarcerated criminal who poses as a respected citizen, than we can the man behind the walls. Both are a function of our society; both, and other types as well, have arisen from a social milieu, which can be understood only in terms of a history which considers social, political, religious and economic processes.[9]

---

[6] Logan Wilson, *Public Opinion and the Individualized Treatment of Criminals,* Journal of Criminal Law and Criminology, Vol. XXVIII. No. 5 January, February, 1938, p. 679.

[7] *Ibid.,* p. 678.

[8] Ferdinand Lundberg, *America's Sixty Families,* The Vanguard Press, New York, 1937.

[9] See, Donald R. Taft, *Human Migration,* The Ronald Press Co., New York, 1936, pp. 224–257.

In twelve chapters we have painted a sorry picture of the prison community. It is what it is, because of what it has been in the past. It is what it is because of the influences which have played upon the men who make it up. It has been a commonplace to say that prisons are behind the times, decadent, and that they have not kept step with advances on other frontiers. But we wonder if this is actually true. Now, in 1940, international murders are raging on two continents. A brown shirted fanatic is menacing the peace of the world! Mighty nations build mighty guns. Diplomacy among nations is largely the same class conscious maneuvering it always has been. In our own country there is scarcity in the face of plenty; there is unemployment by millions; there is strife and conflict. Can we say that the prisons are far behind the times when conditions in more important world sectors, are what they are? Probably not. In fact some few prisons are ahead of the times when we give attention to the present plight of the world. This does not mean that our *total* system of criminal justice is not decadent, to be sure, and its faults and the faulty assumptions on which it is based have been well set forth.[10] The point we are attempting to make is that the better prisons with their libraries, vocational training, payment for labor and so on, are, even though a part of a decadent system of criminal justice, in and of themselves, no less progressive than the rest of a disorganized world. For example, the prejudice against race, so prominent in some nations, exists in only the mildest form in most of our prisons. Freedom of speech, though restricted in prison, is curtailed even more so in some supposedly free countries. If graft and swindle exist in some criminal agencies, so do they also exist in many cities. The prisons do not let their men go hungry; they do not let disease go unchecked as many free communities do. It is in this sense, we say, that the prisons are no more decadent than other institutions in society.

Yet, it is impossible to view the immediate future with much optimism.

"The prospect for greater efficiency on the part of the police, the courts and the other agencies for dealing with criminals is not encouraging. A principal limitation of the increased efficiency of these institutions is 'politics.' A second limitation is the unwillingness of the public to pay taxes sufficient to make efficiency possible. And a third limitation is the localistic restrictions on the agencies of justice by the American framework of government. Perhaps these limitations may be removed by a further increase in crime or by a succession of startling crimes.

"Crime might conceivably be reduced by fundamental changes in social organization, such as the minute police regulation of behavior found in certain continental countries or the identification of individual with public

[10] Frank Tannenbaum, *op. cit.*, pp. 474–478.

interests seen in the Marxian ideal, or a return to the simple and slowly changing social organization of fifty years ago, when behavior was controlled largely by the pressure of the intimate group of neighbors and other associates. But nothing except a cataclysm is likely to produce such fundamental changes in the social organization at least in the near future. Whatever improvement is made in the control of crime must be made within the framework of the present developing social organization and with the limitations mentioned in the last paragraph." [11]

Within the framework of the present developing social organization, improvement can be made. The principles as shown in resolutions developed through many years by the American Prison Association, can be applied to our prisons in greater or less degree with beneficial results. As for the more pressing aspects of the criminal problem, let every dollar spent for improvement of prisons, be increased three fold for the development of Probation systems, and increased five fold for study and an integrated service in the communities from which the heavy majority of our inmates come.

---

[11] *Recent Social Trends, op. cit.*, p. 1167.

APPENDIX A

METHODOLOGICAL NOTE

This volume, intended as a contribution to the literature of penology, would be incomplete without mention of the methodological frame of reference. To be sure, the methods used have become largely self-evident, but a few additional explanations may prove helpful. Subsequent studies of the prison community should refine the exploratory and oftentimes hypothetical problems brought forth here. No one can be more aware of the limitations of the studies than the writer.

Most important, perhaps, as a phase of method, has been the writer's routine, daily, service work. In the prison which this study describes, he has examined sociologically over 2,500 men and has learned in greater or less detail the themes and activities of the 2,500 lives. Substituting for the psychologist the writer has conducted over a thousand intelligence test routines and has administered several hundred individual psychometric examinations. As colleague and friend of physicians and psychiatrists, he has assisted with medical treatment, with surgery, with spinal punctures, with the care of the violently insane and the mildly neurotic. He has seen prisoners work, sleep, eat, fight, play and die. He has purposefully affiliated himself with officials and guards in order to understand their point of view. In short, the experiences and observations brought about through the writer's job are important aspects of the method. Additional years of experience in two other penitentiaries of the same state have added maturity to his experience and thousands of sociological examinations and interviews to his general knowledge. Investigations of prisoners' homes, communities and hangouts have furthered integrative speculation concerning the problem of the prison community. Continued contact of long-standing with inmates who have been discharged from the prison has provided additional insight. Particularism has been avoided by the writer's interest and deep concern with human activities divorced from the prison world. National and international affairs, civil liberties, music and athletics have served to aid him in avoiding a too heavy specialization, and these facts are mentioned here only because portions of the study are interpretative, and the reader has the right to know something of the interpreter's orientation.

To return to the more concrete problem of method, the *purpose* of this volume must be appraised. Purpose and method go hand in hand. Had we been attempting to prove or disprove an exactly phrased hypothesis, the methods would necessarily have been different. But our purpose has not been specific, but general. It has been to show in sociological form all the important phases in the social life of the prison. Not intended as an objective or hypothesis, however, there has nevertheless evolved from the data, long after the observations for the study began, a somewhat specific hypothesis. And this hypothesis refers to the degree and extent of consensus among prisoners. Contrary to impressions and writings of other investigators, this study has found and reported considerable evidence to indicate that consensus, solidarity, we-feeling among prisoners has been previously exaggerated. Important as this fact is (it might well form one basis of new penological treatment), it was not sought for but arose out of the more general purpose of presenting for the first time a sociological study of the prison community. In terms of purpose and method, then, our studies most closely approach the method of cultural analysis, or in another sense, the method may be thought of as the case method, in which the *case* is the prison community.

Perhaps more precise information might have been obtained if statistical methods had been used, but the broad purpose of the study has been to view the prison as an organic inter-related whole, and while statistical techniques can well contribute to this end, the data of the prison community do not easily lend themselves to such methods. The writer experimented with some standardized attitude and value scales. For example, the reader can well imagine a thick-necked robber who has served ten years in prison struggling to evaluate the following proposition, using numbers 1, 2, and 3 to show partial or complete agreement or disagreement: *"The world would be a much better place if we took to heart the teaching, 'Lay not up for yourself treasures upon earth . . . but lay up for yourself treasures in heaven, where neither moth nor rust doth corrupt, and where thieves do not break through and steal."* [1] Similarly, the reader can understand the emotional tension which an inmate will develop in agreeing or disagreeing with the following statement: *"The individual who refuses to obey the law is a menace to civilization."* [2] To be sure, scales could be developed which would be suitable for the measurement of prisoners' attitudes and values, but

[1] Gorden W. Allport and Philip E. Vernon, "A Study of Values," Houghton Mifflin Co., New York, 1931. The material quoted is one of forty-five propositions in refined questionnaire form.

[2] L. L. Thurstone, "The Measurement of Social Attitudes," The University of Chicago Press, Chicago, 1931, From "Attitudes Towards the Law by L. L. Thurstone and Daniel Katz.

it is doubtful if in the present state of our knowledge the results of such techniques would be any more revealing that the sympathetic interview techniques used for the collection of most of the data in this study.[3] Refined statistical methods are the next step.

It is evident that much of our material has resulted from interviews with inmates. Space need not be taken here to describe the intricate aspects of the sociological interview.[4] It is sufficient to state that the goal of the interview is to break down distrust and build up rapport. Numerous means and techniques are employed to this end, but fundamental to all is a condition of empathy on the part of the interviewer. In over 30,000 various conversations with inmates, only three have flatly refused to coöperate, and only a dozen or so have shown an unfriendly attitude. It has been possible to develop positive friendly relationships of long standing with a large number of men. The social warmth of such relationships has been the entree to the material for our studies. When close rapport is gained with men in prison and when one understands the conditions which has made them what they are, it is no easy matter to keep a calm, impartial perspective. Thus, though the writer as a human being has developed sympathy and understanding, he has made every effort, as the pages of the book will show, to keep an objective, dispassionate viewpoint.

As one result of the rapport developed through interviews, it has been possible to have the men write their experiences and attitudes on a wide variety of subjects. Over fifty lengthy autobiographies have been prepared, some of which refer primarily to prison life. Over two hundred various descriptions, character sketches, and expoundings upon conditions have been collected over the years. Such materials have legitimate research value if the atypical and sensational is avoided, and if the statements are fairly representative of the population in general. The point should be made here that the written materials of prisoners which have been shown in the volume are fairly representative of all aspects of the prison population, except that inmates of low intelligence have been unable to produce written materials. This seems to be an unavoidable difficulty although the writer has attempted through his own words to show the ideations and activities of inmates who, because

---

[3] Illuminating insight into method may be found in the following studies of high merit: Hans Riemer, *Socialization in the Prison Community,* Proceedings of the Sixty-Seventh Annual Congress of the American Prison Association, 1937, pp. 151–155, and, Norman S. Hayner and Ellis Ash, *The Prison Community as a Social Group,* American Sociological Review, June, 1939, pp. 362–369.

[4] Pauline V. Young, *Interviewing in Social Work,* McGraw-Hill Book Co., New York, 1937, pp. 282–292. See also, Saul D. Alinsky, *A Sociological Technique in Clinical Criminology,* Proceedings of the Sixty-Fourth Annual Congress of the American Prison Association, 1934.

of a low I. Q., are unable to express themselves in the written word.

Inmates who were able and willing to write were given a wide range of topics. Among the subjects upon which information was sought were the following:

Other Suggested Topics for Investigation

1. The Monotony of Prison Life
2. Methods of Punishment
3. Attitudes of Inmates from Cities
4. Provincialism of Rural Inmates
5. Songs and Poems of Inmates
6. Slang, Profanity, Epithets, and Nicknames used by Inmates
7. Incidents of Fooling the Guards
8. Incidents of Kindness by Guards
9. Penal Atmosphere on the Night of an Electrocution
10. Character Sketches of Guards
11. Character Sketches of Inmates
12. Church and Religious Attitudes of Prisoners
13. Homosexuality: Its Cause, Development, and Effect
14. The Use of Narcotics by Prisoners
15. The Grapevine System
16. Routes, Hot Letters, and Kites
17. Old Time Yegg Men
18. Education and Acquirement of Culture by Inmates
19. Reading and Creative Writing by Inmates
20. Attitudes toward Inmates with Syphilis
21. Christmas Eve in a Penitentiary
22. Stool Pigeons: Methods, Status, Effect
23. The Effect of Dull, Drab Days on Convict Temperament
24. The Meaning of "Bum Rap"
25. Good Times in a Penitentiary
26. Gangs and Intimate Groups behind Gray Walls
27. Exploitation of Old Inmates by New
28. Exploitation of Old Guards by New
29. Exploitation of New Inmates by Old
30. Character Sketch of the Fish
31. Learning the Ropes
32. Awaiting Electrocution and Stir Simpleness
33. Description of My Work Gang
34. Cell House Customs
35. My Cellmate

Other suggested topics produced valuable information and provided leads for more intensive investigations.

Numerous schedules were used in collecting data. The study of boyhood ambitions, group affiliations, leadership, occupational adaptation, and other subjects lent itself to the schedule technique. In questioning inmates considerable care must be taken. Jockeying is frequently necessary and indirect techniques are more likely to procure truthful answers than direct questions. So, in using the schedule technique the type of information was clearly defined before interviewing and consequently the writer needed only a brief outline before him during the actual questioning. The following outline, for example, refers to some of the data shown in Chapter XI on the social significance of work:

Schedule Outline

Status of Worker:

1. Outside trade?
2. How long served?
3. Number of prison jobs?
4. How long in present job?
5. Hours loafing per day?

Social Interrelationships at Work:

1. How many men talk to each day?
2. How long, how much conversing?
3. Frequency of speech with guards per day?
4. Frequency of speech with Superintendent?
5. Content of talk with inmates: case, crime, prison events, etc.?
6. Extent of grouping: how large, how often, conflict, cohesion?

Individual Aspects of the Work:

1. Day dreaming?
2. Content of day dreams?
3. Learned more on this job than on jobs outside?
4. Intent to put training to use; work upon release?
5. Any interest in the work; pride in accomplishment; why?
6. Does prison labor help men reform—opinion?

Perspective:

1. Admire Henry Ford, Rockefeller?
2. Define: machine age, profit system, socialism?
3. Do you believe in labor unions?
4. What is done with the goods you make?

The replies to the series of questions outlined above were placed on cards and tabulated later. A fairly complete explanation of the schedule technique has been given in Chapter V.

Questionnaires have also been used. Two of them are shown here. The first one has reference to the inmate's leisure time usages before incarceration, and the second one was used anonymously for the study of group relationships.

Name............................RHO..........................
Number..........................RHO ETA....................

RILT Inventory

1. How many ways may a batter reach first base?............
2. In dice what numbers are called "naturals?"..............
3. Name your three favorite movie stars.......................
4. Who won the World Series in 1934?.........................
5. In dice games what does *fade* mean?.......................
6. Who is Lionel Barrymore?......................................
7. Who is the present manager of the Detroit Tigers?..........
8. In dice what numbers are *craps*?..............................
9. Is Jean Harlow a blonde or a brunette?.......................
10. Who is Gabby Hartnett?...
11. In dice does the shooter or the fader have the best odds?..........
12. How old is Shirley Temple?......................................

1. How many points for a basket in basketball?...............
2. In pool what color is the eight ball?...........................
3. Who is known as America's March King?.....................
4. How many men on a basketball team?........................
5. In pool what is the *break*?..
6. Name your three favorite songs..................................
7. How many fouls before a basketball player is ousted?.........
8. What is the average weight of pool and billiard cues?.........
9. Who is Arturo Toscaninni?.......................................

1. How many points for a touchdown in football?...............
2. In poker does a flush beat a straight?..........................
3. Who is Sinclair Lewis?...
4. How many men on a football team?.............................
5. In draw poker how many cards are dealt?......................
6. Name your favorite book..
7. Who was the universally selected All-American half-back this year?..
8. Name three prominent American authors.......................
9. What card games can be used for betting?.....................

1. Who is the heavyweight boxing champion now?................
2. What is the average cost of whiskey per pint?.................
3. Name the two largest broadcasting chains.......................
4. How many pounds must a 140-pound boxer lose for the lightweight division? ....

5. Who are your favorite radio stars? . . . .
6. What percentage of alcohol is in whiskey? . . . .
7. Who was known as the "Manassa Mauler"? . . . .
8. Do you prefer beer, whiskey, or gin? . . . .
9. What type of radio program do you dislike most? . . . .

1. For what is Johnny Weismuller best known? . . . .
2. Who won the 1935 Kentucky Derby? . . . .
3. What is your favorite newspaper? . . . .
4. What is the flutter kick in swimming? . . . .
5. What is good time for 6 furlongs in horse racing? . . . .
6. What part of the newspapers do you like best? . . . .
7. Name three strokes used by swimmers . . . .
8. Who is William Randolph Hearst? . . . .
9. Name four prominent jockeys . . . .

The foregoing questions, bearing the title of RILT, which is the abbreviation of "recreation, interests, and leisure time," have been referred to in Chapter IX. The following questionnaire was used for the collection of data presented in Chapter V and proved valuable, not only in furnishing information, but as a means of introducing discussion by the inmates on the general topic of prisoner relationships.

Social Relations Questionnaire

Explanation: Knowledge is needed regarding the social life of men in prison. Your name and number will not be considered. We are asking you to answer these questions as frankly as possibly. Words of possible double meaning will be explained and explicit directions will be given as to the method of answering the statements. . . . We begin the study by assuming that men in prison make social adjustments in one of the following ways:

I. (A) *The Complete "Clique-Man":* This is a man who is one of a group of three or more men who are all very close friends. They share each others' luxuries and secrets and have accepted, or are willing to accept, punishment one for the other. The "Clique-Man" is so closely associated with his group that he thinks in terms of "we" rather than "I" and he acts as the group acts. The Clique has some permanence.

(B) *The "Group-Man":* This is a man who is friendly with a certain small group of men but who does not entirely subject himself to the wishes and acts of the group-as-a-whole. He would share his luxuries, tell some of his secrets, but would not "go all the way" for those with whom he is friendly. While he is particularly friendly with a group, he also freely mixes with a number of other men and is, at least casually, friendly with these others.

(C) *The "Two-Man" Group:* This is the man who is friendly with other inmates but who never becomes close except with one other man, usually the cellmate or a gangmate. With this one man he forms a relationship that is characterized by the same situations as the "Clique-Man" has with his members.

(D) *The "Semi-Solitary" Man:* This is the man who, while civil with other inmates never really becomes intimate with them or shares with them any thoughts or acts except of the most casual nature. He is the man who is *almost* playing a "lone-hand."

(E) *The "Complete-Solitary" Man:* This is the man who keeps almost constantly to himself and shares nothing with other inmates. While he may talk with other men, he is generally alone and seeks no one.

Please check the group into which you most closely fit.

II. *Attitude Concerning Social Life in General:* Think in terms of what you know of other inmates rather than your own relations. If the following statements seem true to you mark them with a plus. It they seem false, mark them with a minus sign. Plus equals yes and minus equals no.

1.——All prisoners are loyal to each other.
2.——All prisoners are loyal to some few other prisoners.
3.——Most prisoners have no sense of loyalty.
4.——Cliques in prison (as above described) do not exist.
5.——Only a small percentage of men are members of cliques.
6.——A large percentage of the men are members of cliques.
7.——Most prisoners are more interested in themselves than in any other prisoner.
8.——The men in cliques are so loyal to each other that they think in terms of "we" rather than "I."
9.——Friendships in prison are of short duration.
10.——The longer I am associated with prisoners, the more do I realize that they possess many manly and honorable qualities.
11.——Every clique has a leader.
12.——The "Semi-Solitary" man (as above described) is the type of man most prisoners are.
13.——Friendships in prison result from the mutual help that man can give man rather than because of some admired quality.
14.——Familiarity in prison breeds contempt.
15.——Inmates usually make the closest friends among those with whom they work.
16.——The most important item in the code of a prisoner is:

III. *My Own Attitudes and Relations with My Fellow-Inmates:*

1. I have —— very close, loyal, friends.
2. I have —— other friends.
3.——I would accept punishment for *any* inmate regardless of justice or cause.
4.——I would accept punishment for a few fellow prisoners who are members of my group regardless of justice or cause.
5.——I would share half my luxuries with any inmate.
6.——I would share my luxuries with the men in my group.
7.——I would have no objection to any prisoner marrying my sister.
8.——I would want no man who has been in prison to marry my sister.
9.——I would not object to those in my group marrying my sister.
10.——Upon release I will avoid all friends I have here.
11.——I tell all my private secrets to the members of my clique or group.
12.——I never tell any inmate anything that is important.

Finally, a word should be said about documentation. This study is essentially a laboratory investigation and as such has made no effort to refer to the vast literature of criminology. Many outstanding contributions have been mentioned in footnotes, and while the writer has appreciated the significance of many studies not mentioned, such studies are not closely related to this more or less pioneering effort, and do not treat the prison from the same frame of reference.

APPENDIX B

PRISON ARGOT

Among the 1,200 words and phrases included in the "dictionary," many are so infrequently used that they cannot be considered as comprising a working vocabulary. Thus, only the words and terms whose meanings are generally known among the inmates, are presented here.

A

ACES HIGH, n. Trustworthiness; a term reflecting trust and reliability in a person of the underworld

ACE, n. A dollar.

ALKY, n. Contraction for alcohol.

ANGEL, n. A heroin pill.

ANGLE, n. An aspect of a proposition; also a method of figuring out a difficulty.

ANNIE OAKLEY, n. A free admission.

APPLE KNOCKER, n. A farm boy.

ARM, vt. To attack a man from the rear; to hold a person in the bend of the arm; "put the arm on him"; to rob.

AUNTIE, n. An elderly, male homosexual.

B

BABY GRAND, n. A five hundred dollar bill.

BACKER, n. A lawyer or other person of influence with the authorities.

BADGER, n. A man who dresses as a woman and exploits other men for money.

BAG, n. 1. A down and out prostitute working in streets and alleys. 2. Any woman.

BANG, n. 1. A copulation. 2. A shot of dope. vi. To copulate.

BANK, n. A solitary cell in prison.

BEANS, n A copulation. vi. To copulate.

BED UP, vi. To go to bed with someone (obscene).

BEEF, n. A complaint or protest. vi. To complain or to protest.

BEHIND THE EIGHT BALL. An expression indicating one to be in bad luck.

BETSY, n. A pistol, a six-shooter.

B. I., Contraction for Bureau of Identification.

BIG HOUSE, n. A penitentiary.

BIG SHOT, n. A person of importance. vt. To imitate, to simulate the attributes of a superior.

BIT, n. 1. Sentence in prison, "time." 2. A thief's share of loot: "I got my bit."

BLOTTO, adj. Intoxicated.

BLOW, vi. 1. To depart, to leave: "he had to blow." 2. To "blow a mark" is to be unsuccessful in thieving either through the arrival of the police or through some blundering.

BLUE JOHN, n. Thin or skimmed milk such as is found in prison.

BO, n. A bum, a hobo.

BOILERMAKER, n. A prostitutes lover.

BOOK, n. A life sentence.

BOOSTER, n. A shoplifter; some of the best boosting is done by women; also, a steerer, a shillaber.

BOX MAN, n. A take-off man in a dice game; also a safe blower.

BRAT, n. A boy used for sex purposes, a "punk."

BRIARS, n. Hack saws, used in reference to sawing bars in jail or prison.

BRIG, n. A solitary cell in prison.

BROWNING, n. The act of sodomy.

BUCK, n. 1. A Catholic priest. 2. A dollar.

BUG, n. 1. An insane person. 2. A burglar alarm. 3. vi. To talk together, to conspire.

BUG DOCTOR, n. A psychiatrist.

BULL, n. A detective.

BUMP OFF, vt. To kill, to murder.

BURN, vi. 1. To become angry: "he burned up." 2. To become infected with gonorrhea. 3. To cheat one's partner in crime 4. To execute in the electric chair.

BUSY, n. A watchman, a plain clothes detective.

BUY, n. A purchase of liquor or drugs by a "stool pigeon," to be used as evidence by an officer.

BUZZARD, n. 1. A hijacker who preys upon other criminals for the loot of a successful robbery. 2. An unattached old bum who appears uninvited in the jungles.

C

CALENDAR, n. One year (sentence).
CAN, n. A jail or prison.
CANNED HEAT, n. Any solid alcoholic fuel, purchased in tins.
CANNON, n. A pickpocket.
CAN OPENER, n. An instrument used to strip the front layer of steel sheet from a safe.
CASE, vt. 1. To shadow, to follow or to watch. 2. To study a "lay out" or projected robbery; to learn the habits of the watchman or other employees of the place and adjacent territory.
CASEMAN, n. A lookout or an observer for a gang of robbers; see verb "to case."
CAT, n. A stool pigeon.
CENTURY, n. A hundred dollar bill.
CHIP, n. A till in a cash register.
CHISEL, vt. 1. To bargain for a better price or terms; to hold out or take advantage of: "he chiseled me out of ten bucks." 2. To supplant, to horn in, to crash the gate, to ingratiate one's self.
CHOPPER, n. A machine gun or its operator.
CLEAN GET, n. A successful escape.
CLIP, vt. To hold up, to rob.
CLOCK, n. A life sentence in jail: "doing time the clock around."
CLOUTING, inf. Stealing, especially shop lifting.
CLOWN, n. A village constable or policeman.
COKIE, n. A cocaine addict.
COLD SAUSAGE, n. A heartless killer.
COLD TOMATO, n. A murdered person.
COLD TURKEY, n. Caught in the act: a right charge, an open and shut case.
CON, n. 1. A convict. 2. A conspiracy. 3. A confidence, a confidence game.
CON MAN, n. A person who uses deceit in his racket, gaining confidence and then committing a fraud.
CONNECTION, n. A good introduction to influential officials.
COOK, vt. 1. To distill alcohol. 2. To kill by legal electrocution.
COSHED, vt. To be knocked out, especially by a blow on the head.
COWBOY, n. A young inexperienced gangster.
CRACKER BOX, n. An easily blown safe.
CRASH A JOINT, or CRASH, vph. To smash the glass window or door of a place of business, snatch an armful of merchandise, and escape in a motor car.
CROAKER, n. The prison physician.
CRUSHER, n. A broad-shouldered and weak-minded thief.

D

DANCE HALL, n. In a prison, the electrocution room.
DEAL, n. Any transaction between thieves.
DEALER, n. A narcotic peddlar.
DECK, n. A quantity of narcotics sufficient for one dose.
DINERO, n. Stolen money of any description.
DINGE, n. A Negro inmate.
DIP, n. A pickpocket.
DITCH, vt. To cache or hide loot.
DO A BIT STANDING UP, vph. To serve a prison term without bad effect.
DOG CATCHER, n A deputy warden in a prison.
DOUBLE SAWBUCK, n. A twenty-dollar bill.
DOZENS, n. A slighting rhyme relating to one's parentage; series of vulgar and profane epithets.
DRAW, n. Facility with a pistol.
DRINK, n. A charge of nitro-glycerine: "give her a drink," i.e., "pour the soup."
DRUM, n. An old-fashioned vault with the safe (keyster) within.
DUCKET, n. 1. A card or letter, usually a physician's certificate, advising of some disease or affliction which excuses an inmate from duty. 2. A ticket from the parole board announcing the amount of punishment.
DUG OUT, n. A big eater of institution food.
DUMBY, n. A bottle of milk on a doorstep and easily stolen.
DUST, n. 1. Cocaine. 2. Tobacco.
DUSTER, n. A cash box in a safe.

E

EASE, vi. To enter cautiously, "to ease in."
EDGE, n. An advantage.
EDGE IN, vi. To ease in, to advance cautiously.
ELEVENTH COMMANDMENT, subs. A prison term meaning, "Thou shalt not get caught."
END, n. A portion of a split: "did you get your end?"
EQUALIZER, n. A pistol.
ERASE, vi. To wipe out, to kill.
EYE, vt. To scrutinize closely. n. A watchman.

F

FADE, vi. To leave, to disappear.

FAIRY, n. A male prostitute.

FALL, vt. To be arrested and sent to prison: "he fell in Chicago."

FAN, vt. Frisking by a pickpocket in an effort to locate the pocketbook.

FENCE, n. A receiver of stolen property.

FIN, n. A five-dollar bill.

FINGER, vt. To accuse, to place under suspicion; to be identified: "I caught three fingers."

FINGER MAN, n. An informer.

FINISHING SCHOOL, n. A reformatory for young girls.

FINK, n. 1. A strike breaker. 2. Also a stool pigeon. v. To "squeal."

FISH, n. One newly arrived in prison.

FLATTIE, n. A "flat-foot"; a policeman.

FLOATER, n. A release from jail with admonition to leave town immediately: "he gave me a floater."

FLY MUG, n. A railroad detective.

FRAME, vt. To accuse falsely.

FRISK, vt. To search, to shake down.

FRONT, n. A legitimate business which serves as a disguise for predatory undertaking.

FRONT MAN, n. A man that will go to the defense of one in trouble.

FRUIT, n. A male homosexual whose perversion is fellatio. When an invert is attracted to young men or boys he is called "kid fruit," or "K. F."

FRY, vt. To electrocute.

G

GAFF, n. Pressure, third degree: "he stood the gaff."

GALLERY, n. The collection of photographs and files in the detective bureau.

GANG SHAG, n. Sexual intercourse between a woman and a group or gang of young men.

GAPPER, n. A piece of mirror used as a periscope to watch the guard, used by inmates in prison when cooking or handling other contraband.

GATO MONEY, subs. The ten dollars given a convict upon release.

G-MAN, n. A Federal officer.

G-NOTE, n. A one-thousand-dollar bill.

GERBER, n. A pickpocket.

GET, n. An escape or a get away.

GETTING SHORT, vph. A term applied in prisons to men whose sentences are nearing an end; the "whisper."

GLIM, n. 1. A light. 2. A glimbox is a contraption of burned rags, a piece of emery stone and a steel button which is used as a cigarette lighter.

GLOM, vt. To arrest a law-breaker in flight.

GONE COOL, vph. A gangster phrase meaning that one of the mob has been killed.

GONIFF, n A gunman, a thief; a Yiddish term.

GOOD GO, n. Something easily successful, a good break in life; a comfortable job in prison.

GORILLA, n. A gangster.

GOWED UP, par. Full of "gow," i.e., under the influence of a narcotic.

GOW JOINT, n. A place where opium is smoked, or any place where any narcotic is sold.

G. GRAND, n. A one-thousand-dollar bill.

GRAPE VINE, n. The underworld system of communication.

GREASE, n. Nitroglycerine.

GREASE BALL, n. 1. A dirty, greasy person; used contemptuously. 2. Also an Italian. 3. A kitchen worker in prison.

GRIFT, n. A petty racket; sometimes picking pockets.

GRIFTER, n. A small-time grafter, usually with a circus or carnival.

GUFF, n. Insolence, back talk to officers.

GUNSEL, n. A young, male homosexual.

GUZZLE, vt. To strangle.

GYP, vt. To cheat.

H

HACK, n. A night policeman.

HALF A CENTURY, n. A fifty-dollar bill.

HALTER, n. A hangman's noose.

HAND JIG, vi. To masturbate.

HARNESS BULL, n. A town policeman.

HEAT, n. 1. A pistol. 2. Pursuit or suspicion, also danger: a police car is a "load of heat." 3. A town or resort may have so much "heat" directed upon it that it is described as "burning up."

HEATER, n. A pistol.

HEAVY MAN, n. 1. A safe blower. 2. A person who guards gambling houses, etc. 3. A bruiser or killer for a mob.

HEEL, vt. To investigate, or to look up; "to heel the joint"; to shadow, to follow.

HEIST, vi. To rob; to stick up.

HEISTMAN, n. A highway robber.

HEP COP, n. An officer who knows what is going on about him.

HIDE OUT, n. A place of refuge.

HIJACK, vt. To hold up and rob.

HIJACKER, n. A highwayman who specializes in the robbery of shipments of liquor in transit.

HOG EYES, n. Skeleton keys.

HOLD THE BAG, vph. To take punishment.
HOLE, n. Punishment cell in prison.
HOOD, n. Contraction for hoodlum.
HOOSGOW, n. 1. A farm boy, an ignoramus. 2. Used as an expression of contempt, anyone undesirable. 3. A jail.
HORNET'S BULL, n. A railroad policeman.
HORSE, n. A trick or an advantage: "you have a horse on me."
HOT, a. 1. Stolen goods. 2. Wanted by the authorities; in a state of being watched.
HOT SEAT, n. An electric chair.
HUMMER, n. An arrest on a false charge; a "bum rap."
HUMMINGBIRD, n. The electric chair.
HUNG UP, vi. Suspended by the wrists to bars; a method of punishment for infractious prisoners.
HUNK OF ICE, subst. A large diamond obtained by theft.
HUSTLER, n. 1. A thief or racketeer. 2. A prostitute.

I

ICE, n. Diamonds.
ICE BOX, n. The prison morgue.
IN, adv. Having easy entree; having inclusion: "I was cut in."
IRON, n. A pistol.

J

JAMOKE, n. Coffee.
JIG, n. 1. A Negro. 2. Also used in the plural for burglar tools.
JOB, n. An act of unlawful business.
JOBBED, vi. To be convicted on a false charge.
JOCKER, n. Usually the active party in homosexual behavior; the male rôle.
JOHN LAW, n. A police officer.
JOINT, n. 1. A saloon. 2. Any place of shady character, a house of assignation. 3. Also the penis.
JUG, n. 1. A bank. 2. A jail. 3. The "hole" in prison. vt. To deposit money in a bank.
JUNGLE, n. A meeting place of hoboes, usually along the railway tracks, near fresh water, and provided with trees for shade, and grass.
JUNK, n. Any narcotic.
JUNKING, inf. To steal small articles from a junk yard, such as seltzer bottles, etc., which may be disposed of at drug stores and the like.

K

KALE, n. Money.
KEPTEE, n. A kept woman.
KEYSTER, n. A steel safe, usually enclosed in a vault.
KICK, n. 1. A pocket, "I have it in my kick." 2. vi. To object.
KICKOUT MAN, n. An escaped convict.
KID, n. A young male prostitute.
KITE, n. An illicit note or letter passed between inmates.
KNOCK OFF, vt. 1. To kill. 2. To close by violence, as a place of business. 3. To dynamite, also to rob or to burglarize.
KNOCK-OUT DROPS, n. Chloral hydrate.
KNOWLEDGE BOX, n. A country school that is available and easy of ingress so that hobos may enter and sleep.

L

LAY, n. A copulation. 2. A prospect for a robbery: "he got the lay while still in stir."
LEAD-OFF MAN, n. The leader of a predatory gang.
LEATHER, n. A pocketbook or wallet.
LEGGINS, n. A simulation of coitus between two males.
LOAD, n. A loaded truck used in speaking of illicit liquor.
LONG GREEN, subs. Money, contraction for green back.
LONG TOM, n. A sawed-off shotgun.
LOSE HIS MARBLES, vph. To become insane.
LOW DOWN, n. A piece of correct information.
LACE UP, vt. To tie up, to bind: refers to hand cuff or straight jacket, but more to "lacing up" the victim of a theft.
LAM, vi. To depart in haste, to escape from prison: "he is on the lam."
LAMSTER, n. A fugitive from justice; also an escaped convict.
LAW, n. A police officer, a prison keeper.
LIFTED THE JACK, vph. To steal the money.
LINED; WELL LINED, adj. Condition of being flush with money.
LUG, n. An uncouth or clumsy person.
LUNCH HOOK, n. The human hand: "get your lunch hook out of my kick."
LUSHING, inf. To drink heavily; to stay drunken.

M

MACHINERY, n. An invert.
MAKE, vi. To obtain a desired end: "I made him for his poke."
MAN (the), n. A prison keeper.
MAP A GET, vph. To plan a get away from a robbery: "we have a get already mapped."

MARK, n. 1. A job, usually criminal: "look up a mark." 2. An intended victim. 3. A safe which may be opened with an explosive.
MC COY, n. Genuine liquor; anything genuine: "It's the real McCoy."
MERCHANT, n. One who practices fellatio (invert).
MOB, n. A criminal gang; see "troup."
MOBSTER, n. A gangster.
MOLE, n. A bank robber who tunnels under the vault.
MOLL, n. A criminal's sweetheart.
MONKEY CLOTHES, n. A policeman's uniform.
MONTH IN CONGRESS, subs. A spell in solitary.
MOPE, n. A departure, a leave-taking.
MOTHER SUPERIOR, n. A term sometimes used in fun in connection with an elderly male homosexual, especially if popular with a number of young customers.
MOUTHPIECE, n. A lawyer.
MUSCLE, vi. To compel, to intimidate, to force one's self in.
MUSICAL FRUIT, n. Beans.

N

NAIL, vt. To capture, to arrest.
NARK, n. A stool pigeon for the police.
NEWSPAPER, n. A thirty-day jail sentence.
NOSE, n. A stool pigeon for the police.
NOSE TROUBLE, n. Prying curiosity.
NUT, n. Overhead expense; the "nut" is the money paid to a sheriff or a prosecutor for permission to run a gambling game, speakeasy, or other illicit project; protection money.
NUT DOCTOR, n. A psychiatrist.
NUTS AND BOLTS, adj. Looney, feebleminded.

O

OBBIE, n. A post office which might be robbed.
OFF CHILD, n. A child born out of wedlock.
OLD RALL, n. Syphilis.
OUT, n. An escape: "he made an out from stir."
OUT ON A LAY, vph. Out working up a racket.

P

PACKAGE, n. A parcel of narcotics; a small amount of liquor.
PAPER, n. A worthless check.
PAPER HANGER, n. One who passes fictitious paper, a check passer.
PASS, vt. 1. To be excused for violation of a rule "I got a pass." 2. To permit egress without molestation: "I paid the copper for a pass."
PAY OFF, n. 1. Money or goods received from thefts. 2. The end of anything, the final event.
PERSUADERS, n. Guns, pistols.
PETE MAN, n. A safe blower.
PENITENTIARY AGENT, n. A shyster, or double crossing lawyer.
PIG MEAT, n. A young dusky Negress; applied usually to one whose appearance hints of prostitution.
PILL ROLLER, n. A physician.
PINCH, n. An arrest.
PINEAPPLE, n. A bomb.
PLANT, n. 1. Money or loot which is hidden because of danger, or for protection.
PLAY HOUSE, n. A prison with a small population.
PLUG, vt. To shoot.
POKE, n. A roll of money, a purse or a wallet.
POKE UP, vt. To stick up.
POKE-UP ARTIST, n. A professional highwayman.
POLITICIAN, n. A convict who has a good job in prison with privileges.
POTATOES, n. Money.
POT SHOT, n. A light charge of "soup" (nitroglycerine).
POULTICE, n. A bread spread with butter and jam or any two types of spread.
PROWL, vi. To ransack, usually refers to burglars who are called "prowlers."
PULL A GOPHER, vph. 1. To burrow or tunnel under a bank vault. 2. To hibernate, also to disappear.
PULL THE LEATHER, vph. To take out one's purse.
PUNK, n. 1. An adolescent boy thief. 2. Also a young male prostitute, the passive agent in pederasty (invert). 3. Also bread. 4. adj. Condition of being unacceptable: "punk food," "punk booze."
PUSH OVER, n. 1. An easy theft for criminals. 2. Boy or girl easily induced to be used sexually.
PUT ON THE BEE, vi. To beg; to make a touch; to borrow.
PUT ON THE SPOT, vph. To lure a victim into seclusion and work damage upon him.
PUT THE FINGER ON, vph. This phrase is used by convicts to designate that suspicion has been directed toward some person.
PUT UP, vi. To serve time at a prison: "I put up eight years at Sing Sing."

R

RACKET, n. Any illegitimate enterprise.

RADIO, n. A convict that talks loudly and frequently.

RAP, n. An arrest, blame, accusation, as: "I beat the rap." vt. To accuse, to indict, to arrest.

RAPPER, n. A term applied to a person who makes a protest about an inmate's release to the parole board.

RAT, n. A stool pigeon.

RATTING, vb. n. Tale bearing.

RIB, vt. To prepare a "sucker"; to convince a victim that he is going to get something for nothing.

RIGHT, adj. A person who is faithful, trustworthy; opposed to tale bearing or "snitching."

RIGHT COP, n. A police officer who is in on the graft; one who will "do business."

RING, vt. To surround as to screen. A man is said to be "ringed" when a trick is played upon him by other prisoners who encircle him so that what is being done to him may not be detected.

RINGER, n . Information which proves to be false.

RING TAIL, n. An informer; a stool pigeon; a squealer.

ROCK, n. A diamond; sometimes other gems.

ROD, n A gun.

RODDED, vi. Armed with a revolver.

RODMAN, v. A gunman.

ROLL, vt. To steal from the clothing usually during sleep, or during intoxication or after the use of knock-out drops, as "jack-rolling."

ROUND BOY, n. A spherical type of safe used in small banks in which the door is screwed fast.

ROUTE, n. A go-between in the delivery of contraband.

RUMBLE, vt To learn or come upon information: "we got a rumble the guards were wise."

S

SACK, n. The human stomach.

SALLY, n. The Salvation Army.

SAWBUCK, n. A ten-dollar bill.

SCATTER MAN, n. A saloon keeper; a banker or depository for a thief.

SCORE, vt. To succeed, to make good: "he scored for two grand."

SCRAM, vi. To leave suddenly or in haste. Often used as a command.

SCREENS, n. A solitary cell in prison which is enclosed by fine meshed wire netting which precludes the passing of any contraband article.

SCREW, n. A guard; a key to a lock.

SECONDS, n. Coffee grounds which have been twice boiled for economy.

SHAKE DOWN, vt. To search; also to enforce payment for protection: "the coppers shook me down." n. A search, blackmail

SHEETS, n. Cigarette papers; newspapers.

SHIEVE or SHIV, n. A knife, usually hand-fashioned and contraband.

SHILL, n. A steerer or "come along man" for a show or a racket.

SHINE, n. A Negro.

SHORT, n. A stolen auto; sometimes a street car.

SHYSTER, n. A cheap or dishonest attorney.

SIL UP, vph. To affect a silly or foolish attitude; used to attract attention in begging, or to disarm a policeman after an arrest.

SING, vi. To confess or to complain.

SISTER, n. A male homosexual.

SKIN, n. A purse, a leather bill fold.

SLEIGH RIDER, n. A user of "snow," i.e., cocaine

SLOUGH UP, vt. To arrest, to place in solitary.

SLUM, n. Plunder, loot.

SLUM DUMP, n. A jewelry store.

SLUM GULLION, n. A stew made of meat and vegetables common in prison.

SNITCHING MOON, n. A full moon, making detection of burglars easier.

SNOW BIRD, n. A cocaine addict.

SOLDIER, n. A watchman for robbers while on a theft.

SPEAK, n. Contraction for speakeasy.

SPEED BALL, n. Gum opium rolled into a pill and placed under the tongue; sometimes refers to mixture of morphine, heroin, and cocaine.

SPRING, vt. To secure a release from prison: "the mouthpiece will spring me."

SQUAWK, n. A complaint. vi. To inform, to complain, to squeal.

SQUEAL, vi. To confess upon oneself, also to carry tales about others: to tattle; to betray a pal.

STALL, vi. To feign, to malinger, to detract attention from; n. A person that detracts the attention of the victim while his pocket is being rifled.

STASH, vt. To hide: "he stashed the loot."

STIFF, n. 1. A letter or note. 2. A corpse. 3. An intoxicated person.

STIR, n. A penitentiary.

STIR BUG or STIR SIMPLE, n. A convict insane from confinement.

STOOL, n. A stool pigeon; an informer, usually for self-profit.

STOOL PIGEON MOON, n. A full moon.

STOOL PIGEON PARADE, n. The prison warden's court.

STRETCH, n. A term served in prison.

STRING, n. A piece of rope, usually referring to escape plans.

STRIP, vt. To take money from a wallet; to rob.

STRIPES, n. Punishment garb worn by prisoners for serious infractions of the rules.

STRUNG UP, vi. See "hung up."

SYNDICATE, n. A money pool for operating a racket. A group of convicts in prison which, by means of bribery of officials or other sinister methods controls the better jobs and privileges among the convicts.

T

TAIL, vt. To shadow; to follow a person to learn their habits or home.

TAKE, vt. To rob. n. The proceeds of a robbery.

TAKE FOR A RIDE, vph. To invite a person to accompany one so as to be able to kill or dispose of him in secret.

TAP, vt. To empty: "to tap the till."

TEND BAR, vi. To stand handcuffed to the bar in solitary.

TENNER, n. A ten-dollar bill given to a prisoner upon release from prison.

TIP OFF, n. A revelation or disclosure.

TOUCH, 1. vi. To connect; to make good. 2. n. An easy theft; a "soft touch."

TRAFFIC, n. A man or boy invert.

TRIM, vt. To rob; to acquire by chicanery.

TROUPE, n. A gang of pickpockets, safe blowers, or other thieves who steal together.

TURNOVER, n. A transfer to another prison.

TURN UP, vph. To discharge from court.

TYPEWRITER, n. A machine gun.

U

UNDERGROUND, n. A method of smuggling letters or other contraband from prison or into prison; something contraband.

UP AND UP, adj. Reliable, dependable.

W

WEEPER, n. A pistol: "carrying a concealed weeper."

WELL BRITCHED, adj. The condition of being well supplied with funds: "well heeled."

WHISPER, n. A term denoting the last few months of a prisoner's sentence.

WHITE CAP, n. A deputy warden.

WHIZ, n. The pickpocket racket: "on the whiz."

WHING DING, n. A simulation of illness for some deception, a sham: "he pulled a whing ding."

WIPE OUT, vt. To erase, to kill.

WIRE, n. The person who actually picks the victim's pocket.

WOLF, n. An active pederast.

WORKOUT, n. A beating.

WORKS, n. The third degree; the entire list of physical tortures.

WRONG, adj. Unreliable, unfaithful, untrustworthy: "he's a wrong guy."

Y

YAP, n. A term of contempt for a disliked person, a farm boy, an ignoramus.

YEGG MAN, n. A wanderer, a hobo, a safe blower.

YEN, n. The desire of a drug addict, both physical and mental, for his drug.

INDEX *

* Compiled by Rose Emelia Clemmer.

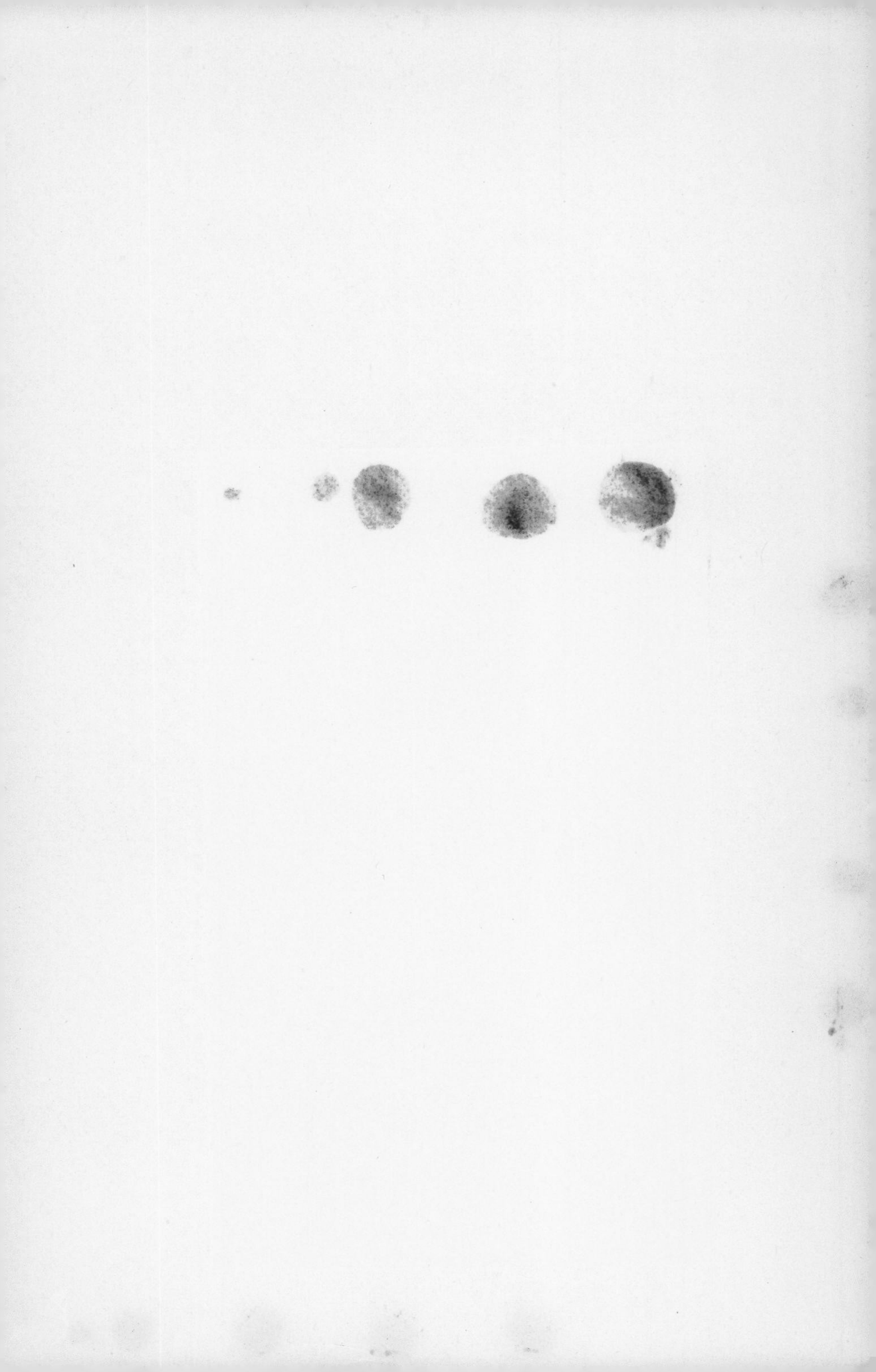